The Path
of
Wisdom

Background Books   3

The Path of Wisdom

Biblical Investigations

by

Bruce Vawter, C.M.

Michael Glazier
Wilmington, Delaware

About the Author

Bruce Vawter, C.M., received his doctorate in Scripture from the Pontifical Biblical Institute, Rome, 1956. Since 1968 he has taught Scripture at DePaul University as Professor in and Chairman of the Department of Religious Studies. His many publications include *Path Through Genesis; The Conscience of Israel;* and *Amos, Hosea, Micah, with Introduction to Classical Prophecy,* volume 7 of the *New Testament Message* series.

First published in Background Books in 1986 by Michael Glazier, Inc., 1935 West Fourth Street, Wilmington, Delaware, 19805.
© 1986 by Michael Glazier, Inc. All rights reserved.
Library of Congress Card Catalog Number: 85-47756.
International Standard Book Number: 0-89453-466-1.
Cover design by Brother Placid, OSB.
Printed in the United States of America.

CONTENTS

INTRODUCTION

Bruce Vawter needs no introduction to students of the Bible. For three decades he has been at the forefront of scholarship. His contributions, in more than a dozen books and pamphlets and nearly a hundred articles, have ranged from Genesis to Paul and the Gospel of John. His service to the public and the scholarly community by his editorial work was recognized in 1980 when he received the Herbert Gordon May Award from the Society of Biblical Literature. He was honored with the presidency of the Catholic Biblical Association as early as 1961, and with that of the Chicago Society of Biblical Research in 1975. He participated in the translation of the New American Bible and is one of those entrusted with the revision of the RSV. He has also been active in the inter-disciplinary projects and publications of *Concilium* and *Listening*.

The context of Fr. Vawter's work has been primarily in the Catholic Church, but never in a narrowly denominational way. He was himself a convert to Catholicism at age 16. In the years leading up to and following the Second Vatican Council he was one of the pioneering figures who introduced the methods and conclusions of ecumenical critical scholarship to English-speaking Catholics, and fostered the revival of interest in the Bible in the Catholic Church. The task was of course facilitated by the Dogmatic Constitution on Divine Revelation in 1965. In later years it has not been necessary to justify the use of critical methodology in Catholic scholarship. In his pioneering work on Genesis in 1956 Bruce Vawter still wrestled at length with the traditional claim of Mosaic authorship. He concluded that "We have not yet reached the point when we can give a wholly satisfactory answer to this question" (p.17), but added that "substantial Mosaic authorship may be seen to be rather of the order of quality than of quantity" (p. 18). In his "new reading" *On Genesis* twenty one years later he could say that

> Mosaic authorship no longer forms a problem for practically anyone . . . In whatever diluted a sense we may continue to talk about a Mosaic influence on the Pentateuch . . . we are not discussing authorship as our contemporaries understand authorship. Historical and literary criticism have ruled on this matter once and for all and finally . . . There is no point in trying to breathe new life into an ancient formula by inventing new meaning for either "Moses" or "authorship."
> (*On Genesis*, p. 15)

The liberation attested in this development was achieved through the patient work of Vawter and his colleagues in the years before the Council. It is now recognized that ruling on a question of authorship or provenance is the province of critical scholarship, not of tradition or ecclesiastical authority.

In an early, pre-Conciliar, publication *The Bible in the Church*, Fr. Vawter undertook to expound "the Catholic position" on the Bible. At heart, this was an affirmation of the need for a mediating tradition and the impossibility of treating the Bible as a sole, sufficient norm. Yet his perception of "the Catholic position" was neither polemical nor simple. He was too well informed of the various opinions which have held sway in the history of the church, and which he elegantly reviewed in his book on *Biblical Inspiration*. His view of the role of tradition was not only supported, but undoubtedly illuminated by the recent (mainly Protestant) recovery of the layers of tradition within the Bible itself. The affirmation of tradition required a view of revelation as a living and ongoing process, a view not always regnant in the Church. So he found it—

really astounding that for so long the Church has contented itself with a theology of inspiration that not only paid no attention to the continuing life of the Biblical word . . . but even in some respects, led to conclusions that have seriously hampered and inhibited productive thinking about the dynamism of the word . . . No theory of Biblical truth, on the Church's premises, should have been permitted to envisage an inerrant letter that would, logically, rule out the possibility of a Sermon on the Mount updating the Law and the Prophets. . . . (*Biblical Inspiration*, 155)

His concern for the role of tradition is evident in his persistent interest in the question of redaction in both Testaments (see chapters 8 and 19 below). It retains its relevance in the current ecumenical debate about the status of the canon in Biblical Theology.

Concomitant with the concern for tradition is the emphasis on history. If the Bible is a product of tradition it is a product of history, of changing circumstances and forms of expression. This emphasis is evident in Vawter's demand that the prophets be read in their historical context, but most conspicuously, perhaps, in his book on *This Man Jesus*:

The assumption of this book is, then, that if there is anything of value to be preserved in the way of life and thought that we rightly represent as Christian, there is required of us that lively interest in the circumstances of the historical Jesus . . . It is the means whereby we are prevented from creating a mythical Christ out of pious experience and imagination or, more commonly today, out of our own aspirations and the way we would have things be . . . (*This Man Jesus*, 23).

It is also an indispensable means of continuity with the roots of tradition. Vawter's emphasis on history was undoubtedly influenced by the so-called Biblical Theology Movement which dominated Protestant scholarship in the fifties and sixties. The theme of history has subsequently receded, but Vawter's concern to provide some standard of objectivity, some way of distancing our exegesis from whatever we happen to be doing at the moment, remains important.

A concern for history should not be confused with an insistence on historical accuracy or facticity. More often it is a matter of retrieving those loose ends of the tradition which do not fit neatly in our theological systems. Bruce Vawter's recent book on *Job and Jonah* is a celebration of such loose ends and an insistence that the tradition not be reduced to uniformity. Much of his work has been an appreciation of the human character of the Bible with all the attendant flaws and imperfections that it entails. The issue at stake in the Catholic debates about Scripture was . . .

> the very character of the Bible as the work of man, as one of his greatest works, done in the language and thought-forms of man, bearing the stamp of its origins that can be dated and placed in the world of man and in its history. Theoretically, the humanness that belonged to the Bible had never been denied, the rare exception noted. But practically it had often been submerged. (*Biblical Inspiration*, 126)

It has been the achievement of Bruce Vawter and of the scholars of his generation to restore an appreciation of the human character of the Bible to the Catholic Church. It remains for the next generation to probe more fully the sense of the traditional affirmation, which Fr. Vawter could take for granted, that it is also the Word of God.

John J. Collins

1. The Bible in the Roman Catholic Church

In Concert with most other traditional Christian bodies, the Roman Catholic Church has proposed, in its official formulations of faith, a view of Scripture as *norma normans et non normata* (a standard which sets the standard without being subject to any other standard) of belief. Also, in concert with the formulations of the other bodies, those of the Roman church still reflect, to some degree, even now, the theological controversies of the fourteenth to sixteenth centuries that culminated in Reformation and Counter-Reformation. The theological tensions reflected in the formulations have, in these ecumenical times, provoked difficulties for those respective bodies that wish to disembarrass themselves of polemics no longer useful. I am thinking, on the one hand, of the Faith and Order Conference of the World Council of Churches which grappled with the traditional *sola Scriptura* formula in its discussions at Montreal in 1963 and whose findings were published under the intriguing title *Tradition and the Traditions*. With that side of the problem I am, of course, not presently concerned. I am, however, concerned with the correlative problem that has been presented to the Catholic Church, with its traditional "Scripture *and* tradition" formula.

The concept of Scripture presumed in the Catholic formulations represents that of the medieval theologians, which was, in turn, an inheritance, broadly speaking, from the Fathers of the Church of the third century onward. For the Fathers, Scriptures were, first and foremost, divine oracles—teaching communicated by God to men by means of human writers imbued with a prophetic spirit.[1] This concept owed something to the New Testament (the *theopneustos* of 2 Tim 3:16, esp.) but probably much more to the image of the mantic oracular prophet that had prevailed in the Hellenistic world and to the precedent of such figures as Philo of Alexandria, who had explicitly identified the biblical process with the divine possession of mantic prophecy. This tendency to equate the Bible with oracular revelation carried with it at least two other associated tendencies, which also were inherited by the medieval church and caused problems for it and for later generations, not excluding our own. The first was the prejudice against consideration of the Bible as human literature subject to the literary conventions of man. The second was the recourse to a multiplicity of scriptural "senses" in order to extract religious significance from a text that did not possess it obviously on the surface.

These were tendencies, not absolutes. Augustine, to take a random example, could quite straightforwardly assert that there were statements in Scripture *nulli saluti profutura*, having no bearing on salvation, and that by that same token, the Scripture was not to be bent to pretend to the teaching of biology or physics.[2] Such would be the basis for a later principle laid down by Aquinas, that scriptural writers had dealt with matters of profane science simply according to appearances, utilizing popular figures that even those who knew better still found convenient to employ for understanding.[3] Chrysostom, Augustine's contemporary in the East could employ the concept of *synkatabasis*, condescension, an idea that pervades his writing, to ac-

---

[1] I have summarized the patristic notion of the Bible in Vawter, *Biblical Inspiration*, Theological Resources (Philadelphia: Westminster Press, 1972), pp. 20-42.

[2] Augustine, *De Genesi ad litteram* 2.9, Migne, *PL* vol. 34, p. 270.

[3] Aquinas, *Summa Theologiae* (hereafter cited as *ST*), Ia, q. 70, art. 1 ad 3.

count for adjustment of the divine authorship of Scripture to the human hearts, minds and circumstances that eventually had produced it. Yet we know that when Theodore of Mopsuestia (c. 350-428) – one of the early Christian writers with whom a modern exegete would feel most comfortable – tried to systematize such practical conclusions in a theory that would have distinguished prophecy from other spiritual gifts that had gone into the production of Scripture, he was rewarded in 533 by a posthumous condemnation by the Second Council of Constantinople.[4] As for what commonly is called the allegorical or tropological interpretation of Scripture (not to mention the "typological" or other "spiritual" senses discerned in it), there is no doubt that from Philo through the Alexandrians and Antiochenes, down through the Middle Ages and into modern times, dissatisfaction with the historicocritical method of getting at biblical meaning has been motivated by reluctance to accept the plain sense that the biblical author intended his words to have.[5] I recognize that a present-day synchronic exegetical approach to the biblical text which relies heavily on the structures that emerge from comparative literatures may have a great deal to contribute to our understanding of the Bible. Such an understanding, however, I am sure can only supplement, never substitute for the diachronic study of a text that is a part of human history. Literature is a human phenomenon to be investigated in its own right, and religious literature is only one part of human literature. But on the other hand, some of the religions that have produced literature wish to be judged not on *what* they have written but on *why* they wrote it. I think that we are asked to view the Scripture first of all as a record of what God has done at determined points of time: This is the essence of historical revelation, that God has *acted* (the ṣidqôt Yhwh, "justices of the Lord" [Mic 6:5, etc.]). It was in this posture of enquiry that in the thir-

[4]J. D. Mansi, *Sacrorum Conciliorum nova et amplissima collectio*, reprinted and cont. by L. Petit and J.B. Martin (Paris: n.p., 1889-1927), vol. 9, p. 223.

[5]Cf. Bruce Vawter, "The Fuller Sense: Some Considerations," *CBQ* 26 (1964): 85-96.

teenth century, at the height of the Middle Ages, Thomas Aquinas appeared on the theological scene.

Aquinas was one of those persons who appear every millennium or so—or in these times of geometric progression, perhaps every century or decade or so. He revolutionized contemporary theology, however, more than any Barth, Wellhausen, Bultmann, or Dalman ever has done in his own time. When Aquinas died on March 7, 1274, on his way to the Council of Lyons—forty-nine years of age and in ill health, summoned to the council by the Pope—he was under condemnation by the universities of Oxford and of Paris: The archbishops of both Canterbury and Paris, renowned theologians in their own right, had run athwart Aquinas on purely intellectual grounds. There was then no Inquisition or Holy Office or Congregation for Sacred Doctrine; Aquinas died as thoroughly rejected in high ecclesiastical circles as one could have been in the thirteenth century. Despite this, of course, and despite the fact that the influential Franciscans declared his teachings unacceptable in their schools, Aquinas shortly was canonized and declared a doctor of the church. He is now customarily termed the *doctor angelicus*, or *doctor communis*, the very standard of orthodoxy, particularly for those for whom any later Aquinas is an unthinkable prospect and whose acquaintance with him, in any case, is likely to be quite superficial.

It is not directly pertinent to our discussion, but indirectly very pertinent to note that Aquinas was the first of the medieval theologians to characterize *faith* as an *intellectual* virtue. This, totally apart from the fact that for Aquinas, no less than for Luther, there was a rigorous distinction between faith and reason. It was this theological position that put him into sharpest opposition with John Peckham, Archbishop of Canterbury, and Stephen Tempier, Archbishop of Paris—a position that was due to Aquinas' acceptance of Aristotelian realism in contrast with the Platonism and mysticism inherited from earlier theology. Our discussion is affected by the degree to which this theological determination reinforced the persuasion derived from the Fathers: to treat revelation, which was the object of faith, and Scripture, which was revelation in concrete form, as *doctrina sacra*, sacred teaching. Such an approach resulted in the fact that for Aquinas, *sacra doctrina, sacra Scriptura,* and even *sacra theologia* could be synonymous terms.[6] But by the same token, since Scripture was a teaching, it was not the text of the Scripture that was most important, but rather the meaning of the text—what it was understood to signify through the distillation of more than a millennium of Christian tradition. The text was involved, of course, both for what it plainly said and for what it plainly excluded. But what it plainly said was the same thing tradition had made plain, and of course, a doctrine became no less scriptural simply because tradition had found better words to express the reality intended than the scriptural text itself possessed. Thus Aquinas found it both appropriate and scriptural to use, in relation to God, a term such as "person," not found in the Scripture but also not *Scripturarum sensu discordans*, contrary to the meaning of Scripture.[7]

A theologian of the Middle Ages was primarily an expositor of the Bible. Only after becoming established as proficient in this area could one be presumed worthy to compose *sententiae* or *summae* of various kinds. The tradition continued long: Martin Luther's initial theological essays were commentaries on the psalms, which he produced while still lecturing as an Augustinian monk in his German university. (It might be noted that, until quite recently, a nervous post-Vatican I Roman Catholic administration had quite reversed this ancient rule, requiring a candidate for a "biblical" degree first to acquire one in "theology.") The Bible that the medieval theologian presented was, of course, the Bible of Christian tradition. It was the Bible, for all that—the only Bible that existed. Yves Congar has put it accurately:

> The theological thought of St. Thomas, as of the Middle Ages, at least up to his time, was based essentially on the Bible and tradition. We can never stress too much the fact

[6]Cf. Erik Persson, *Sacra Doctrina; Reason and Revelation in Aquinas,* trans. Ross Mackenzie (Philadelphia: Fortress Press, 1970), pp. 83-90. See also Aquinas, *ST,* Ia, q. 1, art. 2 ad 2; q. 1, art. 3.

[7]Aquinas, *ST,* Ia, q. 29, art. 3 ad 1.

that in those days theological teaching was profoundly biblical. The ordinary lecture of the master was a commentary on Sacred Scripture. That is why the scriptural commentaries of St. Thomas represent his ordinary public teaching as a master.[8]

And, if one who has studied both Aquinas' commentaries and his theological tractates may be permitted an added note, it is in the commentaries (especially, I would think, in those on Romans and Galatians, where he anticipated Luther's doctrine of *sola fide*) that he is at his scriptural best, in contrast with the fairly casual way he uses Scripture in his *Summa*.

If I seem to dwell unduly on the biblical orientation of pre-Reformation Catholicism, I apologize, but do not repent. It remains a fact that there is enormous ignorance of this matter even among theologians and church historians. I will not pursue it further, but only recommend to those who do not know it the work of Beryl Smalley on *Study of the Bible in the Middle Ages*.[9] There is also a little book of my own in which I begin with Geoffrey Chaucer (a contemporary of John Wycliffe and the Lollards) to suggest that the Bible was quite as much a waybook in Catholic England as it became later in Protestant England.[10] Only the circumstances were different.

The circumstances, of course, were those produced by history. If, in the words of an earlier Roman Catholic enthusiast, the thirteenth was "the greatest of centuries," it seems appropriate to agree with a modern historian's view that the fourteenth century was indeed "calamitous."[11] The melancholy story needs no rehearsing. It is a tragedy of errors—political, civil, and ecclesiastical—abetted by numerous acts of God. What is most important for our consideration is that, by reason of ecclesiastical

[8]Yves Congar, *A History of Theology,* trans. Hunter Guthrie, S.J. (New York: Doubleday & Co., 1968), pp. 113-14.

[9]Second ed. (Oxford: Basil Blackwell, 1952).

[10]Vawter, *The Bible in the Church* (New York: Sheed & Ward, 1959).

[11]Barbara W. Tuchman, *A Distant Mirror: The Calamitous 14th Century* (New York: Alfred A. Knopf, 1978).

schism, heresy, and disruption, the notion that any authentic ecclesiastical "tradition" regarding the Scripture had been safely handed down from of old simply disappeared. There remained only manmade "traditions" which had grown up about the Scripture and which could easily be seen as being contrary to it. When people came to believe that there was no longer a reliable tradition resulting from the decisions of a thousand years of Christianity as to the meaning of a scriptural text, the way was open for any interpretation one wanted to make. Of course, such a potentially anarchic situation did not always occur: Various Protestant orthodoxies with traditions of their own were soon established.

We come back to the *sola Scriptura* principle. It is certain that no Fathers of the church, no medieval theologians of the church, would have been uncomfortable with the formula *sola Scriptura*. According to their lights, that is exactly what they were dealing with. They were dealing with it, they thought, when they took the Scripture for what they thought it meant, as centuries of tradition had taught them its meaning. What became incredible to them, but very credible to the Reformers, for whom the church itself had become incredible, was that the proverbial ploughboy with the vernacular Bible in his hand was a match for the pope of Rome with all the councils of the church behind him. We really should try to understand this position as the enormity it must have appeared in Catholic eyes in the fifteenth century. It was as though, in our time, a fresh translation of the United States Constitution, independent of judicial interpretation from 1789 onward, should be presented in 1989 as the basis of the establishment of an American Republic with all the authenticity attaching to that name, disregarding two centuries of history.

It should be noted that the Scripture that had been adapted by the church — the Old Testament, which it had inherited, and the New Testament, which it had created largely on the precedent of the Old Testament — was also exclusively a matter of tradition. As for the new Testament, Augustine's principle is well known: He would not have accepted the truth of the gospel, except for the authority of the Catholic Church. The determination of the Old Testament had been even more traditionally tied. The Christian Old Testament—which is not the Hebrew Bible—is a genuine creation of proto-Christianity, growing out of Judaism (Palestinian and Diaspora) into something new. That new something was, in one respect at least, standard Christianity. It is not necessary to take a stand on the accuracy of the Septuagint as a faithful translation of the Hebrew Bible (to the extent that it was, indeed, a translation of the Hebrew Bible) to come to the conclusion that in any case, translation or otherwise, the Septuagint was the Bible of the New Testament and of early Christianity. (At least three-quarters of the citations of the Old Testament in the New Testament are from the Septuagint. It is a well- known fact that in early Christian times, the Septuagint had become so "Christian" that the new translations of Aquila, Symmachus, and Theodotion were called for in the Greek-speaking Jewish community.) The Septuagint "canon," in any case, is in reality the Old Testament of the Christian church as it was eventually determined by the Council of Trent.[12] The "Protestant" canon of the Old Testament, ultimately a determination of copy editors rather than of biblical scholars, was the result of a misunderstanding which began with Jerome concerning the authentic text of "the Word of God," together with a lack of factual information about the historical process that had led to a collection of works which would be finally denominated as canonical.[13] The so-called Protestant canon of the Old Testament is ultimately a Renaissance construct based on insufficient knowledge of the past. In a rather different area, but out of a similar faulty reconstruction of the past, the Renaissance scholars popularized the *textus receptus* of the New Testament—the averaged, Byzantine text—which long enjoyed pride of place in Protestant Bibles in preference to the better

[12]Henricus Denzinger and Adolfus Schönmetzer, S.J., *Enchiridion Symbolorum* (hereafter cited as DS), 34th ed. (Barcelona: Herder & Herder, 1967), §§ 1501-503.

[13]Cf. Jack N. Lightstone, "The Formation of the Biblical Canon in Judaism of Late Antiquity: Prolegomenon to a General Reassessment," *SR* 8 (1979): 135-42.

text tradition that underlay the Vulgate Latin, and which has in recent times been replaced only with great difficulty.

And so we return to consideration of Scripture as the determinant of faith, Catholic or Protestant, as represented in the various formulations. *Sola Scriptura*, for reasons that now should be apparent, was a formula made impossible for Catholic orthodoxy by the Reformation movement. A century—even a half-century—earlier, it would have been possible, but now it had become, in Catholic eyes, little more than a slogan of Protestant intransigence. Hence the decree of the Council of Trent, in its Fourth Session of April 8, 1546, determined, first of all, that the source (*fons*) of

> all salutary and moral discipline [is] the gospel promised before by the prophets in the holy Scriptures, promulgated by the very mouth of our Lord Jesus Christ the Son of God, then to be preached by his Apostles to every creature [and that] this truth and discipline is contained in written books and unwritten traditions which were received by the Apostles from the mouth of Christ himself or by the Apostles themselves under the inspiration of the Holy Spirit [*Spiritu Sancto dictante*].[14]

In retrospect, this formulation certainly could have been happier. Had it put tradition in the singular rather than the plural, it would have been more pleasing to any present-day Catholics properly attuned, as they think, to the belief and profession of their church: that tradition is not a rival source of doctrine to that contained in Scripture, but that it is the interpretative envelope in which Scripture has been transmitted as *sacra doctrina*. However, as everyone must surely know, conciliar language is committee language, the language of compromise. The concept of tradition and of traditions was as much confused— that is, subject to variant interpretations—at the Council of Trent as it was in Montreal in 1963, where the words of Kristen Eynar Skydsgarard were remarkably like those of Trent:

[14]DS § 1501. On the propriety of translating "under the inspiration," see n. 17 below.

Naturally Luther agrees that the church existed before the
Scripture, but he also insisted that the word of God itself
already was before the church and before the written book
. . . . The living word of God is before every Gospel . . . a
word which first of all is not to be written and read, but it
is absolutely necessary that this word be spoken and heard
. . . . Christ has not called us to write, but to preach.[15]

At Trent the concept of tradition(s) was variously understood:
as traditions which were apostolical or merely ecclesiastical;
as being on a par with or subordinate to Scripture; as interpretative of or supplementary to Scripture; as relating only to
practice or to doctrine itself; and in many other ways. We should
hardly expect this council, under the pressures it then experienced, to have accomplished in the sixteenth century successful ecumenical formulas which have not yet been produced by
the twentieth. One formulation it did avoid—for whatever
reason—was that which had been proposed in pre-Tridentine
Counter-Reformation theology at the council itself and which
subsequently would appear in some post-Tridentine theology—
namely, that divine revelation was the possession of Scripture
and tradition(s) *partim . . . partim*, partly in the one, partly in
the other. This formula disappeared entirely in the delibera-
tions of the council. And thus it appears that George H. Tavard
is quite correct in his final assessment of the achievement of
Trent as the most and the best that could be expected at that
time of any ecumenical council: Compared with pre-Tridentine
theology, the decree of April 1546 makes it impossible to hold
that new doctrines may still be revealed to the Church [the
thought that postapostolic traditions could be intruded into the
articles of faith]: the stress on apostolicity is too well marked
to be compatible with such a view. It remains neutral on a notion of Tradition (in the singular), which would include Scripture and be identified with the life or conscience of the Church:
the rationale of the Council precluded consideration of this problematic but did not gainsay the underlying theology. It finally

---

[15]Cited in Eduard Stakemeier, *Die Konzilskonstitution über die göttliche
Offenbarung* (Paderborn: Bonifacius-Druckerei, 1966), pp. 27-28.

respects the classical view: Scripture contains all revealed doctrine, and the Church's faith, which includes apostolic traditions, interprets it.[16]

Vatican Councils I and II, the two councils of the Roman church that have occurred since the Council of Trent, have added nothing essential to the determinations of that council (composed mainly of Italian and Spanish bishops, never more than a hundred or so) with regard to this vital question. The First Vatican Council did no more than reiterate Trent's definition of Scripture, interpreting that *Spiritu Sancto dictante* should be read in more modern terms: *Spiritu Sancto inspirante*.[17] In either case, of course, we are dealing with gross anthropomorphisms. "God dictates"—I need not remind you that dictation in the modern sense, or at least in the sense we like to think modern, when the one dictated to is totally passive to the dictator, is the product of a recent world of shorthand pads and electronics. "God inspiring" calls us back to an even earlier frame of reference, to the concept of a vital essence that can be breathed into a passive recipient. I will not enter here into the question of the mechanics of biblical inspiration. My only point at this juncture is to insist that Vatican I did nothing further than the Council of Trent, except to change its terminology slightly.

Nor did Vatican II much affect the question. Vatican II accepted the "new" terminology of *inspired* to characterize the sacred Scripture, but beyond this and the specific note that these books of Scripture contain "revelations without error" and attest to "God as their co-Author," nothing much more was said— certainly nothing more than had been suggested by both Protestant and Catholic theology in the interim.[18]

The only real question that arises, therefore, from the stand-

---

[16]George H. Tavard, *Holy Writ or Holy Church, The Crisis of the Protestant Reformation* (New York: Harper & Brothers, 1959) pp. 208-209. Tavard's summation of the situation at the Council of Trent is excellently excised from the minutes of the sessions, see pp. 195-209.

[17]DS § 3006.

[18]W.M. Abbott and J. Gallagher, eds., *The Documents of Vatican II* (New York: Guild Press, 1966), pp. 119-21.

point of the Catholic reader of Scripture is this: Who indeed determines the traditional meaning of the Scripture, the meaning that should appeal to us in an existential sense; the meaning that commands us to take action, that reveals to us the *Sachgehalt*, content, of the Word of God?

In the Catholic Church we talk about the magisterium, the teaching authority of the church, the ultimate determinant of what is to be believed and not believed – in these days, at least, what the pope and his bishops have determined to be the norm of faith. It was not so always. I have no intention here of invading the realm of the ecclesiastical historian, who will tell you that there was a time when an ecumencial council of the church could stand up against the pope and say him nay without recrimination. It is very obvious today that a pope can stand up against an ecumenical council and say it nay without recriminations. In the Middle Ages, the magisterium of the church referred to: the authority of the pope, which was always respected; the accumulated authority of the bishops, which was respected only slightly less because it was harder to garner; the *consensus theologorum*, the common agreement of those who were supposed to devote themselves professionally to the study of the meaning of revelation; and the *consensus fidelium*, the common belief of all Christians, against which deviations and heresies could be measured. All these constituted the magisterium of the church when there was, for all practical purposes, only the one church which was coextensive with the body of Christian believers.

None of these components of magisterium was judged to be absolutely imperative of itself. The famous formula of Vincent of Lerins: *quod semper, quod ubique, quod ab omnibus,* the commonality of Christian faith, was called into question long before John Henry Newman's *Essay on the Development of Christian Doctrine,* and certainly before Walter Bauer's *Orthodoxy and Heresy in Earliest Christianity.* "Athanasius against the world" of Arianism is a far earlier precedent. Theologians, as we have seen, could stand fairly well against a consensus of their peers, and yet almost within their own lifetimes be styled "doctors of the church." Pope could and did anathematize pope, council could anathematize council, and, for good measure, pope could anathematize council–and council, pope. Together, however, these components were constitutive of the beliefs of the church in regard to its constitutional documents, the sacred Scripture of the Old and New Testaments.

Historical circumstances have radically altered this rather free and easy approach to magisterium. Both the Reformation and a more respectable papalism which eventually developed in reaction to the Reformation resulted *within the Catholic Church itself,* and not merely with regard to those outside its fold, in the concept of an *ecclesia docens*, the teaching church, superior to the *ecclesia docta*, the church that is taught, the faithful.

There has been no doubt, in recent times at least, according to textbook theology, about who it is that constitutes this "teaching church." It is the bishops of the church and, more specifically, the bishop of Rome, speaking with or without the consultation of the other bishops, who, in practice, serve as his appointees throughout the Roman Catholic world. To be even more specific, the teaching church generally finds its exercise through the decisions of the largely anonymous decrees of the congregations or bureaus of the Roman curia, which officate in the name of the Holy Father, sometimes with and sometimes without his explicit advertence.

Actually, the situation does not affect individual Catholic consciences as much as one might think. The First Vatican Council on July 18, 1870, defined the infallibility of the Roman pontiff in matters of faith and morals under certain sharply defined conditions.[19] His decisions, it was decreed, should be regarded as definitive of themselves, and not from the consent of the church. This is what the textbooks call the extraordinary magisterium of the church. It would, I think, be difficult to find any contemporary Catholic theologian who would defend the proposition that the Catholic Church, either prior to or subsequent to the First Vatican Council, has ever submitted the Scripture in whole or in part to this "extraordinary magisterium" for

---

[19]DS § 3006.

any effect that would not find general agreement with most of those who consider themselves Christians.

We are left, therefore, in the main with the church's "ordinary magisterium," which, as I have said, in post-Reformation times has come increasingly to mean the utterances of the pope or of his surrogates in the Roman congregations. Especially in the nineteenth and twentieth centuries, there came into existence the papal "encyclical letter," a pronouncement made in the pope's own name and above his signature, carrying with it, no doubt intentionally, a greater than usual approbation of the Apostolic See. The encyclicals, as far as they have affected biblical studies, have been very liberal and enlightened. The *Providentissimus Deus* (November 18, 1893) of Leo XIII, for example, while it treated the newfangled "critical" approach to the Bible with some horror, at the same time recognized–against the fundamentalism of biblical inerrancy–that the biblical authors had intended to write nothing about profane matters (*nulli saluti profutura*, in the words of Augustine), but only saving truths; that therefore their observations on physical realities and the like must be judged in accordance with the opinions of their age. In a special paragraph, Leo noted that the same principle of interpretation might "especially be applied to biblical history."[20] When the largely unsung but profoundly influential Austrian Jesuit Franz von Hummelauer (1842-1914) took up this historical challenge, he succeeded only in provoking several decisions by the Pontifical Biblical Commission in 1905, under Pius X, which condemned all his views–the courtesy extended, however, of no reprobation by name.[21] (Mercifully, no encyclical on biblical studies was ever issued in the reign of Pius X.) The *Spiritus Paraclitus* of Benedict XV (pope 1914-1922), a pope hardly remembered today, was a truly pedestrian enterprise–little more than a series of commonplaces on Scripture, together with an affirmation that Pius X had not been wrong when he insisted that Leo XIII had never authorized any conception of biblical history as "relative" rather than "absolute." Both these terms

[20]DS §§ 3288-90.
[21]Cf. *DBS* 4, 144-46.

were qualified as "so-called" and "according to common parlance," whatever this may mean.[22] Nothing further really happened in the papal area until the *Divino afflante Spiritu* of 1943, which was appropriately termed by French scholars *l'encyclique libératrice,* the liberating encyclical, which, among other things, endorsed wholeheartedly the Hummelauerian principle that *"jede literarische Art hat die ihr eigentümliche Wahrheit,"* which was acceptably translated into the Latin of Augustin Bea as *"sua cuique propria est generi litterario veritas."*[23] The anathema and unacceptable of one age thus became the *doctrina communis* of another. Since 1943 there has been no additional papal encyclical expressly on the Scripture. It must be admitted, however, that the *Humani Generis* of 1950, an encyclical of the same Pius XII who had authored *Divino afflante Spiritu,* in the process of criticizing certain contemporary tendencies in the sacred sciences found it necessary to reprobate "in a special way" the "too free interpretation of the historical books of the Old Testament."[24] The mistake, the encyclical noted, was due this time to misinterpretation of a letter sent by the Pontifical Biblical Commission in 1948 to Cardinal Suhard, then the archbishop of Paris. This leads us to consider the other media through which the "ordinary magisterium" of the church has been exercised in respect to the Bible.

Since the Council of Trent, three Roman congregations or commissions have had to do with official ecclesiastical pronouncements regarding the Scripture. First, there was the Congregation of the Council, which initially was instituted to provide authentic interpretations of the decrees of the Council of Trent. It did not last long in this capacity; there is still a Congregation of the Council in the Roman curia, but it is concerned with other matters and has nothing more than the name in common with its predecessor. Second, there is a group originally called the Congregation of the Inquisition (not connected with the Spanish Inquisition); for most of its recent life, it was termed

[22]DS § 3653.
[23]See Vawter, *Biblical Inspiration,* pp. 122, 177.
[24]DS §§ 3898-99.

the Congregation of the Holy Office and now most recently has been renamed the Congregation for the Doctrine of the Faith. Its purpose was and is the preservation of the purity of Catholic doctrine; the change of names doubtless reflects in some measure the difference of approach to this preservation through the centuries.

Finally, there was the Pontificial Biblical Commission established in 1902 by Pope Leo XIII (who included among its first consultors both Franz von Hummelauer and also Marie-Joseph Lagrange, O.P., who had been equal sufferers under Roman scrutiny) partly at least in answer to a wave of protest that had greeted a response of the Congregation of the Inquisition in 1897 regarding the so-called Johannine comma (1 John 5:7). Could the authenticity of this passage be called into question? No, was the response of the Congregation, even though to every critical eye of the time it was already obvious that it was a Latin interpolation into the Greek text, inserted no earlier than the fourth century. Leo XIII intended to avoid future embarrassments of this kind for church authority by assembling a corps of consultors who were competent to rule on such critical matters. But in 1903, Pius X began to rule, and from that time on the Biblical Commission outdid the Inquisition at its own game, piling up a collection of authoritarian decrees–on implicit citations in Scripture, on the species of scriptural historiography, on the Mosaic authorship of the Pentateuch, on the authorship of the four Gospels and Acts, and so on–in a total vacuum of naked authority isolated from the scholarly world. (It is to be remembered, of course, that in this same period appeared the decree of the Holy Office *Lamentabili* and the encyclical *Pascendi* in which the Modernist crisis was faced by the Roman Church.) Not until the time of Pius XII and under the secretaryship of J.M. Vosté, O.P., did the Biblical Commission resume the positive directions that originally had been intended for it. It should be acknowledged, however, that in 1927 the Congregation of the Holy Office did reconsider the 1897 decision on the Johannine comma, and it explained that its intention had not been to inhibit free and critical discussion of the text, but only to vindicate the teaching authority of the church against mere private opinion. As I once wrote, "Given the literary form of Roman curial documents, this amounted to a handsome apology for having made a precipitate and unnecessary intrusion into the arena of scholarly discussion."[25] Only in 1979, after all, did Pope John Paul II find it opportune to declare that the same Congregation of the Inquisition had erred in its seventeenth-century condemnation of Galileo–a matter to which we shall return.

Most of the early decrees of the Biblical Commission were framed from the assumption of an adversary situation between church tradition and critical acceptation of the Bible. The more the critical view of the Bible prevailed in the western world, the less credible some of these decrees appeared as applicable to the Universal Church. In 1955 the Roman curia recognized this fact and, within its *stylus curiae*, corrected the bad situation that had developed. On the appearance in that year of a new edition of the *Enchiridion Biblicum* (a more or less official Roman collection of ecclesiastical documents pertaining to the Scripture), both the secretary and the undersecretary of the commission simultaneously published an identical article, indicating that in their minds those prior decrees, to the extent that they did not touch on essential matters of faith and morals, ought not to inhibit the free exercise and use of critical method and its results in coming to quite opposed conclusions.[26] Since that time the Biblical Commission has, by and large, not only refrained from negative inhibitions on critical biblical research but, on its own initiative, also has suggested avenues of research in which biblical science can and should assist in the *magisterium ecclesiae*. It has not, to be sure, suggested very many of these,

---

[25] Vawter, *Biblical Inspiration,* p. 123 n.

[26] Athanasius Miller, O.S.B., "Das neue biblische Handbuch," *Benediktinische Monatschrift* 31 (1955): 49-50; A. Kleinhans, "De nova Enchiridii Biblici editione," *Antonianum* 30 (1955): 63-65. Kleinhans later incorporated this interpretation in "Bibelkommission," *LTK* 2: 359-60. See also *CBQ* 17 (1955): 50-53, 450-51; E.F. Siegman, C.Pp.S., "The decrees of the Biblical Commission," *CBQ* 18 (1956): 23-29; J. Dupont, O.S.B., "A propos du nouvel Enchiridion Biblicum," *RB* 62 (1955): 415-19.

nor have there been too many other invitations from the hierarchical church for exegetical assistance in its pastoral mission. Nevertheless, the climate of the present is vastly different from that which preceded the Second Vatican Council.

Thus for example, in 1964 the commission issued an "Instruction on the Historical Truth of the Gospels,"[27] which effectively distinguished the levels in the Gospel narratives that frequently are called the *Sitz im Leben Jesu* (the origin within the circumstances of the historical Jesus of Nazareth), the *Sitz im Leben Ecclesiae* (the area covered by form criticism), and the *Sitz im Evangelium* (the area of redaction criticism), and it invited exegetes to consider the implications of these distinctions as they affect the question of the historical character of the New Testament.[28] The substance of this instruction was accepted into the New Testament section of the *Dei Verbum* constitution of the Second Vatican Council.[29] In more recent times we have witnessed a ruling by a majority vote of the members of the commission to the effect that there is no peremptory argument to be extracted from Scripture that would prohibit the ordination of women to priestly ministry within the church, a position which, to say the least, has not proved acceptable to the higher exercise of the magisterium.[30]

It was probably this once quasi-adversary symbiosis of church authority with theology/exegesis that accounts for, or at least contributed to the involvement of the authoritarian levels of the Roman Catholic Church with a concept of total biblical inerrancy in the nineteenth and early twentieth centuries. This concept, as James Barr has correctly maintained, is essentially a Protestant concept–a more or less modern Protestant concept, for that matter–a reaction that emerged among people whose only guide of life, the Bible, plain and unencumbered by any

---

[27]*AAS* 56 (1964): 712-18.

[28]Cf. Joseph A. Fitzmyer, S.J., "The Biblical Commission's Instruction on the Historical Truth of the Gospels," *TS* 25 (1964): 386-408.

[29]Abbott and Gallagher, *Documents of Vatican II*, p. 124.

[30]"Women and Priestly Ministry: The New Testament Evidence," *CBQ* 41 (1979): 608-13.

traditional refraction, suddenly was found to be in apparent conflict with the revelation of a newfound science and history.[31] Some years ago Karl Rahner also raised the question: What is the point of proposing an infallible Bible in a church that professes to already have an infallible teaching authority in faith and morals?[32] I am less interested in Rahner's response than in the pertinence of his question.

The concept of biblical inerrancy is not to be confused with the venerable Jewish and Christian affirmation that the Bible is the true Word of God communicated without falsehood. *Falsehood*, not *error*, is the antinomy of the *truth* of the Bible that was sustained by the Fathers and the theologians of the medieval church.[33] As we have seen before, it was the conviction of these earlier generations of Christians that the Bible, throughout, was a document of divine revelation relating to salvation, not an encyclopedia of useful information concerning matters that could be ascertained through the natural means of human observation or record. Apparently purely "profane" *dicta* of Scripture either were researched for the "spiritual" religious sense that lay beneath their surface or were dismissed as *obiter dicta*, peripheral to the divine message, a natural accompaniment to it conditioned by the circumstances of the times.[34] It was not assumed that there was, apart from a salvific context, a biblical utterance about anything whatever that could be called inerrant.

The notorious Galileo case of 1633 is no exception to this rule, unless to prove it. Some years ago, I spent a bit of time looking at the exegetical principles employed by some of the most respected Catholic exegetes of the late sixteenth and early seventeenth centuries and compared them with those employed

[31]James Barr, *Fundamentalism* (Philadelphia: Westminster Press, 1978), pp. 40-41.

[32]Karl Rahner, *Studies in Modern Theology* (Freiburg: Herder, 1965), p. 31.

[33]Cf. Oswald Loretz, *Galilei und der Irrtum der Inquisition* (Kevelaer: Butzon & Bercker, 1966), pp. 182-209.

[34]There are exceptions, of course, but the rule is exemplified in such citations as those which appear in n. 2, 3 above.

by Galileo.[35] Incidentally, in the case at hand, Galileo was not, as some secondhand apologists have tried to maintain, a mathematician who foolishly had tried to play the theologian without learning the rules. On the contrary, Galileo's exegesis (which was, by the standards of the time, entirely to the point and unexceptionable) differed in no respect from the exegesis of those who opposed him.[36] It was as hard then as it is now for me to avoid the conclusion that Galileo's ecclesiastical condemnation was a matter of contemporary convenience, in conformity with the judgment of Giorgio di Santillana (*The Crime of Galileo*). That is to say, it was the academic conservatism of the dominant Aristotelianism, more than anything religious, that decided Galileo's fate. Academe then spoke with a religious voice rather than with another, for this was the seventeenth and not yet the eighteenth, nineteenth, or twentieth century, but it was an academic voice for all that. The admixture of the academic with the religious is evident in the Inquisition's decree:

> The proposition that the sun is the center of the world and does not move from its place is absurd and false philosophically, and formally heretical because it is expressly contrary to Holy Scripture. The proposition that the earth is not the center of the world and immovable, but that it moves and also has a diurnal motion, is equally absurd and false philosophically and at least erroneous in faith.[37]

This was neither the first nor the last time the secular arm returned the compliment the church had frequently conferred upon it by impressing it into the service of doing its dirty work.

The fact is that in no council of the Universal Church, either before or after the Reformation, has the formula of inerrancy been applied to the Bible. The formula was applied, to be sure, by various popes and papal commissions, but only subsequent

---

[35]Vawter, "Biblical Interpretation and the Positive Sciences," *Homiletic and Pastoral Review* 71 (1961) 1127-38.

[36]Loretz, *Galilei*, pp. 72-100.

[37]Santillana, *Crime of Galileo* (Chicago: University of Chicago Press, 1955), p. 307.

to Vatican I. By Vatican II, it was expressly rejected, though it appeared in its crassest form in the original draft presented to the conciliar fathers, and it clung there tenaciously until the fourth and penultimate redaction of what finally would emerge as the constitution *Dei Verbum*.[38] Through this process the original, truly fundamentalistic assertion that "divine inspiration by its very nature excludes and rejects every error in every field, religious or profane" yielded at last to the conclusion that, concerning inspiration, "it follows that the books of Scripture must be acknowledged as teaching firmly, faithfully, and without error that truth which God wanted put into the sacred writings for the sake of our salvation."[39] This was the voice of authentic Judeo-Christian tradition, rather than a reaction to the displacement of scriptural omniscience exploded by the Enlightenment or to the danger of exegetes' infection by the spirit of skepticism.

Another anomaly from which Roman Catholicism has been protected by its tradition is Marcionism, whether in its original or in its latter-day manifestations–namely, the position that Old Testament history and theology are irrelevant to Christian faith. This position, in modern times, without recriminations, I perceive to be characteristic of German rather than of other continental scholarship–certainly not of Anglo-Saxon. In any case, no doubt owing to the well-deserved acclaim of German scholarship, it is a much respected position in Protestant circles (and also, of course, in some Catholic circles, which are no less immune to the prestige attached to German scholarship). There are many chapters and verses I could cite, but I shall cite only one, a quite recent one. Franz Hesse, a truly distinguished biblical scholar, at the conclusion of an excellent commentary on the book of Job, finds it necessary to note that its sublime message is, after all, obsolete for Christians, since it appears in a part of the Bible that is not normative for Christianity.[40]

[38]Otto Semmelroth and Maximilian Zerwick, *Vaticanum II über das Wort Gottes,* SBS 16 (Stuttgart: Katholisches Bibelwerk, 1966), pp. 28-34.

[39]Cf. Abbott and Gallagher, *Documents of Vatican II*, p. 119, esp. n. 31.

[40]Franz Hesse, *Hiob,* Zürcher Bibelkommentare AT 14 (Zürich: Theologisches Verlag, 1978).

Such a position would be impossible for one sensitive to the Catholic tradition, not only because of papal statements such as the *Mit brennender Sorge* of Pope Pius XI, which reaffirmed the *Heilspädagogik* of the Old Testament and was sent to the German bishops in the heyday of Nazi superstition;[41] but more important, because of an unbroken succession to which one feels he belongs, a succession that stretches from its earliest written records, perhaps in the Muratorian canon, down to its latest, such as the *Dei Verbum* of Vatican II.

Let us conclude. If the *norma normans* of Scripture on the official teaching of the church is to be measured ideally in terms of the immediate effect produced on it by the consensus of its exegetes, we are not as advantageously positioned in this present century as was the church of the Fathers or of the Middle Ages. The adversary condition between authority and scholarship still exists to some degree, manifested now not as much in repression of the one over the other as in the former's choice to ignore what the latter may be saying. Any number of doctrinal and moral issues presently troubling the church could be alleviated and not further confused were the "teaching" church only more receptive to the words of those who manifestly possess from the Spirit the charisma of teaching rather than of government. Still, in the long run there is much more reason to rejoice than to despair. The same issue of *L'Osservatore Romano* which reports the censure of Hans Küng also contains an allocution of the currently reigning Roman pontiff on the Yahwistic creation story of Genesis 2-3 which depends on an impeccably critical appreciation of the biblical text. The Council of Trent, which desiderated a restoration of a Latin Bible *quam emendatissime*, corrected to the extent possible, for the liturgical and doctrinal usages of a Latin church, has, in this last year, finally seen the realization of its aspirations in the appearance of a new Vulgate–an entirely new version done by an international corps of scholars from the original texts, mandated by Pope Paul VI and promulgated by Pope John Paul II. In turn, this has pursued a policy inaugurated by Pope Pius XII, who

---

[41] *AAS* 29 (1937): 151.

never cited a biblical text in Latin unless the translation was in accord with the original. And it would be hard to imagine, despite all the prognoses that dictated otherwise, a more satisfactorily scriptural emphasis in the official utterances of any Christian body than that which emerged in the decrees of the Second Vatican Council. Such is providence, an even more trustworthy companion than scholarship.

2. The God of Hebrew Scriptures

Uncertainty is the law of this life. It is a law that is learnt only reluctantly, even by those who should best know how inexorable a law it is. One may recall how the great H.H. Rowley deplored the passing of critical consensus on the book of the prophet Ezekiel, some twenty-five years ago. It was, he said, a passing "certainly calculated to fill the student with wonder as to whether present-day scholarship has any objective standards" (Rowley). The present writer applauded this sentiment at the time, and complacently contrasted the stability of the rest of OT studies with those of the NT. (As a matter of fact, that "seamless robe of Christ" which was supposed to be the Gospel of John just about at this same time, in great similarity with Ezekiel, was being tentatively regarded as a work of complex redaction, as it has proved to be with many subsequent refinements of the scholars). Now, however, we have seen how many other OT consensuses have appeared only to disappear as though they had never been, to have had once an ephemeral success that brooked no respectable opposition only to vanish utterly in our days as objects of undeserved derision on the part of later scholars, many of whom never even paid their proper dues to entitle them to assist at the obsequies. One will think immediately, of course, about the source-criticism of the Pentateuch/Hexateuch/Tetrateuch, an enterprise which might even be said to have created modern critical method, which engaged in the past scholars probably of a calibre superior to any of those whom we possess today.

One may also think of other consensuses which other OT studies have dislodged from a previous position that a dozen years or so ago seemed to be unassailable. Martin Noth's reconstruction of the Israelite *amphictyony*, for example, which made so much sense a short generation ago, today can be dismissed even in a deeply conservative journal not on peremptory grounds of infidelity to a revealed word but on eminently historico-literary principles according to which the hypothesis simply does not correspond to fact (Hauser). And what are we to say with regard to even more recent hypotheses which may or may not survive the next decade of scholarly enterprise? With regard to George Mendenhall's notion of the real circumstances of Israel's "conquest" of Canaan, for example, according to which the *Landnahme*, the taking over of the land, essentially is transmuted from foreign invasion into a proletarian revolt of an indigenous population? Or with regard to Margaret Barker's notion of the circumstances of the postexilic Judahite "restoration" in Palestine? If I read her rightly (Barker), she tends to suggest that the canonical text of the OT represents rather a botch of a *pis aller* of historical challenges that should and could have been greeted by far preferable solutions.

These scholarly reversals and revisions present no problem for historical positivists, to whom history is simply a series of unrelated events, a story that has no patterns, no plan, no direction, and is only the record of what supposedly actually happened. They do present problems for those who, without ceasing to be critically historical in their thinking, also wish to believe–on grounds which admittedly are not historical in the positive sense–that there is a theology of history, or, to put it more aptly, that in history the grounds for a biblical theology have been revealed.

Let us consider two propositions, the first of which is somewhat paradoxical. It is paradoxical because it seems that only now it the scholarly community beginning to recognize that OT criticism affects Christian faith quite as much as, if not more than, the criticism of the NT. Along with many others, I once

thought somewhat naïve the decision of the ecclesiastical authorities made after the publication of Marie-Joseph Lagrange's *La
méthode historique* in 1903 that he should confine himself to
the "safer" and less "controversial" area of NT rather than of
OT research. I am not so sure, now, that the Roman wallahs
were not on the right track: the OT did and does present for
Christian faith a problematic that is antecedent to and far more
complicated than anything that is contained in the NT. To dismiss the enormous problems with which the OT confronts Christian belief requires a complete disdain of history, whether this
is expressed by a fundamentalism which has constructed a "salvation history" acceptable to itself but to no disinterested historian, or by a neo-gnostic reinterpretation of Christianity which
regards its historical presuppositions to be nothing other than
flotsam on the sea of circumstance out of which Christian faith
emerged.

The second point is, of course, that the OT does not present
one single problem for NT belief in God, but many. Put in
another way: the challenge which the OT seems to present to
us rises less from the inacceptibility of its God-construct than
it does from the incompatibility of multiple constructs which
may be at war with one another. Before the Christian accepts
OT theology as a *propedeuticon* of his own belief, in other
words, it appears that he first must put together from the OT
documents a theology which the OT itself never produced. This
is to ask a good deal.

The problem does not disappear for us simply because it was
no problem either for the Tannaim or for the Fathers of the
Church. The Tannaim and the Fathers were conditioned by the
syncretism of their age to acquiesce in judgments which the
pluralism of our age can never permit. Though the judgments
which we do make should certainly never be made with any
disdain of those made by our fathers in the faith, whether of
the NT or the patristic era, of Chalcedon or the Middle Ages,
of the Reformation or the Enlightenment, still, in every case
we have to do with time-conditioned statements of varying
degrees of authority, which however authoritative they may be
remain nevertheless time-conditioned according to the recog-

nizance of a time that is not our own, and which leave us, therefore, always with the duty to solve our own problems for ourselves without any easy bypass of once-for-all solutions frozen
in ancient consecrated words of human devising. The Second
Vatican Council said no less than this in its decree *Dei Verbum*
when it noted of OT revelation the element contained there which
is "incomplete and temporary" (Abbott: 122), and also acknowledged that in relation to the Scripture the church is "the pupil
of the Holy Spirit, concerned to move ahead daily toward a
deeper understanding" of the Bible–a paragraph in which the
Council insisted upon the vital necessity of up-to-date scholarship *in re biblica* (Abbott:126). I assume, of course, that what
is "incomplete and temporary" has not been so demonstrated
once and for all but may be patient of the continued demonstration of ourselves or of subsequent generations assisting the
church in its docility to the better comprehension of the meaning of the word of God, which mainly is a word about God.

Diversity of the God Concept

The foregoing is prefatory to the proposition that the diverse
characterizations of the God of the OT as presented in the OT
documents do not add up to a minus but to a plus. For one thing,
they carry with them the ring of authenticity as regards divine
revelation. If we take as a classic definition of divine revelation that it is the word of God communicated to man in human
terms, then we must certainly expect that the communication
has come to us in all the vagaries of which the human mind
and heart are capable. Capable of encompassing God as of all
else, naturally, since God is unknowable to man except in his
metaphysical essence, which is a construct of the human mind.
And secondly, the variety of OT testimony to God should be
cherished as a protection against the human temptation to *hybris*,
to the gnostic pretension of total awareness of the divine, an
illusion which can provoke disaster not only religious but also,
perhaps, civil and political, as our own times may demonstrate.
Ignoring this variety may also result in heresy in the most

etymological sense of the word, a *hairesis*, a choosing, whether perverse or well-intentioned, which results in what can only be considered a perversion of the message of the OT.

In an article of over a dozen years ago, Morton Smith offered as a definition of the Yahweh of the OT–a god in whose existence "nobody, as far as I know, believes," "a North-Arabian mountain god who traveled in thunderstorms and liked the smell of burning fat" (Smith: 1969, 21). At that time I suggested that if Morton Smith was serious in this summation of the meaning of the God of the OT, either his collection of a "body of documents from the ancient Mediterranean world" (his term for the OT) happened to miss some folios that were in my collection, "or he has gravely misconstrued the character of the literature to whose study he has dedicated his scholarly life" (Vawter: 1974, 477). Smith's reading of the OT testimony I cannot with all charity consider to be anything other than in its own way a perverse *hairesis* and a travesty of history. Had the Yahweh of Israel been nothing more than what he called him, this Yahweh would surely have taken his place simply as a problematical cypher among the 500 or so other divine names which Mitchell Dahood has discerned in the Eblaite pantheon (Dahood). It is hard for me to believe that by a totally random process Christians' worship of God under the title of "Lord" = "Kyrios," which is in turn an "Adonai" or "Yahweh" of the OT, took place in a vacuum of other contenders for supreme lordship in the Ancient Near East. Such a conclusion, however, I admit depends as much, or at least almost as much, upon a presumption of faith as it does upon the empirical evidence.

To pursue the consequences of my proposition: we do not have from the OT a consistent portrait of God as we would expect to have from, let us say, a *Summa* of the Middle Ages or a *Dogmatik* of the twentieth century. Anyone who thinks that we have such a consistent portrait is either ignorant of the OT evidence or has, on grounds of his own, decided to bend the OT evidence to conform to a model of his own construction, which is generally a model that he has extracted less from the NT, from which he thinks it comes, than from a syncretistic "God" concept which is as alien to real history as was the "Theos"

of Hellenistic myth or as is the "God" of American civil religion.
The second proposition I would like to make is that we have
no reason to expect any such consistent portrait, that in fact
such a consistent portrait would be a certain sign that the OT
sin of idolatry has been committed, namely that we have sought
to create God according to our own image and likeness. As I
have said, when we speak the word "God" we enunciate a human
construct, a philosophical metaphysics. No one who is unprepared to think in metaphysical terms has any right to expect
his idea of God to be given respectability as a term capable of
being grappled with by anyone else. This principle applies
equally I am sure, to a pre-Kantian medievalist to whom "cause"
is the same whether it occurred before time in the beginning
of all or refers to a present rearrangement of furniture in his
own apartment. Equally it applies to the biblical fundamentalist
whose God is grandfather writ large, the God who frowns on
extra-tribal vices but certifies the ways of the tribe as most
righteous. It applies as well to thinkers for whom "history" is
a univocal concept, despite all the qualifications that the past
couple of centuries have taught us to apply to it.

As far as the first point is concerned, it is hard to see why
there should be problems. Why should the Yahweh of Israel,
a Deity worshipped in the north as in the south in the days of
the prophets Amos and Hosea at approximately the same time
in the eighth century B.C., have been precisely the same in the
popular religion of the two nations anymore than he was
separately for these two charismatic men? Amos looked out on
a world, which included Israel, that he could regard only as
a *massa corruptionis*, a world for which there could be no
redemption. His proclamation of God, therefore, certainly justified by Israel's experience of Yahweh, was one of inexorable
retribution, for the nations as well as for Israel. He made a great
contribution to theodicy thereby: justice has its demands which
are not to be countered by sentimentalist parodies of theology,
and if we figure God as the epitome of justice, he cannot be
a God who is less than rigorously just. It is hard to agree with
various recent commentators who have tried to temper Amos'
message by holding as "authentic" such passages as 9:11-15

which earlier commentators instinctively recognized to be ac-
commodating gestures towards a comfortable postexilic theological synthesis. The God of Amos, the God of total justice,
is not, to be sure, the only God, but he is God for all that and
he should not be confused with other Gods.

And what of the God of Hosea, Amos' contemporary? There
is no reason to think that Amos and Hosea consciously served
other than the one Yahweh of Northern Israel. Quite apart from
the biblical records, the stela of Mesha King of Moab confirms
for us that it was only this Yahweh who was the Deity of Israel.
[For what it is worth, I find convincing the contention that the
original name was Yahw (two syllables; the source of the latter Yahu/o, etc.), that the *h* terminal of the Mesha stela is a
possessive pronoun, and that the tetragrammaton was tenden-
tiously formed. So Martin Rose (Rose).] Yet What does Hosea
tell us about this God, what revelation of him that had never
been made known to the mind and heart of an Amos? What
was revealed in Hosea, to adopt the phrase of John L. McKenzie, was a God of "divine passion" (McKenzie).

One can hardly read Hosea 11:8-9 in its context without
becoming convinced that in these verses we have the heart of
Hosea's experience of the God of Amos' wrath expressing an
anguish over his wrath which I am sure would have shocked
Amos and disconcerted him.

> How can I give you up, O Ephraim,
>   how deliver you up, O Israel?
> How can I treat you like Admah,
>   or make you like Zeboiim?
> My heart recoils within me.
>   my pity is stirred.

These are the words of a God not eager but rather reluctant
to punish, uncertain in fact of the consequences of what he can
do and what he should do. The following lines reinforce this
conclusion as this God argues with himself in the same inter-
rogative way:

> I cannot let loose my fury,
> I cannot turn about and destroy Ephraim:

for I am God and not man,
the Holy One in your midst.

And yet, of course, Hosea's God did destroy just as surely as
Amos' did.

Are these separate Gods, the Yahweh of Amos and of Hosea,
or are they discrete manifestations of a one God? If this is a
hard question for us to decide with all the resources we have
of fine distinction and refined hermeneutics how hard must the
question have appeared to an eighth-century B.C. audience–
which did not have even a canon of Scripture to fall back upon?
What prophet was to be believed? Who had, in Jeremiah's words,
stood in the *sôd* of the Lord?

It would be tempting to pursue further the varieties of prophetic religious experience, since it is from the prophets of Israel
first of all that we expect the confident affirmation: Here is the
word of the Lord, here is God revealed. Was the God of the
confident, aristocratic Isaiah quite the same as the one who summoned into his service a reluctant Jeremiah and then had to sub-
mit to a series of harangues from this unwilling servant that
could have been suffered only by a truly divine patience? Were
the odd things that Ezekiel did–his so-called "prophetic acts"–and
the odd imaginings in which he and later prophets like Zechariah
clothed the word of God entirely compatible with the stern and
straight-forward image of the God projected by a Nathan or
an Elijah? Is, in fact, the God of the postexilic Israel proclaimed
by Ezra and Nehemiah, the selfsame Deity which Israel had
left behind in Palestine and only recovered by the decree of
Cyrus the Persian? If so, it was only by a strange metamor-
phosis in biblical terms, in which not man but God is strangely
changed.

Some of the other later literature of the Bible indicates this
change. Ezra and Nehemiah, and the Chronicler with them if
he is not the same person, have turned Israel into a race rather
than a people (which it had been in patriarchal or tribal times)
or a nation (which it had become after David and Solomon),
or even a religion, which seemed to have been desiderated by
the indigenous Palestinian population–certainly larger than the
body of "returnees" from Babylonia–who wanted only to join

with their now distant cousins in restoring Israel on earth. The ecumenical attempt failed, we know. The book of Ruth, among other documents, is monument to the failure, which registers its canonical dissent from not only Ezra and Nehemiah and the postexilic Deuteronomic law but also joins forces with the Pentateuchal traditions to affirm proudly the mixed origins of Israel, united by nothing other than acceptance of a common religious tradition. The tradition, whether fictive (by the Chronicler, certainly: but who can say?) or real (but who, at this remove, can realistically say?) is the all. "In many and various ways God spoke of old to our fathers by the prophets."

Much fairer game, of course, is to be captured in the pursuit of the wisdom literature of the OT. By definition, almost, the wisdom writers do not pretend to utter a "word of the Lord." All that they offer is an opinion. This fact, I suggest, points up the fatal flaw in the theory of "canonical criticism" which has been proposed by, among others, Brevard Childs as a supposed solution to the alleged impasse presented by "biblical theology." For the wisdom literature is certainly part and parcel of the canon, by anybody's definition of the canon. In a review of Childs' *Introduction to the Old Testament*, Robert P. Carroll, after rightly noting that Childs' position amounts to a canon-within-the-canon dogma, observes:

> Given the stress laid on the revelation of *Tora* to Moses on Sinai what difference does it make to that dogma if bound up with it is a copy of Qoheleth with his insistence that the work of God is beyond finding out?. . . If the canonical reading of Job is used as a correction to Proverbs and Ecclesiastes, why should Ecclesiastes not be used as a corrective to Deuteronomy (Carroll)?

Why not indeed? Both Job and Qoheleth were confronted by a *deus absconditus*, but were they appealing or complaining to the same God? One may be permitted to doubt it. For that matter, is the *gōʾēl* of Job 19:25 the God of Israel's redemption as later piety has made him to be? One may be tempted to doubt this very much. But if not so, for whom was Job hoping? Did the Lord create wisdom, build it into his universe, and reveal it to us his creatures, or is the wisdom which governs the world a secret known only to God and forever hidden from man (Vawter: 1980)? When the psalmist says (Ps 37:25)

> Neither in my youth, nor now that I am old,
> have I seen a just man forsaken
> nor his descendants begging bread,

we may well envy this true believer whose life had been happily sheltered from the adverse experiences of other psalmists, from those of a Jeremiah, a Job, or an Ecclesiastes; but we might also wonder why then his God did not more resemble than theirs the God of Sirach or the God of most of the comfortable platitudes of Proverbs.

A fair look at the diversity of the God concept in the OT can, perhaps, save us from some very wrong decisions. Years ago, George Ernest Wright pointed out the incompleteness of the OT notion of God (Wright). He did not do this in the spirit of some other modern scholars, who seem to think that there is a total discontinuity of this concept with the God of the New Testament. That God was revealed to Israel in fragmentary and varied ways does not imply that he was not truly revealed. He was revealed to the extent that he could be revealed, namely to the extent that the mind of man at any one time was capable of his conception. At the same time, the NT has not suddenly rendered pellucid and univocal the opaque and equivocal image of God it inherited–mainly–from the OT. I am sure there is no profit in attempting to reconstruct from the NT the mind of Jesus with regard to his notion of God in terms of the OT which was his scriptural revelation. The God of the NT who is the Father of our Lord Jesus Christ we accept from Paul or John or from some other transmitter of the gospel. He is one or another or several of the Gods of the OT, and he is also doubtless the God–another amalgam–of Hellenistic monotheism. Whoever he is, he does not resolve the problem of OT theodicy.

I think it unnecessary to drive this point farther into the ground. Was the God whom the Gospels represent as Jesus' Father the same as the God whom the same Gospels represent as the object of the worship of the Pharisees? Is the God of

Qumran the God of the OT, let alone the God of the Gospels? Has any Christian ever read Louis Ginzberg's monumental *The Legends of the Jews* without being made vividly aware that he frequently intrudes there upon a totally alien religion with a totally alien God? Is the God of Islam–whose Islam?–biblical and koranic, similar in any fashion to the God whom we have extrapolated from whatever parts of the Bible we have chosen?

I offer no solution to these many problems. I merely repeat that God is what we make him: the old Italian expression is *Dio ha bisogno di uomini,* God has need of men. Without men's thinking and striving, God would remain a mere *noumenon* in an unreal world of Platonist idealism. The Bible, in its record of history and of thought, word and wisdom, has given expression to the God idea in many fruitful ways which challenge us to recognize in them not only the Ground of our Being but also our Savior from meaninglessness. Were it not for the variegated image of God as he appears in the OT, however, we should be unprepared for such a challenge. For it is the variety of the OT's religious experience rather than any alleged basic homogeneity that accounts for its endurance into our time, a mirror in which men and women continue to see their authentic selves seeking to identify God.

I would like to end this excursion with some apposite words of Herbert Haag, part of his farewell discourse on retiring from the University of Tübingen:

> Not only is the image of God in the OT more personal than that of the NT, it is also incomparably more complex. The OT knows of a God who is near as well as far off, a God who reveals himself and who hides himself, a God who is humanly comprehensible and at the same time menacing, contradictory, unpredictable, and incomprehensible. It is in such complexity and contrariety, however, sometimes in one form and sometimes another, that man experiences life itself and in such complexity he also experiences God (Haag).

Source Material

Abbott, W.M., ed. 1966. *The Documents of Vatican II* (New York: Guild Press).

Barker, M. 1977. "The Two Figures in Zechariah," *HeyJ* 18:38-46.

———1978. "The Evil in Zechariah,"*HeyJ* 19:19-27.

Carroll, R.P. 1980. *SJT* 33:288-9.

Dahood, J. 1979. "The Ebla Tablets and Old Testament Theology," *TD* 27:303-311.

Haag, H. 1980. "Vom Eigenwert des Alten Testaments," *TQ* 160:13.

Hauser, A.J. 1979. "Unity and Diversity in Early Israel Before Samuel," *JETS* 22:298-303.

McKenzie, J.L. 1955. "Divine Passion in Osee," *CBQ* 17:287-299.

Rose, M. 1979. *Jahwe, zum Streit um den alttestamentlichen Gottesnamen. Theologische Studien,* 122. Zurich: Theologischer Verlag), 1953/54.

Rowley, H.H. "Ezekiel in Modern Study," *BJRL* 36:146-190.

Smith, Morton, "The Present State of Old Testament Studies," *JBL* 88 (1969) 21.

Vawter, B. 1974. "History and Kerygma in the Old Testament," in Howard N. Bream et al., eds., *Old Testament Studies in Honor of Jacob M. Myers* (Philadelphia: Temple, 1974) 477.

Vawter, B. 1980. "Prov 8:22: Wisdom and Creation," *JBL* 99:205-16.

Wright, G.E. 1950. *The Old Testament Against Its Environment* (London: SCM Press).

3. Salvation Is a Family Affair

A difficulty for Christian piety which has also often been the occasion of unhappy distortions of Christian theology is that otherwise beautiful word in the vocabulary of salvation which we know as "redemption." "Redemption," of course, when we look it up in a dictionary, means "to buy back," to regain something or someone that has been held in bond against a price that has now been paid. "You are not your own," Paul told the Corinthians. "You have been purchased, and at a price" (1 Cor 6:19-20). And in the somewhat parallel 1 Pet 1:18-19 it is said that the purchase price of our redemption was neither silver nor gold but the far more precious blood of Christ.

To say that the concept of redemption has disturbed Christian piety and distorted Christian theology may sound very negative in the face of the demonstrated fact of how much it has also enriched and nourished them both: "I know that my Redeemer liveth!" One would certainly not want to belabor or to exaggerate the negative. Nevertheless, who has not at times been uneasy when praying to a merciful Father who—we were told—had relieved his creatures of the terrible burden of their sins only after he had exacted a satisfactory price which they were unable to pay and which had to be paid for them instead by the death of his only Son? The same Son, be it noted, who exhorted his followers to treat friends and enemies with equal love, to return good for evil, to forgive without counting the times or the merits of those who must be forgiven. Surely the Christian must sometimes have come to the conclusion that a rather higher degree of disinterested compassion was expected of him or her than had been demonstrated by the divine Being who is Author of the Christian existence.

What caused this malaise in popular piety and, as we have said, sometimes in serious theology as well was the fallacy that comes so easily to us—the fallacy of trying to turn metaphor and analogy into literal reality. A kindred example of the misunderstanding of metaphor that has led both piety and theology down ways that are now seen as undesirable despite original good intentions is the masculine language habitually applied to Deity in the Bible and the religions derived from it. God as our Father, for instance, was certainly a figure of speech intended first and foremost to epitomize divine love in a way that could hardly be equivalently conveyed by expressing the relationship as one of Creator to creatures; and, in Christian theology at least, the figure of God the Father cannot be separated from that of Son and Spirit as manifesting an archetypal love that is exemplary for the Christian life. Yet we know, when we think about it carefully, that God is neither man as male nor man as human, that God is sexless, that God is not, therefore, a father as we know fathers in our human condition. But we do not always think carefully, and as a result we can ignore the presence of analogy and therefore confuse the analogy with the truth that it was only pointing to. That is what has happened too often when we thought about "redemption."

What does it really mean when we say that God or Christ has "redeemed" us? According to the New Testament, the redemption we have in Christ is the forgiveness of our sins (Col 1:14), a gift of God to us (Rom 3:24). It is an act of grace and mercy, not the result of a commercial transaction, and if, by metaphor, some price is mentioned, it has been only to insist, as our better theologians have always understood, that redemption was and is a serious business which therefore *cost much* (again an unavoidable metaphor).

The New Testament has had no source for its redemptive language, for the way in which it figures redemption and salvation, other than the Old Testament. Therefore it may prove to be instructive if we consider one of the more important of the Old Testament metaphors of salvation, that of *gā'al,* redeem, *gō'ēl,* redeemer, and *gĕ'ullâ,* redemption. Not only will this consideration help put the theological concept of redemption in proper perspective, it will soon become evident that there are dimensions to it as appear from its Old Testament roots that are all too often lost in its casual use in Christian language. It is not, be it noted, the only Old Testament term and concept employed in the language of redemptive salvation, but, as will immediately appear, it is certainly one of the most suggestive and theologically rewarding.

Gā'al, gō'ēl, and *gĕ'ullâ* are, we acknowledge at the outset, commercial language, and the metaphor they apply to salvation is a commercial metaphor; but it is commercial in a very special way, unlike, for example, other terms and concepts used with equal frequency, like *qānâ,* which merely means to buy or acquire, or *pādâ,* which means to free, that is, to free a slave, which was done customarily by purchase. This commercial metaphor with which we are dealing came out of no highly organized mercantile society such as was Israel in its imperial days or even in its less imperial days when it was nevertheless part of the ancient Near Eastern imperial system of Assyria or Babylonia or Persia. It came, rather, from the simpler days of Israelite society when the family, and the extended family in clan or tribe, were all that made up society. As far as we know, *gĕ'ullâ* was something peculiarly Israelite, and the term did not exist in the other Semitic languages cognate with Hebrew.

One of the best examples we have of *gĕ'ulla* in action — here not directly in a theological sense — is in chapter 32 of the Book of Jeremiah. In this instance, while the city of Jerusalem was under siege by the Chaldeans who would eventually conquer it and lay it waste, a certain Hanamel, cousin to the prophet Jeremiah, came to him and said: "Please buy my field in Anathoth [the town near Jerusalem which was Jeremiah's ancestral home], in the district of Benjamin; as nearest relative, you have the first claim to possess it; make it yours" (Jer 32:8). Jeremiah, though he had prophesied a Chaldean triumph and, in fact, had been taken into custody for his pains by the Jerusalemite king who regarded him as a defeatist and a national liability, acceded to his cousin's request. He did so to testify that though now his people must suffer foreign domination in punishment of their sins against their God, the time of restoration would also come through the mercy of this same God. "Just as I brought upon this people all this great evil, so I will bring upon them all the good I promise them. Fields shall again be bought in this land, which you call a desert, without man or beast, handed over to the Chaldeans. Fields shall be bought with money, deeds written and sealed, and witnesses shall be used in the land of Benjamin, in the suburbs of Jerusalem, in the cities of Judah and of the hill country, in the cities of the foothills and of the Negeb, when I change their lot, says the LORD" (Jer 32:42-44).

What we are interested in here is the familial background of this transaction. The "nearest relative" of whom Hanamel spoke is our *gōʾēl*, literally, "redeemer" or "vindicator," or, as we shall see in a moment, even "avenger." In a society which predated centralized authority and depended for its stability on that of the family, maintenance of the family inheritance was a prime consideration. Society was threatened when family property was alienated, when the family unit of society was put in jeopardy by being deprived of the natural means of its independent subsistence and exposed to the sufferance of outsiders. So it was that the "nearest relative," like Jeremiah in this case, had the moral obligation to "redeem" the family property from the threat of alien hands. It is this same concern that motivates the property-redemption legislation in about twenty-five passages of Lev 25 and 27. Also the action of Boaz with regard to the inheritance of Naomi in a score of passages in Ruth 2–4 a situation complicated in this instance by the concurrent issue of the marriage of Boaz with Naomi's daughter-in-law Ruth, something that probably originally had nothing to do with *gěʾullâ*.

The *gōʾēl*, however, did not play the merely passive role of stepping in to prevent by his prior claim a family embarrassment. His function could be also quite positive, employing force, if need be, to stave off alien encroachments (see Prov 23:11). And his obligation extended to the family honor as well as to its property, for the "name" which was the identity of the family consisted in more than the material things it possessed. Thus, in an age which pre-existed courts of law, judicial processes, and orderly punitive processes, the *gōʾēl* might be called upon to take the only measure that could guarantee some semblance of vindictive justice by becoming the "avenger" of a slain kinsman (see Jos 20:3, 5, 9 and 2 Sam 14:11). The mingling of property "vindication" with blood "vengeance" in the legislation of Num 35:12-27, Dt 19:6, 12, etc., indicates how closely associated and even identified these functions were in the thought of ancient Israel.

And so, with this background, we come to understand how the God of Israel could come to be regarded as Israel's *gōʾēl*, and how, centuries later, the New Testament could in the same spirit conceive of a redemption by this same God that would affect not the Hebrew people only but a people of God which, potentially at least, is the whole of the human race he created.

When did this metaphor first come to be applied theologically in relation to God's salvation of his people? First of all, it is very easy to say who was the first to make a great thing of it, to constitute it a cornerstone of his theological edifice. That person, beyond question, is the anonymous prophet of Israel's exile whom we customarily term the Second Isaiah, who is responsible directly for chapters 40-55 of the Book of Isaiah and also, directly and indirectly, for some passages in the so-called Trito-Isaiah sections of Is 56–66 or even such a "Proto-Isaianic" verse as Is 35:9. This prophet, who was also, as far as we know, the first thinker to conceive of God's creative action as a work of salvation—an idea that was taken up by the Priestly author of the "first" creation story in Gen 1:1–2:4a—likewise in about twenty-five instances figures the God of Israel as its *gōʾēl* in redeeming it from captivity. (It may be thought interesting that the Second Isaiah always uses in this connection forms of the verb *gāʾal* but never the substantive *gĕʾullâ*. The phenomenon would doubtless reward investigation. (Neither does the Gospel of John, much concerned with faith, ever employ the substantive for this concept but always the verb "believe.")

Was the Second Isaiah (who must have flourished sometime

between the years 587–535 B.C.) anticipated in this theology? The response to this question, unfortunately, must remain uncertain because the evidence is ambiguous. The concept appears in a number of Psalms (Pss 19:15; 69:19; 72:14; 74:2; 77:16; 106:10; 107:2; 119:154), most of which, if not all, are of postexilic composition and subject, therefore, to the influence of Second Isaiah. It appears in Jer 31:11, which could be authentically the work of Jeremiah, written out of a situation not unlike the Second Isaiah's but also, like Jer 50:34, could be a later addition to the Book of Jeremiah. It appears in Ex 15:13, as part of the "Song of the Sea," an ancient poem which, nevertheless, has undergone a great deal of later elaboration, and in Ex 6:6, a "Priestly" passage which, we have already noted, manifests a theology much dependent on the Second Isaiah. It appears in Lam 3:58, beyond question a postexilic passage that could hardly have escaped the influence of the great exilic prophet. But it also appears in Gen 48:16, and in Hos 13:14 and Mic 4:10, passages which nobody will lightly dismiss as obviously recent additions to the Old Testament documents and which instead may be very ancient indeed.

(We are leaving out of consideration possibly the most famous theological usage of *gōʾel* in the Old Testament, that of Job 19:25. "I know that my Vindicator lives," reads the New American Bible, indicating by its capitalization that God is the *gōʾel* that Job had in mind. But did he? The scholars cannot agree on the meaning of this enigmatic verse, and for this reason, if for no other, we are prepared to declare it out of bounds for our present discussion. Job may have had in mind a totally different theology, as unique to that book as the book itself is unique in the Old Testament.)

There is nothing repugnant in the view that it was, in fact, the Second Isaiah who first thought of Israel's God as its *gōʾel* and, in doing so, reached back to authentic Israelite roots that were no less valid for having been neglected for several centuries. After all, it was the Second Isaiah alone of the prophets (except perhaps for his contemporary Ezekiel, one time) who has mentioned the patriarch Abraham. The patriarch Jacob, who gave his name Israel to a people, appears in the prophetic literature notably elsewhere only in Hos 12, and there in a posture that is hardly flattering. Outside the Book of Genesis the patriarchal history of Israel's remote beginnings hardly turns up in Hebrew literature until the time of Second Isaiah.

What we are saying is that in Second Isaiah's time, a time when Israel had lost the sureties of its earlier age that had been summarized in land and temple and kingship, other sureties had to take their place. Such new sureties could be, at first glance, fairly trivial: the Sabbath rest, for example, or circumcision, or other externals such as the dietary laws governing kosher food, all of which served to preserve and emphasize religious identity. The anthropologist Mary Douglas in her study of the "bog Irish" in England has shown how, in a kindred cultural context, such externals have exercised a stabilizing and unifying force that demonstrates them to be anything but trivial. It will be remembered that it is the Priestly creation story of Genesis that represents the Creator God as completing the ordered world in a work-week of six days and then resting on the seventh day, thus sanctifying the Sabbath for humanity by his example. And it is in the Priestly version of the story of the covenant God made with Abraham (Gen 17) that circumcision is featured as the sign and seal of this "everlasting covenant" between God and Abraham's descendants.

Traditional religious externals, a traditional remote patriarchal age to which it was profitable to recall a people's hearts and minds, and language that pictured a saving God acting the role of a traditional family redeemer, all these are parts of a single whole. It would be an exaggeration to pretend, in the last instance, that Second Isaiah represented God as *gōʾel* only to make of salvation a "family" affair. As a matter of fact, the parallels in which *gāʾal* is set in these prophetic writings show that in his theology the word has a far wider and richer significance than this.

For one thing, Second Isaiah's pairing off of the ideas of salvation and creation—another example he set for the Priestly theologian—is in the minds of many a far more suggestive and profound contribution to Old Testament soteriology than this one we have been discussing. Neither, however, should we minimize the importance of this one. When, as he often does (e.g., in Is 43:14), he identifies the *gōʾēl* as "the Holy One of Israel," his hearers could not have failed to be reminded that the God who had created and redeemed them was none other than the God of the patriarchs, the God who was known as the familiar of their fathers Abraham, Isaac, and Jacob (Israel). (Even as the Priestly theologian in Ex 3:15 is careful to have it made known to Moses that Yahweh, the name under which God would be known in the historical experience of the people of Israel, was indeed the patriarchal God of Abraham, Isaac, and Jacob.)

Also, if the late William F. Albright was correct in his interpretation of the divine title used in Gen 31:53 and 31:42, the exilic prophet could also have been evoking by this means a strikingly similar designation of the patriarchal God that had been made long ago. The title, *paḥad* of Isaac, is frequently translated "Fear of Isaac," but few have ever been really happy with this translation. On the basis of some comparative language evidence, Albright thought it should rather be translated "Kinsman of Isaac," and in this opinion he has been followed by numerous other scholars.

It is hoped that this brief exploration of a small bit of Old Testament salvational theology will have been of help to the reader in putting into proper perspective the ways in which the people of Israel thought of their redeeming God, ways which were not always of awe and dread but also of familiarity and family feeling.

4. The Scriptural Meaning of Sin

Etymologies are intriguing, though sometimes misleading, for it is use that really determines a word's meaning. But it is at least instructive to approach a term first through its etymology. When we do this with the words used in the Bible for sin, we find that none of them has that exclusively moral association to which hundreds of years of Christianity have accustomed us.

In the Hebrew Old Testament the word most commonly used for sin is *hattah*, "to miss the mark," and the mark missed is not necessarily a moral one. Proverbs 19:2 uses this verb of the hasty traveler who loses his way through inadvertence to road signs. After *hattah*, the most commonly used Hebrew word for sin is *pesha*, "to overstep" or "to rebel." Here again we find no exclusively moral association; for instance, when 2 Kings 8:20 says Edom successfully "rebelled" against the rule of Juda, the author is passing no moral judgment on the revolt but simply recording a political fact. Nor do other Hebrew words that were used on occasion to signify a moral lapse have an exclusively moral application.

The Greek and Latin terms used to translate the Hebrew have much the same broad meaning. The Greek Old Testament renders *hattah* by *hamartano*, which also means "to miss the mark" and in profane Greek often refers to a man's losing his way on the road. In Latin, *peccare* has as its root meaning "to stumble" and did not originally connote anything moral. So etymology cannot tell us much about the biblical theology of sin.

We must, rather, see how the words are used, as we said at the beginning. A legalistic interpretation of biblical religion could make the notion of sin something purely formal: not a matter of rightdoing but rather of the avoidance of wrongdoing. But Wellhausen was certainly wrong in extending such a conception to the law itself and to the way it was understood in the biblical period. This can be clarified by examining a few passages.

Usage in the Prophets

See, for example, the prophet Amos's use of *pesha*. The "transgressions" of which he speaks include inhumanity, cruelty, social injustice, violation of contract, acceptance of bribes, violation of public trust, greed, lust, and hypocrisy, on the part of the Gentiles as well as of the Israelites (Am 1:3; 2:8). There is obviously no question here of sin as the merely formal, mechanically computed violation of law. For Amos *pesha* is a rebellion against God's moral will, which is known to Jew and Gentile alike as the norm of rightdoing. It is true that Amos does not elaborate a doctrine of natural law, but he does say (6:12) that the rejection of the justice and the rightdoing that God required of Israel was as absurd and unnatural as tracking horses over rocks and ploughing the sea with oxen. Sin for the Israelite was the violated will and law of the Lord, but it was a will and law that found a response in man's mind and heart; it was never arbitrary whim or caprice.

This meaning of *pesha* that we first find in Amos is also common to the rest of the prophets. And it is proper to look in the prophets for an expression of the spirit of the law. The criticism of the past century tried to oppose the two, as though the spiritual, prophetic religion and the priestly religion of the law had been separate, antagonistic developments in Israelite history. We now recognize that in this attempt the critics had also taken the wrong track and missed the mark. Prophecy and law are, of course, two different emphases of Israelite religion, which spoke two different languages. But they were emphases of the same religion and were directed toward more or less the same ends. We do not expect to find the moral and devotional teaching of Catholicism in the Code of Canon Law or the Roman Ritual. Similarly, it is now agreed that we rightly interpret prophetic teaching in the Old Testament as supporting in its way a doctrine that the law upheld in its way.

Meaning in the Law

In the law the favored word for sin was *hattah*, and the "mark" that was missed was that of the Covenant of Sinai. Israel's law was the spelling out of the people's obligations with respect to this covenant, so we must have a clear idea of what covenant meant in the ancient Near East. Whereas the binding force of an ordinary contract is based on legal justice, a covenant obligation was not thought of primarily as one of justice but as one of love. The word customarily used in the Old Testament for the notion of the covenant bond is *hesed*, which may mean mercy, loyalty, devotion, loving kindness, or simply love. The covenant idea was modeled after a familial rather than a legal relationship. When an Israelite committed *hattah* (sinned), his offense was not determined by the letter of the law he had violated but by the familial piety he had ruptured.

Sin Is Positive

To the Semite, sin and evil were not negative (the deprivation of good) but something positive that had been done and that continued to exist until done away with. What we consider "guilt" and "punishment" were to the biblical authors hardly distinguishable from the sin itself. In Numbers 32:23, for instance, we translate the same Hebrew word as both "sin" and "consequences of sin." Because sin was seen as something positive, even those sins committed in ignorance demanded expiatory rites and sacrifices, and whole communities, yet unborn, could share in the guilt of the progenitor or of a fellow member. It was not that they were held "guilty" of another's wrongdoing; they were simply caught up in the consequences of an act in a situation where the consequences were the continued existence of the act itself.

Similarly, punishment was not so much a retribution visited upon the sin as it was the inexorable running of sin's course. God could forestall this consequence–by accepting sacrifices for sins of ignorance and responding to prayer, sorrow, and confession for other sins. But God's forgiveness of sin did not automatically entail his remission of punishment, as can be seen from the famous judgment passed on David's sin with Bathsheba. Catholic teaching on the temporal punishment of sin is a true echo of this biblical doctrine.

We can see from this "objective" view of sin in the Old Testament why what was sinful was broader in extent than what was immoral. Legal purity, which was the external holiness of a people consecrated to God and a reminder of their need for interior holiness, could be violated without any immoral act. A woman had to make a "guilt offering" after childbirth, for instance, even though no question of morality was involved. In this there is a major difference between the Old and New Testaments, for we find in the New Testament no trace of the idea of purely legal holiness. The old formulas are used, but within the new dimension of a salvation and regeneration of which the former figures were but a foreshadowing. The "holy ones" to whom St. Paul writes are those of whom personal holiness is expected as a consequence of the indwelling Spirit. With the entire apparatus of formal sanctity superseded in a new and spiritual covenant, sin and immorality are fully identified. The law of Christians is the code of conduct of a people which has charity as the *ḥesed* of their covenant with God.

Another consequence of the objective view of sin in the Old Testament is that it is represented as an obstacle that stands between God and his people. Expiation is the removal of this obstacle; it is not a matter of "appeasing" God or changing him in any way but of removing the sin from man. If a sin has been willful, the mind and heart must be changed by repentance. In Isaiah 6 we see how clearly the prophet sees sin as such a cutting off of man from God; man is "lost" in the presence of the Holy. Perhaps the same idea is present in the English word "sin," namely that it "sunders" one from the other (as in the German *Sünde*).

Psalmist's Notions

From the penitential psalms, and notably from Psalm 50, the *Miserere*, we gain an even clearer idea of the biblical theology of sin. Three different words are used to express what the sinner begs God to do for him in his sinful state: "blot out," "wash," and "cleanse." All three verbs denote a ritual or declaratory obliteration of sin, but we must recall that the "washing" the second verb alludes to is the washing of clothes–and the oriental flung his soiled clothing in a stream and stomped on it enthusiastically. So the psalmist is asking God for two kinds of cleaning–what a later theology will distinguish into a forensic and a real justification.

In the *forensic* justification, God simply declares the sinner to be a sinner no more. But since it is obvious that no human act can be done away with as though it had never occurred, there must also be a *real* justification. The guilt that has remained in the sinner and prevents his access to the God of holiness must be stamped out and obliterated, like the dirt in a soiled robe. The psalmist calls on the Lord to "create a clean heart" and to "renew an upright spirit" within him. For the Israelite, the "heart" was the seat of all emotion, will, and thought; he thought or "said" things in his heart, not in his mind. And the "spirit" was the power that God put in man to enable him to think and will in his heart. So we see that for the psalmist the justification of the sinner entailed a divine work of recreation, a renewal of a personality that had been distorted and turned aside from its true purposes by the act of sin. Create, he says, a new *me*. Sin was, in his eyes, an involvement from which man could not emerge without an alteration in his inmost being.

The Old Testament background of St. Paul's doctrine of original sin can be seen in Psalm 50:7, "Behold, I was brought forth in guilt, and in sin my mother conceived me." The psalmist says this as a motivation to God to be merciful, as a reminder that man's proclivities are sinful. Biblical authors knew well that the introduction of sin into the world and its continuation were the achievement of human malice against the will of God. Man's disposition to sin was part of a consistent history in which the will of a saving God had been resisted and thwarted from the first.

New Testament Emphasis

Most of the Old Testament theology of sin can be found in the thinking of the New Testament authors, but there is also a decisive difference that results from the new and definitive revelation of Christianity. For while sin was taken for granted and elaborately provided for in the life of the Old Covenant, the New Testament Church saw in itself the fulfillment of the prophets' prediction of a new and everlasting covenant in which sin would have no part. Sin was, therefore, always a kind of apostasy for the Christian. Because the Christian could always relapse into his old ways, sin was an ever present possibility. Yet he could sin only by abandoning the total commitment involved in Christian faith, which he could regain only through the new heart and spirit that must once more be bestowed on him by divine grace.

The sense of horror and of enormity in the presence of sin never deserts the New Testament. If we today can summon a somewhat casual attitude to the function of the confessional in the sacramental life of the Church, undoubtedly this is partly due to the fact that modern man, even Christian man, has to a greater or less extent forgotten what sin really is. Probably man can never really lose his sense of sin, though today he seems to have great difficulty in defining for himself what he means by it. When we look about us at a world in which men give witness to a feeling of rootless and purposeless existence, to a life bereft of meaningful experience in which event follows event in witless sequence and where men can achieve no community together, we perceive in a groping sort of way what biblical man understood by sin.

5. The Biblical Idea of Faith

In the course of his Bamptom Lectures of 1938, Professor Alfred Guillaume has included the eyewitness account of a vindication by ordeal as still practiced, as a last resort, among certain Bedouin tribes of Arabia. In this particular ordeal, a white-hot spoon was licked three times by the accused, with the result that nothing more than a touch of dry ash was found on his tongue, though it has been known for men to lose the whole or a part of their tongues in such experiments. As Guillaume concludes:

"This ordeal, from its beginning to its end, is based on the belief that God will vindicate the innocent and punish the guilty, and though it is so ancient that it cannot be used as an argument for the truth of the central dogma of religion which Jews, Christians, and Muhammadans hold in common, it has real value as a demonstration of what a Semitic people understand by faith."

What a Semitic people understand by faith is, of course, also what the Bible understands by faith.

Things are usually what they are said to be: *nomen est omen,* said the ancients. It is doubtless due in part to our deriving our word "faith" from *fidere,* "confide in," "credit," that we tend to think of it as pretty much exclusively concerned with the mind. It is not quite the same, I think, with our verb "believe," which we use to indicate the exercise of faith.

"Believe," which is cognate with words used in other Germanic languages for "faith" (*Glaube, geloof*), is related to the obsolete verb "belove," found now only in the passive. When we say, therefore, that we believe–or, to be sure, when our ancestors said it–we express much more than a mere intellectual assent. We express commitment, engagement, that giving over of the whole self that is entailed in what we call "love."

By a kindred association of ideas, the biblical authors indicated much the same thing as their understanding of faith. The Hebrew words which we translate "fidelity," "faith," and also "truth," are all derived from the verb *aman*, which has the meaning "be firm, sure." We are all quite familiar with one form of this word, the liturgical affirmation "amen," which is to say "this is most certain." To signify belief in someone or something, Hebrew uses a causal form of this verb ("make firm") together with the preposition "in" or "to."

Scholars are not fully agreed what was the underlying thought-pattern, whether the person conceived himself as being made strong in relation to the object of his faith, or whether he declared this object of faith a firm foundation. In either case, it is plain that in this Semitic acceptance there is a more personal involvement than is really adequately described in terms of "subject" and "object." In faith, one does not merely accept a proposition, he sets his whole being in relation to another.

This Semitic idea of faith is also that of the New Testament. The writers of the New Testament preached a faith which had a new content and new direction, but which was in nature the same. What the Old Testament Israelite had professed with regard to Yahweh, in the New Testament was a profession of the Holy Trinity and of the Lord Jesus.

An engagement of the entire person involves, naturally, intellectual assent. As has just been noted, there has been a Western tendency to emphasize the intellectual side of faith. Apart from the reason I suggested, there have been good historical causes for this emphasis: the anti-intellectualism of the Reformation was one, and in more recent times Modernism's subjectivism has been another, both of which encouraged us to insist on the objective reasonableness of the act of faith.

Such an emphasis also has authentic biblical roots. The Jews at various times, particularly in their contacts with the intellectual ferment of Hellenism, were impelled to the same emphasis, as were the writers of the New Testament. No one who reads the biblical authors without prejudice could ever think that for them faith is anything short of an act in which the human mind, far from abdicating its office, is performing what is most worthy of it, wholly in keeping with its nature and dignity.

But the isolation of man's mind, after all, however useful to the philosopher in the analysis of a human act, is not a reality in everyday doings. "After all," as Newman rightly said, "man is *not* a reasoning animal; he is a seeing, feeling, contemplating, acting animal." What engages his faith is not what engages his mind only, or what he may apprehend primarily in intellectual terms.

He is more apt to believe "in his bones," as we say, or "in his heart of hearts." The absolute and irrevocable commitment that is expressed in martyrdom we do not think of primarily as an intellectual act, though of course it is that ultimately. We think of it, and the martyr thinks of it, as an act of faith performed by his whole being.

Catholic theology has always avoided what is sometimes implied, unfortunately, in some of our popular treatments of faith, which might give the impression that it is (as the Book of Common Prayer called it) a "persuasion," merely the inheritance of a traditional body of doctrine.

A Personal Encounter

Theology has always insisted that faith is a personal encounter of the believer with the first, the divine truth. It has always stressed the intervention of the human will in the act of faith: precisely because faith is faith, and not knowledge, the will must command the assent of the mind. *Credo quia impossibile*—"I believe because it is impossible," may or may not have been said by the Church Fathers, but whether said or not, it expresses — taken rightly, of course — a truth proper to faith, which is not anti-intellectual but super-intellectual.

That faith is the act of the whole man, not only of his mind, explains the Church's traditional horror of the heretic, a horror so difficult to explain nowadays to those for whom faith is the equivalent of opinion. Goodness and malice reside in the will, not the intellect. A heretic, in the true sense of the word, is not one who merely shares an erroneous conclusion about what is revealed truth, as saints and even Doctors of the Church have done. He is, rather, one who has willfully cut himself loose from the Author of his supernatural existence.

When the writer of Hebrews says that "it is impossible to bring back to repentance those who were once enlightened, who have tasted the heavenly gift, who have been made partakers of the Holy Spirit, who have tasted the good word of God and the power of the world to come, and then have fallen away," he says what every pastor of souls knows by daily experience. And he knows equally well the reason: "For they have again crucified for themselves the Son of God and held him up to mockery" (Heb 6:4-6). How often–and how often vainly–have we reasoned with the "fallen away" about his abandonment of the faith! And how often is anything intellectual really involved? An apostate has not changed his mind only, he has wrenched his entire person into a new, and wrong, direction.

"Of Small Faith"

Our Lord's frequent rebuke of his disciples as *oligopistoi*, "of small faith" (Mt 6:30; 8:26, etc.), evidently was not to question how much they believed statistically, but how deeply. They believed, but not consistently, not wholeheartedly, not with complete commitment.

They were what the father of the boy whose cure is described in Mark 9:13-28 humbly confessed to be: "I believe; come to the aid of my unbelief"–meaning, as Father Lagrange has pointed out: "come to my aid, even though I do not believe strongly enough." Similarly, when our Lord said of the centurion, "such faith I have found with no one in Israel" (Mt 8:10), the sting of the comparison derives from the fact that the uncircumcised centurion, greatly at a disadvantage in respect to his acceptance of formal revelation, nevertheless displayed better than the recipients of that revelation the attitude of soul which in the Bible means faith.

Anyone who has read the New Testament knows how much broader is the scope of "faith" than that which we are apt to give it. Often the New Testament word will have to be translated, or at least understood by us, now as "confidence," now "trust," now "hope," now "conviction," now "assent," and even, as St. Paul uses it in Romans 14:22, something like "informed conscience."

It is well to remember, however, that these distinctions are ours, in accordance with a psychological view of man that is not found in the New Testament. The distinctions may be very useful, even necessary to our thinking, but neither should we permit ourselves to become the victims of our own method. We should not lose sight of the fact that to the authors of the New Testament revelation, who had one word for all these things, faith was such an all-embracing idea.

Though the New Testament authors inherited their idea of faith from the Old Testament, faith itself has a far greater significance in the New Testament than it ever did in the Old. This is the result not only of the new revelation which had made better known than ever before the extent of the tremendous mysteries of God. Even more importantly, it is the result of an entirely new dimension given to faith in God's ultimate revelation of himself in his only Son.

The newness of this dimension is strikingly reflected in the expression, common in John's Gospel, but likewise found throughout the New Testament, "believe *into* Christ (or God)." This formula, impossible to reproduce in good English, has been preserved in our creeds, where *Credo in Deum* is a strictly Christian form, replacing the *Credo Deum* or *Deo* of classical Latin. Scholars are agreed that this unusual terminology reflects the new theological thinking of the primitive Christian Church.

Christian Revelation Unique

It is not simply an imitation of the Old Testament formula mentioned above (the preposition "in" with the verb *aman*), for the Greek Old Testament on which the New Testament writers largely depend for their theological language had never tried to reproduce this Semitic idiom in Greek. It is, rather, an attempt to express the unique character of the Christian revelation, which is essentially of a Person. St. Thomas caught the drift of this formula in Scholastic terms when he wrote that *credere in Deum* properly expresses the act of faith as commanded by the will, since the will inclines to the divine truth as to its end (*Summa*, II-II, 2, 2).

In the New Testament God, or Christ, is much more personally the object of faith than in the Old Testament. There is, in a sense, less to believe "about" him, since he is now apprehended personally, who is the end of our natural and supernatural being. The word of God made known in the fragmentary utterances of the Old Testament is in the New Testament possessed incarnate.

Christian faith is not just a means to God, "a shadow of the good things to come," but the possession of God and his divine Son.

It is this personal direction of Christian faith which explains the Pauline formula "faith of Jesus," that is, "faith which is (of) Jesus," the equivalent of "faith in Jesus." John contrasts the mediacy of Old Testament religion with the immediate possession of divine life shared by those who have faith in Christ: "The Law was given through Moses, while grace and truth have come through Jesus Christ" (1:18). "He has given them the power to become sons of God, those who believe *into* his name" (1:12). This is real, not merely imputed sonship (cf. 1 Jn 3:1), as real as the Christ to whom we are joined by faith.

Because of the object of Christian faith, it becomes clear how Paul can regard it as justifying. In his famous teaching on justification by faith the Apostle builds on Genesis 15:6, where it is said that Abraham "believed (in) God, who accounted it in him as righteousness."

Justification, says Paul, is God's free gift, "according to grace." In this Abraham became the father of all who believe, that his faith was accounted justice in him, just as our faith is accounted justice in us, coming from the gratuitous act of God's mercy in saving us from sin through Jesus Christ. The text of Genesis signified that Abraham's faith was accepted by God as possessing a value it did not have of itself: such is the sense of the Hebrew word used for "account."

In virtue of Abraham's faith, God justified him, accounted him righteous, bestowed on him his friendship and thus endowed him with a righteousness he could not have had of himself. Such was the value of Old Testament faith, and such is the effect of Christian faith, but to the latter Paul ascribes even more, in keeping with the new dimension of faith.

For Christian faith is directed not to a promise, but to a fulfilled reality. By Christian faith we are not only united to a God who promises, as he did to Abraham, but to him "who has raised Jesus our Lord from the dead, who was delivered up for our sins and rose again for our justification" (Rom 4:25). Our justification from faith (5:1) results in our now having reconciliation (5:11). Faith in him who raised Jesus is also faith in Jesus himself: "We have also believed in Christ Jesus, that we may be justified by the faith of Christ" (Gal 2:16).

Christian faith, in other words, actually is righteousness, since it connects the believer with the source of his salvation. Hence St. Thomas in his commentary on Romans 4:5 observes that the justice accounted to the believer is "not indeed that by faith he merits justice, but belief itself is the first act of justice which God works in him. For inasmuch as he believes in God who justifies, he submits himself to his justification, and thus receives its effect."

Total Commitment

This justifying faith, in Genesis and in St. Paul and in St. Thomas, is more than an assent to a truth. It is a total acceptance of *the* truth, who is God, even against every human consideration, a whole-hearted commitment which is the beginning of a new way of life. "He did not waver through lack of faith concerning the promise of God, but he grew strong in faith giving glory to God, fully convinced that he was able to do what he had promised. Therefore it was accounted to him as righteousness" (Rom 4:20-22).

It is equally plain from the teaching of the New Testament that the faith *versus* works controversy posed by the Reformation was a false issue. Faith is both something less and something more than the early Reformers taught, in proportion as the righteousness achieved through faith is a reality and not the imputation that they believed. What God declares, is. "God gives life to the dead and calls into being things that were not" (Rom 4:17). Because faith is a commitment of life, not just a frame of mind, it necessarily entails good works. Because the justification of faith is real, the works of faith also God accounts as righteousness.

Admittedly the Epistle of James begins from a different standpoint than Paul's, but there is no conflict in its complement of the Pauline doctrine of justification: "Was not Abraham our father justified by works, when he offered Isaac his son on the altar? You see that faith worked together with his works, and by works faith was made complete. Thus the Scripture was fulfilled: 'Abraham believed God, and it was accounted to him as righteousness,' and he was called the friend of God. You see that a man is justified by works, and not from faith only" (Jas 2:21-24).

It is just as important today as it has been in the past for us to lay stress on the objectivity and the reasonableness of faith, to lay stress, therefore, on its intellectual aspect. The concept of faith professed by existentialist theologians like Rudolf Bultmann, rejecting as it does all objectivity, all motives of credibility, all verification of historical revelation, is less acceptable to Catholics than the original ideas of primitive Protestantism. This is fideism rather than faith, a concept hardly to be ascribed to the New Testament whose authors were the heirs and witnesses of a continuity of divine revelation within history.

At the same time, however, when Bultmann and others speak

of the here-and-nowness of faith, they are on firm biblical ground. If our faith is not our way of life, the principle of our every action, our very life with God, then we do not understand faith as the Bible understands it.

It is not enough that we "make an act of faith" in the divine mysteries, we must *believe* them. It is not enough that we believe that Jesus Christ was raised from the dead, we must believe *in* the resurrected Christ. It is by such faith that the New Testament teaches Christians to live in this life, till faith yields to vision.

6. The Jerusalem Bible

To understand the considerable success, as well as the virtues and shortcomings of The Jerusalem Bible, one must make the effort to recall, or to learn for the first time, as the case may be, what was the situation facing English-speaking Roman Catholics a quarter-century ago when they wanted to read the Bible. I speak of making an effort, for in these relaxed and ecumenical days it is hard to conjure up that quarter-century ago from the ashes of the past. It is worth the effort, though, and not only for English-speaking Roman Catholics. I intend to make critical remarks about that unecumenical and unrelaxed time in respect to my own church (Roman Catholic), since it is of course the one I know best. If I might venture one fascinating speculation, it would be to wonder about what additional travails might have been experienced by a Revised Standard Version then being burnt in fundamentalist pulpits and raising questions on the floor of a McCarthyite Congress, had Catholics been sitting on its board of editors and translators as they do now.

What was the situation that confronted Roman Catholics in their access to a vernacular Bible? First of all, at least officially they were forbidden any translation (or, for that matter, edition of the biblical text in the original languages) that had been brought out under non-Catholic auspices. That was, and is, the provision of canon 1399, 1° of the Code of Canon Law.[1] It is true, canon 1400 effectively nullified this proscription by permitting the use of such books "only to those who are engaged *quovis modo* (= in any manner whatever) in theological or biblical studies."[2] This is an instance of that built-in dispensational characteristic of Roman law that is often bewildering to people accustomed to a common law that does not take into account privilege. The purpose of these seemingly conflicting laws was to allow relatively free access to the Bible, but only after it had been asserted in uncompromising language that its publication and divulgation were regarded as an exclusive prerogative of the Roman church. Judged in this light the law of the Code was, in fact, quite liberal: at least a reversal of purely negative legislation inherited from pre-Reformation heresy-hunting in the late Middle Ages.[3] On the other hand, as anyone who was teaching Scripture in Catholic schools at that time can readily

[1] The *Codex Iuris Canonici,* a codification in 2414 separate *canones* of centuries of ecclesiastical legislation, took effect in the Latin church May 19, 1918, a year following its promulgation. Theoretically it is still in effect, subject to subsequent specific revisions (such as those which have virtually abolished the *Index Liborum Prohibitorum* and seriously modified the *censura praevia* of books and other writings), pending an overhaul that may or may not come to fruition in our times.

[2] A commentary on the Code, much used in Catholic seminaries at the time, further made it quite clear that the provision applied to anybody: "omnes, tam sacerdotes *quam tirones* [my emphasis] et alumnos, qui habitualiter studia biblica et theologica, sive in scholis *sive privatim* [again my emphasis], seria mente excolere et augere nituntur." See Uldaricus Beste, *Introductio in Codicem* (Collegeville: St. John's Abbey Press, 1946) on can. 1400.

[3] An interesting example typical of many others was recently called to mind by the 500th anniversary of the Bible in Catalan, printed at Valencia in 1478 (and translated a long generation before). Though proclaimed in its colophon to be "the most true and Catholic Bible" and published with the highest available ecclesiastical approbation, it fell prey to the Spanish Inquisition which was extended to Valencia in 1484 and which consigned to the flames vernacular Bibles along with Jewish Talmuds and Arabic works of alchemy. Cf. Guiu Camps, "Cinccents anys de la primera edició catalana de la Bíblia," *Revista Catalana de Teologia,* 3 (1978), 3–16.

testify, when the law came to be implemented on the level that affected most people, it was often enforced by those who knew all about canon 1399, 1°, but had never heard of canon 1400 or did not understand it, and this despite the fact that in the Roman as well as in other systems of law, doubtful laws are no laws at all and the presumption of the law is supposed to favor freedom from the law.

Secondly, another canon, no. 1391, managed by its negative phraseology to give the impression that access to the Bible should be made difficult rather than easy. Translations were forbidden, said the canon, "unless they be approved by the Apostolic See, or unless they be published under the bishops' supervision and with notes taken principally from the holy Fathers of the Church and from learned and catholic writers." Quite properly, of course, a Latinate and Italianate Holy See had not to that point, and has not subsequently, "approved" any translation of the Bible into English, French, German, Flemish, or Choctaw. The "bishops' supervision" of which the canon spoke probably envisaged nothing more complex than the imprimatur of a local ordinary (such as took place, for example, in 1965 when Cardinal Cushing of Boston authorized a "Catholic edition" of the RSV New Testament). It was popularly assumed, however, that such translations could be approved only for "private devotion," and that any "official" version would require a more general approbation of the church. Specifically, it would have to be in conformity with the Bible used in the church's liturgy which, by and large and with slight differences, was the Sixto-Clementine Vulgate of 1592. (It must be remembered that at this time the liturgy of the church was in Latin and that the reading of the scriptural word in the vernacular — usually made from the altar and not from a pulpit — was a dispensable concession to the better understanding of the Latin liturgy, simply translating the pericopes in the Roman Missal.) As for the requirement that a translation have notes, the intention of course was to safeguard orthodoxy from the perilous possibility of "private interpretation" which would arise from study of the unadorned word of God. In these days and times, however, there is hardly need to argue the merits of an annotated Bible, when even the Bible Societies have recognized their "without note or comment" formula to be sadly unreal.[4]

Finally, as has already been suggested, there was a persuasion that to be really serviceable in the church and not merely a scholarly curiosity or private source of study, a biblical translation had to be based upon the Vulgate, which the Council of Trent[5] had declared "authentic for public lectures, disputations, preaching, and explanation, so that no one should dare or presume to reject it under any pretext." There is no doubt that this persuasion was very well founded in the letter of the law, which continued to emerge from Rome from time to time almost till the eve of *l'encyclique libératrice* of Pope Pius XII, the *Divino afflante Spiritu* of 1943. It was only then that Catholics of the Anglo-Saxon world discovered that a revisionism had been going on in the law of the church on whose intellectual and ideological periphery they had long been habituated to dwell. Suddenly it was revealed to them that the intention of Trent had been to confer on the Vulgate only a "juridic," not a critical, authority, so that the Vulgate might be textually corrected with impunity, and that even "official" national or regional vernacular translations could and should be made from the original biblical texts without respect to the Vulgate.[6] The Catholic Biblical Association of America, founded in 1937 with one of its principal aims to provide the English-speaking Catholic world with a more serviceable Bible than it then possessed, was at that moment (1943) in process of biblical translation—from the Vulgate, of course. Immediately after *Divino afflante Spiritu* came a shifting of the Association's gears, and a decade later would see the emergence of the beginning of what would eventually become

---

[4]Article I of the Constitution of the American Bible Society established in 1816, states that the sole object of the Society shall be "circulation of the Holy Scriptures without note or comment." See Creighton Lacy, *The Word Carrying Giant* (South Pasadena: William Carey Library, 1977), pp. 10, 16-17, 84-95, 252-253, 256, 259-260, 262, 288. —Ed.

[5]In its Fourth Session, April 8, 1546. Cf. Denzinger-Schönmetzer, *Enchiridion Symbolorum* (34th ed.; Freiburg: Herder,1967),§§1504,1506.

[6]*Divino afflante Spiritu* in Denzinger-Schönmetzer, § 3825.

the New American Bible, translated completely from the original biblical languages. Apace, however, in more fruitful and sensitive soil, had already been sown the seeds of The Jerusalem Bible.

Besides the law concerning it, the actuality of Catholic biblical publication must also be known in order to appreciate properly what The Jerusalem Bible brought in its time. The Bible used by English-speaking Roman Catholics then was variously called the Douay Version, the Douay-Rheims, or the Challoner-Rheims. None of these titles was especially accurate. What had happened was that English Catholics in exile under Queen Elizabeth I, Oxford scholars all, had produced at Rheims in 1582 an English translation of the New Testament, and again at Douai in 1609 a translation of the Old Testament. Both of these had been made from the Vulgate—out of principle and not because texts in the biblical languages were unavailable, as in the case of the old Wycliffite versions. The translators of the Authorised (King James) Version of 1611 make reference to the Douay-Rheims version disparagingly in their famous preface, neglecting to note how much they had profited from its precedents, especially from its rendering of the Greek definite article that lay behind the anarthrous Latin of the Vulgate by means of the English definite and indefinite articles. (This was a petty conceit on their part, to be sure, since every translation of the Scripture has been in debt to its predecessors, at least from the time of the Targumists and the Septuagint onward.)

The "Douay Bible" that was in the possession of Catholic families in our generation, however, was actually largely the product of Bishop Richard Challoner (1691–1781). Challoner, who was innocent of the biblical languages, "revised" this version in 1749, again in 1750, drastically in 1752, and later as well. His aim was to make the language more readable which, generally speaking, meant that he adjusted it to that of the Authorised Version. Subsequent to his time the text entered upon a recensional history of its own, picking up variants from the carelessness of printers and the deliberate changes introduced by copy-editors. In England the text tended to be printed as a blend of the first two Challoner revisions, while in America more of the changes from the third revision were included. Probably no two publishers ever produced precisely the same "Douay Bible."[7]

So at length we come to 1966 and the appearance in England and America of The Jerusalem Bible, the realization of an idea whose time most everyone probably agreed had come. There was officially available for the Catholic reader only the Challoner mishmash just described, filled with childishly apologetic footnotes, and hardly the work of "learned and catholic writers." Efforts to replace it had been unsuccessful, and alternatives to it were still aborning. To be sure, at least in the United States, a better edition of the New Testament was available. In 1941 members of the Catholic Biblical Association under the patronage of the episcopal committee of the Confraternity of Christian Doctrine had published a revision of the Challoner-Rheims which was, in effect, a new translation still officially of the Vulgate (but of critical editions, this time) but with consultation of the Greek so that all major variants between Greek and Latin were noted. Various American publishers of the "Douay Bible" printed this revision for their New Testament. There was also, from England, the version of the entire Bible, made from the (Sixto-Clementine) Vulgate by Monsignor Ronald Knox, the New Testament first published in 1945 and the Old Testament in 1949. The Knox Bible was adopted by the Catholic hierarchy of England and Wales as an official version and also enjoyed considerable success in America. But there was no version done from the original texts. What would eventually become the New American Bible (then known as the CCD or Confraternity Version, begun in 1943) was appearing part by provisional part, but the *editio princeps* of that completed Bible would not be published until 1970. Other "private" translations of the original Greek or Hebrew — such as the New Testament of Aloysius Spencer, O.P., posthumously published in 1936, the New Testament of James Kleist, S.J., and Joseph Lilly, C.M., published

[7]More particulars than the reader may be interested in knowing about this history can be found in Hugh Pope, O.P., *English Versions of the Bible* (2d ed.; St. Louis: Herder, 1952), 355-378, 386-441, 464-496.

in 1954, the Westminster Version of the entire Bible begun in 1913 and never completed—enjoyed limited circulation and were mainly regarded as curiosities, though each had its own merits.

What The Jerusalem Bible did, therefore, was, precisely at the right time, to present the English-speaking Catholic world with a version of the Scripture done from the original texts, turned into a dignified and highly readable form of our mother tongue, under impeccable Roman Catholic auspices (including, therefore, those Old Testament books and parts of books traditional in the Catholic canon and excluded from the "Protestant" and the Jewish). The introductions and annotations were both critical and scholarly, rarely apologetic. Its success was immediately assured.

The Jerusalem Bible also wisely chose to guarantee its ecumenical acceptance by eschewing the parochial "Catholic" spelling of proper names that had long challenged the good will of non-Catholics seeking to make use of scholarly articles and reference works done by Roman Catholics. The spelling of the biblical names of people and places is, of course, purely conventional. Hardly any normal reader would recognize who is meant by names like Yirmyahu or Yesha'yahu, which is the way they read in the Masoretic (Hebrew) text. The Septuagint had rendered them as Ieremias and Isaias (the final *s* to make them declinable) and thus they passed into the Vulgate. Thus they passed also into most modern languages. The early English translators, however, restored to them a bogus Hebrew flavor by substituting an *h* for the final *s*. The spelling of the names was already too well established for more to be done than this. For less well established names, however, more could be done, and generally it was to turn them into a rough-and-ready equivalent of the Masoretic spellings, using some equivalences that were probably lost on even their first readers, such as the *z* which was to stand for the Hebrew *ṣadê* (a Yiddishism). (Though even in the Authorised Version, in the New Testament at least, such forms remain as Elias in Mk 9:5 [RSV, Elijah] and Zacharias in Lk 1:5 [RSV, Zechariah].) Now in many cases the Vulgate, following the Septuagint, had preserved more authentic pronunciations than those devised by the Masoretes.

Nabuchodonosor, for example, is certainly closer to the Babylonian Nabukudurusūr than is the Nebuchadnezzar or even the Nebuchadrezzar of our English versions. On the other hand, many of the Vulgate spellings simply reflected the inadequacies of Latin or Greek to reproduce Hebrew aspirate sounds. When such forms were then mechanically "Englished," this resulted in sounds not originally intended — Lachis, Ezechias, Osee [Hosea]. Other spellings had become transmogrified into bizarre forms with no etymological justification in any language, such as Aggaeus [Haggai] and Eliseus [Elisha]. Compounding these confusions in Catholic biblical language were others inherited from the Septuagint which were not really the fault of the Vulgate: Paralipomenon, for example (a Greek genitive plural for works Jerome had called the books of Chronicles), and I–IV Kings (the Septuagint actually had "Kingdoms") for the books Jerome had distinguished as I–II Samuel and I–II Kings.

All academic questions aside, the point was that a conventional English rendering of biblical terminology had been arrived at over a period of some centuries, and the alternate "Catholic" usages could only co-exist with it as some kind of ghetto dialect. The Jerusalem Bible led the way in producing a Catholic version of the Bible, English in its spelling as in all else. The Confraternity Version did not adopt this principle until 1969 (at the publication of its final portion of the Old Testament, the historical books from Samuel through Maccabees), one year before the *editio princeps* of the New American Bible which would extend the principle to the Bible throughout. Up to this point only half-hearted gestures in this direction had been made, resulting in such anomalous forms as Isaia, Jeremia, Abdia (from Abdias = Obadiah), Sophonia (from Sophonias = Zephaniah in conventional English), etc. It was with these anomalous forms that the *New Catholic Encyclopedia* was caught when it appeared in 1967, and thus it is locked in with an English biblical vocabulary that is now gone forever.

What primarily made the Jerusalem Bible possible, however, was nothing English at all, but something quintessentially French.

During the late '40s and early '50s there appeared in 43 separate fascicules what was originally conceived and was eventually accomplished as an entirely new, highly critical, translation into French of the complete Bible from the original languages, Each fascicule was the work of at least one internationally recognized biblical scholar. Hardly at that time could any other part of the Catholic world than the francophone have gathered such a cadre as that which produced this Bible. Some of the fascicules were eventually to go through as many as two subsequent revisions, revisions which would be substantive and by no means confined to mere stylistic niceties. Style was, it is true, very important, as one would expect in a French publication, and each fascicule had passed the test of good language as well as good scholarship. What made this Bible of such import in the Catholic world outside of France, however, were the extensive introductions and notes that accompanied each biblical work, amounting in effect to a series of biblical commentaries. (Indeed, for many of the biblical books the best commentary available at that time produced under Catholic auspices was to be found in these fascicules.) In 1956 a one-volume edition was published, understandably with highly compressed introductions and notes, but also with the addition of an admirable system of marginal cross-referencing. This was *La Sainte Bible traduite en français sous la direction de l'École Biblique de Jérusalem.* The title recognized the great part played in this production by members of the Dominican biblical school in Jerusalem, a part that was proportionately even greater in the publication of the one-volume edition than in the fascicules, which represented the collaboration of some forty translators and editors. It is this Bible, of course, that is the basis of what was published in English in 1966 under the title The Jerusalem Bible. It is not to denigrate the qualities of the twenty-eight "principal collaborators" named in the credits of this latter publication to add that a comparable version in English would have been impossible without dependence on the French. English-speaking Roman Catholicism simply had not yet had the time to gather the resources which had been longer possessed by their numerically superior Continental coreligionists. The necessary dependence is, therefore, clear and undisputed. What is not altogether clear is the degree of dependence, acknowledged or unacknowledged.

An unsigned note following the imprimatur of Cardinal Heenan in the first edition of The Jerusalem Bible states that

> The introduction and notes of this Bible are, with minor variations and revisions a translation of those which appear in *La Bible de Jérusalem* [actually this was not, as yet, an official title] published by Les Editions du Cerf, Paris, (one volume edition, 1961) [actually, as we have seen, 1956] under the general editorship of Père Roland de Vaux, O.P. [The 1956 French Bible lists a far more complex Comité de revision.] The English text of the Bible itself, though translated from the ancient texts, owes a large debt to the work of the many scholars who collaborated to produce *La Bible de Jérusalem,* a debt which the publishers of this English Bible gratefully acknowledge.

In the Foreword by Alexander Jones, General Editor of the Jerusalem Bible, the source of which "this present volume is the English equivalent" is correctly identified as the one-volume 1956 French version "known popularly as *La Bible de Jérusalem.*" The introduction and notes are acknowledged to be "a direct translation from the French, though revised and brought up to date in some places — account being taken of the decisions and general implications of the Second Vatican Council." [No explanation has ever been given of the meaning of the last clause.] The Foreword continues:

> The translation of the biblical text itself could clearly not be made from the French. In the case of a few books the initial draft was made from the French and was then compared word for word with the Hebrew or Aramaic [we are therefore speaking of at least the books of Daniel and Ezra?] by the General Editor and amended where necessary to ensure complete conformity with the ancient text. [Amending an incorrect translation of the French? Or a translation of the French that had incorrectly rendered the originals?] For the much greater part, the initial drafts were made from the Hebrew or Greek and simultaneously compared with the

French when questions of variant reading or interpretation arose. Whichever system was used, therefore, the same intended result was achieved, that is, an entirely faithful version of the ancient texts which, in doubtful points, preserves the text established and (for the most part) the interpretation adopted by the French scholars in the light of the most recent researches in the fields of history, archaeology and literary criticism.

There follow some rather sensible words on the Englishing of the Bible in general and the defense of an editorial decision to reproduce the tetragrammaton throughout as "Yahweh," even in the Psalms which were translated with an eye to Catholic liturgical use. It might be noted, incidentally, that only in this respect did The Jerusalem Bible depart from its sensible decision to stick to the proper names that had become conventional in English. In contrast, in the French original "traditional" French forms like Sédécias, Josias, and Nabuchodonosor rub shoulders with exotica like Hilqiyyahu, Miçrayim, Çeboyim, and Shéneaç-çar, which must be as perplexing to a French reader as they are to any other.

What is not clear from the unsigned note combined with Alexander Jones' Foreword is the extent to which The Jerusalem Bible admits to being a translation of the 1956 French archetype and where it claims to have depended on an improved text. Much more controllable in this regard are the pretensions of another satellite of the French text, the so-called Jerusalem Bible in German.[8] In this case there was an already existing German translation for most of the biblical books (the translation for the Herders Bibelkommentar plus the Beuron translation of the Psalter); only the books of Joshua, Judges, and Ruth were done afresh by the German translators. The translation was simply changed, where necessary, to conform with the reconstruction of the text presupposed by the French notes and introductions, which were reproduced quite faithfully.

---

[8]*Die Bibel. Die Heilige Schrift des Alten und Neuen Bundes. Deutsche Ausgabe mit den Erläuterungen der Jerusalemer Bibel* (Freiburg: Herder, 1968).

The question of the independence of the English Jerusalem
Bible from the French translation is, of course, very important, as is the question of the extent to which the English translators "revised and brought up to date" and otherwise improved
on the French of 1956. As has already been mentioned, the
fascicule edition of the French Bible continued in multiple revisions after 1956, culminating in another one-volume *nouvelle
édition revue et augmentée* in 1974, by which time *La Bible
de Jérusalem* was at last accepted as the official and not merely
the popular title of the translation. The 1974 one-volume edition not only incorporated but went beyond the fascicule editions subsequent to 1956 and therefore there is no point in comparing its text with that of The Jerusalem Bible of 1966 as a
standard of the improvements that should have been registered
by the English. Nevertheless, there were fascicule changes,
sometimes in rather important areas, which were in existence
when The Jerusalem Bible was being prepared, and which
it obviously chose to ignore in favor of sticking to the 1956
version.

Thus, for example, the fascicule of Matthew's Gospel had
passed through two subsequent revisions in French before The
Jerusalem Bible appeared. "Je ne parle pas de la fornication"
was the way the "Matthean exception" had first appeared in the
translation of Matt. 19:9, and "I am not speaking of fornication" is the way it runs in The Jerusalem Bible (along with a
note to match, which is a verbatim translation of the French).
Meanwhile a second edition of the French had substituted "con-
cubinage" for "fornication," and in turn this yielded to "prostitution," which also is the reading of the 1974 version—"pas
pour prostitution"—along with a new note that reflects a quite
different interpretation of the text. The 1968 German "Jerusalem
Bible" also has a form of the 1956 French ("ausser wegen Un-
zucht") and the same note. Other random examples where both
English and German have followed the 1956 text without regard
to second thoughts which had been already expressed in the
fascicules are the episode which begins with Josh. 7:2 and the
translation of I Sam. 1:23. In the first instance, beginning the
narrative of the conquest of Ai, the two derived versions re-

produce the footnote of 1956 acknowledging that the site was uninhabited in the time of Joshua but suggesting that it could have served as a refuge for the people of the Bethel region. As early as 1958, however, this attempt to salvage history from the story had been abandoned by *La Bible de Jérusalem* and the note had been radically altered. I Sam. 1:23 in the French of 1956, the German, and the English has the possessive pronoun in the second person, justified by "versions" (the German also noted the agreement of 4QSam^a). But the later editions of the French have restored to the text the third person pronoun of the Masoretic Text.

It is instructive to compare Isa. 2:2–3, first in the French of 1956 and 1974, and then with the English of 1966.

1956	*1974*
Il adviendra dans l'avenir que le mont du Temple de Yahvé	Il arrivera dans la suite des temps que la montagne de la maison de Yahvé
sera établi au sommet des montagnes et s'élèvera plus haut que les collines.	sera établie en tête des montagnes et s'élèvera au-dessus des collines.
Toutes les nations y afflueront, des peuples nombreux s'y rendront et diront:	Alors toutes les nations afflueront vers elle, alors viendront des peuples nombreux qui diront:
"Venez, montons à la montagne de Yahvé allons au Temple du Dieu de Jacob,	"Venez, montons à la montagne de Yahvé, à la maison du Dieu de Jacob,
pour qu'il nous enseigne ses voies et que nous suivions ses sentiers.	qu'il nous enseigne ses voies et que nous suivions ses sentiers."
Car de Sion viendra la Loi et de Jérusalem l'oracle de Yahvé."	Car de Sion vient la Loi et de Jérusalem la parole de Yahvé.

These are, rather obviously, different translations of Isa 2:2–3. The 1974 *Bible de Jérusalem* acknowledges that its translation of Isaiah has been "entièrement retraduit." More precisely, there has been an effort to make the translations of Isa. 2:2–3 and Mic. 4:1–2, which differ very little in the Masoretic text, agree correspondingly in the French, though there remain some subtle differences even in the 1974 version which could be of interest to us if we were concerned with the French rather than the English. We are concerned with the French only to point out that both in words and in punctuation the translations represent separate interpretations of the original text. Only to this extent are we involved with the French text, not to suggest in any way that the English Jerusalem Bible should have anticipated a revision of the *Bible de Jérusalem* that did not then exist.

What the Jerusalem Bible has, however, for Isa. 2:2–3 is this:

> In the days to come
> the mountain of the Temple of Yahweh
> shall tower above the mountains
> and be lifted higher than the hills.
> All the nations will stream to it,
> peoples without number will come to it; and they will say:
> 'Come, let us go up to the mountain of Yahweh,
> to the Temple of the God of Jacob
> that he may teach us his ways
> so that we may walk in his paths;
> since the Law will go out from Zion,
> and the oracle of Yahweh from Jerusalem.'

It would be difficult, I think, to conclude that the Jerusalem Bible here is anything other than a translation – admittedly a translation into very idiomatic English – of the French of 1956. Word choices, verb tenses, punctuational and other interpretations, all agree, far and beyond the need to adjust the translation to any significant footnote, which in this instance does not exist. The German *Jerusalemer Bibel* can serve as a control, providing a translation of its own for the same commentary:

> In der Folge der Tage wird es geschehen: Da wird der Berg
> des Hauses Jahwes festgegründet stehen an der Spitze der

Berge und erhaben sein über die Hügel. Zu ihm strömen alle
Völker. Dorthin pilgern viele Nationen und sprechen:
"Auf, lasst uns hinaufziehen zum Berge Jahwes, zum Hause
des Gottes Jakobs! Er lehre uns seine Wege, und wir wollen
auf seinen Pfaden wandeln. Denn von Zion wird ausgehen
das Gesetz und das Wort Jahwes von Jerusalem."

Here is where The Jerusalem Bible is most vulnerable from
the critical standpoint. There is no doubt that an exhaustive investigation would show that it has gone its own way in various
instances independently of the French. (An example is present
in this very passage, as a matter of fact, since it chose to harmonize its translation of Isa. 2:2–3 with Mic. 4:1–2 by reading
debar Yhwh in both cases as "the oracle of Yahweh," whereas
the latter text in the 1956 French had "la parole de Yahvé"—
the formula which of course was chosen for Isaiah and Micah
in 1974.) For the most part, however, and quite understandably
in view of the limitations imposed by its times, it has reproduced
accurately and in creditable English a work of French scholarship of the middle '50s. And while the French scholarship of
the middle '50s, particularly the French Catholic scholarship
represented by the École Biblique, was as critical as any that
then existed, it continued to develop not only from its association with other scholarly groups but also from its own internal
development and growth.[9] To take another random example:
The initial note on Genesis 14 in the English Jerusalem Bible,
acknowledging that it "does not belong to any of the three great
sources of Genesis," maintains that "behind it lies a document
of great age" and that "all we can say is that the narrative finds
its most natural setting in the conditions of the 19th century
B.C." This is a faithful translation of the note in the 1956 French
Bible. In the 1974 *Bible de Jérusalem,* however, all that is left
of the note is the negative part: the passage is neither J,E, nor
P. Further, it seems to be "a late composition making a pastiche

---

[9]In *Bibel und Kirche* 32 (1978), 135, Anton Steiner, responding to the
familiar question "welche Bibel kaufen," also chides the "Jerusalemer Bibel"
for having acquiesced in introductory material and annotation that was already
outdated in 1968.

of ancient material"—much of which is "historically impossible." While the earlier judgment in this matter might be held equally as respectable as the later, that is hardly the point. The point is that The Jerusalem Bible has frozen *La Bible de Jérusalem* at a stage of its development which did not represent the maturest thinking of those responsible for it.

Both the actual translation as well as the annotation given it differ from 1956 to 1974, as we have seen. Nor do these, of course, affect only matters of detail. In Gen. 1:2 "God's spirit hovered over the water" according to The Jerusalem Bible, here faithfully echoing the French of 1956 and translating the note referring to Deut. 32:11 to justify this understanding of the verb *merahepet*. But by 1974 the *Bible de Jérusalem* was expressing what is probably the prevailing interpretation today: "un vent de Dieu tournoyait sur les eaux" ("a wind of God was swirling over the waters") and in a footnote explicitly denied that there is any mention here of the "spirit" of God. The French of Gen. 3:22 is the same in 1956 and 1974 and is faithfully rendered in English by The Jerusalem Bible. But while the note in 1956 had it that "immortality was a pure gift of God which man's disobedience forfeited," the 1974 note says no such thing, rather that the earthly paradise is an image of the immortality to which man aspires. The difference is considerable. The earlier edition reflects a period of apologetics in Catholic biblical studies when there was still a felt obligation to defend a traditional exegesis that had gone into dogmatics regarding the "preternatural gifts" possessed by our "first parents" prior to their fall from grace. In the later edition the attempt has been abandoned in favor of a more relaxed and objective exegesis.[10]

Although the explanatory notes and introduction were a decisive factor in the initial acceptance and success of The Jeru-

---

[10]Cf. Herbert Haag, *Biblische Schöpfungslehre und Kirchliche Erbsündenlehre* (Stuttgarter Bibelstudien 10; Stuttgart: Katholisches Bibelwerk, 1966), 49-54, referring also to pp. 13-37. There is an English translation, *Is Original Sin in Scripture?* (New York: Sheed & Ward, 1969), but in the substitution of English for German sources the force of the contrast has largely disappeared.

salem Bible, it is undoubtedly in its status as a good readable version of the Scripture that its continuing reputation stands. This is apparently the status on which the editors themselves wished their version to stand or fall. In 1968 a "Reader's Edition" was published, doubtless the edition now known to most of those who use it in this country. The notes and introductions were reduced to a bare minimum, in view of an announced intention to impede the ordinary reader with as little as possible of the marginalia that are of interest to the more professional student. At the same time, in this edition, the spelling was Americanized: "honour," "labour," "favourable," and the like, became "honor," "labor," and "favorable"; "gaol" and "gaoler" became "jail" and "jailer." However, whatever was the grain (*bar* or *seber*) that Joseph's brethren brought from Egypt to Canaan, this edition is more British than American when it has them bring it in "corn-sacks" (Gen. 42:28).

Among the collaborators acknowledged in the original edition of The Jerusalem Bible are several whose area of competence was obviously that of sensitivity to the best resonances of the English language, such as Robert Speaight and J.R.R. Tolkien. There is no doubt that they and the rest of the editors and translators in this respect performed their task with distinction. The Jerusalem Bible is in English what *La Sainte Bible de Jérusalem* is in French, a credit to the challenging capabilities of the language. It is particularly good in its narrative passages and reporting of familiar dialogue: stories are told the way good stories should be, and conversations sound like real people talking together. "Today God has put your enemy in your power," says Abishai to David. "So now let me pin him to the ground with his own spear. Just one stroke! I will not need to strike him twice" (I Sam. 26:8). "To Job they spoke never a word," goes the old folktale about Job's friends in 2:13, "so sad a sight he made." The Jerusalem Bible has made a clean break with "Bible English" while at the same time avoiding folksiness and respecting the genre of the text it is translating. "Better a poor man living an honest life than the adept at double-talk who is a fool" (Prov. 19:1). This is not only better than other English versions earlier and later, it is also superior, to the extent that

I can judge, to its French prototype. "In fact, this seems to be the rule, that every single time I want to do good it is something evil that comes to hand. In my inmost self I dearly love God's Law, but I can see that my body follows a different law that battles against the law which my reason dictates. This is what makes me a prisoner of that law of sin which lives inside my body" (Rom. 7:21–23). There is a temptation to multiply the examples of translations which are just right. Nor is it necessary to temper this praise by acknowledging the presence here and there, as in any other version of the Bible, of the odd word or phrase or idiom that could have been better handled.

We have already noted the excellent cross-referencing system reproduced in the margins (omitted, however, in the "Reader's Edition"). This, together with the system of headings, sub-headings, and paragraphing—an important interpretive device, surely—has been borrowed from the French along with the other more overt notations. A further decision of format marked a definite improvement on the French, namely the relegation of verse numbers to the unobtrusive inside margins (when the division falls within a printed line it is marked in the text by a large dot). While chapter numbers are noted, they are also similarly set apart as the items of convenience they were originally meant to be and not hindrances to the sequence of the text. Also, perhaps alone of modern English versions, The Jerusalem Bible notes marginally the variant chapter-and-verse indications that occasionally occur among the versions ancient and modern (in Job 39–40, for example, or in Hosea 1–3, in much of Ecclesiasticus, etc.), which can easily confuse the reader attempting to consult more than one translation at a time. The only serious exception to this rule—and here there has been a noteworthy deviation from the French—has been the decision to follow in the Psalms the verse enumeration as it occurs in what is called "the English Bible." In this acceptation "the English Bible," I suppose, means what simply "the Bible" meant to Henry Higgins when he counted it along with Shakespeare as one of the noblest products of the English tongue, that is to say therefore, the King James Version. It seems that practically every modern English version of the Bible, even those which have consciously broken with the Authorised Version translation-tradition (such as the New English Bible and Today's English Version, both of which omit the Psalm titles in the bargain), have elected to perpetuate this eccentric system which can hardly matter much to the casual reader but which continually frustrates anyone trying to follow a commentary or work of reference written in any other language than English. One must always remember that the English text is one verse out of kilter, even as Roman Catholic commentaries on the Psalms in a bygone age were usually a whole Psalm out of kilter when they followed the Septuagint/Vulgate enumeration rather than that of the Hebrew. Only the New American Bible in recent days has refused to perpetuate this parochial "English" enumeration of Psalm verses.

In his *Trials of a Translator* Ronald Knox insisted that good translation required a better knowledge of the receptor than of the donor language, and he confessed to having had more recourse in his own work to Fowler and the Oxford Dictionary than to the standard lexica and concordances of the biblical languages. He was probably right in every respect. The Jerusalem Bible, by this test, needs no apology. No one would want to take from it the credit that is its due for having so capably filled a void that then existed in 1966 in the English-speaking Catholic world, hungry for reasonable access to the word of God. It is a monument.

As long, however, as it bears the name The Jerusalem Bible, explicitly borrowed from *La Bible de Jérusalem*, it is a monument to a biblical tradition that no longer exists. That biblical tradition has been done away with effectively through the later development of *La Bible de Jérusalem* in fascicule and in the one-volume edition of 1974, a Bible which is in many essentials altogether different from the French archetype of 1956.

If, on the other hand, The Jerusalem Bible wishes to declare itself free of the French archetype and to persist in its own right as an English version on the plane of the New English Bible, the New American Bible, the Revised Standard Version, or the like, then it seems that something must be done for which there is no evidence that anything has been done. That is to say, there is no possibility of achieving ever what a publisher's blurb in 1966 claimed for The Jerusalem Bible: "This is *the* Bible for the twentieth century." Ronald Knox insisted, again quite correctly, that the Bible should be translated afresh for every succeeding generation—and in these days of geometric evolution we know that generations overtake one another with increasing frequency in even the small portion of the twentieth century we are destined to experience. There is no such thing as a perfect translation of the Bible in any language that is destined to have a responsible life for more than a decade or so. Every existing version that has a claim to responsibility has already built into itself the machinery of future revision. Is there such a machinery built into the continuing existence of The Jerusalem Bible? If there is not—and all the indications are that there is not—then The Jerusalem Bible is destined to remain the monument that it is, a faithful reproduction of some of the best biblical scholarship of the late 1950s. It would be doubly unfortunate if the casual reader, invited to adopt the Jerusalem Bible, were led to believe that nothing of significance had occurred in the past generation to constitute it a less acceptable option in response to the perennial question, "Which Bible is best?"

7. History and Kerygma in the Old Testament

Recently, in criticizing a book dealing with some aspects of the contemporary theological posture, a reviewer[1] commented on its author's alleged

> preoccupation . . . with trying to make sense out of biblical passages for modern man. A common reaction among the young would certainly be; "So what? If it makes sense, fine; but if it doesn't say anything to us, don't try to twist it for the sake of saving it.". . . Instead of "reinterpreting," why not move on?

This kind of question is being raised more and more these days, and — such is the erosion of the common ground on which theology once stood — it is becoming increasingly harder to answer in terms that are mutually intelligible. The biblical theologian — by which I mean here simply the theologian who takes the biblical word as his *point de départ*, who would define the theological task as having an initial stage at least in "trying to make sense out of biblical passages for modern man," — will no doubt be puzzled as to what he is supposed to move on to: what has displaced Scripture as the *norma normans* which will now only tolerate Scripture if it "makes sense," and which indulges

[1] Mary Daly, on Gregory Baum's *Man Beginning*, in *National Catholic Reporter*, July 10, 1970, p. 12.

"reinterpreting" more as a concession to nostalgia than as a necessary step in methodology? If he is told that the social and behavioral and phenomenological sciences constitute this norm, he may be old-fashioned enough to inquire whether the roles of philosophy and theology have not been dramatically reversed. A decent and dynamic humanism suitably illustrated by biblical parallels—the sort of thing that Erich Fromm, for one, has done very well—can faithfully depict a world of man which theology must take into account; but it is not theology itself, not Christian theology, unless the humpty-dumpty school of linguistics now prevails and words mean what we choose to make them mean, no more and no less.

There is little point in belaboring this issue. Most of those who consider themselves theologians working within the (Judeo-) Christian tradition will mainly agree that "the Bible is in a peculiar way the foundation of all theology, of all thinking about Christianity. No form of Christianity can afford to dispense with the Bible . . . the foundation document of the Christian faith."[2] Such an affirmation will be made by Catholics as well as by Protestants and, along with conservatives, by those who believe that the Bible must be radically de-mythologized and/or that its canon must be sharply circumscribed. Even those whose theology *de facto* was or is not biblical—the medieval scholastic for whom *scriptura* was in reality patristic tradition, the post-Tridentine Roman Catholic who began with conciliar or papal formulas and eisegeted biblical tags to fit them, the present-day philosopher of religion whose conclusions turn out to be corroborated by the Scripture rather than inspired by it—did and do believe themselves to be biblical theologians in the sense defined above. Theoretically at least, it is agreed that theology is subject to the judgment of the biblical word, however minimal this word may be conceived to be, and it is not at all a question of twisting the word to accommodate it to something else of whatever provenance.

At the same time, what so-called radical theologians are pre-

[2]R. P. C. Hanson, in *The Pelican Guide to Modern Theology*, Volume 3, *Biblical Criticism* (Penquin, 1970), p. 15.

pared to deny to the Bible as a whole, many of those who qualify eminently as biblical theologians in the above sense are cheerfully prepared to deny to the OT in particular. That is to say, they view OT history and/or its kerygma as having nothing whatever to do with NT faith.[3] The reasons for this attitude are various and not invariably Marcionist. One of the more respectable of them, which has also suggested the topic of this present paper, is the disparity which critical study of the Bible has revealed to exist between the *bruta facta* of ascertainable history and the kerygmatic version of that history.[4] The disparity is not of course confined to the OT; it also poses an acute problem for the NT, as, most recently perhaps, the discussion provoked by the Pannenberg-*Kreis* has made very clear. The OT difficulty, however, is compounded by associated factors: exotic literary forms, the extreme distance that separates us from most of Israel's formative experiences, and—above all—the new direction into which NT faith has shunted the OT kerygma. Research into the kernel of fact that may lie hidden in a cult

[3]Rudolf Bultmann ("To Christian faith the OT is no longer revelation"), "The Significance of the OT for Christian Faith," in B. W. Anderson, ed., *The Old Testament and Christian Faith* (London: SCM, 1964), p. 31. Friedrich Baumgärtel ("The OT is a witness out of a non-Christian religion; its self-understanding is not identical with evangelical prior understanding"), in Claus Westermann, ed., *Essays on OT Interpretation* (London: SCM, 1963), p. 135. Franz Hesse ("Der alttestamentliche Zeugnis ist in seinem Selbstverständnis ein fremdes Wort aus einer fremden Religion, ein Wort ausserhalb des Evangeliums"), "Kerygma oder geschichtliche Wirklichkeit," *ZTK* 57 (1960), 17-26. See the discussion in my "History and the Word," *CBQ* 29 (1967), 512-23. See also the sensitive study of G. E. Wright, "Historical Knowledge and Revelation," in *Translating and Understanding the Old Testament*, Essays in honor of Herbert Gordon May, ed. by H. T. Frank and W. L. Reed (New York and Nashville: Abingdon, 1970), pp. 279-303.

[4]Hans-Joachim Kraus is not extremely helpful on this point in the revised edition of his *Geschichte der historisch-kritischen Erforschung des Alten Testaments* (Neukirchener Verlag, 1969). After bringing the discussion only to the point of von Rad's *Theology* and its sequelae, he asks (p. 509): "Wird ein Weg gefunden werden, auf dem die Spaltung überwunden kann? Das ist jetzt die Frage."

legend or in the saga of a thirteenth-century tribal chieftain can much more readily be made to appear meaningless for Christian faith than can research into the circumstances of the historical Jesus, though, to be sure, the latter appears equally meaningless to many Christians. In any case, and whether or not one is disposed to make a point of it, the disparity between what Abraham, let us say, was according to his putatively contemporary lights—at last account, a donkey trader (and smith?) resembling the Ibsha of the celebrated wall painting from Beni Hasan—and what he is in the book of Genesis, not to mention Galatians and Romans, is more than considerable.

So much more, in fact, that the discovered discrepancy readily encourages both ridicule and caricature. In a rather gloomy view of the prospect of OT studies, Morton Smith has indicted biblical faith as the culprit responsible for a perverse approach to what he characterizes as a "body of documents from the ancient Mediterranean world."[5] His approach is obviously that of an historian who sees his discipline threatened by the aprioristic view of so many who deal with this body of documents, who are ideologically committed to making the biblical construction of events square anyhow with the history of scientific method: *die Bibel hatte doch recht!* With fine impartiality, he scores the conservatism displayed in reproducing biblical texts, some desperate efforts that have been made to wrest meaning from a corrupt textual tradition through recourse to comparative linguistics, romanticizing biblical history on meagre archeological evidence while failing to acknowledge how thoroughly archeology has vindicated the substance of Wellhausen's hypothesis (an ingratitude of which I believe OT study is really guilty), claiming uniqueness to the OT of religious motifs that are not unique at all, and so forth. Only about OT theology does he not speak, because it is "unspeakable." As we will recall, most of these points were given attention in a much milder fashion several years ago at separate stages by that valuable gadfly James Barr.

Smith's article is often incisively witty and of course often quite on the target. No one is unaware of the effort that has

[5]"The Present State of OT Studies," *JBL* 88 (1969), 19-35.

been made to prove the Bible right by the naïve use of archeological and other evidence. It is part of the price that has had
to be paid to the concerns that made those Mediterranean documents objects of study in the first place, that endowed the chairs
of learning and underwrote the publication of the texts and
funded the digs. Without those concerns, and despite their incidental aberrations, it is very doubtful that there would have
ever been the resources, let alone the occasion, for either Morton
Smith or me to be writing at this juncture. Critical method, after
all, has not been something lately imposed on biblical studies
after having been tested and proved in alien areas. It was the
study of the biblical texts that only later led to the idea of extending textual criticism to other literature.[6] It is at least arguable
too that it was biblical archeologists who did the most to convert what began as a treasure hunt into an organized discipline
making sense out of—*faute de mieux*, perhaps—shards and walls
and queer scratchings. It is true they have dug by the Book,
as Schliemann, for example, dug by his book rather than look
for Troy in, say, the forests of Swabia. But I do not really find
with Smith the unmasking of a sinister plot in "Solomon's cop-
per foundry that turned out to be a granary, Solomon's stables
that were built by Ahab, a Maccabean fortress that turned out
to be Solomonic," and the rest. No more sinister, at least, than
the canals of Mars that disappeared with better telescopes or
that extra pair of human chromosomes that float about in limbo
now that microscopes have improved. It might be remembered
too that Nelson Glueck, who, after all, corrected his own mistake—a thing that is not lightly done in scholarship—went looking in the Ghor for neither smelters nor granaries, but for the
docks of Ezion-geber, which he never found.[7]

---

[6]Cf C. F. Evans, "The Inspiration of the Bible," *Theology* 59 (1956), 11-17.

[7]For a much more balanced and informative essay of the role of archeology
in controlling "tradition," and *vice versa*, see the article of one who is well
informed of both: Roland de Vaux, "On Right and Wrong Uses of Archaeology," in *Near Eastern Archaeology in the Twentieth Century,* Essays in
honor of Nelson Glueck, ed. by J. A. Sanders (Garden City: Doubleday,
1970), pp. 64-80.

At all events, on both sides we are being urged to cease trying to find religious meaning in the OT, either because the quest leads nowhere, as far as the presuppositions of Christian faith are concerned, or because it interferes with the serious study of an otherwise significant corpus of written materials. On the contrary, however, I believe the quest to be both legitimate and necessary — necessary too not only for faith but for basic and minimal human understanding. If Morton Smith is serious when he sums up the OT portrayal of Yahweh as "a North-Arabian mountain god who traveled in thunderstorms and liked the smell of burning fat" — the late Colonel Robert Ingersoll lacked the erudition to phrase it quite this well — I must conclude that either his collection of the documents is missing some folios that are in mine or he has gravely misconstrued the character of the literature to whose study he had dedicated his scholarly life.

For the God whom Jesus revealed was very different from this, while at the same time he was the God of Israel, the very God of the OT. "Revelation of God in Christ" cannot but be meaningless unless it takes into account both a prior knowledge of the God whose fullness came to be seen in Jesus and the expectation of his manifestation which was the sum of Israel's history and the substance of Jesus' proclamation.[8] This is true not only of the situation of Jesus' original preaching to the Jewry of his time and place (or of the perhaps comparable situation of a later Jew who hears the kerygma of the gospel), it is likewise true of that of most Christians, who come to a knowledge of Israel's God and its expectation only through the Jesus of the church's preaching: there is always a logical if not a temporal "prior." It is true too, even when it is conceded that Judaism has legitimately retained its own interpretation of the OT based on the Torah which "by no means leads to the companion of taxgatherers and sinners, to the Pauline doctrine of justifica-

---

[8]Cf Wolfhart Pannenberg, "The Revelation of God in Jesus," in James M. Robinson, John B. Cobb, eds., *Theology as History,* New Frontiers in Theology 3 (New York: Harper & Row, 1967), pp. 102-5.

tion, or to the Johannine assertion of the divinity of Jesus."[9] It is not necessary to denigrate Judaism in order to affirm that for Christian faith the prior of the OT and the direction of its history have found in Jesus an interpretation that is its own, an interpretation, however, that the earliest church considered to be an extension rather than a denial of Judaism's. At least, what is of key concern in the one acceptation of the OT kerygma is of key concern in the other:

> The New Testament does not deny that the Jews pray to the same God as the Christians. Even if we are children of Abraham in a special sense, we are yet subject to the same God and represented by the obedience of the same patriarch. At the same time that Abraham was promised a son and heir, he was also assured that he would become father of many nations. His faith is set before the Romans and Galatians as the decisive type of the faith by which men are justified.[10]

The promise and the God of the promise constitute the one inspiration of both Judaism and Christianity.

Now the one God common to Christians and Jews, the God whom Jesus revealed in fullness, is the God who first came to be known in Israel's history. Lately we have been warned against making too much of this historical factor,[11] to the detriment of revelation through the spoken word, which is likewise at-

---

[9]Ernst Käsemann (critique of the 1967 report of the Dutch church on the authority of the Bible), in *Das Neue Testament als Kanon* (Göttingen: Vandenhoeck & Ruprecht, 1970), pp. 347f.

[10]Markus Barth, *Israel and the Church* (Richmond: John Knox Press, 1969), p. 16.

[11]Notably by James Barr, "Revelation through History in the OT and in Modern Theology," *Interp* 17 (1963), 193-205; then in his *Old and New in Interpretation: A Study of the Two Testaments* (New York: Harper & Row, 1966). Barr is much better at puncturing exaggerated claims and conclusions — a valuable function — than he is at articulating positively what he believes the fair assessment of the situation to be. However, it seems evident that he does not intend to deny that history has been *a* chief vehicle of the knowledge of God in the OT.

tested to by the OT; but it still seems to be an unassailable fact
that history throughout has been the determinant of OT revelation in a way that nothing else has, and to it everything else
has been subordinate.[12] The earliest bearers of the prophetic
word in Israel of whom we have any firsthand acquaintance
already presuppose the decisive deeds of Yahweh in history—
basically the kerygma of the Pentateuch, in fact—as having
revealed the God in whose name they speak: prophecy is a consequent, not the determinant, of this historical process of revelation (Amos 3:9–12; Hos 9:10; 11:1–4; etc.). It may be rejoined
that the prophetic word was required to give interpretation to
the historical event in the first place before it could become a
medium of revelation, and this in a sense may be true; but if
it is true, it is unverifiable from the prophecy we know: as with
all history, event and interpretation have come down together
and are encountered together in the ancient "cultic credos." A
prophet may, indeed, give a prior interpretation to a coming
event,[13] but, whatever may be the source of his word, it is intended to set that event in corroboration of a primary one that
is presupposed: *ky 'ny yhwh*. There is no purpose in denying that
the OT represents God as being encountered other than through
the indirect mediation of history. Yet it is doubtless not without
significance that even the priestly Torah has at all turns been
worked into the framework of Israel's history. Neither is the
wisdom literature, with its alleged lack of interest in history,
usually concerned with the God of Israel's revelation. However,
wisdom did display an interest in the history of Israel. Not only
has it strongly influenced the didactic, so-called secular histories

[12]Cf Hans Lubsczyk, "Die Einheit der Schrift. Zur hermeneutischen
Relevanz des Urbekenntnisses im Alten und Neuen Testament," in *Sapienter
Ordinare*, Festgabe für Erich Kleineidam, ed. by F. Hoffman *et al.* (Leip-
zig: St Benno-Verlag, 1969), pp. 73-104.

[13]Cf Walther Zimmerli, "Das Wort des göttlichen Selbsterweises (Erweis-
wort), eine prophetische Gattung," in *Mélanges Bibliques rédigés en l'hon-
neur de André Robert* (Paris: Bloud & Gay, 1956), pp. 154-64.

of Joseph and the Davidic succession narrative,[14] its motifs have probably entered into the portrayal of sacred history as well.[15] It is worthy of note too that the apocalyptic view of eschatology which, after much reluctance, present-day scholarship is willing to ascribe to Jesus as well as to the early church, a perspective which gave Israel's history universal and cosmic dimensions,[16] is with some probability attributed to the wisdom tradition as having played a predominant role in its formation.[17] In its end as in its beginning, therefore, the OT presupposition of NT faith has had a strong historical orientation.

And thus we are brought back to the question of the tension between the data of history as we are able to know them and history as it has been told in the kerygma. To be concerned about the facts of OT history as relevant to biblical faith, to find other than philological significance in literary and historical criticism and what is turned up by the archeologist's spade, is not, as some seem to take it, the reversion to a religious historicism. It is, simply, to take the Bible seriously in its claim to represent a history of revelation—to take that claim seriously, that is, with the same critical approach and resources one is expected to bring to bear on other claims to credence. The claim is not taken seriously in the existentialist *als ob* acceptance of the OT kerygma seemingly favored by, among others, Gerhard von Rad, much in the manner of Martin Kähler's repudiation of historical criticism in relation to the kerygmatic Christ.

---

[14]See, most recently, R. N. Whybray, *The Succession Narrative: A Study of II Sam. 9-20 and I Kings 1 and 2, Studies in Biblical Theology,* Second Series 9 (Naperville: Allenson, 1968).

[15]See Martin J. Buss, "The Meaning of History," in *Theology as History*, p. 149.

[16]Cf Jürgen Moltmann, *Theologie der Hoffnung*, 5th ed. (Munich: Kaiser Verlag, 1966), pp. 120-24.

[17]Cf Gerhard von Rad, *Theologie des Alten Testaments* (Munich: Kaiser Verlag, 1960) II, 319f. Without sharing all of the author's assumptions (e.g., his conviction of an absolute dichotomy between prophetic and apocalyptic eschatology), one can nevertheless agree that he has made a good case for wisdom influence.

History and interpretation are inseparable — granted — and the one comes to us only by means of the latter; but to exhibit no curiosity over what has been interpreted is hardly to enter into the spirit of the OT, which from first to last is concerned with things that happened or would happen. No necessary distinction between the historic and the merely historical should be allowed to obscure the fact that, in the biblical view, history always contains something that is *einmalig*, and that something cannot be dispensed with.

Morton Smith has justly praised an article by Roland de Vaux on historical method in which, it should be observed, de Vaux, qualifying von Rad's *Theology of the OT* as rather a history of Israel's religion, maintains:

> The theologian takes for his starting point the conclusions of the historian of religions, and he judges of their validity, not only according to the criteria of rational science, but according to their conformity to the established truths of his faith. He then goes beyond these conclusions by integrating them into the whole of revelation. The connection between religious history and objective history, between the history believed by Israel and the true history of Israel, is apparently more difficult to establish; however, it must be established in the eyes of the believer, for if the historical faith of Israel is not in a certain way founded in *history*, this faith is erroneous and cannot command my assent.[18]

I see no realistic option to this one. It involves what Helmut Thielicke has called "the irrevocability of anti-criticism."[19]

By this expression, Thielicke designates the task of historical research in relation to faith as not to define the territory in which

---

[18]"Method in the Study of Early Hebrew History," in J. Phillip Hyatt, ed., *The Bible in Modern Scholarship* (New York and Nashville: Abingdon, 1965), p. 16. Parallel in "Les patriarches hébreux et l'histoire," *RB* 72 (1965), 7: "Si la foi historique d'Israël n'est pas fondée dans l'histoire, cette foi est erronée, et la nôtre aussi."

[19]"The Resurrection Kerygma," in *The Easter Message Today* (New York: Nelson, 1964), p. 82.

faith can settle down but, rather, to come to grips with those historical-critical considerations that would, if validated, deprive faith of any ground on which to settle. Oscar Cullmann has recently seen the force of this kind of argument in his response[20] to the (unconscious) challenge thrown down by, among others, S. G. F. Brandon's *Jesus and the Zealots.*[21] There must be no mistake about it: if Brandon's (re)construction of the Jesus of actual history is peremptory as well as merely plausible, then Christianity has lost the basis of its kerygma. There can be no talk of adjustments or of reinterpretations or of higher truths; it must only be admitted that the doctrine of the cross, behind which, as a *brutum factum*, lies the event which Brandon calls "the most certain thing known about Jesus of Nazareth," was, by a colossal mistake or by one of the most successful deceits known to history, a groundless myth created out of the routine execution of a convicted λῃστής by a second-string civil servant in one of the backwaters of the Roman empire. (I am by no means denying the undoubted contribution which Brandon has made to *Leben Jesu-Forschung* but, rather, acknowledging, as he has not explicitly, that the conclusion he has drawn from it quite negates the Christian gospel.) The historical validity of Israel's kerygma is of course not as intimately connected with NT faith as is the person of Jesus, but the connection is no less real for being of relatively less importance. If historical research should force us to acknowledge that there had never been those *ṣdqwt yhwh* in which Israel had found its God, it is not merely that Jesus addressed himself to a mythical Father; there simply was, by definition, no God for him to reveal, no God reconciling us to himself in Christ in culmination of a *Heilsgeschichte* that never was.

It is not, obviously, that we are called upon to make history out of the cult-inspired recitals of the conquests of Jericho and Ai, or whatever literary form we are supposed to assign these

---

[20]*Jesus und die Revolutionären seiner Zeit* (Tübingen: J. C. B. Mohr, 1970).

[21]Manchester University Press, 1967. Also in articles and books previously and subsequently.

perennially interesting etiologies, or to ask ourselves whether the axe head really floated. Solomon's granary is all one with his foundry, which is to say that it matters neither more nor less nor at all. Considerations of this kind are irrelevant to the question of whether we may continue to regard the OT as a record of historical revelation, and no service is paid to the cause of reasonable discussion when such considerations are dragged in as though they were entirely germane to that issue. Neither is the issue changed in the least because earlier Christians, who lived in an uncritical and unhistorical age, did mistakenly believe such considerations to be germane to it. We know, as they usually did not, that the OT, like history in the mass, contains its share of myth and legend, and we have learned, in part through their mistakes, to disengage the question of historical revelation from the outmoded category of biblical inerrancy.

Neither is there question of historical criticism being expected to confirm that God covenanted with Israel, thereby somehow proving right the prophets and the pentateuchal histories in the moral and religious implications they discovered in his having revealed his mercy and loving-kindness. Historical criticism cannot do such a thing; as we have said, its task is the much more modest one of ascertaining the facts, as best it can recover them, of which history has been fashioned. History itself is not facts but the interpretation of facts. The best — or worst — that historical criticism can do is to establish that the interpretation is or is not, as the case may be, compatible with the facts. This is not to reduce the function of historical criticism to a purely negative one, as though it served its purpose only by not coming up with data that would make a peremptory judgment against biblical history inevitable. Its business is with facts, and the more facts we have the better we are able to understand how the history came about and what are its virtues and shortcomings, how we must qualify it if we still choose to accept it. But even if we should someday find a record from, let us say, the nineteenth Egyptian dynasty telling of a flight of Asiatics through the Sea of Reeds, though for some reason we might think that our biblical history had been proved to be more "factual" than we had hoped it to be, actually we should be not much affected

in regard to our disposition to accept or reject the history of
the exodus. I have chosen an example which, though highly
unlikely, is not entirely inconceivable: there was a time, after
all, when far more recent happenings, such as the Babylonian
captivity, and the Ezran-Nehemian restoration, and the prophet
Ezekiel, could all be written off as so much romanticizing provoked by theology, until the Babylonian chronicles turned up
to present their own version of certain facts that were indisputably the same. Facts again, not history. To have the Babylonians confirm independently that King Jehoiachin was, indeed, one of their guests in exile did clear the air a bit. It did
not, however, speak to the evaluation of Jehoiachin made by
Jeremiah or Ezekiel or the Deuteronomic historian, or to the
meaning of the exile ventured by any of these or by the Second
Isaiah or Ezra and Nehemiah and the Chronicler. We have Sen-
nacherib's version of his siege of Jerusalem and his bottling up
of Hezekiah in the capital (probably recounting the first of two
campaigns which the OT has united into one). It is good to have
this agreement on facts; yet what could be further removed than
the separate interpretations that have been given the facts? The
excavator of an Israelite town of the age of Amos and Hosea
may be able to show, by the mute evidence of archeology, the
glaring contrast of rich and poor that called forth the prophetic
denunciations of these eighth-century spokesmen for human
rights,[22] but the evidence, which is undoubtedly far less abun-
dant than that which will be available to the same effect to the
remote archeologist of twentieth century America, must have
been as ambiguous to men of good will then as it remains to
men of good will now. Who wrote the proper commentary on
the agreed facts? Historical criticism, it seems to me, can mainly
offer interesting suggestions, the value of which should not be
minimized; but it can offer no final solutions. And thus we must
reluctantly conclude that its findings, in any positive sense, are
usually of far more interest to the biblical scholar in his capacity

[22]Cf Roland de Vaux, "La quatrième campagne de fouilles à Tell el- Far'ah,
près Naplouse," *RB* 59 (1952), 566. Parallel in "The Excavations at Tell el-
Far'ah and the Site of Ancient Tirzah," *PEQ* 88 (1956), 133f.

as student of Near Eastern culture and religion than as biblical theologian.

Still, since history is an interpretation of facts, the facts are always a comforting thing to have, and thus must be of interest to the biblical theologian. Has the possession of the facts damaged, in any way that we now know, their interpretation as offered by the OT? I am not aware of any, or at least of any that is significant. Recognition that the facts are patient of interpretations other than that of the Bible, even that a contemporary interpretation of them, as in some instances mentioned above, would have inevitably differed from it, constitute no apodictic argument against the OT kerygma. Not, first of all, in point of principle. As Alan Richardson has correctly stated, history does not automatically become "truer" the closer it is brought to the events it chronicles and interprets. He uses as an example the meaning of Bismarck in history, which could be accurately appraised only in the light of what happened in 1933 and 1945.[23] The thing is, history simply cannot be written by contemporaries, a fact that seems to be generally accepted by practically everyone except biblical critics.[24] It is probably the most respectable of the reasons for the *loi de cinquante ans* governing access to the French national archives, a provision understandably frustrating to a journalist like William L. Shirer in his recent inquiry into the 1940 collapse of the Third Republic, yet indirectly given some sort of justification by Shirer's own decision to make the first act in his drama the Dreyfus case of 1894.

Neither in point of principle nor in point of specific detail do I conceive of the facts' having dislodged the biblical interpretation. Certainly we know that the history of Israel was a far more complicated one than the kerygmatic version of it we find in the Bible. We have learned to separate the exodus tradition from the wilderness tradition, and both of them from the tradition of Sinai, and to trace the paths by which they came

[23]*History Sacred and Profane* (Philadelphia: Westminster, 1964), p. 222.
[24]*Ibid.*, p. 235.

to be united.[25] Or, alternatively, we have left Sinai with the exodus complex but separated it from the cultic credos and the promise of the land, stressing in the process the importance and the complexities of the patriarchal traditions.[26] We have agreed that the major components of what came to be the people Israel were three or perhaps four, that for all practical purposes this people came to be in the land of Canaan, that the *Landnahme* might with some justice be better termed an insurrection than a conquest. In many ways, therefore, our reconstruction of what happened must be quite different from the story which Israel told of itself. Yet when we reconstruct, we go back to the same facts that Israel presupposed in its story. So far as I know, no responsible research into biblical origins has done other than confirm that there was an exodus, that there was a wilderness experience, that something important took place at Sinai. Is the historical reality of these events diminished by their being assigned to only one element or other of the forebears of the covenant people Israel? I do not see how, unless at the same time we must deny any relevance of the events of 1776 to other than the relatively few descendants of certain Dutch and English colonists who now inhabit thirteen of our southern and eastern states. In the biblical view of history, Israel was created by covenant granted it by its God. I do not know of any finding of critical history that invalidates such an interpretation; I do know of some that support it, to the extent that they suggest Josh 24 as a scene taken from life, even though what is represented there as a renewal may well have been a beginning. Here as well as elsewhere in scholarship, there have been false starts and necessary corrections. Albrecht Alt's seminal work on Israel's laws has been modified by the studies of Erhard Gerstenberger, and George Mendenhall's pioneer recognition of the relevance of the treaty form has had to undergo numerous refinements. But it would be hard to think of an area where research has been

[25]See, most recently, Brevard S. Childs, "A Traditio-Historical Study of the Reed Sea Tradition," *VT* 20 (1970), 406-18.

[26]So Horst Seebass, *Der Erzvater Israel und die Einführung der Jahweverehrung in Kanaan* (*BZAW* 98 [Berlin: Töpelmann, 1966]).

more rewarding,[27] offering a realistic alternative to the Well-hausenian synthesis of the past century. More and more too, it is taking us back to the kernel of historical fact which underlies the patriarchal legends, which may in the long run prove to be a more fruitful field for biblical understanding than the Nuzi parallels have been.

When I say that historical criticism, thus far at least, has served the study of the Bible not by validating the history of the OT but, rather, by not invalidating it, I recognize that I am subject to various objections. The discrepancy between interpreted event and the often recoverable facts that have been mentioned above has to be admitted by even the most conservative biblical theologian. It is a question, I presume, as to whether the discrepancy has become so wide that the one must exclude the other. I do not see that it has become so wide in any significant instance, but others may well disagree. Some scholars there are of course whose concept of the discrepancy is far more radical than the majority of their peers, and it is safe to assume that they would consider the scientific evidence to have ruled out rather thoroughly the biblical construction. The late and great Martin Noth, for instance, to all practical purposes eliminated the not inconsiderable figure of Moses from his purview of the history of Israel. I doubt that most OT scholars would agree with Noth in this respect, but his and other extreme positions do tell us of the continuing need we have for rigorous critical study of Israel's traditions. Would the OT interpretation have to go if we had to discard Moses as an historical character? In his brief study of the Moses question of a few years back, which in my view demonstrated the need of common sense as the climate required to save scholarship from absurdity, Rudolf Smend[28] concluded, if I read him rightly, that Moses could be

[27]See, among recent studies, Gene M. Tucker, "Covenant Forms and Contract Forms," *VT* 15 (1965), 487-503; and M. Weinfeld, "The Covenant of Grant in the OT and in the Ancient Near East," *JAOS* 90 (1970), 184-203. Also the interesting work of R. E. Clements, *Abraham and David,* Studies in Biblical Theology, Second Series 5 (Naperville: Allenson, 1967).

[28]*Das Mosebild von Heinrich Ewald bis Martin Noth* (Tübingen: J. C. B. Mohr, 1959).

dispensable: he contrasted his case with that of Jesus, who is identified with the gospel in a way that Moses is not with the OT kerygma. Certainly critical study has forced us to reduce the figure of Moses, though not so much the Moses of the OT as the one of later legend and mysticism. Not Moses but the exodus is represented in the OT as the event in which God was revealed, just as the conquest—or whatever we are to call it, in fidelity to the facts—of the land is represented as the fulfillment of divine promise, not the Ephraimite chieftain Joshua, whom the biblical historian has transformed into Moses' successor and leader of a united Israel. Moses' case is somewhat different from that of Joshua, it is admitted, but I think it fair to say that the OT kerygma is never concerned with persons or dates or geographical routes to any of the degree that it is definitely concerned with the deeds of the Lord. The deeds of the Lord certainly involved all these, but in ways that the biblical traditions had often forgotten and which we may sometimes rediscover only with difficulty. Even where in the OT revelation is presented as separated from historical event (the prophets serve as a partial example here just as they serve as a partial exception to what follows), the characteristic of the divine "inbreaking" into human consciousness is remarkable for its anonymity.

Another objection may be that historical criticism has, indeed, invalidated much of the OT historical kerygma, and that I am simply refusing to acknowledge the fact by taking refuge in an idealized and selective anamorphosis of the OT that bears little resemblance to the real article. I do not believe this to be the case, however. When I speak of the OT kerygma, I mean the kerygma of the OT canon. To accept a canon of Sacred Scripture is to make an act of faith, but, as an historical phenomenon, the formation and composition of the Biblical canon are matters for critical study. It has become a truism to say that the biblical canon testifies to a unity of diversities. Those who hold to a canon-within-the-canon principle have stressed the undeniable diversities, contradictions, indeed—at least incompatibilities—to conclude to the necessity of taking one's stand on one or another enunciation of the canon at the expense of the rest. That this stand may not appear to be merely an ar-

bitrary choice, appeal has been made to the hermeneutical
principle[29] — resulting, however, in what many will judge to be
a choice which, if not arbitrary, is still highly personal. I think
that the argument may fairly be turned in the opposite direction. What is wrong with the assumption that the hermeneutical
principle was operative in the formation of the canon, that it
is this that accounts for what unity the canon possesses? For
a unity of some kind, the canon demonstrably is: a selected body
of materials gathered of set purpose with full awareness of its
inner tensions. Earlier, I objected to the caricature of the God
of the OT as "a North-Arabian mountain god who traveled in
thunderstorms and liked the smell of burning fat." If such were
the kerygma of the OT, I doubt very much that its word would
have much to say to me. But it is not the kerygma of the OT,
or even of one part of the OT, though I am perfectly aware
that all the terms of this composite portrait are to be found in
its pages. Many years ago, Otto Eissfeldt made some sound
observations on the interaction of OT theology and historical
criticism which seem to be entirely applicable at this point.[30]
Historically considered, the OT is a corpus of writings produced
over many years and subject to all the changes that time and,
it is hoped, the development of the human spirit inevitably bring.
Within this historical perspective, it is not hard to see how the
patriarchal legends, or the Davidic theology of the Yahwist,
or the Chronicler's retrojection of post-exilic Judaism into the
era of David and Solomon, could have had meaning and significance proper to the age of their devising and have lost them
in a subsequent generation. The same history that first made
them relevant might also later declare them superseded. This
is not simply to decide in favor of the most recent, but to sub-

---

[29]Käsemann, *op. cit.*, pp. 355f.

[30]"Israelitische-jüdische Religionsgeschichte und alttestamentliche Theologie," *ZAW* 44 (1926), 1-12 = *Kleine Schriften* (Tübingen: J. C. B. Mohr,
1962) I, pp. 105-14. For a much more negative view of Eissfeldt's article,
cf Norman W. Porteous, "Old Testament Theology," in H. H. Rowley, ed.,
The Old Testament and Modern Study (Oxford University Press, 1951/61),
pp. 318ff.

mit the canon as a whole to the judgment of history. The early prophets had already in principle examined and rejected the more naïve kind of covenant theology manifested in the doctrine of holy war or the schematic outline imposed by the D author on the portrayal of Israel's past in the book of Judges. Historical criticism, no less than the balance of the OT canon, rules in favor of the prophets: history does not recur in the cyclic fashion described in Judges, however useful it may have been at the time to think of it so doing. In the same way, when the canon of the OT is seen as the record of an historical process, the God who emerges from its kerygma has assumed more subtle attributes than those once ascribed to Baal Zaphon. The fault of the rabbis and the fathers of the church was not, as I see it, their acceptance of the whole OT canon, which they then felt obliged to interpret as having uniform weight throughout, despite all its internal tensions. Living in an uncritical and unhistorical age, they simply did not have the impulse to read the OT historically, to see what by the historical nature of the case was residual and what had been merely provisional.

Neither is it a question, as far as I can see, of having to take the NT as the standard of interpretation of the OT—of beginning with the OT from the standpoint of its position in the church's canon, in other words.[31] In the first place, while the NT presupposes an OT scriptural canon, it is not of one mind concerning either the dimensions of that canon or, except in general terms, the details of its kerygmatic message. There is more about the OT that the NT presupposes than that it attempts to define and assimilate, so that its invitation is for us to seek the meaning of the OT with the means at our disposal rather than to find a ready-made interpretation of it at hand. Further, as Eissfeldt pointed out, it is not through the NT, but rather through historico-critical method, that much of the authentic message of the OT has been recovered. For example:

---

[31]Despite my basic agreement with Brevard S. Childs, I much prefer to his idea of the OT as emerging from the Christian canon my notion of its canon as validated by its own internal history. See his *Biblical Theology in Crisis* (Philadelphia: Westminster, 1970), pp. 99ff.

The prophets as personalities, as religious figures in their own right, remained unknown to Christianity for eighteen centuries. They lived and functioned—one need only think of the frescoes of the Sistine Chapel—as those who had prophesied Christ, and thus a few of their words were of significance. But as personalities they remained not understood and inoperative. It was the historical research of the 19th century which taught us to understand the grandeur of the prophetic figures by entering into a living experience of their proclamation. And who would deny that this newly discovered value in recognition has also enriched the life of faith?[32]

We do not, as I see it, take our interpretation of the OT from the NT, even though we take a general direction from it, just as Judaism has proceeded to the OT from another general direction. Our understanding of much of the kerygma of the OT and of what is really central to it depends on interests and means that were not always those of the NT and its age. This is the more positive side to the function of historical criticism in relation to OT understanding, and one which can often reach conclusions acceptable to Jew and Christian alike.

I would like to conclude on this note. Far from being superfluous or detrimental to the faith which approaches the OT seeking to hear a word, historical criticism serves the dual function of setting its critical affirmations in credible relief and of bringing to its text the resources necessary for the better understanding of its message. Without destroying its value for faith, historical research helps us to define the kind of history, and its limitations, that has been made the vehicle of revelation. It has become a commonplace to designate this as history become myth: "The Exodus from Egypt is a historical datum, it becomes a matter of religion only when myth has portrayed

---

[32]*Loc. cit.*, 7 =110. Eissfeldt goes on to argue that historical criticism also helps in other ways to separate the perennially valid from the unacceptable in the OT—for example, by pointing out the kind of narrow nationalistic motivation which Israel itself outgrew.

it in paradigmatic terms."[33] I remain not entirely convinced of the aptness of this category. It is true that by now we have long been schooled away from a simplistic conception of myth as stories about disreputable goings on among the gods; we have learned that this is a distortion of myth, that myth is in fact a genuine, if not an empirical or strictly rational way of attempting to get at a truth. There are, we are told, good as well as bad myths, and even just harmless myths which, nevertheless, give men direction and motivation: myths of race and of nationhood, the American dream and Yankee know-how, the lost Eden to be regained or the utopia to be achieved, and so forth. It may be that in this sense we will have to understand kerygmatic history as myth—that is, all history that man lives by as a faith can be called myth.[34] But it seems to me that we are in danger of taking away myth's distinctive meaning by making it mean too many different things. Also I would prefer a term for biblical history other than one which, to the extent that the Bible uses it at all—which is rarely—it sets precisely in opposition to its kerygma.[35] Nor is this usage merely a reflection of an unsophisticated appreciation of myth, since the same wealth of meanings now attached to myth was available to the biblical authors

[33]Theodor H. Gaster, *Myth, Legend, and Custom in the Old Testament* (New York: Harper & Row, 1969), p. xxxvi. Also Joseph Jensen, in "What Happened to Moses?" *CBQ* 32 (1970), 404-17 (an article with which I am in almost total agreement), ends by accepting "myth" as a valid designation of the kerygmatic history of the OT.

[34]So, apparently, R. A. F. MacKenzie, "The Problem of Myth and History," in his *Faith and History in the Old Testament* (New York: Macmillan, 1963), pp. 69-81).

[35]In the NT, μῦθος occurs late in 1 Tim 1:4; 4:7; 2 Tim 4:4; Tit 1:14; 2 Pet 1:16, always in the sense of fable, deceptive story, the very opposite of what is historically true. In the intertestamental literature, it might seem to have been given a more neutral sense: Sir 20:19 has it equal *mšl* (cf. Gustav Stählin in *TWNT* [IV], 787); still, the fact that it is here ascribed to a fool has doubtless determined the translation. The μυχός reading at Wis 17:4 B S is doubtless preferable to the Λ μυθος. In Bar 3:23, μυθολόγοι occurs in the sense of sloganists, manufacturers of empty tales.

as well. I would prefer, in other words, a term that did not apply equally well to the biblical kerygma and to those cleverly concocted tales (2 Pet 1:16) that the Bible sets against it. If myth is to be the phrase, we no longer have a means of distinguishing what the Bible calls myth—and is myth, by anyone's definition—from that which it sets in the most profound opposition to it, and we set on one and the same level an historical faith in election with its caricature in *Blut und Boden* superstition. Faced with the same option some years ago, G. E. Wright preferred to define the OT idea as one of history interpreted by faith.[36] This is the way I believe the Bible would want to describe itself, and that I believe is what historical criticism assists us in defining more precisely.

The scholar who is being honored in these present pages has, among the many other contributions he has brought to biblical studies, always evinced a concern for theological interpretation, pointing out the enduring value of biblical meaning once it had been wrested from the text. (I think, for one thing, of his work on the Chronicler's history in the AB series, dealing with material that has not always been judged to hold much promise for the Christian reader.) Whether or not he will approve of the views expressed in the article preceding, I trust that he will accept them as having been uttered in appreciation of and in the same spirit with which he has always approached the OT.

[36]*God Who Acts,* Studies in Biblical Theology 8 (London: SCM, 1952), pp. 126ff.

8. Prophecy and the Redactional Question

The problem which perennially faces the conscientious translator of the bible or its commentator is: which bible does he translate, on which bible does he comment? The problem looms largest for the Christian exegete of the OT; but it is no less a problem for the Jewish expositor of the OT and even, in some sense, for the Christian interpreter of the NT. The problem is common because it is constituted by the common historical fact of redaction, and the historical fact of redaction is that it dates almost from the first moment when the biblical word began to be committed to writing. The fact explains the phenomenon noted by Elias Auerbach:[1]

> the deeper one probes into the composition of the Hebrew Bible, the more he is confronted by a phenomenon unique in world literature: There are, in fact, two Bibles.

However unique the phenomenon may be, we are not prepared to say; but a phenomenon it undoubtedly is. Furthermore, on Auerbach's own principles, the number of bibles involved probably cannot be limited to two. He went on in his remarks:

> Even to the present day the reader's comprehension of the Bible as far as the important developments of Israel's exter-

---

[1]"Die grosse Überarbeitung der biblischen Bücher," VTSup 1 (1953) 1-10.

nal and spiritual history are concerned comes rather through
the redaction than through the original traditions and the accounts of the older original sources.

Auerbach was concerned only with the "great" redaction of
Israel's sacred literature, the rereading and recasting of its history
that took place in the wake of the national disaster we call the
Babylonian captivity, in the long generation that produced the
deuteronomic history structured about a rigid (one might even
say, deterministic) theology of covenant, and the Priestly theology and history with its somewhat different concerns and
preoccupations. But just as it may be doubted that the redactional activity of this era may properly be reduced to one alone
in inspiration and intent, it must also be observed that this particular "great" redaction was neither the first nor the last in the
long process by which most of the OT writings have come down
to us who read them today.

The complexities of the redactional process present the biblical translator and expositor with his dilemmas and trilemmas.

What is to be said, for example, in reply to the apparently
reasonable stance assumed by "conservative" translators, Jewish
or Christian, who profess to render the OT texts as precisely
as possible "as they stand" or "in their canonical form"? In this
form, we are told, the OT is truly scripture, the finished product of a faith community. In this form, it is further alleged,
the texts must be wrestled with in preference to all conjectural
emendation however likely: as long as sense can be extracted
from the texts in this form they are in presumptive possession
against all the alternatives. We are confronted, we see, by two
assumptions, one involving historical fact and the other deriving from it a methodological principle. But the fact, on the one
hand, is not all that certain, while on the other hand the
methodology begs the question in view of a history of transmission of the OT texts that is, indeed, certain.

Even in its finished form, it is doubtful that the entire Hebrew
OT can be reduced to the status of a single canon. Rather, there
are in it the residues of several canons, several redactions, which
have not always been harmonized one with another. That harmonization which did take place, which justifies our speaking

of *a* bible, is the working of a later tradition which most certainly sprang from the OT and continued its process, but just
as certainly was subsequently imposed upon it. Therefore when
we approach the OT not simply as a collection of ancient literary
documents but as religious literature, it is necessary either that
we select one canon of this literature at the expense of others
or that we assume them all together, along with all of their internal tensions. In some instances, when redaction has not merely
manipulated a received text but has actually altered it internally,
we have only the option of choosing our canon.

An example of this necessary choice occurs in Amos 8:3,
a line from the fourth of Amos' visions of the doom of Israel,
which both RSV and NAB on "conservative" principles render:
"The songs of the temple shall become wailings in that day."
Contrast NEB and SBJ: "The singing women in the palace shall
howl." RSV and NAB have chosen to translate the text as it
was meant to be read by the Masoretic editors of the Hebrew
OT, while NEB and SBJ have stripped it of its redaction and—
admittedly by conjecture—have translated what the prophet
Amos (or *his* editor) originally said.

There would seem to be no question about this.[2] The word
šîrôt as "songs" would be an anomaly in this text. While it is
true that there is a feminine singular form of *šîr* which turns
up a number of times in the OT (never in Amos), it is likewise
true that a feminine plural form never (otherwise) occurs. Always the plural is masculine: *šîrîm* (and so in Amos 5:23 and
8:10). The redaction on which the Masoretes depended produced the anomalous form by altering an earlier *šārôt* (cf. 2
Chr 25:35) in order to adjust to a post-Exilic Jerusalem scene
a text that had at first applied to an eighth century Samaria situation. The same process forced an entirely new meaning upon
the verb of the sentence.[3] There was no need to change the word

[2]Cf. J. F. A. Sawyer, *Semantics in Biblical Research* (SBT 2/24; Naperville: Allenson, 1972) 5-6.

[3]In every other instance of the use of **yll* hif in the Hebrew OT (all of
them in the prophetical literature) the meaning is of a person or a personification actively engaged in weeping or wailing. See the lexica.

hêkāl (ultimately derived from the Sumerian *ê-gal*, "great house"), since it already meant equally well palace or temple (in the latter acceptation, originally conceived as the palace of a god). Now that royal palaces were no more and *hêkāl* was replacing older expressions to designate the Jerusalem temple, it could not be allowed that there should be singing women there in defiance of the post-Exilic law which assigned the music of the temple firmly and exclusively to the male voices of the Levitical choirs. Thus this present redaction had a theological as well as a chronological motivation.

It might be objected at this point that the redaction in question has affected very little if at all the development of the human spirit, and that tracking it down is a matter chiefly of archival and philological interest. The objection has its measure of truth. However, there is some value in treating of an example of this kind, both to show how pervasive has been the influence of redaction, extending down to minutiae which at this remove may be thought trifling and of little practical consequence, and also to underscore the time-conditionedness of the redactional enterprise. The theological bias that first provoked the redaction and that may have addressed itself to what was then a significant issue, may no longer respond to any such issue at all. Instead, the theological issues of a later age may require quite different biases, including, perhaps, the one that was originally intended by the author of the redacted passage. We are cautioned, in other words, against assuming that the development of any given text within the life of a faith community has invariably reached some peak of relevance at the stage that has come to be designated "canonical." That peak, for a given age, might have been achieved earlier in the process, or it may be yet to come.

All of the prophetic works, Amos' included, have through redaction been made into books for the comfort and consolation of Israel, however inexorable may have been their original message of doom and condemnation. There can be no doubt about the necessary and vital function that these redactions served in nourishing the spiritual wants of a people during trying and perilous times, and of the hope that they offered in the face of every contrary human sign; but it would be obviously disastrous to interpret the whole of Israel's prophetic experience simply in the light of its postexilic redactional adaptation. To do this would be not only to cancel out an essential chapter in the history of Israel and of religion, it could also, in a time of other exigencies and imperatives, lead to an unintended triumphalism and unjustified self-righteousness, to a *Herrenvolk* conception of divine election from which the indispensable ingredients of judgment and service have been extracted. And if such a resultant caricature of prophecy has held perils for Judaism, how much more has it held them for Christianity! In their redacted form uncritically assimilated and with the accretion of an unbiblical and anti-biblical mythology of prophetical experience, the prophets for long in Christian history were oracular ciphers, at one with the Sibyls as providing chapter headings to a catalogue of putative predictions thought to have been fulfilled to the letter in NT times, with their historical individuality and reality almost totally obliterated in the process. Otto Eissfeldt has rightly claimed for modern critical biblical study the credit for having restored Israelite prophecy to its proper place not only in genuine history but also in the record of genuine religious experience,[4] a thing which it did and could do only by seeking the *ipsissima vox prophetae* behind the words of canonical redaction. Particularly in connection with the prophetical literature, indeed, has the biblical expositor found himself frequently in tension with the biblical translator; for if the latter felt it his duty to render the "canonical" text at every turn, the former knew that this could be universally done only at the expense of biblical misunderstanding. What is true of the prophetical literature, nevertheless, is true also in other measures of most of the rest of biblical literature.

We can add another twist of the screw of canonical complexity. Since canon was only begun in the bible and completed only after it, it could be fairly argued that the Christian has no

---

[4]"Israelitisch-jüdische Religionsgeschichte und alttestamentliche Theologie," *ZAW* 44 (1926) 1-12 = *Kleine Schriften* (Tübingen: J. C. B. Mohr, 1962) 1, 105-14.

business at all in translating as his bible the Hebrew OT. It could be fairly argued, that is, if we were willing to pursue down to its last logical conclusion the argument for translating a "canonical" text. When the Jewish translator takes for his basic biblical text the *masora*, to be rendered critically and discounting its occasional errors and lapses, he is acting consistently within a tradition—a Jewish, not a Christian tradition, of course—reflected and elucidated not in the *masora* alone but also in other Jewish sources that grew up together with it. Not so with the Christian translator of the MT. He approaches this text (as some Jewish commentators are careful to point out) as an alien, both factually and historically. Factually, because as it stands the *masora* testifies to a religious experience outside his own and usually outside his scholarly competence as well. It must be accounted passing strange, as Morton Smith has correctly observed,[5] that the so-called critical editions of the Hebrew OT most used today by scholars, which have been published under Christian auspices, are in reality reproductions of the *masora* down to its last synagogic detail, and that they make no attempt whatever, except by way of footnotes, to suggest the restoration of an original text—the conventional acceptation of the task of a critical edition of any document—even when the MT is clearly wrong and a suggested emendation is clearly right.[6]

---

[5]"The Present State of Old Testament Studies," *JBL* 88 (1969) 19-35. See pp. 22-23: with most of the rest of the article the present writer does not find himself in much agreement.

[6]Preservation of the "literal" Hebrew text is taken to the limits of reproducing the suspended *nun* in Judg 18:30 where pious censorship transformed the name of Moses into that of Manasseh; in retaining what even the Masoretes noted as *tiqqûnê sōf rîm*, scribal "corrections," i.e., intentional deformations of the text; the "bless" instead of the obviously original "curse" of Job 1:5, 2:9, and like passages; preservations of the *k^etîb*, the erroneously written consonants which the Masoretes refused to change even though marginally and by punctuation they noted the *q^erê* that they thought should be read, etc., etc. See D. M. C. Englert, "Bowdlerizing In the Old Testament," *A Light Unto My Path: Old Testament Studies in Honor of Jacob M. Myers* (ed. H. N. Bream; Philadelphia: Temple University, 1974) 141-43. It is interesting that the new BHS which is now replacing BH³ shows a tendency to shrink

Historically, the Christian stands outside the MT tradition, because the OT of the early Christian church was not the Hebrew bible, let alone its *masora*, but rather the Greek LXX.

Obviously, we do not intend to argue, as some have argued,[7] that on the basis of its having formed the NT and the early Christian church the LXX is somehow a Christian or the Christian OT that ought to be preferred to the Hebrew. The LXX is a translation, sometimes accurate and sometimes inept, of another literature; and when it is inept a translation does not become right simply through the sanction of usage or because it has inspired Christian thoughts. Jerome's hardly won struggle for the *hebraica veritas* in the early fifth century,[8] which finally prevailed in the Reformation, was certainly no misdirection of energies. An historical religion like Christianity seeks contact with its literary origins, which are reflected only mediately through a translation. At the same time, the LXX is often deliberately "inept" in its translation: which is to say that it is also frequently a redaction—a Jewish redaction, as it happens, yet

the truly critical apparatus appended to the text at the expense of expanding the Masoretic apparatus and includes with each fascicle a portable table of the 48 Masoretic accents which the vast majority of its users will find serviceable only as a bookmark. All such efforts are admirable when directed towards the preservation of postbiblical Jewish tradition, but they can only impede the reconstruction of a genuine edition of the Hebrew bible. Translators who work from these texts customarily ignore the evident excrescences, usually without indicating their departures.

[7]In the most extreme form, perhaps, D. Barthélemy, "L'Ancien Testament a mûri à Alexandrie," *TZ* 21 (1965) 358-70, for whom the Hebrew OT stands in relation to the canonical OT of Christianity (i.e., the LXX) precisely as the J source of the Pentateuch stands in relation to, say, the book of Genesis, namely as a *propaedeuticon*. There is a considerable literature on the subject, mainly the work of some esteemed French colleagues, which the present writer must regretfully assess as an excursion into futility and a defence of the indefensible.

[8]For an engaging appreciation of the impact of Jerome's effort over against the LXX establishment represented by Augustine, Bishop of Hippo, see the opening pages of the article by J. A. Fitzmyer, "A Recent Roman Scriptural Controversy," *TS* (1961) 426-44.

more proximate to Christianity than some of the redaction of the *masora*—representing the same kinds of adaptation and alteration that have occurred within the purely Hebrew transmission of the biblical text. Rigorous adherence to the principle that the text to be translated should be the redacted text of a faith community might seem to demand, therefore, that the LXX be heard in preference for its redactions, unless we are arbitrarily to set limits on the time, the geography, and the language of the redactional tradition.

Rigorous adherence to the principle we have never had, thank God. The Greek-speaking church, understandably, has retained the LXX for its OT, and Jerome never really succeeded in dislodging the LXX from the liturgical usage of Western Christianity. A conception of the "inspired," i.e., the canonical character of the LXX redaction/translation was certainly operative in both these instances, along with other considerations that doubtless add up to nothing more edifying than the inertia of custom. Jerome himself, despite his insistence on the *hebraica veritas* (which, to be sure, he understood in a rather naïve fashion), produced in the Vulgate a "Christian" OT which frequently owed to the LXX—or to the NT, indeed—as much as or more than it did to the Hebrew and Aramaic he had learnt through such toil and pain.[9] Martin Luther also professedly translated a "Christian" OT, sharing many of Jerome's presuppositions,[10] but he also thought it more important to get back to the language of the initial scriptural inspiration. Even modern biblical versions occasionally lapse into the habits of the past, as when, for example, the *'almâ* of Isa 7:14 is rendered "virgin" (NAB, RSV mg) in deference to the LXX and Matt 1:23 rather than to the evident sense of the Hebrew. Even when the LXX was widely accepted as possessing a normative tradition, the church was never of a single mind concerning the extent to which it determined or presupposed a canon of scripture. While the

[9]For what was Jerome's idea of a "literal" translation, see my *Biblical Inspiration* (Philadelphia: Westminster, 1972) 29.

[10]Cf. H. Bornkamm, *Luther and the Old Testament* (Philadelphia: Fortress, 1969) 219-46.

Council of Hippo in A.D. 393, for example, upheld in the West the longer, "Alexandrian" canon based on the LXX,[11] in the East the Council of Laodicea of about 360 had already restricted itself to what is essentially the "Palestinian" canon of the Hebrew OT and had explicitly rejected as noncanonical various of the books long contained in the LXX.[12]When during the Reformation and Counter-reformation the Roman church finally decided in favor of most — not all — of the additional books and parts of books that had been introduced into the canon through the LXX, while another course was followed by most of the Reformed churches, the basis of the choice in each case was a (disputed) Christian precedent.

We should hardly want the situation to be otherwise than it is. Obviously, no one would dream of translating the verbs in the second verse of the book of Amos into a past tense, as the LXX did, rather than into the present or future indicated by the Hebrew. This, despite the fact that the LXX choice was not done in ignorance but was doubtless deliberate, indicating the conviction of the translator concerning the relevance of the prophecy to his time. The LXX amounts here to a faith-inspired redaction, in other words, quite as respectable and as worthy of consideration as the post-Exilic Hebrew redaction of Amos 8:3 already noted. Our instincts rebel against the idea of reproducing what has been an obvious change of an original text. At least, they rebel in the case of the prophetic literature: in other areas of the bible acknowledged redactional alterations are accepted as a matter of course as constituting the ultimate

---

[11]*EB* §§ 16-17.

[12]*EB* §§ 14-15. Actually, it is probably incorrect to think of separate canons as far as these councils were concerned, except to the extent they had come to embody Christian rather than Jewish tradition. Though the two questions are often confused, it is by no means evident that acceptance of the LXX as inspired scripture carried with it acceptance of the LXX's "canon." Indeed, as we have just indicated, where the LXX was most firmly established at the time, in the East, the tendency was to adopt a narrower canon of the OT, whereas in the West the longer canon became the rule. As is known, Jerome in opting for the canon of the Hebrew OT was an exception to the western rule.

text of the "final author." And, as we have shown, they do not rebel even in the case of the prophet's literature as long as it is a question of the received text of the *hebraica veritas*.

Proponents of our "conservative" translations of the OT, that is, those who for all practical purposes want to translate the *masora*, rightly point to the fact that it is only in this form that the substance of the Hebrew bible has been transmitted to the present-day translator. Unlike most of the other documents of antiquity – the Greek NT and the LXX pre-eminent within this other majority – the Hebrew OT was not allowed to descend through the normal process of a manuscript tradition, the process which results in the evidence of variants and recensions and which calls for proper critical editions, but instead was rigorously controlled and artificially standardized through the suppression of contrary witnesses so that only one form of the text survived: the *masora*. Essentially, of course, this contention is correct, or has been correct until quite recent times; and it alone can be the justification for perpetuating "critical editions" of the Hebrew OT which are in reality simply critical editions of the *masora*. The manuscripts, really only scraps and snippets of manuscripts, which had escaped the vigilance of the Masoretes and come down by other routes, were so insignificant as to deserve little or no attention. Indeed, the earliest of the Qumrân discoveries, which almost unbelievably revealed generous portions of the pre-Masoretic Hebrew bible, did so only to strengthen the case for the soundness of the *masora*. Both 1QIs[a] and 1QIs[b] differ from the MT very little, and only in a handful of cases does it appear intrinsically likely that they witness to a preferable reading. However, the evidence which has continued to flow from the same source during the past twenty-five years has also begun to unsettle the privileged place once enjoyed by MT in its splendid isolation. The evidence is, as it happens, largely corroborative of scholarly speculation that required only the positive proof that comes from manuscript testimony alone. For example, a fragment of the Hebrew of Samuel found among the earliest of the Qumrân documents has tended to confirm the hypothesis that the LXX of this work with its variants and "expansions" is in reality the rather faithful translation of *a* Hebrew recension of the text that must have coexisted with the one that was eventually adopted by the Masoretes.[13] It has become evident that the text of Samuel was in a rather fluid condition at the beginning of the Christian era, and that what has been handed down in the MT has no clearer title to being considered the "original" than to be recognized as an abbreviation of the "original." Conversely with the book of the prophet Jeremiah.[14] In this case the evidence of 4QJer[h] also appears to confirm what was long suspected, that this book existed in diverse redactional forms represented separately by the LXX and the MT. In this instance the MT chose to hand on the long form of the text; and while essentially both redactions must go back to the same school or circles (i.e., the deuteronomic redactors who are responsible for so much of the OT in its received form); the new textual evidence verifies the suspicion entertained by literary criticism, namely that most of the *plus* found in MT is secondary, created from and inspired by the "original" text of Jeremiah, but not properly part of it.[15]

All of the foregoing merely exposes the tip of an iceberg of available and weighable facts that enter into our present dis-

---

[13]See F. M. Cross, "A New Qumran Biblical Fragment Related to the Original Hebrew Underlying the Septuagint," *BASOR* 132 (1953) 15-26.

[14]Cf. E. Tov, "L'incidence de la critique textuelle sur la critique littéraire dans le livre de Jérémie," *RB* 79 (1972) 189-99.

[15]An easy instance from literary criticism: Jer 33:14-26 is the longest continuous passage of this book in MT that is lacking in LXX. The style is anthological: vss. 14-16 are a pastiche of 29:10 and 23:5-6; vs. 17 comes from 35:16; 31:35-37 have served as the model for vss. 19-22 and vss. 25-26; and there are other reminiscences. Jeremiah's words have been used partly in a sense different from that of the authentic passages: the *Yhwh ṣidqēnû* and *ṣemaḥ ṣaddîq* of 23:5-6 turn up in vss. 14-15 (the received MT actually has *ṣemaḥ sᵉdaqâ* in vs. 15, but at least four MSS testify to *ṣaddîq* instead, and this was read by Theodotion); but the former now means Jerusalem rather than the king thereof, and the latter in turn refers to the kingship itself rather than to a scion of David. This passage is discussed at the beginning of my "Levitical Messianism and the New Testament," *The Bible in Current Catholic Thought* (ed. J. L. McKenzie; New York: Herder & Herder, 1962) 83-99.

cussion. To expose the whole iceberg might seem to be self-defeating: we should end by demonstrating the practical impossibility of translating the OT at all. The Holy Bible invoked by fundamentalist piety with such confident and untroubled assurance simply does not exist. What bible there is must be reconstructed, always laboriously and often enough with ambiguous and indeterminate results.

Obviously, however, biblical translations are to continue, as they should. The bible will continue to be, in whatever a refracted form and in whatever a vernacular approximation, a source of inspiration and life to the many, who are the most who will ever read it, who have no firsthand acquaintance with the bundle of unsolved and insoluble questions which trail in the wake of every new translation, nor with the linguistic and other tools by which these questions are raised and got at. Responsible translation, on the other hand, will doubtless increasingly have to call attention by whatever means to those same questions, and will have to give an account of the degree to which it has resolved them. Measures of this kind ought to be taken not in any hope or desire of unsettling biblical fundamentalism, which they will not do, — in the worship of his non-historical bible the fundamentalist is the purest of the existentialists—but simply from the intention to deal candidly and honestly with the literary foundations of biblical religion.

There is a limit, nevertheless, to the cautions and controls that we can reasonably expect a translator to incorporate into his copy. A translation is not a commentary, even though a good translation ought to be the beginning of commentary and, indeed, in many instances eliminate the need of commentary. It cannot be expected to reflect line by line the many complexities of textual and literary criticism which the translator cannot ignore and of which he cannot permit his reader to remain entirely ignorant. There are obvious restrictions on footnotes and other critical apparatus which can be introduced into the translation of a biblical text to impede and annoy the progress of the ordinary reader. For a biblical translation, after all, is designed primarily for the ordinary reader, and a version whose idiosyncrasies must repel the general public would not only be self-defeating in terms of intention and effort, it would also deny the affirmation of biblical faith which holds that the bible mediates the word of God to men in the understood words of men.

The provisional resolution of this impasse has been to permit the translator and the expositor to go their separate ways, the one presenting at each juncture more or less arbitrarily that form of the text which seems right or convenient to him, the other supplying all the nuances in the lack of which even the best of translations must often be misleading. We should hope that there are better solutions than this one. For one thing, translations must undoubtedly become more forthright in acknowledging their presuppositions, and consequently require more sophisticated readers. Above all, however, we need studies of the biblical text, of the individual books of the bible, which will show how those messages which were once uttered orally came through the process of writing to be made into a living literature nourishing the spiritual aspirations of a people through continual adaptation, a process which is in turn the precedent for their subsequent adaptation in the preaching and hearing of the later communities of faith. Thereby we might hope to understand what is really entailed in the concept of biblical "inspiration," a rather different thing from the unreal and static irrelevancy that has so often been made into its caricature.[16]

The prophetical literature above all is suited to and requires such studies. True, it cannot be said that commentators on the prophets have failed their duty to point out the alterations that separate the putatively original words of the prophet in question from the received Hebrew text in which he has to be read. Only, they have generally undertaken this task with the intention of separating the "authentic" words of the prophets from the "deformations" introduced by the various editors of the prophetical books. And frequently enough the selfsame editors who are responsible for the "deformations" are precisely the ones

---

[16]For the ongoing character of inspiration, see again my *Biblical Inspiration*, esp. 95-131.

to whom we are indebted for the preservation of the prophetical collections in the first place. Secondly, while the commentators have been adept at pointing out the editorial additions to the prophetic text that form one very important type of redactional change, they have not been equally sedulous in tracking down and interpreting internal alterations of the kind we have verified above in treating of Amos 8:3. And finally, in one or the other of these redactional situations, or that of the transfer of thought that occurred in a translation-redaction such as the LXX, the approach has been mainly lexicographical rather than from the standpoint of the sentence which is ultimately the true expression of theological thought.[17]

The book of Amos, it would seem, is one of the sections of the prophetical literature best adapted to the kind of studies we have just suggested.[18] It is this for several reasons. For one thing, this book represents one of the oldest collections of poetry and prose to be found in the OT. Certainly there are in the OT other segments of literature far older than Amos, not only the

---

[17]Here we recall the position of J. Barr, *The Semantics of Biblical Language* (Oxford: Oxford University, 1961), who devoted the conclusion of his book to this thesis after having propounded it several times previously in passing. He later returned to the same topic in "Hebraic and Greek Thought-forms in the New Testament," *Current Issues in New Testament Interpretation* (ed. W. Klassen and G. F. Snyder; New York: Harper and Row, 1962) 1-22. As he sometimes does, Barr somewhat overstated his case (which was formulated against such works as the Kittel-Friedrich *TDNT*): what the semanticists call "full words," which account for the great majority of the entries in the theological dictionaries, can have significance in themselves even apart from context; cf. S. Ullman, *Semantics. An Introduction to the Science of Meaning* (New York: Barnes & Noble, 1962) 44-49. It is "form words" which cannot be regarded of themselves as having theological significance and take on meaning only when they are part of a phrase or sentence. Both types of word are obviously involved in our discussion, but the commentators do not always advert to the distinction and its implications.

[18]J. A. Arieti's article. "The Vocabulary of Septuagint Amos," *JBL* 93 (1974) 338-47, even though exclusively lexicographical, offers many suggestive observations on the LXX adaptation of Amos which point to the new nuances which it introduced into the prophetic text.

smaller units found in isolated psalms, songs, proverbs, and the like, but also such major efforts as the Yahwistic history (itself a redaction of even older material) that has been incorporated into the Pentateuch or Hexateuch. Amos, however, stands aloof in this company as being the longest sustained unity of its kind that has been largely retained for its own sake rather than for what it could contribute to other purposes: through all its redactions, it has remained substantially a document of the eighth century B.C. and has kept its identity in a way that other ancient bits of the bible have not. Furthermore, for all its antiquity, Amos is one of the best "preserved" of the books of the Hebrew OT. That is to say, its text has suffered relatively little from the unintentional alterations that have been introduced through human error and which, in their most desperate state, have sometimes ended in a jumble of letters which have preserved no thought at all. (The fact that Amos has been affected by so little of this as over against the roughly contemporary work of Hosea, which contains so much of it, has suggested to some authors that greater care was exercised over the text of Amos which had attained an earlier "canonical" fixation.) And lastly, as we already suggested, while Amos like all books is a work of redaction, it is not a redactional work. That is to say, by way of example, while some additions to the book of Amos may be ascribed to the influence which we customarily call deuteronomic,[19] there was never any attempt to bend either its content or format into the well-known deuteronomic pattern; and the same may be said of other recognizable redactional influences. (The only exception, as already noted, would be the post-Exilic redaction which has converted Amos into a salvation prophecy. But this purely mechanical and readily detectable addition has scarcely affected the interpretation of the book since the beginning of critical study.) It would appear, therefore,

---

[19]As *certain* additions of this kind, we would doubtless have to instance 2:4-5 and 3:7 among others. See T. R. Hobbs, "Amos 3, 1b and 2, 10," *ZAW* 81 (1969) 384-87, criticizing W. H. Schmidt, "Die deuteronomische Redaktion des Amosbuches," *ZAW* 77 (1965) 168-92, regarding the delicacy of the application of "deuteronomic" to these and other redactions.

that this straightforward text would be an ideal area in which to view the varied redactional activity of the people of faith among which it was preserved in the successive ages when it was found to have relevance.

The present writer hopes to be able to pursue these objectives in some limited way at a future date or dates.

9. Israel's Encounter with the Nations

In his *Essay on the Development of Christian Doctrine* John Henry Newman made a great point of the assimilative powers of the Church as providing one of the notes of its authentic development in contrast with doctrinal corruption.[1] The corollary of the process of assimilation was, of course, the value of all that had been assimilated. Rather than a reproach that could be held against Christianity in general by a new and as yet immature science of the history of religions, or against Catholicism in particular by an historically naive 19th-century Anglo-Saxon Protestantism, Newman recognized that the Church's absorption of so many 'pagan' elements was its boast and glory, a sign of catholic authenticity. "So far then from her creed being of doubtful credit because it resembles foreign theologies, we even hold that one special way in which Providence has imparted divine knowledge to us has been by enabling her to draw and collect it together out of the world, and, in this sense, as in others, to 'suck the milk of the Gentiles and to suck the breast of kings' ". The church is, to a depth unknown to Ulysses, a part of all that she has met. Because of what he knew of her past, Newman could contemplate with complete equanimity a church

---

[1] See *Essay* (Doubleday Image Book edition, 1960), esp. 348-360 also "Milman's View of Christianity" in *Essays Critical and Historical* (rev. ed., Longmans, Green & Co. 1891), Vol. 2, pp. 186-248.

of the future as much tributary to China or Japan as once she had been to Canaan, Syria, Greece and Rome. He was prompted, in other words, to a vision of the church's mission in which he saw beyond the conventions of his time, as he did in so many of his visions, for all that this was not a new vision. The mission of the Church to the heathen has for its true model not the colonialism of the white man's burden. But rather a congress of man, a universal body into which all men of all nations are incorporated as equal members who give life to the body as well as receive it, the life of the whole which is to be the full stature of Christ.

What Newman discerned as the genius of the Church from his study of the Fathers, we have learned to discern also from the contemporary study of the New Testament. A pre-eminent past in this study has been played by Form-and-Redaction Criticism, by which is meant the isolation and identification of the many variant traditions that have conspired to make up the New Testament canon, the reconstruction of the sometimes conflicting interests and influences that account for the separate theologies represented by the traditions, and reflection on all that is entailed in the transformations and adaptations undergone by the traditions in their passage from one New Testament author or school to another. We shall not presume to deal with this vast subject in the modest compass and the context that have been set for us, but it would seem that there are at least three more or less assured conclusions from this study that have a direct bearing on the subject we do intend to discuss. First, that as we encounter it from the beginning in its own canonical documents of origin, there was never an utterly monolithic, homogeneous Christianity from which any deviation could be only an aberration. Though he may have been guilty of some exaggeration and special pleading, Walter Bauer was very nearly correct almost forty years ago when he analysed aboriginal Christianity as a disparity of beliefs; certainly it was a disparity of theologies with more than trivial differences.[2] The moulds

---

[2]Bauer's *Rechtgläubigkeit and Ketzerei im ältesten Christentum* was first published in 1934 (Tübingen, Mohr) and was reedited with supplements by Georg Strecker in 1964, four years after Bauer's death. An ET *Orthodoxy*

in which the Christian message was cast were as diverse as the syncretic world in which the message was first spoken and heard. Secondly, that one of these moulds, and a chief one, was provided by the venerable gnostic or wisdom tradition of thought endemic in the world into which Jesus was born. Though the gnostic interpretation of Christianity could degenerate into heresy, it was also able to produce an early Christology which, by its lack of national ties and the cosmic sweep of its vision, was most congenial to the universalist concerns which the gospels have ascribed to the author of the Church.[3]

It was precisely this kind of New Testament Christology to which appeal was made by Asian delegates to the 1961 Conference on *Faith and Order* held at New Delhi when they censured what they regarded as the "church steeple" mentality of Western theology. Thirdly, that the phenomenon of the New Testament canon, seen in its own internal history, does not permit us to declare this kind of Christology marginal simply because it has on occasion been redacted into another more dominant, or alternatively, to declare those whole works marginal which have it as their dominant Christology. Redaction, which has played so large a role in the formation of the canon, was always basically more of an acceptance than a rejection.[4] To reject one part of the canon on the basis of another of its parts[5] is not really to respect the undeniable diversity of the canon but to measure the canon by a yard-stick other than its own.

and Heresy in Earliest Christianity (Philadelphia, Fortress) was published in 1971. Catholic reviews of Bauer's work through the years have been critical but rather generally favourable.

[3]Cf. André Feuillet, *Le Christ sagesse de Dieu d'après les épîtres Pauliniennes* (Paris, Gabalda, 1966). Also Richard N. Longenecker, *The Christology of Early Christianity* (Studies in Biblical Theology 2/17, 1970) 25-62.

[4]As the present author has argued in "The Colossians Hymn and the Principle of Redaction," *Catholic Biblical Quarterly,* 33 (1971) 62-81.

[5]Most recently on "the canon within the canon" see Ernst Käsemann (ed.), *Das Neue Testament als Kanon* (Göttingen, Vandenheeck & Ruprecht, 1970): fifteen authors arguing with Käsemann over the propriety of narrowing the canon to fit "the essence of the gospel".

That yardstick cannot be the Spirit, if indeed the Spirit was the first unity of the canon.

These principles and facts, we have said, are altogether relevant to the topic of our discussion, which is Israel's encounter with the nations. We may briefly summarize their relevance as follows. First of all, Israel no less than the primitive Christian church was, both in origins and through most of its historical life, a heterogeneous mixture taken literally from the nations. The religion of Israel which formed its unity manifested the same note of assimilation that we have predicated of the Christian Church; long before a postexilic prophet wrote its song, Israel had, in Newman's sense, "sucked the milk of nations" (Is 60:16). Secondly, the same wisdom tradition which affected the infant church had long been operative in Israel, through many transformations, with all the same implications of a universalism transcending national and ethnic limitations. The tradition had become, it is true, thoroughly Israelite; wisdom had come to dwell in the tents of Jacob (Sir 24:8); but if this was a marriage in which she forsook her father's house in favour of glorious sons (Ps 45:11-18), still her dowry enriched Israel for ever. And finally, though the Old Testament canon is a work of redaction which has subordinated a myriad dissident elements to a dominant and eclectic *Heilsgeschichte* which became particularist and national, it was a canon formed on the same principles as those of the New Testament, which bid us hear all the dissonant voices. Christians too easily admit to no problem in this area, since they are habituated to taking from the Old Testament what they will at random, or indeed nothing at all as they choose; yet it was not as a collection of miscellaneous documents that the Church inherited the Old Testament, but as a canon of Scripture, the record of how a people of God had heard and responded to his word. We shall look briefly at the first of these points and reserve most of our attention for the other two.

The mixed character of a people that would later set such a high price on the purity of bloodlines is well known and needs little comment; it was acknowledged by the earliest biblical texts and has only been confirmed and explicitated by later studies.

(The association of religious orthodoxy with a necessarily highly idealized ethnic integrity in postexilic Judaism cannot, unfortunately, be lightly dismissed as of no enduring consequence, since it affected some influential theologies; but it can and must be seen in its proper historical context, as we shall try to see it). "A roaming Aramean was my father," began the ancient creed (Deut 26:5), and only now are we beginning to suspect how wide the fathers roamed and from how far. The Bible itself brought them from Chaldea, Arabia, Syria, Egypt, Asia Minor; the main contribution of modern study has been to sort out the separate origins of its traditions, to indicate that what eventually came to be called Israel was the result not of only one but of multiple histories, which have become one only as a vehicle of religious kerygma.[6] It was not a common ancestry or even, in its totality, a common historical experience that brought about the phenomenon of Israel, but the dynamism of a new faith that polarized a religious and social revolution on the soil of Palestine.[7] Not the least significant note of its dynamism was its demonstrated power to assimilate into a new and unique thing the many disparate elements it had found along its paths and to which its many disparate components contributed and continued to contribute.

If venerable cult objects such as the Ark seem to go back to the nomadic origins of some of Israel's ancestry, and if traces of the same beginnings can be discerned in its chief feasts which survived many retranslations, still the bulk of its ritual life and its priestly traditions were taken in through amalgamation with Canaan. From Canaan came the psalmody of which we shall

---

[6]The classic study of modern times is Gerhard von Rad's *Das form-geschichtliche Problem des Hexateuch* of 1938, reprinted in *Gesammelte Studien zum Alten Testament* (Munich, Kaiser, 1958) 9-86; ET in *The Problem of the Hexateuch and Other Essays* (Edinburgh, Oliver & Boyd, 1965).

[7]The position defended by George Mendenhall in "The Hebrew Conquest of Palestine", *Biblical Archaeologist* 25 (1962) 66-87. It has been adopted substantially by John L. McKenzie in the best current work on the period, *The World of the Judges* (Prentice-Hall, 1966).

soon be speaking, from Canaan too the cultic and royal traditions which sustained psalmody. Solomon's temple was Phoenician, David's court was Egyptian. Egypt and Arabia were the
routes by which wisdom entered the mainstream of Israelite life
and was eventually assimilated to its covenant theology of a
priestly people. The covenant itself, though it took on in Israel
a distinct moral dimension owed to a less unclouded vision of
the covenant God and to the preaching of the great prophets,
was based on models developed into analogous forms by the
contemporary peoples of Canaan and Asia Minor. Israel's laws,
which spelt out its covenant duties and formed their commentary, were drawn, as we have long known, from principles of
justice and equity which Israel shared with her neighbours of
the Near East, with Assyrians and Babylonians, Sumerians and
Hittites; even the so-called apodictic laws which Albrecht Alt
once thought were unique to the Mosaic codes are now recognized to have had their parallels among other peoples in other
religions. Prophecy, whose achievement in Israel was quite
literally unlike that of any other people of the times, nevertheless
had in Israel the same humble beginnings that it had in Phoenicia,
in Canaan, and in Amorite Mesopotamia, and pursued to the
end many of the same interests with the use of similar techniques.

All this kind of thing is much more frankly acknowledged
and even approved in the earlier sources of the Old Testament
than in the later. The patriarchal traditions make nothing special
of Israel's early place among the nations: the father of the
Hebrews is hidden in Genesis ch. 10, a flotsam in a sea of in-
termingled and inter-related peoples. The Midianite provenance
of the cult of Yahweh is more than hinted at by the major Pentateuchal traditions, even though in conflict with some of their
other interests. The priestly tradition, for all of its other par-
ticularisms, still retains an older spirit of openness, as when
it looks all the way back to Noah for the beginning of the covenant which God struck with Israel. The distinction between "nation" and "people", as a matter of fact, that is, between Gentile
and Israelities in any ideological sense, is characteristic of the
later literary history of the Bible, not the earliest. A particularism
there always was, of course, since it was taken for granted that

every people had its own God and its own traditions. Particularism became exclusivism, however, only under the stress of peculiar historical developments.

Israel's cultural assimilation was, on the one hand, necessitated by the poverty of its own native resources. "The one thing we know for sure about the peoples who invaded Palestine from the thirteenth to the eleventh centuries is that they came from the east and south and were not of high culture".[8] It was inevitable that they should draw, and continue to draw, on the superior societies that surrounded them on all sides, especially from the two ancient centres of civilization between which Palestine formed the land-bridge and meeting-point, Egypt and Mesopotamia. Yet this undeniable dependence does not tell the whole story. Israel knew how to reject as well as to accept; assimilation, not uncritical adaptation, was the rule in most of the things that counted. The struggle with the Baals of which we read in Judges, Samuel and Kings was a real one, even though it has been coloured by the Deuteronomic historians with the hues of other struggles waged on other grounds and with other weapons. In the give-and-take of the religious ferment which Israel instigated in Canaan, Yahweh did more than war against the centres of cult-prostitution, the immolation of infants, the superstitions of magic and necromancy. He also appropriated names and places where men had come to know God under other forms and images, forms and images which tempered the sternness of Israel's desert God without destroying his identity. The Yahweh of Israel who could become the Lord of the Christian Old Testament was a revelation to which Canaan also contributed with its cult of El and Baal,[9] a High God who also acted in history, a combination virtually unique in the theologies of man.[10]

---

[8]Morton Smith, in a somewhat jaundiced view of "The Present State of Old Testament Studies," *Journal of Biblical Literature* 88 (1969) 19-35.

[9]Cf. Otto Eissfeldt, "El und Jahwe,"*Kleine Schriften* (Tübingen, Mohr, 1966) III, 386-397; ET in *Journal of Semetic Studies* 1 (1956) 25-37.

[10]Cf. E.O. James, *The Worship of the Sky-God* (University of London, 1963) 56.

Something of what was entailed in this assimilative process can be seen in Psalm 29, one of the Psalter's three pre-eminent "cosmic hymns". Though all of those psalms have been frequently assigned to a relatively late date in Israel's history,[11] there is good reason to concur in the judgment of numerous modern commentators for whom Ps. 29 at least is very ancient indeed. It is a hymn that was sung in the Jerusalem liturgy (and, if we may credit the Septuagint title, sung at the conclusion of the Feast of Booths) celebrating a theophany of the Lord of Israel, but a theophany unlike others in that his power and voice are seen and heard in nature, in a storm, and in a storm, for that matter, which sweeps not the land of Israel but the Phoenicia of the north.[12] If it has not been adapted from an original hymn to Baal-Hadad, as many scholars believe, it has at least been closely modelled on such a hymn. In any case, what is significant is that we have to do with a divine manifestation that is *per se* universalistic.[13] At least in this one instance, and probably through insights gained by dialogue with the nations, the Old Testament has recognized that the word of its God was also to be read in the nature that was the book of all mankind; a word, furthermore, not of judgment in plague or pestilence, but a word of glory and peace.

The other two psalms in this category have other values to offer. Psalm 8 is likewise a hymn, but not a theophany. It is, rather, a meditation on the implications of the priestly creation story in Genesis, or at least on a conception of creation that was also shared by the priestly author. It speaks of a universal God, but this was no novel thing for the Old Testament in speak-

[11]Lately by Alfons Deissler, "Zur Datierung und Situierung der 'Kosmischen Hymnen' Pss 8, 19, 29," *Lex Tua Veritas: Festschrift für Herbert Junker* (Trier, 1961) 47-58.

[12]Thus Artur Weiser is wrong in his commentary in finding "a link with the Israelite Sinai tradition"; the Kadesh of vs. 8 is not that of the wilderness tradition but the Syrian desert as so designated in the Ugaritic texts.

[13]The *hadrat* of vs. 2 does not mean "(holy) attire" (variants: "splendour," "court," etc.) as usually in the translations, but "appearance (of the Holy)", as recognized by Cross, Dahood, Weiser, Kraus, et al.

ing of Yahweh (Ps 24:I, Is 6:3, etc.); it does not speak of a universal manifestation of God (unless something of this nature is hinted at in the obscure vs. 3). What is unusual, however, is its introspective attitude taken towards human creation, unusual for Israel and reminiscent of the interests of the wisdom writers. Of the same nature is Psalm 19, which is really two psalms that have been meaningfully united by a post-exilic author. The first part of Ps 19 resembles the nature theophany of Ps 29, but in reality its thought appears to be of a more elusive and mystical strain. It, too, seems to be a hymn that has studied from exotic models: Vss. 5b-7 look very much like a sun-god hymn which has been divested of its myth and fitted to the preceding verses which speak of the created heavens. The heavens and the firmament, says the psalmist, testify to the divine glory, to the creative power of God, but not in words that are patient of human understanding. The resolution of this seeming paradox which contradicts rather than confirms the sentiment of Ps 29 is to be found in the reluctant conclusion reached by the later Israelite practitioners of Wisdom: nature is a book in which God has written his name, but *de facto* man does not read it there (so the Wisdom of Solomon, ch. 13). Appropriately, then, has been added the praise of the Law which now make up vv. 8-15 of the psalm: the knowledge of God which man has not acquired through wisdom he has safely in the revealed word. The joining of ideas present in this psalm also follows another precedent of the later wisdom, which was to pair off with the wonders of nature Israel's own *Heilgeschichte*; thus, for example, Ben Sira's climactic "praise of the fathers" (Sir 44-50) following 42:15-43:33.[14] Wisdom, we can see from these examples, spoke with an assimilated and multiple voice in Israel.

In connection with these psalms we have already used the term "wisdom" somewhat ambiguously, and unavoidably. Unavoidably, because there is an ambiguity inherent in the concept itself, which can with equal justice apply to a defined school with its proper literary traditions and genres or to a more general

---

[14]Cf. Edmond Jacob, "L'histoire d'Israel vue par Ben Sira," *Mélanges Bibliques André Robert* (Paris, Bloud & Gay, 1956) 288-294.

theological attitude which was capable of expressing itself in various literary forms. It is with the attitude that we are most concerned, though it cannot be understood fully as an historical phenomenon without reference to the more rigid tradition which partly controlled it. Because they span so many of the schools and traditions which Israel produced in the long history of its canon, and practically every age of its literary life, the Psalms offer one of the best means of examining this attitude. (The editing of the Psalter itself may preserve one of its effects in that at one stage in its formation the name of Yahweh was replaced, sometimes even quite mechanically, with the neutral word Elohim in the collection made up by Pss 42-83). In the Psalms, too, of course, this kind of thinking must be measured against its known development in the wisdom literature properly so called.

The theological attitude which we wish to associate with wisdom was, first of all, one which worked independently of Israel's peculiar experience of covenant and election, which had its point of departure in man himself standing in relation to God and to his fellows in the universe. We may safely adopt von Rad's definition of this attitude as a blend of anthropocentrism and piety without wondering over much whether there was an even "older" wisdom than the one he envisages which was totally profane in its humanism.[15] If there was, it is not such a wisdom that has penetrated the canonical books of the Old Testament. In keeping with its extra-Israelite origin and international character wisdom in Israel retained an openness to the outside both for the ideas and its heroes . . . Job, Amenemope, Enoch, the Ezrahites, Lemuel, Agur . . . while at the same time striving for ecumenicity in its religious views. These same qualities were still preserved in wisdom's later stage, when it had been thoroughly integrated with covenant theology and had become, in R.N. Whybray's phrase, the "handmaid of orthodox Judaism."[16]

---

[15]See William McKane, "On the Definition of Old Wisdom," in *Prophets and Wise Men* (Studies in Biblical Theology 44, 1965) 48-54.

[16]*Wisdom in Proverbs* (Studies in Biblical Theology 45, 1965) 21. But his example Ben Sira was not all that "orthodox": his theology would later be called Sadducean. If Ben Sira's Judaism is closed, it is with the conserva-

Then it continued to be open to the ideas of the Gentiles, though it could judge their wisdom by the Law as easily as the other way round. All these traits we have noted in the three psalms we have already seen.

In the Psalter wisdom may celebrate the ecumenicity of Yahwistic piety in its contact with the universal human condition: the founding of a house and family (Ps 127) or the joy in the company of one's fellows (Ps 133). It may, as one of its favourite themes, inculcate the commonsense and practicality of moral righteousness on the basis of common human experience (Pss 1, 37, 112, 128), an experience, alas, which other wisdom writers would testify was not as common as it ought to be. Alternatively, like Job and Ecclesiastes the spirit of wisdom in the Psalms can question the traditional and easy equations and, like the author of the Wisdom of Solomon, be receptive to other answers that had occurred to questing spirits outside Israel. It is hardly by chance that only in the wisdom Psalms 49 and 73 does the Hebrew Bible contemplate the possibility of a survival of physical death, contrary to the otherwise almost unbroken tradition (including that of Pss 6:6, 88:11-13).[17] The Old Testament doctrine of hope found an especially poignant expression in the wisdom psalms.[18]

What was implicit in this attitude speaks more eloquently, perhaps, than do the explicit reference to the nations in the Psalms. The Psalms, because they embrace all theologies and ages, are capable of saying terrible things about the Gentiles (Ps 137); they are capable of the triumphalistic eschatology of the Jerusalem cult whose universalism envisaged a subjugation

tion of Ben Sira, just as Ecclesiastes' is closed with the pessimism of Qoheleth. The Wisdom of Solomon has also put wisdom to the service of Judaism, but with quite different results, more typical of wisdom.

[17]"Intimations of Immortality and the Old Testament," *Journal of Biblical Literature*, 91 (1972) 158-171.

[18]Cf. Walther Zimmerli, "Statements about Hope in the Psalms," in *Man and His Hope in the Old Testament* (Studies in Biblical Theology 2/20, 1971) 26-41. Also Alfons Deissler, "Das Israel der Psalmen als Gottesvolk der Hoffenden," *Die Zeit Jesu: Festschrift für Heinrich Schlier* (Herder, 1970) 15-37.

of the Gentiles (Pss 47, 102:16, the Royal Psalms); and they are equally capable of the gentler universalism, though still triumphalistic, which shares the Second Isaiah's vision of the nations coming to partake of Israel's blessings (Pss 22:28, 86:9, 117). The Psalms are, after all, mainly the song book of Israel and its temple. We are doubtless authorized, however, to equate with the theology of the wisdom Psalms the kind of stance taken by other works inspired by the wisdom tradition which entered into the question *ex professo* in the polemics of the time. At a time when bitter historical tragedy and other circumstances conspired to drive Israel into a serious introversion, to adopt the stern particularism of Ezra and Nehemiah, to write into its laws decrees of inexorable exclusion (such as Deut 23:3), contrary spirits were not lacking to voice opposition. The post-exilic books of Ruth and Jonah, both conceived in the spirit of didactic wisdom, countered Jewish exclusivism by exploiting some of Israel's most ancient literary traditions.[19] The drift of these works is so well known that it is unnecessary for us to go into details. They are all the more significant that they were written in the face of so much that had moved contrary spirits to such opposite conclusions.

To the superficial eye at least, it was Deuteronomy rather than Ruth that put its abiding stamp on the canon; Ezra rather than the lesson taught to Jonah, and idealized (and partly fictional) the history of holy war of extirpation against the Gentiles rather than what had been learnt from them. Yet the intertestamental literature and, indeed, the Judaism to which the New Testament testifies, are silent witness to how much the assimilative process continued. Israel learnt from Persia and the *oikoumene* of Hellenism quite as it had learnt from Egypt and Arabia, and became a part of them forever. And even had this not been so, even had exclusivism prevailed in fact as it was

---

[19]Mal 1:11 (the pure sacrifice among the Gentiles) and Is 19:19f. (the altar in Egypt) are often cited as other steps in the same direction. However, while these passages entertain a universalism of sorts, it is rather one of the expansion of Israel. See the writer's discussion in *The Bible in Current Catholic Thought* (Herder & Herder, 1962) 85f.

held so widely in theory, the canon itself stands as mute evidence
to a tradition that did not die and that was not allowed to die.
Wisdom did in fact become the handmaid of orthodox Judaism,
but the effects of its free-ranging spirit were not stifled. The
canon, with all its inner conflicts and difficulties, is the record
of a dialogue that had once taken place and that had to go on
because of the living ideas to which it had given harbour. The
Christianity to which Judaism gave birth, and which had to
overcome its own temptation to turn in upon itself, eventually
achieved a universalism in principle which far exceeded that
of the parent religion. This universalism did not spring full-
formed from the mind of its genius, however. It had been her-
alded, and in many ways it had been anticipated by, and in other
ways it would be incomprehensible without, Israel's prior encounter with the nations.

10. Intimations of Immortality and The Old Testament

I

In the third and final volume of his Anchor Bible translation and commentary on the Psalms, Mitchell Dahood has concluded a brief section devoted to "Biblical Theology" with a reference to an unnamed American scholar who several years ago

> suggested a moratorium on the writing of major works attempting to synthesize the theology of the Old Testament. He maintained that our generation should concentrate on monographic studies of individual problems put in a new light by textual and archaeological discoveries of recent decades. The foregoing observations on the theology of the Psalter seem to corroborate the wisdom of his suggestion. The new readings and analyses — grammatical and prosodic — disclose numerous concepts, motifs, and attitudes that require a more thorough and systematic treatment than is feasible here. I would be gratified if this heavily philological commentary were to elicit monographic studies of some of the ideas uncovered by the systematic application of Northwest Semitic philological principles to the text of the Psalter.[1]

It is a pleasure to take up this invitation in some small way. First of all, because anyone who has any feeling whatever for

---

[1]*Psalms III* (AB 17A; Garden City: Doubleday, 1970) LI-LIII.

biblical theology might wonder whether "a decade and one hundred fifty psalms later" following Dahood's fateful conversation with David Noel Freedman in the library of the Pontifical Biblical Institute in Rome,[2] his long-awaited excursus on the subject might not have been expected to embrace more than a couple of pages of new names of God and a reiteration of the evidence on which he bases his contention that the Psalms testify rather extensively to an Israelite faith in resurrection and immortality. Secondly, this attempt, however modest, to deal with some of the theological issues raised by Dahood's new translation may, by raising questions of literary form and context, suggest the impropriety of getting at the content of historically significant texts by the almost exclusive use of comparative philology. Rather than to conceive of his task as one of simply assimilating new ideas opened up by the philological possibilities, one would imagine that the commentator would think it his duty to control the possibilities by other relevant considerations in the process of his exposition, thus turning them into probabilities or vice versa.

I use the term possibilities because that is what, unsupported by other evidence, so many of them remain. No one who has followed the work of Mitchell Dahood can be unaware of the tremendous contributions he has made to our knowledge of the OT through the erudition he has acquired through the years His commentary on the Psalms is an enviable landmark for any scholar, and there is no one, however adverse to its method and presuppositions, who will not agree that time after time its author has hit the meaning of the text on its ineluctable head. The "Grammar of the Psalter" assembled by him and his research assistant Tadeusz Penar which appears as an appendix to his third volume shows the discipline and system that he has imposed upon his research. But in less disciplined hands, how easily can his method lead to games that anyone can play, anyone with a casual acquaintance with the languages cognate with biblical Hebrew and a little imagination. Anyone who has been persuaded that the Masoretes were appallingly ignorant (and

---

[2]*Ibid.* V.

at times, of course, they were) of the meaning of a text which they nevertheless preserved with almost miraculous literal accuracy, provided only that the letters now be redistributed into more congenial accuracy. This game has been played before, with Akkadian and Arabic before Ugaritic.

And occasionally Dahood seems to be playing the same game. What, for example, are we to make of his translation of Sir 7:36? The text, as we have it, runs as follows:

בכל מעשיך זכור אחרית
ולעולם לא תשחת

ἐν πᾶσι τοῖς λόγοις σου
μιμνῄσκου τὰ ἔσχατά σου, καὶ
εἰς τὸν αἰῶνα οὐχ ἁμαρτήσεις.

The NAB, the only English-language translation which has used the Hebrew text of Sirach, where extant, as its primary base of operations, has rendered Ben Sira's thought thus:

> In whatever you do, remember your last days, and you will never sin.

This translation agrees, substantially, with the NEB, the RSV, the SBJ and its satellites in English and German—and with the LXX.[3] It does so because it has chosen to read the last Hebrew word, as presumably the LXX did, *te͗sahēt*, a piel of *šāḥat* otherwise well attested in this sense in the OT. Dahood on the contrary renders the text:

> In all your works remember the future life, and never shall you descend the Pit.[4]

In doing so, he has seized on a perfectly acceptable meaning of the verb (we shall return later to the question of *'ah͗arît* = "the future life"). In the niphal form *šāḥat* is equally well attested (probably also in the Hebrew of Sir 9:8) in the sense of

---

[3]NAB is more influenced by the LXX than it professes to be, in fact, if SBJ is correct in assuming that the *'ah͗arît* of the Hebrew represents the end of things done rather than of him who does them (the latter is the clear sense of the Greek). However, 11:26-28, also noted by SBJ, should be taken into account as a possible parallel.

[4]Ibid. XLVIII.

moral or physical destruction. To this, however, he has added the overtone which he has derived from the identification of šaḥat as the "Pit" (= Sheol). Now there should never have been any doubt about the meaning of this word in biblical Hebrew: it *can* signify a pit (cf. Ezek 19:4), and on occasion it can signify *the* Pit of Sheol, as Ps 16:10 indicates quite clearly. As a matter of fact, despite the otherwise rich vocabulary assigned to the underworld in the Semitic languages, its presence elsewhere than in biblical Hebrew is not attested, except in one Ugaritic passage where it has been identified as such by Dahood.[5] Northwest Semitic philological principles have, therefore, nothing to do in this case with strengthening the probability of Dahood's translation—and this is to set aside the propriety of making a verbal form out of *šḥt* that includes the idea of Sheol. The translation must be judged, rather, on the score of its correspondence with other factors, certainly not excluding the one of internal probability with the mind of the author.

In Dahood's translation, Ben Sira avers that an eye to the prospects of one's life beyond the grave may serve to persuade a man to order his life so that he may, in God's judgment, avoid Sheol. But this is not the mind of Ben Sira, who holds to the "old" deuteronomic theology which restricted retribution to this life alone and regarded the realm of death in a purely negative light, as the common lot of all men, bad and good.[6] His best advice is that man should live a life of enlightened self-interest, but

---

[5] See Nicholas J. Tromp, *Primitive Conceptions of Death and the Nether World in the Old Testament* (BibOr 21; Rome: Biblical Institute, 1969) 18-19. The passage appears in C.H. Gordon's *Ugaritic Textbook* (AnOr 38; Rome: Biblical Institue, 1965) 607:64-65. In the *editio princeps* Charles Virolleaud identified the Ugaritic *šḥt* with Akkadian *šaḥatu* (a kind of plant): the parallel is *ʿrʿr* = biblical *ʿaroʿēr* or *ʿarʿor* (the juniper tree). Tromp found this identification doubtful, but no more so that that of Gordon and Dahood, which on the one hand supposed a missing parallel and on the other was tenuous (Dahood in *Psalms III*, 25-26).

[6] See Alexander A. DiLella, "Conservative and Progressive Theology: Sirach and Wisdom," *CBQ* 28 (1966) 139-54.

highly moral indeed, helping his brother in the same spirit, since one cannot take one's goods with him on the beyond. Death is inexorable, and in Sheol there are no pleasures to be sought (Sir 14:12-19).[7] It is proper to mourn for a dead man— obviously, a good man—as propriety and piety demand. But excessive grief is not only of no use to the deceased, it can also be of harm to the living. There is no return from death, and death's best office is to remind the living of the fate that is also in his store (Sir 38:16-23).[8] Death (*māwet, thanatos*), it seems, is an eternal sleep (*nûḥat ʿôlām, anapausis aiōnos*, Sir 30:17). It is a bitter thing for man to encounter in the midst of life's fulness, though it can easily be a surcease of sorrow for one who has never really lived, whose career on earth must be deeemed a failure; but in any case, it is a fate that must be faced, as it has been and ever will be, the fate of every creature, from which no inquest is granted in the beyond (Sir 41: 1-4).[9] In death there can be nothing positive, merely a dissolution (vss. 5-10).[10] Immortality:

הבל [בני] אדם בגויתם	11 Man's [men's] body is a fleeting thing, but a
אך שם חסד לא יכרת	virtuous name will never be annihilated.[11]

[7]So the Hebrew and the LXX; contrast the Syr. NAB, NEB, SBJ translate substantially the same.

[8]Here too there is no difficulty between the Hebrew and the LXX, and the modern versions are in concert.

[9]Since the Masada Ben Sira is lacking at this point, we have only negative reasons to confirm that at 41:4d we should read with Genizah B margin: *ʾên tôkᵉhot hayyim biśᵉʾôl* = LXX *ouk estin en hadou elegmos zōēs*. But *tôkᵉhot* = *elegmos* can be variously taken, as the contemporary versions testify.

[10]For some reason Tromp (*Death and the Nether World*, 87, n. 41) alleges Sir 41:10 (meaning 40:11?) and 1 Mac 3:62 (*lege* 2:62) as parallel to Eccl 12:7. But at best there is only a half parallel. Sir 41:10 only says that nothing returns to nothing.

[11]Contrast LXX, followed by RSV, SBJ, NEB. We follow the Genizah B text and margin reconstructed with the aid of Masada; cf. Yigael Yadin, *The Ben Sira Text From Masada* (Jerusalem: Israel Exploration Society, 1965) 19. The Masada text reproduces a dittography of the *lamedh* in vs. 11b.

פחד על שם כי הוא ילוך

12 Have a care for (your) name, for it will stand by you

מאלפי שימות חמדה

better than precious treasures in the thousands.

טובת חי מספר ימים

13 The boon of life is for limited days, but

וטובת שם ימי אין מספר

a good name, for days without number (NAB).

There is an immortality, since a virtuous life remains as a witness that cannot be destroyed. A man lives on because kindness and righteousness survive (*ḥesed* and *ṣeḏāqāh*, Sir 40:17); their eternity is man's eternity: he lives on in what he has done and for what he is remembered.[12] The body of man—and that is verily man—is laid away in peace, but the name of man endures in *saecula saeculorum* (Sir 44:14).[13]

In the context of such thought, is there room for a translation such as the one Dahood has given to Sir 7:36? No one, by any means whatever, escapes Sheol, fails to "descend the Pit." Because he accepted the story in 1 Kgs 17:17-24 as literal history Ben Sira could conceive of a man being brought back from Sheol, i.e., from death (*mimmāwet = miššeʾôl*, Sir 48:5), but only as an extraordinary miracle otherwise unheard of in sacred history, not as a matter of even proleptic eschatology. Eschatology in Ben Sira?

II

I have devoted this much attention to what might seem to be a rather obvious point because I feel that the same sort of mistake in reading a passage according to the philologically possible rather than according to the theologically probable may have been made where the issues are not so evident. What, for

---

[12]Cf. Patrick W. Skehan, "Sirach 40, 11-17," *CBQ 30* (1968) 570-72.

[13]Masada confirms Smend's reading of the mutilated B text and marginal reading of vs. 14b *ûšemām ḥay leḏôr wāḏôr*. Cf. Yadin, *Ben Sira Text*, 37.

example, of Ps 73:24, that passage above all in the Psalms where the possibility of a life beyond the grave is entertained?

Even in a more conventional translation than Dahood's,[14] Ps 73:24-25 has long suggested to various commentators that the psalmist envisaged the possibility of a life beyond the present.[15] But what kind of life, and on what terms? The psalm is of a relatively late date,[16] of a time when Ben Sira and Qoheleth and the author of the Wisdom of Solomon and perhaps many other devout Israelites were grappling with the problem of retribution posed by the traditional this-worldly view of human destiny and were emerging with widely divergent responses. The response of Ben Sira was a fairly intransigent adherence to the old perspective, as we have just seen. The author of Psalm 73, on the other hand, apparently found himself impelled by the logic of his position to look beyond that perspective. Despite the seeming unchecked triumph of the evil-doer and the corresponding degradation of the just, he is inspired by an experience of the divine presence (vs. 17) to affirm that at the end it will not be so. Evil will eventually be destroyed, while he will be taken to God. The language is vague: we have here more of an expression of trust and confidence than a credal articulation; however, it does seem a fair enough assumption that the psalmist is thinking of some kind of divine intervention in the style of Gen 5:24 and 2 Kgs 2:3-12. That "he is convinced that God will assume him to himself, without suffering the pains of death"[17] may be too precise an interpretation of what was

[14]"Lead me into your council, / and with glory take me to yourself. / What shall I lack in heaven with you?/ I shall want nothing on earth." So in *Psalms II* (AB 17; Doubleday, 1968) 187.

[15]Cf. Hans-Joachim Kraus, *Psalmen I* (BKAT XV/1; Neukirchener Verlag, 1960) 509f.; Gerhard von Rad, *Theologie des Alten Testaments I* (Munich: Kaiser, 1957) 403-5; Artur Weiser, *Die Psalmen* (ATD 15; Göttingen: Vandenhoeck & Ruprecht, 1955) 350; *The Psalms* (Philadelphia: Westminster, 1962) 514-15. See, however, the article by M. Mannati, "Sur le quadruple *avec toi* de Ps. LXXIII 21-26," *VT* 21 (1971) 59-67.

[16]At least after Jer 12:1ff.; cf. Kraus, *Psalmen I*, 504.

[17]Dahood, *Psalms 1* (AB 16, 1966) on Ps 16:10, referring also to Ps 49:16 and 73:24. Cf. Tromp (*Death and the Nether World*, 198-200), endorsing this line of interpretation.

in the psalmist's mind. But even if so, what the psalmist envisages is an altogether extraordinary occurrence, underlined by his use of the verb *lqh* in its "pregnant" sense.[18] Psalm 73 may witness to a belief in an other-worldly eschatology, but, if so, as a highly personal and unique response to a particular situation. It can hardly be extrapolated into a dominant idea of the Psalter.

Much the same significance it seems, should be attached to the assertion of Ps 49:16, which also appears in a late sapiential psalm. If this verse is to be taken at its literal face value, the psalmist avers that, in contrast to the wicked who must go down to never-ending death without the comfort of the wealth in which they have trusted, he himself will be "redeemed" from Sheol by Yahweh's "taking" him. Again we have the situation of a man grappling with a problem to which there was no traditional answer, or rather, to which there was a traditional answer which now seemed inadequate. Like the author of the Wisdom of Solomon who contemplated the problematic in a broader context and concluded that God had "taken" to himself (Wis 3:6, *prosedexato autous*) the souls of the just, granting them immortality as his free gift, the psalmist apparently believed that a like intervention would vindicate himself and those like him. Neither in Wisdom nor in the psalm is anything said one way or the other about a resurrection of the body: that eschatological solution was, we know, now developing in the Judaism of Palestine and of the diaspora. It has been argued that the author of Wisdom, whose thinking was entirely Jewish even though his language was Greek, did include the idea of resurrection in his eschatology.[19] The same supposition might be made with even more likelihood for the thought of the psalmist; at least, it is by no means clear that "he is convinced that God will assume him to himself, without suffering the pains of death." He does, after all, while presenting himself as a master of *hokmāh* (vs.

---

[18]That there is a "pregnant" sense of *lqh* there can be no doubt, and the psalmist is doubtless thinking of the way Yahweh "took" Enoch and Elijah. But Yahweh also "took" other men in other ways, as Amos 7:15 testifies. The common denominator was the unusual, the unexpected action of Yahweh.

[19]So DiLella, "Conservative and Progressive Theology," 152-54.

4), proclaim that all must suffer death, the $h^a k\bar{a}m\hat{\imath}m$ along with the senseless and the foolish (vs. 11). Furthermore, we should not be unaware of the uncertainty of our interpretation of the psalmist's mind. Though his opinion may be discounted as less probable, Christoph Barth's arguments may not be simply dismissed when he maintains that the Sheol from which the psalmist awaits deliverance is that created for him by his enemies.[20]

As with the "pregnant" use of the word "take," so with the meaning of "life" in the OT. One may agree with L. Swain that "for the Hebrew mind human life is such an absolute and positive value that it involves eternity. Thus it would be superfluous for the Hebrew to qualify what he knew to be human life in its fulness with the epithet,"[21] without concurring that when "life" obviously connotes more than mere existence something like "eternal life" must be the ultimate meaning. The range of meaning for "life" in the OT is far more comprehensive than that.[22] The life of which Deuteronomy speaks, and which it opposes to death, the long life promised on the land to those who keep the statutes of the Lord (Deut 30:15-20), is obviously a meaningful existence that transcends mere being, but it is just as obviously a this-worldly life with no pretensions to anything beyond. So is it in Psalm 37, a psalm which Dahood rightly recognizes as deuteronomically inspired. Why, however, in vss. 37b-38 does the perspective become, for him, other-worldly, whereas up to that point it has not been?[23] It is, largely, because

[20]*Die Errettung vom Tode in den individuellen Klage- und Dankliedern des Alten Testaments* (Zolliko: Evangelischer Verlag, 1947) 158-160.

[21]Quoted by Dahood in *Psalms III*, XLVI.

[22]See the discussion by Bultmann and von Rad in *TWNT* 2, 833-53.

[23]Cf. *Psalms I*, 232. He has rightly avoided giving the *'ereṣ* of vss. 9, 11, 22, 29, 34 anything other than the deuteronomic sense, though the promise here of an "everlasting" dwelling is in parallel with that of vss. 37b-38, and though elsewhere (in Pss 27:13, 116:9, 142:6) he understands an *'ereṣ hahayyîm* (which most commentators understand to mean this earth in the deuteromic sense) as = paradise. Elsewhere, *'ereṣ*, even absolutely used, is for Dahood a synonym for Sheol, an identification which is accepted by Tromp (*Death and the Nether World* 180-81), but only as a secondary extension of the word (Sheol is part of the earth and therefore can = the earth).

of his identification of *'aḥᵃrît* with "the future life," a matter which we have already noted in passing.

In several of these translations, Dahood has been much influenced by his interpretation of a crucial Ugaritic passage, 2 Aqht VI: 27-38. This mythological selection is deserving of our examination at the present time.[24] The first lines are straightforward enough to form no problem for translation. The "virgin" Anath is speaking to the "hero" Aqht:

irš ḥym watnk	Ask for life and I will give it to you,
blmt waslḥk	immortality and I will bestow it on you.
aš sprk 'm b'l šnt	I will make you number your
'm bn il tspr yrḥm	years with Baal, with the gods you will number months.

Thus far a fairly common mythological theme, reflected alike in the Genesis story of the "fall" and the myths of Gilgamesh and Adapa, to go no further: the offer of immortality to otherwise mortal man, to be granted as a boon or achieved through the ingenuity and manipulation of the favored one.

To the lines that follow, Dahood has given the following translation:[25]

kb'l kyḥwy y'šr	For Baal when he gives life gives a feast,
ḥwy y'šr wyšqynh	gives a feast to the life-given and bids him drink.
ybd wyšr 'lh n'mn	The Gracious chants and sings in his presence.

This, however, fits the context only with difficulty. It is not Baal but Anath whose life-giving is in question: she is to be the bestower of life upon the *n'mn* Aqht, the *ǵzr* (this same parallelism, referring to Aqht, occurs in lines 40-45 of the text

---

[24]I cite the text according to Gordon in *UT*; however, I have redistributed it according to sense lines and normalized it by not indicating uncertain letters where these constitute no difficulty.

[25]*Psalms III*, XLVIII.

below). Therefore it seems more reasonable to construe the sense as follows:

kbʿl kyhwy[26]	Even like Baal, so shall he live;
yʿšr wyšqynh	he shall feast him and give him to
ybd wyšr ʿlh nʿmn	drink, the good one will chant and sing in his presence.[27]

If this is a correct reading, the remainder of the text, which is again fairly straightforward, seems to fall in proper place:

wtʿnynn	And so she says to him:
ap ank aḥwy	Even so shall I give life to Aqht
aqht ġzr	the hero!
wyʿn aqht ġzr	But Aqht the hero replies:
al tšrgn ybtltm	Deceive me not, O virgin,
dm lġzr šrgk	for to a hero your lies are
hhm(?)	thorns(?).
mt uḥryt mh yqḥ	Man: what kind of future does he get?
mh yqḥ mt atryt	What kind of destiny will man get?
spsg ysk lriš	Blight (?) is poured on his head.
ḥrṣ lẓr qdqdy	hoariness (?) on (the nape of?) his skull,
wmt kl amt	and the death of everyman I shall die,
wan mtm amt	for dying I shall surely die.

[26]Reading the intervening *ḥwy yʿšr* of lines 30-31 as a dittography. Cf. Joseph Aistleitner, *Wörterbuch der ugaritischen Sprache* (3. Augfl.; ed. Otto Eissfeldt; Berlin: Akademie-Verlag, 1967) 244.

[27]There is a parallel in *ʿnt* I, an obscure text, where in line 9 occurs *yʿšr wyšqynh*, also of a ceremonial performed before Baal, and in line 18 *ybd wyšr*. What is being described is evidently some rite performed in the presence of the god, providing him with nourishment. Hittite texts may furnish examples of the same or a similar thing; cf. Albrecht Goetze, "Hittite *šipant-*," *JCS* 23 (1971) 77-94. The seventh text cited by Goetze reads: "While the seer is busy libating, the singer stands by. They sing the god's song."

It is not necessary to pursue the course of Aqht's *hybris* further: his male chauvinism compels him to point out that in any case his magic bow which Anath covets and for which she wants to exchange immortality would be of no use to a mere woman. It is sufficient to observe that he rejects the whole possibility of immortality as illusory: immortality is a gift that can never be given since it is not in man's capacity to receive it. Man, by definition, is mortal, and his destiny is to die. The myth, therefore, to the extent at least that Aqht's mind is that of the myth, reflects the same attitude towards life and death that seems to have prevailed throughout most of OT times. "Life" may, indeed, in Anath's protestation have the sense of eternal life, never-dying; but Anath's view of things, here as elsewhere, is rejected. In addition, it ought to be noted that the never-dying of which Anath speaks is precisely that: her immortality is simply the perpetuation of present human existence, not a new life beyond.

It is hard to see, as a consequence, how the myth can be used to support the sense which Dahood wishes to give to '*ah*ᵃ*rît* so often in the OT. On Aqht's lips '*ah*ᵃ*rît* (= *uhryt*, par. *atryt* = "what follows [after]") means the temporally posterior,[28] perhaps even the ultimate posterior, the end (the meaning which it has in Sir 3:25; 11:28; 12:12; 38:20; and, as we have already seen, in 7:36 [logical rather than temporal end?]). It does not, obviously, envisage a "future life," an idea which Aqht finds absurd. (One might, with equally disastrous results, try out such a translation of '*ah*ᵃ*rît* in Sir 38:20, attempting to reconcile it with the immediately following verses.) It lends no support to the view that the concrete future should be understood other than it has traditionally been, as "progeny," in the other texts which are now alleged in support of an eschatological life-beyond: Ps 37:37-38; Ps 109:13;[29] Num 23:10; Prov 23:18; 24:14, 20.

---

[28]See Horst Seebass, *s.v.*, in *TWAT* 1, 224-28.

[29]Dahood takes the parallel *dôr* '*ah*ēr ("the following generation") as = "the age to come," cf. *Psalms III*, 104. There is no doubt that "generation," in Hebrew as in English, had a temporal before it had a concrete, personal

Now it is true that the texts from Proverbs do not infallibly signify—as do texts like Dan 11:4 and Ezek 23:25—that the *'aḥᵃrît* with which they are concerned is so terminal and concrete as to demand the translation "progeny." They do, however, demand a translation that is in keeping with what the word must have meant in the time that it was incorporated into these texts.[30] And, to the extent that we can determine from contemporary parallels,[31] these texts date from a period in which it would have been abnormal to expect anything other than a this-worldly eschatology. Aside from the controversial translations which Dahood has offered for certain verses in the complex of Prov 22:17—24:22 (beginning with the words of Amenemope which have been borrowed fairly substantially from a previously defined text) is there anything that would give aid and comfort to the view that a future life, for good or ill, was entertained for anyone whatever?

---

meaning (though hardly one that responded to the beyond-time). In context, however, vs. 12 seems to define clearly enough the "age" that is meant.

[30]And here, of course, we come face to face with the question, what did the text mean to the author of Proverbs, if, indeed, the author-compiler-designer of Proverbs was one and the same. Cf. Patrick W. Skehan, "Wisdom's House," *CBQ* 29 (1967) 468-86. I have tried to raise the same redactional problem in my article, "The Colossians Hymn and the Principle of Redaction," *CBQ* 33 (1971) 62-81. The author of Prov 1-9 (= the author of Proverbs) may very well have understood by *'aḥᵃrît* (though there is, as far as I know, no evidence that he did) something far beyond what was understood by "the wise." But I take it that Dahood has intended the text to be interpreted as it stands in its original state, independent of redaction.

[31]The "words of the wise" in Prov 22:17—24:22 are generally taken to have been a second stage, at least, of the anthologizing that eventually resulted in the book of Proverbs. They are, it may safely be said, old aphorisms. Cf. B. Gemser, *Sprüche Salomos* (HAT 16; Tübingen: Mohr, 1937) 3-4; J. van der Ploeg, *Spreuken* (De Boeken van het Oude Testament VIII/1; Roermond: Romen & Zonen, 1952) 9-10

III

This observation causes us to examine some of the other earlier texts in which Dahood has found an other-worldly eschatology. In Prov 14:32, for example, it is true enough that commentators have been content to read with the LXX an alternative text for which the MT already offers a sensible reading:

ברעתו ידחה רשע	ἐν κακίᾳ αὐτοῦ ἀπωσθήσεται ἀσεβής,
וחסה במותו צדיק	ὁ δέ πεποιθὼς τῇ ἑαυτοῦ ὁσιότητι δίκαιος.

This means, for Dahood, that the just man finds consolation in his own death.[32] I, too, would be disposed to preserve the *bemôtô* of the MT against the *betummô* presupposed by most of the versions (LXX *hosiotēti*). But it is by no means evident that a blissful state in the afterworld is being promised to the just; rather he is being invited to rejoice in the destruction of the unrighteous. Such a sentiment is admittedly unworthy of later thinking, both Jewish and Christian,[33] but it is there for all that:

> The wicked man is overthrown by his wickedness, and the just man rejoices in his death.

The idea expressed may be contrary to the advice given in Prov 24:17, but it was not alien to many a psalmist, as we well know. Thus seen, the eschatology of the passage differs in no way from that otherwise expressed in the same "Solomonic" collection of proverbs (e.g., 10:27; 11:31; 14:27).

With respect to Prov 14:32 the LXX translator (or the Hebrew scribe on whose work he was dependent) may have been influenced in his reading by the almost unbroken series of an-

[32]Against this view he finds the LXX "tendentious," for reasons I cannot ascertain. Cf. *Psalms III*, XLV.

[33]Though it may, perhaps, be tempered somewhat. "Bij de dood van de boze is de gerechte van iemand die hem onheil kon aandoen bevrijd." So van der Ploeg, *Spreuken, 55.*

tithetic parallelisms that surrounds this verse (although climactic parallelism is also present in this collection, e.g., 10:22; 10:26; 11:22; 12:14; 13:14; 14:10; 15:3; 15:30). All the more interesting, then, is Dahood's rendering of Prov 12:28 as a climactic parallelism where the LXX again offers an antithesis.[34]

בארח־צדקה חיים	ἐν ὁδοῖς δικαιοσύνης ζωή,
ודרך נתיבה אל־מות	ὁδοὶ δὲ μνησικάκων εἰς
	θάνατον

As Dahood notes, R. B. Y. Scott, among others, has concurred in the essentials of the translation he wishes to give this verse:[35]

> On the road of righteousness there is life,
> and the treading of its path is deathlessness.

Nor is this an especially new recognition: GKC (§152*g*), for example, cites this verse to exemplify how *'al-* may be used to form a compound word, "not-death" (the only example, however, which it brings forth). And indeed, on the present state of the evidence it does appear that the MT has the better part of the argument and that LXX has again created an antithesis where none was intended. Its *mnēsikakos*, a hapax legomenon, is not precisely the word we would expect as an antithesis in the first place; and it sounds very much like an expedient to supply for a misunderstanding of the text; the *iter devium* of the Vg seems to be no less. The MT, as it appears, makes good sense, and there is no purpose in altering it.[36]. The efforts of the NAB, RSV, SBJ, and other modern versions, to justify the LXX by reading *tō'ēbāh, me*s̆*ûbāh,* or anything else besides *ne*t*îbāh,* simply do not convince. They would con-

---

[34]Cf. *Psalms II*, XXVII, *III*, XLIV.

[35]*Proverbs, Ecclesiastes* (AB 18; Garden City: Doubleday, 1965) 91-92.

[36]Scott, who takes *ne*t*îbāh* to be a feminine, wants to read *ne*t*îbātô* as a correction of the MT for "its path." But *nātîb* is almost equally well attested in the Hebrew Bible. The *-āh* ending already contains the pronoun (which in any case—*s̆e*d*āqāh* the antecedent—should be feminine rather than masculine), if we recognize with Joüon (§ 94 *h*) how often the Masoretes omitted the *mappiq*.

vince only if it were clear that the MT is hopelessly corrupt, and this is not clear.[37] The NEB manages to combine the MT consonants with an antithesis, but by means of a translation that requires more justification than appears from its text.[38]

Let *'al-māwet* mean "no-death," as I believe it does. It does not, therefore, follow that the Israelite author is thinking of an immortality in the naive sense which Anath proposed to Aqht and which the Canaanite hero spurned as unreal. There is more to the question than this.

The concept of death in the OT is an altogether complicated one, as has been shown no better than in the study of Tromp to which we have more than once referred. If death is—aside from an altogether exceptional miracle such as that vouchsafed to Elijah—the common lot of man, as natural to him as it is for him to have been born in the first place, there is another dimension under which death is considered as a punishment, i.e., as the unexpected, unusual cutting off of a life.[39] This does not mean simply the premature death of the evildoer which was so devoutly awaited by the psalmist and wisdom writer (and prophet) alike; all of these, along with the Deuteronomist and the author of Job, knew that this did not always occur. There are other ways in which death can strike the godless as retribution, be he in advanced age or in youth. Just as life is not mere existence, neither is the quality of death always the same, merely a cessation of earthly life. Capital punishment brings with it the curse of God (Deut 21:22-23). This is the kind of death with which the paradise story of Genesis deals (Gen 2:27; 3:4),[40]

---

[37]Van der Ploeg (*Spreuken*, 50) accepts Gemser's emendation (*mᵉšûbah*) while at the same time confessing that "iets aanders dan een noodoplossing is dit niet."

[38]"But there is a well-worn path to death." The reason for this rendering of *derek nᵉtîbāh* is somewhat opaque.

[39]We do not have reference here to the mythological traits of fire, worms, thirst, etc., sometimes ascribed to Sheol, the major aspect under which Tromp (*Death and the Nether World*, 190-94) considers this question.

[40]In discussing the sense of Gen 2:17, Claus Westermann (*Genesis* [BKAT 1; Neukirchen: Neukirchener Verlag, 1970] 305-6) reviews the five possibilities (six, really) proposed by U. Cassuto and concludes, following Gunkel,

as does the story of Abimelech in Gen 20:7 and 26:11; *môt tāmût* is the formula by which a man is sentenced to death by law.[41] There is no blessedness in death for anyone, but the death of the evil man is a death beyond death: "The memory of the just will be blessed, but the name of the wicked will rot" (Prov 10:7). Death, though inevitable, has nevertheless many faces; much depends on how a man dies (cf. Jer 34:4-5) and how he is remembered, if indeed he is remembered, in the land of the living (cf. Isa 53:9).[42] All these factors should make it plain how the author of Prov 12:38 not only could but, indeed, inevitably would insist that the treading of the path of righteousness is no-death, without the necessity of his having had any theory of a normal fate for man alternative to death. In whatever guise, death is never the fruit of righteousness. In the guise of retribution, as here, it is totally excluded from and by the way of righteousness.

with one of those which Cassuto rejected, viz., that Yahweh did not in the event carry out a sentence of death which he had threatened: "God is and must remain the Lord of his own words." This solution seems preferable in the long run. Cassuto's own interpretation, "At the time you eat of the tree of knowledge the sentence will fall upon you that never can you eat of the tree of life, that is, never can you attain to eternal life, you will be compelled one day to succumb to the power of death" (*Me'Adam 'ad Noach* [2nd ed.; Jerusalem: Magnes, 1953] 82), respects the mythological motif on which the Yahwist's story undoubtedly drew, but hardly the Yahwist's own purposes and his use of the legal formula. See, with separate nuances, Oswald Loretz, *Schöpfung und Mythos* (SBS 32; Stuttgart: Katholisches Bibelwerk, 1968) 128-31; Herbert Haag, *Biblische Schöpfungslehre und kirchliche Erbsündenlehre* (SBS 10, 1966-67) 52-55.

[41]Thus, with verbal variation for the casuistic form, repeatedly in collections of laws like those of Exodus 21, Leviticus 20, Numbers 35, and again Ezek 3: 18; 18:13. Narrative passages like Exod 19:12; Lev 20:2; 1 Sam 14:39, 44; 22:16 undoubtedly reflect the same legal formula. Only a few passages like Judg 13:22; 2 Sam 14:14 (both in the first person plural) seem to employ the infinitive absolute simply for emphasis.

[42]Cf. Barth, *Die Errettung vom Tode*, 64-65.

IV

This brings us back to a more positive consideration of what the OT ordinarily understands by that life which it opposes to death.

Dahood's determination to discover a doctrine of personal immortality operative throughout most of OT times ends, it appears to me, in obscuring one of the OT's primary values for later eschatological right-thinking. This result is only compounded by his persistent use of terms like "beatific vision," "elysian fields," and the like, which admittedly do not occur in the literatures under discussion but were developed under other influences and have a tradition of their own. What is obscured is the distinctive historical process by which Jewish and afterwards Christian eschatology became something quite outside the conventional mythological pattern, quite outside those elysian fields to which Dahood would conduct it. The means of obscuring it is the invocation of language equally plastic to very diverse eschatologies—"live/dwell forever," "see God"—or of literary parallels which, to the disregard of history,[43] are easily promoted from the status of true and legitimate parallels which do deserve some kind of explanation into that of a simple identification *in re* which preempts all explanation.[44]

Whatever is to be said of the contention that a yearning for immortality is innate in man, responding to the very nature of

---

[43]See the remarks of Harry M. Orlinsky, "Whither Biblical Research?" *JBL* 90 (1971) 9-12.

[44]An example might be the title "weigher of spirits/hearts" given to Yahweh in Prov 16:2; 21:2; 24:12, where the sense is the one who is capable of knowing a man inwardly and perfectly in contrast to the human judgment which can only rely on externals and be imperfect. The expression has a parallel, but also an entirely different sense, when used of Re or the underworld god Anubis in Egyptian mythology. Another interesting mythological parallel might be "the book of the living" of Ps 69:29. The fact that there is a parallel, however, is simply an invitation to ask what is meant, in each instance, by "the living": to argue to a common meaning from the parallel is to beg the whole question. The Israelite meaning is elucidated by such texts as Exod 32:32-33; Isa 4:3; 56:5, Dan 12:1.

his being,[45] it seems to be both a fact and a fortunate fact that most of Israel's history was played out in a society which had eschewed this yearning. Which is to say, presumably, that in Israelite society the yearning found fulfillment in other ways than the word whispered in Balder's ear, some of which ways we have already seen.[46] However the fact is to be explained, which acounted for what Père Vincent archaeologically deplored as the "silence of the Israelite tombs," there can be no doubt that it was fortunate. Given Israel's cultural dependence on its Near Eastern neighbors west and east, there can be little question that it would have acquiesced in some form or other of its own to the common other-worldly mythology that issued in the Book of the Dead, the *shurpu* texts, the story of Ea and Adapa. It may well be that Israel would have used the myth creatively and in its own fashion, as the Yawist made creative use of myth in constructing his unique narrative of origins. On the other hand, it is more likely that there would have been in biblical literature a proliferation of stories like the one told in 1 Samuel 28, admittedly a moving product of the storyteller's art, but of questionable theological or religious value. It is an isolated example from popular syncretism of what was kept out of the mainstream of Israelite thought and speculation by the tradition reflected in such texts as Isa 8:19; Lev 19:31; 20:6, 27; Deut 18:11.

Because of its tradition which not only excluded necromancy as a superstition but also discouraged enquiry about as well as of the dead, Israel was compelled to examine the meaning of man's earthly existence to a degree and to a depth seemingly without parallel in the thinking of its contemporaries. Not mere existence but meaningful existence is what the OT understands as synonymous with life. As we know, nowhere better than in what we call the wisdom literature of the OT is this dimension

---

[45]Cf. Wolfhart Pannenberg, *Grundzüge der Christologie* (Gütersloh: Gerd Mohn, 1966) 81.

[46]In Israel's collective hope for the future there was also room for individual hope, as has been pointed out by Horst Dietrich Preuss, *Jahweglaube und Zukunftserwartung* (Stuttgart: Kohlhammer, 1968) 102-8.

of life spelled out in loving detail. The common sense of morality, as contributing to a full, happy, untroubled life, is only one
of wisdom's contributions to this dimension. A healthy materi-
alism, a reverence for the dignity of the body which is human
life in the concrete are others, as is the healthy eroticism of
the Song of Songs. Furthermore, it is doubtful that without such
a concentrated view of the human ideal as a full earthly existence
we should ever have seen the flowering of the prophetic doctrine of social justice, not to mention the recognition of the essential sacredness of the human condition to be found in such texts
as Job 31:13-28. When life is valued so much, long life inevitably comes to be accounted the greatest of blessings (Ps
21:5), even though exceptions are recognized. Again, even
though exceptions are recognized, it must be generally true that
a righteous life will be an enduring life, that righteousness
preserves one's existence in the land of the living (Ps 27:13)
and postponed the common sentence of Sheol (Prov 15:24), that
Sheol which is so certain that every threat to life may be spoken
of as if as present (cf. 2 Sam 22:5-7 = Ps 18:5-7, etc).

We have already intimated the shortcomings of this view of
life, death, and retribution. It did not require the poetry of the
Book of Job to point these out, nor were they first seen only
in Israel's later encounter with alien cultures. It was surely only
a lame response to the problem to insist "better a living dog
than a dead lion. For the living know that they are to die, but
the dead no longer know anything . . . They will never again
have part in anything that is done under the sun" (Eccl 9:4-6).
Also as this same citation might indicate, the standard of what
was a rich and full life of meaningful existence was not always
extremely elevated. A comfortable bourgeois condition, like
Ben Sira's, like that of the diligent housewife of Prov 31:10-31:
"Every man shall sit under his own vine or under his own fig
tree, undisturbed" (Mic 4:4), such might be the modest and
rather unheroic character of the life—and everlasting life—that
was God's gift to be rejoiced in.

Still, the realism of this concept of life was healthy too. It
depended not on the fantasy of mythological speculation but
on empirical fact, on the only experience of life to which man

has been able to testify. It reinforced the analysis of human life as essentially that of a body, an analysis that preserved Judaism and, later, Christianity — barring the occasional aberration — from the intellectual narcissim of Stoicism and its irrelevant morality, from gnostic mysticism, and docetic myth. Without this integral view of life Paul would hardly have countered the sophistries at Corinth as he did in 1 Cor 6:12-14, would never have proclaimed, to the condemnation of Manichean piety both overt and unreflected, that the body is a temple of the Holy Spirit and a member of Christ. Without it the hypostatic heresies with all their moral consequences would have swept rather than simply troubled the patristic church, and the schoolmen, who were always more Platonist than anything else, would have emerged with a vastly different synthesis concerning man in this world and beyond. The degree to which the mythological eschatology did penetrate Judaism and also Christianity both ancient and modern is testimony to the power of temptation that is always possessed. That it was, nevertheless, resisted is testimony to a superior dynamic inherited from the OT, another instance of what G. Ernest Wright has meant in characterizing the OT as the church's bulwark against paganism.[47] The truth that the mythology had sought to convey was eventually assimilated by Judaism and Christianity, but within a view of man that was alien to the myth and had preserved truths that were even more basic. This synthesis could never have occurred, it seems to me, had Israel at any very early age and on any very broad scale simply taken the myth over at face value. We are faced here by a phenomenon of historical religion which is far more eloquent than the philological possibilities of any number of isolated texts.

[47]*God Who Acts* (SBT 8; London: SCM, 1952) 19.

11. Prov 8:22: Wisdom and Creation

What I propose to argue in this paper is (1) that both Job 28 and Proverbs 8 speak of a "wisdom" which is neither God's creation nor his natural attribute but rather a possession which he (unlike man) has acquired. Following on this position it will be further argued (2) that the *qānānî* of Prov 8:22, frequently translated "created me" (or the like), has to do instead with a divine acquisition of wisdom that then played a part in creation. Substantive to this argument will be the contention that in no single instance in the OT or in relevant cognate literatures are we compelled by the evidence to ascribe to the verb *qānâ* in any of its forms the sense "create." Finally, it will remain (3) to suggest how and to what effect according to Prov 8:22 Yahweh took possession of wisdom as "the first of his way(s)."

I. An Uncreated Wisdom

It has been a tendency of recent scholarship, following the lead of Gerhard von Rad, to regard the personified wisdom of Proverbs 8 and Job 28 as a concept developed in Israel to represent a rationale inherent in the world and (in Proverbs 8 at least) perceptible by man, the result of God's creative activity. This wisdom is perceived to be less an attribute of God than it is, in von Rad's words, a "divine principle bestowed upon the world at Creation."[1] Roland E. Murphy has seen in this conception implications for the reconciliation of the biblical idea of revelation with "the faith-possibilities for people who hear God through his created wisdom and have expressed this in extrabiblical literature."[2] Similarly, John J. Collins has proposed that this wisdom as divine gift beyond human control could serve as precedent for a natural theology by which universal human phenomena such as justice could elucidate an otherwise overtly "supernaturalist" theology such as Israel's.[3]

That wisdom is in these passages conceived as a world-principle or rationale seems to be clear enough. It is not equally clear that wisdom is seen as such precisely in virtue of its creation by God. Rather, it appears that texts like Job 28 and Proverbs 8 testify to postexilic Israel's contact with another wisdom concept which had not been tributary to or a development of its older wisdom tradition. Von Rad himself acknowledges the difficulty of tracing the postexilic concept from an origin in the older wisdom. The personification of Lady Wisdom has more than one apparent connection with one who was a goddess in other religion-based ways of thought. "Who finds me finds life" (Prov 8:35) sounds strange in an Israelite context if predicated of anyone but Yahweh; it could be predicated of wisdom, von Rad concludes, only because in Prov 8:22 wisdom "identifies itself with the thoughts which God cherished in creating the world." As for Job 28, he concedes that only an addition (by another hand) at the end of the poem has been able to bring it into the mainstream of conventional Israelite thinking. This addition, as it happens, represents an entirely different idea of wisdom from that of the rest of the poem. Marvin Pope has adequately summarized the several reasons for recognizing as extraneous this "conservative" ending to what he calls an "agnostic" presentation.[4]

---

[1]See the treatment of "theological wisdom" in von Rad's *Old Testament Theology* (New York: Harper & Row, 1962) I. 441-53.

[2]"What and Where is Wisdom?" *CurTM* 4 (1977) 283-87.

[3]"The Biblical Precedent for Natural Theology," *JAAR Supplement* 45 (1977) 35-67.

[4]*Job* (AB 15; Garden City: Doubleday, 1965) 183.

In Job 24 and Proverbs 8 Yahweh is not the creator of wisdom but its discoverer. The pre-existent wisdom which he discovers he then, in Proverbs at least, makes the rationale of his creation of and dealing with man and his world. It may have been the same wisdom-myth that originally lay behind Sirach 24; if so, Ben Sira (or his grandson) has much more thoroughly domesticated it by transforming the *persona* of wisdom into Torah, in the process identifying Yahweh with the Most High who was wisdom's creator. Not the same myth but with affinities to it is that of Deut 32: 8-14, where Elyon is represented as parceling out the peoples of mankind and allotting Israel to Yahweh,[5] a people whom Yahweh then adopts as his own. There is no creation here: Yahweh "finds" Israel ready-made, as in Ezekiel 16. Neither is there any wisdom motif in Deuteronomy. The common denominator of such passages is that something comes to Yahweh from without, something that either testifies to his greatness or permits him to manifest his greatness in subsequent deeds, or both. In Job 28 and Proverbs 8 wisdom is the something that comes in Yahweh.

The sense of Job 28, whether it is read conventionally or with the extensive rearrangement of verses suggested by the *NAB*, is essentially the same. Man, it is said, though capable of great craft and exploration, is totally powerless to attain the abode of wisdom. Indeed, wisdom eludes the grasp of any created thing. Even Death and Abaddon—obviously there is here more than an echo of the popular notion of the superior knowledge possessed by the dead—even these have only heard tell of wisdom; they have it not (v 22). God alone has found wisdom out and mastered the way to its place (v 23). Whether what follows, the divine control and ordering of the elements of the world (vv 24–26 conventionally; in the *NAB* reordering vv 24, 3, 9–11, 25–26), is to be regarded simply as the corollary or rather (as in Prov 8:22) the product of the divine comprehen-

---

[5]The interpretation of the passage is hardly affected whether or not the MT *benê yiśrā'ēl* is allowed to stand in v 8 or, as is preferred by most modern commentators and versions, something like *benê 'ēl[im]* is read following the witness of the LXX (and the OL) and Symmachus.

sion of wisdom is not clear, though commentators tend to take the latter for granted. In any case, Job 28 is not primarily concerned with the creative acts of God but rather with his knowledge; and wisdom is not celebrated as demiurge in however diluted a form but simply as that which God has got and man has not.

When we turn to Proverbs 8, we are immediately confronted with the problem that will engage our attention in part 2 of this paper, namely the meaning of the verb *qānâ*, which plays the crucial role in v 22 of denoting the relationship between Yahweh and wisdom. If, however, we were to be permitted provisionally to assume that *qānâ* retains here the same meaning that it possesses elsewhere in Proverbs, viz., "acquire," "get," "take," then there would be no difficulty in seeing how Proverbs 8 shares the perspective of Job 28. That is to say, wisdom appears here as a being existing before all created things, not a creature, therefore, but a prior to creation, which was attainable and attained by God, who then concurred with it in the creation and ordering of the universe. What is added to the portrayal of wisdom in Job 28 is the explicit note of wisdom's participation in the creation of man's world. There is also an all-important difference, of course. The wisdom that has thus entered into man's world is now as a consequence attainable by man, whereas in Job 28 it remains outside his grasp.

The difficulty facing the provisional assumption we have just made is the apparent consensus of present-day biblical versions and commentators that the *qānānî* of Prov 8:22 must be rendered "created me" or the equivalent. This rendering, to be sure, is ancient. The LXX has in this place *ektisen me*. Could *ektise* here be a misreading of *ektēsato*? There is, as far as I know, no textual evidence at all to encourage such a supposition. Nevertheless, some form of *ktasthai* is the almost invariable translation LXX makes of *qānâ* elsewhere in the Hebrew Bible, and, to show that the confusion was possible, it can be noted that LXX[B] reproduces *ktisthēsontai* for the *ktēthēsontai* of Jer 39(32):15. *Ktasthai* was the conventional translation of *qānâ* employed by the other ancient Greek versions as well. *Ektēsato*, "acquired," "took possession of," was what Aquila, Symmachus, and Theodotion read out of the Hebrew of Prov 8:22, beginning a translation tradition that was continued by the Latin Vulgate and the Syro-Hexaplar. It does seem, however, that LXX produced another translation tradition, in Prov 8:22 and elsewhere only in Gen 14:19, 22 — a passage to which we shall later return — rendering a form of *qānâ* with a form of *ktizein*. Thus, from the interrelated LXX, Syriac, and Targum to Proverbs[6] we have testimony to some such meaning[7] as "create" that was attached to the Hebrew *qāná* in at least one Jewish tradition of the late OT or early post-OT times. It is now proper to ask with what propriety the tradition had been formed.

II. Qānâ in Biblical Hebrew

By my count, *qānâ* occurs in all its forms in the Hebrew Bible a total of 82 times, twelve of these in Proverbs. Claus Westermann is probably representative of those present-day scholars who admit for the word a meaning like "create" in a few instances, those instances being, besides Gen 4:1 on which he is commenting[8] and Prov 8:22 which is under discussion here, the following: Gen 14:19–22 (the meaning here, according to Westermann, is "especially apparent"): Exod 15:16; Deut 32:6; Ps 78:54; and Ps 139:13.[9] The *NAB* might seem to add Ps 74:2

---

[6]On the relationship of these witnesses, see Martin McNamara in *NCE* 2. 433.

[7]"Some such." In view of the variety of verbs which *ktizein* translates in the LXX; cf. Werner Foerster in *TDNT* 3, 1066 and 1026. The Greek verb does translate *bārā* (not, however, in Genesis), but also *yāsad*, *yāṣar*, and *ʿāmad*, as well as *šākan*. The *Vorlage* of the Greek Ben Sira testifies to the same variety, adding *ḥālaq*, the hiphil of *yāṣāʾ*, etc.

[8]See *Genesis* (BKAT 1 5: Neukirchen/ Vluyn: Neukirchener, 1970) 392-97. Westermann as well as McKay and Whybray cited below offer useful bibliographies of the history of the philological research into the Hebrew *qānâ*.

[9]In an earlier contribution to this research, Paul Humbert counted 83 instances of *qānâ* in biblical Hebrew, with a maximum of nine possibly signifying "create." Eventually he retained in this sense only Gen 14:19, 22; Deut

to this list, having rendered *qānîtā* as "you built up." Here, however, the *NAB* seems to stand alone, and indeed the *gā'al* parallel to *qānâ* (as in Exod 15:13-16; Lev 25:23-30, 39-55; Ruth 4:4-10; and Jer 32:7-8) should indicate clearly enough that the metaphor involves acquisition and not building. Let us, then, consider the items in Westermann's list one by one.

Gen 4:1. After an extensive discussion of the question, Westermann concludes that Cassuto has probably come closest to the sense of Eve's *qānîtî* in this verse when he translates her words "I have created a man equally with the Lord."[10] The point can be argued, but I am willing to concede Cassuto's point that Eve is (arrogantly?) comparing her reproductive act with Yahweh's act of creation. Nevertheless, as surely no one will question, the choice of verb by which she has been allowed to voice her exultation in this verse has been made first and foremost in view of its capability as a popular etymology for the name Cain. The sound of the verb, in other words, has more determined its choice than its precise significance. (Cassuto's observation that the Arabic cognate of Cain, *qyn*, "smith," is a secondary development from a verb "fashion, mould, shape," is interesting, but seemingly irrelevant to the Hebrew.) Furthermore, as Paul Humbert has pointed out,[11] procreation is by no means the same thing as creation,[12] and the thesis that Eve has "created" Cain trifles with the role of Adam in a generative pro-

32:6; Ps 78:54 (still qualified with a question mark); Ps 139: 13; and Prov 8:22. See his "*Qānâ* en hébreu biblique," in Walter Baumbartner et al., eds., *Festschrift Alfred Bertholet* (Tübingen; Mohr. 1950) 251-66.

[10]See M. D. (Umberto) Cassuto, *From Adam to Noah* (Jerusalem: Magnes 1953) 132-35. I cite Cassuto's Hebrew rather than the English translation used by Westermann since the Hebrew seems to explain the presence of the *'t* rather than the *ke* which Westermann would have preferred to yield this sense. Cassuto's paraphrase is *"Yhwh yṣr 't h'yš hr'šwn, w'ny yṣrt 't h'yš hšny . . . 'ny 'wmdṭ yḥd 'tw bšwrt hywṣrym,"* which can be rendered: "Yahweh created the first man and I created the second man . . . I stand along with him in the order of creators."

[11]" '*Qānâ*,' " 259.

[12]Contrary to the confusion of the two ideas, which has resulted in the *NAB*'s translation of Prov 8:22, "The Lord begot me, the firstborn of his ways. . . ."

cess which was as perfectly understood by ancient peoples as it is by us. It is sufficient that the woman should have "got" or "acquired" the second man in order to vindicate her claim to a share with Yahweh in the continuation of creation.[13]

Gen 14:19, 22. Why is it "especially apparent" that "create" is the sense of the *qānâ* participle in these verses? I suspect, because it has seemed apparent both to ancient and modern translators of the OT habituated to its creational theology, that *qōnēh šāmayim wā'āreṣ* could mean nothing less than "creator of heaven and earth," not least when such a title was applied to deity.

It should be remembered, nevertheless, that "creator" was not the automatic response to *qōnēh* in all the ancient renderings of these texts. In Gen 14:22 Jerome turned the Hebrew into "possessorem," even though in v 19 his "qui creavit" simply echoes the first of LXX's two *hos ektisen*. It is quite possible that in this instance Jerome was following one of his recognizable patterns: even after he began to translate and comment on the Scripture according to the *hebraica veritas*, his residual attachment to the LXX frequently led him to compromise with his better judgment by retaining in some part at least its translational tradition.[14] His rendering of *qōneh* in v 22 would seem to imply that he understood the word to have been derived from *qānâ* in its conventional sense, i.e., "one who has taken possession." One who has taken possession of heaven and earth is, to use an equivalent term, their "lord" or "master." And that is precisely the word that appears in 1 QapGen to translate the *qōnēh* of Gen 14:19, 22. Evidently the Genesis Apocryphon was manifesting no *Tendenz* in this matter but simply intended to turn a Hebrew expression into current Aramaic.[15]

---

[13]Despite his predeliction for Cassuto's interpretation, Westermann ends by translating Gen 4:1 as "Ich habe einen Mann gewonnen, mit Jahwe!"

[14]Cf. Jay Braverman, *Jerome's Commentary on Daniel: A Study of Comparative Jewish and Christian Interpretation of the Hebrew Bible* (CBQMS 7; Washington: Catholic Biblical Association, 1978) 31-34.

[15]See Nahman Avigad and Yigael Yadin, *A Genesis Apocryphon* (Jerusalem: Magnes, 1956), col. 22, line 16 and 21: *mrh šmy' w'ar'* is the reading.

An excursus. It is necessary at this point, for several reasons, to consider the evidence adduced from cognate Semitic languages that supposedly bears on this question, particularly as regards the association of √*qnh/y/w* with deity.

(1) In one Ugaritic text,[16] Asherah is titled *qnyt ilm,* which has been taken to mean "creatress of the gods."[17] Actually, there is nowhere in this text a context to elucidate the title, which might just as easily be translated "mistress of the gods" or the like (see below).

(2) It has been suggested that behind biblical Hebrew *qānâ* lie two verbal roots, the one **qnw > qnh* = "acquire," by far the more common in the OT, the other **qny > qnh* = "create." This hypothesis has been advanced by Humbert (following Heinrich Zimmern), to account for a *qānâ,* "create," in biblical Hebrew as the "relic of mythological and cultic language, Canaanite and pre-Israelite, attested in the Ras Shamra texts, a rare word with mythological flavor."[18] Without necessarily implying the existence of two roots, Ugaritic specialists do customarily assign a meaning "create" to some occurrences of the verb *qny* in that language.[19] As far as I can determine, however, the evidence adduced cannot sustain the weight of the conclusion. In some of the context cited such a meaning is conceivable, never certain; in others it appears to be definitely ruled out.[20]

---

[16]In 51:I:23; III:26,30,35; IV:32 (Gordon's sigla).

[17]So Cyrus H. Gordon, *Ugaritic Textbook* (AnOr 38; Rome: PBI, 1967), Glossary no. 2249. Von Rad in his *Theology,* 142, cites this among other Ugaritic texts to propose a "Canaanite origin" for the Hebrew *qānâ* = "create."

[18]" '*Qānâ*' " 262, 266.

[19]So Gordon, as already cited in nn. 16-17.

[20]The instances follow. (1) 76: III:5-7: *wy'ny[.]aliyn[.b'l.]/ lm.kqnyn. 'l[ ] / kdrd.dyknn[.* This is translated by Gordon in *Ugarit and Minoan Crete*(New York: Norton, 1966) 89: "And Aliyan Baal declares:/ 'Why, like – upon/ Like – which he causes to be' "; the same translation is in his earlier *Ugaritic Literature* (Scripta PBI 89; Rome: Pontifical Biblical Institute, 1949) 50. In the second edition of *Canaanite Myths and Legends* (Edinburgh: T. & T. Clark, 1978) 133, J. C. L. Gibson does not translate the text (10 iii 5-7, according to the Herdner sigla), but in his glossary he offers "creator" as the

(3) Also, though with a question mark, a √*qny,* "create," has been proposed in Phoenician, on the basis of the Karatepe portal inscription (*'lqn'rṣ* again) and the little Kilamuwa inscription.[21] The former text, however, one of the earlier analysts already had agreed should be read "El the lord of the earth,"[22] and the latter, which is not in Phoenician but in a local Aramaic dialect, yields no conclusive meaning of any kind.[23]

Exod 15:16. As has already been pointed out parenthetically, Exod 15:16 is one of those passages in which the meaning of *qānâ* is explicated by a parallel *gā'al.* The *'am-zû qānîtā* of v 16 succeeds the *'am-zû gā' āltā* of v 13. A redeemed people is a purchased people.

Deut 32:6. The presence of *'āśâ* and the polel *kûn* in this verse has persuaded more than one translator and commentator

meaning of the *qny* there (the full word he transliterates *kqnym*). (2) 1 Aqht:219-221: *š̆t.byn.yš̆t.ila. ilš̆*[ ]*il / dyqny.ddm.yd*[.]*mhṣt.a* [qh]*t.ǵ / zr.* Gordon (*Ugarit and Minoan Crete,* 139; *Ugaritic Literature,* 101): ". . . of the wine *our* god Ilš̆ drinks[ ] / Who created the abode. / The hand that smote the Hero A[qha]t . . . "; Gibson (p. 121-22): "May our god drink of the wine, El[ ], the god who owns (these) mountains! . . . "(3) 2 Aqht: VI:41: *tṣhq.'nt.wblb.tqny* [ ]. Both Gordon and Gibson recognize that Anath laughs, but whereas Gordon leaves the *tqny* [ ] untranslated, Gibson (p. 109) will have it that "in her heart she forged [(a plot)]." (4) Krt: 57 has an isolated *aqny* which Gordon (*Ugarit and Minoan Crete,* 102; *Ugaritic Literature,* 68) renders: "[ ] I shall obtain"; so also Gibson (p. 83), supplying in the text and referring to Gen 4:1: "[ ]sons I would get." (5) In 321:I:21 there occurs a proper name *qnmlk.* There is no way of knowing its meaning. This is, as far as I know, the extent of the Ugaritic evidence. I do not believe that it is persuasive in favor of a *qny,* "create." It may be noted that Gibson takes the *qnyt* of 51:I:23, etc., to mean either "creatress" or "mistress."

[21]So *DISO.* 260.

[22]Cf. Roger T.O'Callaghan, "An Approach to Some Religious Problems of Karatepe," *ArOr* 18(1950)354-65. O'Callaghan pointed out that from the time of Hammurabi, Enlil was known by the title *be-el š̆amē u irṣiti.*

[23]Cf. Paul-Eugène Dion, O.P. *La Langue de Ya'udi* (Waterloo, Ontario: Corporation for the Publication of Academic Studies in Canada, 1974) 26. Divided, the pertinent words are *smr z qn klmw,* which Dion renders: "Timon(?) qu'a orné(?) Kilamuwa."

that *qānâ* here must possess a similar significance. Such was not, however, the persuasion of the ancient versions, which routinely translated *qānâ* as "took possession," even though they *did* ascribe the meaning "create" to *kûn*. Actually, a better key to the precise connotation of *qānâ* in this context might be sought in the *tigmelû* which immediately precedes it. Israel is rebuked for its failure to "repay," to "requite," to "deal reciprocally" with the Lord[24] in respect to what he has done for his people. What the Lord had done for Israel has been expressed more than once in OT tradition by the commercial metaphor "purchase" or "acquire." It is in this same hymn that Yahweh receives Israel as an inheritance from Elyon (vv8-9), that he "finds" Israel in the desert and proceeds to become its guide, leader, protector, its *mitgehender Gott* (v 10 and following). This is the present sense, I suggest, in which Yahweh is the God who "made" Israel (v 15).

Ps 78:54. Most contemporary versions and commentators do not seem to share Westermann's discovery of a creation motif in this passage, regarding the mountain to which Yahweh brought Israel, first having exercised over it the power of his "right hand." "Won," "conquered," or the like, usually renders *qānâ* here, possibly improving upon but still remaining within the same line of thought with the "purchased" of the Authorised Version and the equivalent in the LXX and Jerome's *iuxta hebraeos*. In fact, the explicative parallel to *har-zeh* in this verse is *gebûl qodšô*, and there can be no doubt that the primary idea asserted by *gebûl* is ownership, acquired proprietary right.[25] The thought of the psalmist is that of the poet who authored Exod 15:16-17, namely that the people whom Yahweh acquired and made his own he has firmly established in a place equally his own and special to him. The context is, in other words, soteriological and not ctisiological.

Ps 139:13. This is possibly the most difficult passage of all standing in the way of one who refuses to acknowledge a *qānâ* = "create" in the Hebrew Bible. R. N. Whybray doubtless

[24]See K. Seybold in *TWAT* 2 (*TDOT* 3), *s.v. gāmal*.
[25]See O. Ottosson in *TWAT* 1 (*TDOT* 2), *s.v. gebûl*.

speaks for a legion of exegetes when he finds the sense "form," create," the only possible one here, since "it is meaningless for the Psalmist to say that Yahweh 'acquired' or 'possessed' his kidneys."[26] Certainly it would be meaningless, were we dealing with the psalmist's kidneys in the rather literal way I think he did not intend. It would be equally meaningless, I assume, unless we admitted the presence of unusual and exotic conceits in the Bible to exhort someone to gird up the loins of his understanding (1 Pet 1:13). (This passage, albeit from the NT, someone once called a touchstone for the ability to enter into OT thought.) The "kidneys," often paralleled with "heart" (singular or plural) in the Hebrew Bible, very frequently signify the innermost being of a person, particularly his intellectual and emotive life.[27] The ancient versions, therefore, found no difficulty whatever in translating the *qānâ* of this verse as "acquired." Over a millennium and a half ago Theodore of Mopsuestia was equally capable of digesting a biblical "you have possessed my kidneys" by paraphrasing it: "you have understood my thoughts."[28]

The parallel to *kilyōtāy* in this verse is the suffixed personal pronoun in the verb *tesukkēnî*. The verb *skk*, which appears to be common Semitic (it occurs in Ugaritic, certainly, in the same sense that it conventionally has in biblical Hebrew), deserves attention in its own right, which we cannot presently give it. In the twenty-five or so instances of its occurrence in the

---

[26]See his *Wisdom in Proverbs* (SBT 45; London: SCM, 1965) 100-101, esp. n. 5.

[27]Just as *nepeš*, which eventually came to be synonymous with the person, originally meant simply the gullet, i.e., the place where eating, drinking, breathing, life itself, therefore, went on. Cf. Hans Walter Wolff, *Anthropology of the Old Testament* (Philadelphia: Fortress, 1974) 14.

[28]Theodore's commentary on the Psalms has been preserved only in a Latin translation by his contemporary Julian of Eclanum, the latter part of which is best described as an *epitome*. Thus the *quia tu possedisti renes meos* and *intellegisti cogitationes meas* which I translate above. Cf. CCr Series Latina LXXXVIIIA: *Theodori Mopsuesteni Expositionis in Psalmos Iuliano Aeclanensi interprete in Latinum versae quae supersunt*, auxiliante Maria Josepha d'Hout edidit Lucas De Coninck (Turnhout: Brepols, 1977) 283.

Hebrew Bible it seems to convey the invariable meaning of "cover," "protect," "veil," "shield," etc.[29] In this one particular instance where it parallels *qānîtā* in Ps 139:13, various Hebrew lexica have assigned to it a meaning "knit" or "weave." Possibly the development has been: Since *qānâ* = "create," and *skk* is in parallel, then in this case *skk* must somehow indicate the process by which a protective fabric has been brought about. But if, on the other hand, *qānâ* is taken to mean what it ordinarily means in biblical Hebrew, there is no need for this hypothetical philology involving *skk*. The Lord who has *known* the psalmist's in most thought has also been his *overseer* from the time of his conception.

If one looks dispassionately at this psalm, is not this in fact the meaning that we should ascribe to v 13? Throughout the poet continuously celebrates the omniscience of his God, his all-presence in time and place precisely as it affects him who would wish this protective knowledge and solicitude which began at his very conception to continue and prevail now in his moment of distress. There is, of course, no reason that he should not have called upon Yahweh as his creator in v 13; but it appears that he did not. Rather, he appealed to an identification of interests taken on the divine initiative that he would have continue.

Prov 8:22. I conclude that, as there is no compelling evidence from other OT texts to indicate a Hebrew *qānâ* = "created," neither should the verb in Prov 8: 22 be translated in this fashion, quite apart from the positive contextual arguments against any such reading. I cannot agree with Whybray's analysis of this passage as an assertion merely of wisdom's priority in the order of creation with no real distinction drawn between the manner

---

[29]Job 10:11 forms a special problem. Cf. C. J. Ball, *The Book of Job* (Oxford: Clarendon, 1922) 194 and Paul Dhorme,, *Le Livre de Job* (EBib; Paris: Gabalda, 1926) 136. If the MT *teśōkekēnî,* var. *tesōkekēnî,* represents a polel of √*skk* (rather than, let us say, a poel of √*śwk/swk*), certainly the meaning is not ineluctably "knit" or "weave" as many modern commentators seem to take for granted, often justifying their reading by an appeal to the supposed meaning of the supposedly same verb in Ps 139:13!

of its formation and the formation of other things.[30] To the contrary, it seems to me that here wisdom is said to have pre-existed the created order and therefore to be outside it, though in some fashion it subsequently became instrumental in the production of the created order. The fact that such a picture of wisdom is not immediately reconcilable with the more conventional one of wisdom as God's gift to man (Prov 2:6, etc.) perhaps accounts for the reluctance of scholars to admit the normal meaning of *qānâ* = "acquired" in this verse. William McKane, for example, after a thoughtful weighing of the evidence pro and con, concludes that "although this is a common meaning of the word, it is not apposite here, for we expect some indication of how Wisdom originated and not the bald statement that Yahweh acquired her."[31] We expect this, however, only if we assume that the figure of wisdom has been completely digested by and homogenized in OT thought, which I suggest that it has not been. It is better to agree with Franz Hesse who, after his examination of the kindred portrayal of wisdom in Job 28, concludes that we have to deal with an "un-Israelite," i.e., not conventionally Israelite figurement of wisdom that deserves study in its own right and ought not to be easily assimilated to other more familiar concepts.[32]

Neither do I believe that such an assimilation can be made by turning Yahweh's "possession" of wisdom into one of his attributes, as R. B. Y. Scott would have it.[33] Scott finds "possess" an entirely suitable meaning for *qānâ* in Prov 8:22, in keeping with the meaning of the same verb in 1:5 and 4:5, but in the acceptation that "Yahweh 'possessed' wisdom as an attribute or faculty integral to his being from the very first." Scott is en-

---

[30]*Wisdom in Proverbs*, 101.

[31]*Proverbs: A New Approach* (Philadelphia: Westminster, 1970) 351-58, see p. 352.

[32]See *Hiob* (Zürcher Kommentare AT 14; Zürich: Theologischer Verlag, 1978) 158. Hesse recognizes the problem without offering a solution: "Woher diese besondere, im Grunde sehr unisraelitische Auffassung von Weisheit letzlich stammt, hat sich noch nicht eindeutig klären lassen."

[33]*Proverbs. Ecclesiastes* (AB 18; Garden City: Doubleday, 1965) 71-72.

tirely correct in seeing that Prov 8:22 does not speak of wisdom
as Yahweh's creation and that, in fact, it considers wisdom to
be something prior to creation. When, however, "possessed"
becomes equated with "was possessed of," or something like
it, I fear we are engaged more with the ambiguities of English
syntax than with Hebrew grammar. In Hebrew *qānâ* is not a
stative but a very transitive verb. In the qal perfect it does not
mean "was in possession of" but rather "took possession of."
Biblical Hebrew has ways of attributing to someone an habitual
trait or property (the preposition *le* with *hāyâ*, which *is* a stative
verb, would be one of those ways), but such a thing has not
been done in Prov 8:22 by the use of *qānâ* in the qal perfect,
nor in the aorists and the perfects, respectively, that have been
employed to translate the verb in the rendering of the ancient
versions. The acquisition (here imperfect) of the *taḥbullôt* of
which Prov 1:5 speaks is obviously inceptive, and the admoni-
tion to "get" wisdom in 4:5, 7 obviously demands the equivalent
of an aorist imperative. Here we have no invitation to "be wise"
in the sense of developing or exercising a latent or innate talent,
but rather to acquire a quality that one does not yet have.

III. Wisdom and Creation

If, then, according to Prov 8:22 Yahweh once took possession of wisdom before he began to create, what role did wisdom
play in this subsequent creation: in what sense is wisdom called
the *rē'šît darkô*? Certainly not the "firstborn" of his works
(*NAB*) or even the "beginning" or "first" of his works (*RSV,
NEB,* etc.), even though the *derek* in question does undoubtedly
refer to Yahweh's creative "way," his *modus operandi.* (With
the ancient versions the plural of *derek* may very likely be read
in place of the singular, though there is no cause to look for
some forgotten "Canaanite" sense that has been obscured by the
MT.) I believe that Jean de Savignac was altogether on the right
track when, a number of years ago, he suggested as the meaning of *rē'šît* in this context "the principle" of Yahweh's cre-

ative activity,[34] or, as I might more concretely phrase it, "the model" of Yahweh's ways or works. There is nothing particularly abstruse about the discovery of such a sense for the word in its present context.[35] The inherent meaning of *rē'šît*, that which makes it so appropriate to mean "first fruits" in a cultic acceptation, is that which marks it as the logical or chronological prior, qualitatively the most important or the best of a series that will presumably follow.[36] The exact manner in which this first or prior is related to what follows and therefore exact determination of what his first or prior should be called, depends on what is made of it in the specific context in which it is found. Thus, the *rē'šît* (LXX *archē*, Vg *principium*) of Nimrod's kingdom (Gen 10:10) was Babel, Erech, and Accad, the cities of Shinar first in the series of those which would eventually constitute his empire. Lachish was the *rē'šît* (LXX *archēgos*, Vg *principium*) of the sin of Zion (Mic 1:13), the first (in time and importance) of Judah's cities to experience the Assyrian devastation, the exemplar and model of the consequence of Jerusalem's sin soon to be visited upon it. The *rē'šît* of wisdom is: get (*qeneh*) wisdom! (Prov 4:7): wisdom is its own *rē'šît*. I say merely that the Hebrew *rē'šît* seems to cover about the same semantic spread as the Latin *principium*; and there is no reason it should not, since the words seem to correspond with a common mode of human thought. If so, and then if the *qānâ* of Prov 8:22 really meant something like "created" or "begot," the *rē'šît* of this verse would have to be a "first fruits" or "firstborn" or the like. But if, on the other hand, *qānâ* means what I think it means here, namely that Yahweh took possession of a wisdom that he then proceeded to utilize in his work of creation (whatever the meaning of the further *'mwn* personi-

---

[34]Note sur le sens du verset VIII dans Proverbes," *VT* 4 (1954) 429-32.

[35]DeSavignac appeals to Philo. *De confusione linguarum* 63 and Eccl 6:10. Philo, allegorizing out of Zech 6:10, related the *anatolē* of that verse to the *prōtogonos* (the term he preferred to the LXX *prōtotokos*) which *mimoumenos tas tou patros 'odous, pros paradeigmata archetypa ekeinou ta eidē*. Cf. J. G. Kahn, *Oeuvres de Philon d'Alexandrie* 13 (Paris: Cerf, 1963) 75-77.

[36]See J. de Fraine. "Prémices," in *DBSup* 8, 447-48.

fication of v 30), then we shall have to translate the word as "principle" or "model" or the like.

I do not propose to speculate further about the provenance of this wisdom concept or about its assimilation to the other wisdom concepts of Israel, and certainly not about its use (or misuse) in the later Jewish quasi-deification of a pre-existent wisdom = Torah or the christology of Col 1:15-20.[37] In sum, we are here presented with the concept of a pre-existent wisdom or at least of a wisdom not of the ordinary created order, in Proverbs 8 personified and in Job 28 not obviously so, in Proverbs 8 utilized in creation and in Job 28 not obviously so; in either case a wisdom which is not a native attribute of God but a reality accessible to him alone and acquired by him. It is sufficient to recognize that in these passages occurs a distinct wisdom concept that ought not be confused with other wisdom concepts of the OT.

There has grown up a considerable literature which seeks to derive this wisdom figure, particularly as it appears in Proverbs, from that of the Egyptian goddess Maat. Lately, however, scholarly opinion seems to have adopted a fairly negative response to this hypothesis. McKane, in particular, is unsympathetic to the idea, since his own study of Proverbs has led him to the conclusion that Canaanite rather than Egyptian mythology underlies its ventures into wisdom personification.[38] A. Barucq, for his part, after deploring the fact that we really do not know enough about Canaanite wisdom to permit us to draw large conclusions, properly warns against trying to reduce the various figures of wisdom in Proverbs to a single one.[39] Perhaps Whybray has made the most intelligent contribution to this discussion when he pointed out that while the deification of *maat* was fairly inevitable in Egyptian polytheism, such

---

[37]Cf. Franz Zeilinger, *Der Erstgeborene der Schöpfung: Untersuchungen zur Formalstruktur und Theologie des Kolosserbriefes* (Vienna: Herder, 1974) 128 (n. 90 with references), 196.

[38]*Proverbs*, 344, 269-70.

[39]"Proverbes," in *DBSup* 8, 1421 and 1464.

a development would have been much more difficult for the sages of Israel grappling with the same concept.[40]

What Egypt insisted on under the term *maat* was the autonomy of order, justice, reason in the universe. Must we imagine that Israel was less capable of such an idea? Even if, to assert it, it was necessary to figure wisdom as much in control of God as controlled by him? (Centuries later, Anselm of Canterbury would have to do something similar with "justice" in order to explain *cur deus homo*.) If this was the intention of those who accepted this wisdom concept into the religious literature of Israel, the insight should be valued in its own right, however exceptional it may be in the OT, and not too easily be assimilated to the truism that God created the universe wisely.[41]

---

[40]*Wisdom in Proverbs*, 54-56. On pp. 83-87 he also disposes of the Canaanite goddess construct proposed by W. F. Albright.

[41]Eduard Nielsen, "Homo faber—sapientia dei," *SEA* 41/42 (1976-77) 157-65, makes the further interesting point, assuming that both Job 28 and Proverbs 8 agree that wisdom is the principle of existence, both passages appear in appropriate contexts, since in Job wisdom is considered to be inaccessible to man whereas in Proverbs it is accessible. He then compares (without suggesting any dependency) Job 28 with the Yahwistic and Proverbs 8 with the Priestly stories of creation.

12. Postexilic Prayer and Hope

1 Lord, you have been a refuge for us in every generation.

2 Before the mountains were yet born, when earth and land had not been birthed,[1] and from everlasting to everlasting, you are.

3 Turn not men back to dust, nor say,[2] "Return, children of man."

4 For a thousand years in your eyes are like yesterday when it has passed, or a watch in the night.

5 When you cut them off in sleep, by morning they become like drying grass:[3]

[1]Accepting the *polal* rather than the *polel* of the verb as presupposed by the ancient versions.

[2]With LXX and Vg, reading *'al* in place of *'el* in vs. 2, and construing the verbs as jussives.

[3]This conjectural translation presupposes: (a) a temporal or conditional particle ellipsed; (b) there is a root *zrm* having the sense "shorten"; (c) the final verb is equivalent to an adjective. Cf. the LXX, also Charles F. Jean-Jacob Hoftijzer, *Dictionnaire des inscriptions sémitiques de l'ouest* (Leiden: Brill, 1965) s.v. *'zr*, and M. Dahood, *Psalms II* (*AB* 17; New York: Double-day, 1968) 324.

6 in the morning it sprouts, then begins to dry, by evening it has faded and withered.

7 Truly, we are consumed by your anger, and by your wrath we are overcome.

8 You have set out iniquities before you, our hidden sins are brought to light in your sight.

9 Truly, all our days have passed away in your wrath, we have ended our years like a sigh.

10 The span of our lifetime is seventy years, or, if we have vigor, eighty years, but all they can boast of is toil and trouble, for quickly all is gone and flown away.

11 Who can understand the power of your anger, and who can perceive the measure of your wrath?[4]

12 So teach us to number our days that we may gain a heart of wisdom.

13 Come back to us, Yahweh! How long? and have pity on your servants.

14 Fill us at morning with your mercy that we may be merry and rejoice all our days.

15 Make us rejoice as many days as you have grieved us, as many years as we have seen distress.

16 May your works be made manifest to your servants, and your majesty unto their children.

17 Be upon us the grace of the Lord our God, and establish[5] the work of our hands!

So prayed a pious Jew in postexilic Palestine,[6] speaking in

---

[4]Reading with many scholars *my r'h tk* in place of MT's *wkyr'tk*.

[5]Omitting *'lynw wm 'sh ydynw kwnnhw* in vs. 17b as an obvious dittography.

[6]Cf. H.-J. Kraus, *Psalmen II* (*BKAT* 15/2; Neukirchen: Erziehungsverein, 1960) 627-633. Dahood, 322, represents the minority in characterizing the psalm as pre-exilic (ninth century!), largely because of its "resemblances with" Dt 32 and the J story in Gen 2-3.

the name of his people then undergoing an unspecified national disaster, in the words, or in words very like them, which we now read in our Ps 90. It is a beautiful prayer, perfectly worthy of Israel's most ancient traditions; yet it departs from these traditions in interesting ways. Artur Weiser has correctly put it in his commentary[7] that in this psalm "the worshipper finds his firm support in the faith of his forefathers." Nevertheless, it is a faith that has expressed itself in somewhat unusual terms — unusual, that is, when this psalm is compared with various others which, like it, are national laments, e.g. Pss 44, 60, 74, 79, 80, 83, 106, or 137. These latter psalms, some of them early and some late relative to the exilic period, all bear to a greater or less degree traces of what Manfred Weippert has recently[8] defined as the twin conviction that determined Israel's historical consciousness, namely, its sense of non-autochthony in the land, and of the land as the gift of its Lord. Ps 90 does not bear these traces. It has been formed, rather, within the tradition of a developing wisdom speculation.

We do not intend to suggest, of course, that wisdom was merely a post-exilic development in Israel, or that it was in any way out of keeping with all that was authentic in biblical religion. Recent studies which have signalled a renewed interest in Israelite wisdom have also tended to stress its right to be included within the mainstream, or one of the mainstreams, of biblical thinking.[9] What we do intend to suggest, however, is that in the postexilic age the wisdom which had begun as a cohabitant of Israelite religion or which, indeed, had earlier or later been identified with it in some part, now undertook to guide its further development.[10] This evolution was due, one may assume,

[7] *The Psalms* (tr. Herbert Hartwell; Philadelphia: Westminster, 1962) 596.

[8] "Fragen des israelitischen Geschichtsbewusstseins," *VT* 23 (1973) 415-442.

[9] Cf. R. E. Murphy, "Assumptions and Problems in Old Testament Wisdom Research," *CBQ* 29 (1967) 407-418.

[10] In the view of Gerhard von Rad, Israelite wisdom was pietistic from the beginning and already had in it in germ the characteristics associated with its later manifestations: see his "Josephsgeschichte und ältere Chokma," *VTS* 1 (1953) 120-127 = 5 *Gesammelte Studien zum Alten Testament* (Munich:

to the gradual disappearance of prophecy which had been the most effective means of stimulating Israelite growth, and therefore to the accession of *ḥokmâ* to assume the role of *rûaḥ*.[11] The process of development into which wisdom had come provoked it not only to criticize the rest of Israel's religion in relation to the changing world that now confronted it, it also persuaded wisdom to criticize itself, to recognize its own inadequacies relative to its need to reply to what was now demanded of it. This process was, in fact, the beginning of theology as we have come to understand the term, that is, a criticism and rationalization of the *data*, the *tradita*: the *dābār* revealed in word and history now evaluated in its confrontation with the *ʿēṣâ* revealed by the mind of man. The confrontation resulted in numerous responses, some valuable and some less so, and various antinomies, one of which is Ps 90, and others of which are to be found in Job, in Qoh, in the first chapters of Prov, and in Sir, to name only the foremost works of wisdom that we know emerged in the Palestine of the postexilic age.

Let us consider, in order to see better what we mean, the development of Ps 90. The psalmist begins by making his only — and passing — reference to Israel's historical experience: "You have been a refuge for us in every generation." Immediately, however, his attention is focused instead on the un- or prehistorical, on the transcendent realm of an eternal God who dwells beyond the generation of the earth and the world of man. It is not precisely true to say with Kraus[12] that the psalmist's notion of cosmic origins contradicts that of the Gen creation

Kaiser Verlag, 1957) I, 415-439. In our opinion, W. McKane, *Prophets and Wise Men (SBT* 44; Naperville: Allenson, 1965) has made a better assessment in distinguishing as "older" an earlier humanistic or secular (but not thereby irreligious) wisdom which later yielded, still in pre-exilic times and under the influence of the great prophets, to a wisdom that incorporated Torah into its teaching. What in our view is the last stage of the development we indicate above in the text.

[11]Cf. P. van Imschoot, "Sagesse et esprit dans l'Ancien Testament," *RB* 47 (1938) 23-49.

[12]Kraus, 630.

stories, since even the P author of Gen has not bothered to dispense entirely with the myth of the generative power of earth and sea (Gen 1:20,24); but it is true that in this respect his imagery — and, indeed, the viewpoint of the entire psalm — has closer affinities with the poetry of Job 38:8 than with anything else in the Bible.[13] But in any case, it is not with man as creature in relation to his Creator that the psalmist is concerned, but with man the transitory over against the Eternal. The undetermined national disaster into which Israel had fallen provoked him to reflect on human frailty in general, on man who is bound to a limited lifespan and ever subject to the base elements from which he sprang. The "motivation" which the psalmist proffers to the Almighty to urge him to spare his people is not, as in other psalms of impetration, a reminder of the great divine acts that formed the people, the merciful election that established a precedent for continuing mercy; it is, rather, an appeal to the One who need not count his years to show generosity to those whose end is always in sight, whose little play on life's stage extends at best to the duration of a sigh.

What is the best hope that the psalmist can hold out to an afflicted people, the salvation by which they can adjust to, if not solve, the riddle of life? It is entirely predictable, and entirely within the wisdom tradition. Give us wisdom: wisdom which, if it does not give understanding, at least makes us understand why we do not understand. Wisdom cannot really bring man to know God and his designs, but it can bring man to know himself in relation to God, to know that he is a sinful creature and that his lot is weakness. His destiny is to live briefly, and his best hope is to live wisely, that his days of joy may be at least the equal of his days of pain.[14] Such is the grace that God can bestow.

---

[13]Be it noted, however, that Job 38:8 which has the sea "burst forth from the womb" is also like the passages in Gen 1, set in the context of the workings of a Creator God (cf. vs. 4).

[14]Is there a connexion between the wisdom tradition of the psalm and the folk-story of Job 42:16, according to which the protagonist, in recompense for "all the evil which the Lord had brought upon him" (vs. 11), received a twofold recompense, including twice the seventy years of Ps 90:10?

And so, the lesson of wisdom in Ps 90 is that the recognition of his own transitoriness man achieves a meaningful existence in the presence of his God. God is all that man is not: the eternal and the holy. Man is fleeting, and a sinner. To recognize these oppositions is to find true wisdom, to be saved by wisdom, for paradoxically the wisdom that saves is that which acknowledges that man cannot be wise, cannot really penetrate into that cosmic, divine wisdom by which all came to be. Thus our psalmist would doubtless have concurred with the author of Job 28:28 that "the fear of the Lord, *that* is wisdom, and to refrain from evil is understanding."[15]

If this is one view that wisdom could bestow on man to inspire his prayers, it was not the only one, as we have already indicated. Let us now turn to another wisdom-inspired prayer, doubtless from a later time and certainly from another place, and written in another language, but no less imbued with the authentic spirit of Israelite faith. In the book we know as the Wisdom of Solomon, an Alexandrian Jew of the diaspora, sometime in the first century before our era, included this prayer as part of what was essentially a work of consolation for a people again afflicted, this time by religious persecution.

> 9:1 God of the Fathers and Lord of mercy, who made all things by your word,
>
> 2 and by your wisdom formed man that he might rule over all the creatures made by you
>
> 3 and order the world in piety and righteousness, and in uprightness of soul pronounce judgment:

---

[15]On the role of Job 28 in the transformation of the Job-legend into the final wisdom message of the *Deus absconditus*, see the conclusions of H.-P. Müller, *Hiob und seine Freunde* (Zürich: EVZ-Verlag, 1970) 55-59. An alternative view of the relation of the passage to the rest of the book is available in M. H. Pope, *Job* (*AB* 15: New York: Doubleday, 1965) xviii and 177; but all would doubtless agree that vs. 28 means that "the divine wisdom by which God created and regulates the cosmos is beyond man's grasp and ken. For man there is only the practical wisdom of piety" (Pope, 183).

4 give me the wisdom that sits by your throne,[16] and do
not cast me out from among your servants.

5 For I am your slave and the son of your handmaid, a
weak and short-lived man, and deficient in the understanding of judgment and laws.

6 For even if anyone is expert among the sons of men,
if he lacks the wisdom that comes from you he will be
counted as nothing.

[The prayer continues in a paraphrase of Solomon's prayer in
1 Kgs 3:6-9, then concludes:]

13 For what man can know the counsel of God, or who can
discern what the Lord wills?

14 For the thoughts of men are worthless, and precarious
are our devices;

15 for a perishable body weights down the soul, and the
earthly tent burdens the inventive mind.

16 And we can hardly guess what is on the earth, and what
lies in our hands we discover only with toil: who, then,
has traced out what is in heaven?

17 Who has ever learnt your counsel, unless you gave him
wisdom, and sent your holy spirit from on high?

18 And thus the paths of those on earth were set straight,
and men were taught what pleases you, and by wisdom
they were saved.

[In the same spirit, the author's prayer continues later on:]

15:1 But you, our God, are kind and true, longsuffering and
ruling all things in mercy.

2 For even if we sin, we are yours, knowing your power,
yet we will not sin, knowing that we are accounted
yours.

[16]In the Greek, plural with a singular meaning.

3   For to come to know you means complete righteousness, and to understand your power is the root of
immortality.

The initial resemblances between the two passages are obvious. Like the Palestinian psalmist, the Alexandrian poet was
profoundly conscious of the gulf that separated him and all
human beings from the God enthroned on high. He did dwell
upon and paraphrase the creation tradition, especially, it would
appear, the P story of Gen; but again, the theme of creation
he invoked mainly to underscore human inadequacy. Of his own,
and without the special gift of God's wisdom not given in the
act of creation, man was not capable of fulfilling the role in
which the Creator had cast him. So much did the author prize
wisdom, he was willing to say, in effect, that God was unable
to carry through on what he had first conceived in the creation
of man, that man was subject to a fault in basic design from
the beginning.[17] It is to be noted, too, that, as before, what man
should strive to become if he would live as a man—and what
only wisdom can teach him to do—was put in ethical terms,
or rather, terms of piety. There is a touch of the Greek dichotomy of body and soul that would be quite foreign to the Palestinian author of Ps 90, but in his own way the author of Wis also
acknowledged a *Deus absconditus* before whom he must stand

---

[17]This is not really a new or revolutionary idea in biblical religion. The
J story of man's beginnings acknowledges that God repented of having created
man (Gen 6:5f.) after witnessing a really unexplained series of human fail-
ings subsequent to the creation; and even after the "corrective" episode of
the flood, God more or less admits his defeat and his resignation to live with
the man whom he cannot improve (Gen 8:21). The P author, on his part,
describes a creation over which God pronounces a sevenfold "good" (Gen
1:4,10,12,18,21,25,31), yet mysteriously, with only the intervention of the
somewhat ambiguous ch. 5 of Genesis, we are apprised with the unexplained
fact that the whole earth—all creation, and not only man—had become corrupt and evil (Gen 6:11). Where God went wrong is never a question that
is explicitly faced, but it seems to be taken for granted. The only extraordinary thing is that it should have been a live question in the more sensitive
theology of the later postexilic period.

mute and inefficacious, naked and a sinner, whose lot it is to
suffer frustration and suffering.

Yet there are two significant differences between the wisdom
of Ps 90 and the wisdom that has instructed the pseudo-Solomon.
The first is an easy transition, for it involves a development
that had also occurred to Palestinian Jews in the postexilic period, even if not to the author of Ps 90, namely, the identification of divine wisdom with Torah.[18] Man need not only acknowledge his need for enlightenment into what is the right and proper
way; he does in fact know this way when he possesses that
wisdom which has taken up residence in Israel at the command
of God, namely, the law of the covenant (cf. Sir, ch. 24). There
is nothing hazy or abstract, then, in this author's mind as regards
the nature of the divine wisdom: it is tangible and concrete,
counsellor, guide, mistress, or what the author of Ps 119:105
called a lamp to his feet and a light to his path.

The other difference between Ps 90 and Wis is, quite obviously, more arresting. For now we are told that yet in another
way, or at least in the specification of a way not previously
manifest, is wisdom man's salvation. As the pseudo-Solomon
exposes his thought: the knowledge of God which is the way
of righteousness is in turn an understanding that offers the hope
of immortality. With an explicitness not equalled by anything
in the Hebrew Bible, this author proclaims as the ultimate gift
of divine wisdom the power whereby man can transcend the
mortality in which he has suffered so many ignominious limitations. No longer need resignation and acceptance of his lot be
the last resource of the wise man. These retain their value, of
course, for the manifestation of true faith. But in addition there
is hope, and the man of faith who is wise in the sense just defined
may literally hope for the stars. Hope it is, and not a surety;
but it is a hope that relies as well on the logic of the way of
wisdom as it does on the power of a merciful God who has
revealed himself in wisdom.

It is vital to observe, as we just have, that the immortality
envisaged by the author of Wis is a hope and not an inevitabil-

[18]See fn. 11 above, also W. F. Albright, *From the Stone Age to Christianity* (Garden City: Doubleday, 1957) 368-371.

ity. It is the working of a power that was not given in creation but comes through grace. Wisdom has taught this author—and, to be sure, his language and thought milieux have given him the means to express what he has been taught—a more articulated form of the aspiration which other students of wisdom such as the authors of Ps 49 and 73 may have tried to utter much more tentatively and gropingly.[19] His notion of life beyond the grave, in other words, is verbally but not conceptually connected with the Greek paradigm of the essential person who is concealed by the body ($\sigma\tilde{\omega}\mu\alpha = \sigma\tilde{\eta}\mu\alpha$), the dichotomy of the (mortal) body *vs* the (immortal) soul which has affected the thought of both later Judaism and later Christianity. This, despite the fact that the language has made the text susceptible of other interpretations. To put it formally, the idea of immortality here is not ctistiological but soteriological.[20] It is true, the author says that God did not make death (Wis 1:13): in much the same way, the P author of Gen 1 deliberately refrained from having him called Creator of darkness as well as of light (Gen 1:3-5). Nevertheless, not man but "righteousness is immortal" (so Wis 1:12-16, 3:1-9).

The doctrine of the Wisdom of Solomon is, therefore, a product of the later *ḥokmâ*, not of Greek but of Jewish speculation. It takes its place along with the notion of resurrection in its various forms, with the conceptual and literary form that came to be known as apocalyptic,[21] and with certain other alternatives that need not be examined at the present time, all as expressions of the confidence in divine providence which the

---

[19]See the discussion in my "Intimations of Immortality and the Old Testament," *JBL* 91 (1972) 162f.

[20]So, seemingly, was that of much of early Christianity, despite the fact that it, no less than the Wisdom of Solomon, spoke the dualistic language of Hellenism. Many early church fathers considered the soul to be mortal. Origen (ca. A.D. 185-254) found it necessary to defend the *natural* immortality of the soul in order to support his belief in the pre-existence of all spirits. The church, it seems, came to follow Origen in the by-issue without sustaining his main thesis. Cf. P. Bissels, "Die frühchristliche Lehre von der Sterblichkeit der Seele," *TTZ* 76 (1967) 322-329.

[21]Prejudice may call into question the right of apocalyptic to be considered an improvement of the human prospect dictated by the wisdom speculation. However, "apocalyptic was, at the first, the assertion of pious Jews that the

wheel of time had evoked from prayerful men whose ultimate refuge was faith in the God of Israel. They were new evocations, to the extent that new circumstances had demanded them by demonstrating at the same time that the old answers were no longer adequate or convincing. But they were also traditional, to the extent that they were premised on the precedent of a God who controlled events and was not to be controlled by them — not even by events which he himself had brought about — who could and would, therefore, grant immortality, endless days, as a boon, a gift, even as he had once granted long life in the land, after the land itself, to his covenant people.

When we say that these expressions were both new and traditional, we insist, therefore, on two things. First, that though the changing times and scenes and cultures had prompted them and in part given them voice, they relied more on native resources than on alien models. They were, in a word, traditional. But also, and secondly, they were new: they had not been anticipated in Israel's earlier experience,[22] and they had not been borrowed from or shared with Israel's earlier neighbors.

I have recently[23] defended the thesis that Israel's early tradition excluded inquiry about as well as of the dead, and that as a result Israel was compelled to examine the meaning of man's earthly existence to a degree and a depth seemingly without parallel in the thinking of its contemporaries. I have also sug-

Scripture was not to be broken, that a God who was Lord of history would and could bring about all he had promised, despite all worldly signs to the contrary." See my "And He Shall Come Again With Glory," *Studiorum Paulinorum Congressus . . . (AnBib* 17-18; Rome: Pontifical Biblical Institute, 1963) I, 143-150, and consult the included bibliography. See also K. Koch, *The Rediscovery of Apocalyptic* (tr. Margaret Kohl; *SBT* NS 22; Naperville, Allenson, 1972).

[22]For a view of what life and death meant to the earlier *ḥokmâ*, which was quite different from a latter view, see W. Brueggemann, "Life and Death in Tenth Century Israel," *JAAR* 40 (1972) 96-109.

[23]In "Intimations of Immortality," 158-171.

gested that by eschewing the speculation about an afterlife Israel had deliberately rejected the kind of irrelevant myth that supported the sanctuaries of Babylon and created what are now the magnificent ruins of Karnak and the Valley of the Kings. In a genial demurrer, Herbert Chanan Brichto has, among many more important considerations, called me to task for, as I understand it, oversimplifying the situation by denying a belief in an afterlife that undoubtedly did exist.[24] Oversimplification can probably be admitted; but I do not think the admission affects the substance of the views previously expressed. First of all, I think it evident that Ps 90 and most of the other examples of Palestinian *ḥokmâ* indicate that the concept of immortality was not simply a tradition inherited from of old that had proved to be capable of development and enrichment. Secondly, and as I think Brichto himself does not deny,[25] the salvific immortality of Wis and of other later Jewish tradition is not the result of an earlier Israelite assimilation of Near Eastern mythology.

What may have been oversimplification was the perhaps implied assumption that one Israelite attitude covered all others. To say that Israelite tradition discouraged inquiry about the dead obviously must exclude the one that was responsible for 1 Sam 28:5-25. But on the other hand, to insist that there was no Israelite tradition which discouraged such inquiry[26] would appear to ignore texts like Isa 38:18, Ps 6:6, and especially Ps 88:5-13: the "shade" which is forgotten by God and which has no way of achieving contact with him — is there any encouragement given here to speculate on such a non-occurrence? I persist in regarding 1 Sam 28:5-25 as rather isolated and marginal in the Hebrew Bible, since I know of nothing else there that is really like it. Therefore I consider the normative tradition

---

[24]"Kin, Cult, Land and Afterlife," Cincinnati: Hebrew Union College, 1973, pp. 105. This article, to appear in *HUCA* 44, I have reviewed in prepublication form kindly supplied by Prof. Brichto who has also given me leave to make public use of it. My quotations are from this unpublished typescript.

[25]Cf. Brichto, p. 105 (fn. 81).

[26]So Brichto, p. 12.

to have pointed in the opposite direction, and I think the overt scepticism of Qoh and Sir has more realistically portrayed Israel's traditional thought concerning "life" in Sheol than does the sprightly imagery of Isa 14:9-21.[27] Sheol did admittedly involve the concept of some kind of survival beyond the grave, a concept which the Israelites shared with their neighbors and which, in the Bible, doubtless cannot be reduced simply to poetic license, making it one with Rahab and Mot. That there was never any genuine development of the concept beyond the negations of earthly existence, however, I think illustrates what I mean when I say that Israel's tradition discouraged inquiry about the dead. The forbidden practice of necromancy certainly testified to a popular belief in powers possessed by the dead which was perhaps little different from the officially sanctioned beliefs of the Gentiles,[28] but I fancy that the proscription of the practice was as much to contradict the underlying belief as it was to control it. In any case, superstition, if it was in this light that such a practice was regarded, of itself does not necessarily speak to what is false or unreal, but to what is vain observance, dangerous, idle, misleading. The gods of the Gentiles, we know, were first called "false" not to deny their existence, but to classify them as unreliable.

If there was any development at all in Israelite thinking about the state of the dead and, consequently, about Sheol, it seems to have consisted in assembling further negative notes, not positive ones. The development was definitely "not progressive."[29] Later Israelites came to distinguish what they evidently considered the death worse than death reserved for some of

[27]Which text, *pace* H. L. Ginsberg (cited by Brichto, p. 70f.), I do not necessarily consider to be of the same authorship as Isa 8:19, at least in its present form. The point is not important. In any case, the "lively" conduct ascribed to the shades in this poetry is a device to rebuke the *hybris* of the king of Babylon now snatched from life and made one with the shadow existence of the rest of the dead (cf. vs. 10). Isa 14:9-21 no more than Lk 16:19-31 had as its purpose to offer a serious description of the geography or other circumstances of the afterworld.

[28]Cf. F. Vattioni, "La necromanzia nell'Antico Testamento," *Augustinianum* 3 (1963) 461-481.

[29]Cf. J. L. McKenzie, *Dictionary of the Bible* (Milwaukee: Bruce, 1965), *s.v. "Death."*

Sheol's denizens, for the "evil dead,"[30] but they do not seem to have looked in the other direction, towards a state of reward or happiness there. From first to last, it is hardly any exaggeration to claim that Israel's view on death was to see it as an unmitigated misfortune, however inevitable and inexorable it might be, so that the only thing worse than death was premature death. Correspondingly, life was the real gift, and there could be no greater blessing than a long life. Burial practices in the biblical period, both those which were allowed and those which were for one reason or another were forbidden (Lev 19:27f., Dt 14:1, Sir 30:18, Bar 6:26, etc.), testify at best to that vague notion of perdurance which popular superstition and the mythologies of the Gentiles developed and exploited.[31]

And thus I would conclude by stressing the real contribution that was made by postexilic *ḥokmâ* in Palestine and the diaspora when men of prayer came to it for solace and strength in the face of new problems and anxieties and perplexities. Wisdom in Israel had always striven to teach man to live sensibly in tune with the circumstances in which he found himself. Part of its task had come to be that it taught man to pray for the right things, for the attainable, in other words, as God had made known what was attainable and what should be obtained. When the spirit of God melded more and more with the wisdom of God and the two were recognized more and more to be the same because they now spoke the same language, *ḥokmâ* revealed new avenues of hope that were no less distinctively and traditionally Israelite for all that they were in fact new. These latter achievements of wisdom which, from one point of view, substituted for the revelation of the spirit, were possible only because of a long and protracted prior hearkening to the spirit. And these achievements should in no way be minimized by us through any attempt to construe them as other than new. To wisdom, which instructed Israel and the world through Israel, we owe this much and more.

[30]Cf. O. Eissfeldt, "Schwerterschlagene bei Hesekiel," in *Studies in Old Testament Prophecy* (T. H. Robinson Festschrift; Edinburgh: T. & T. Clark, 1950) 73-81 = *Kleine Schriften* III (Tübingen: Mohr, 1966) 1-8.

[31]See R. de Vaux, *Ancient Israel: Its Life and Institutions* (tr. John McHugh; New York: McGraw-Hill, 1961) 61.

13. Realized Messianism

In a recent published lecture[1] Henri Cazelles has traced the messianic idea from its ancient Near Eastern origins in the concept of divine kingship through its acclimation into Israelite Yahwism (the pros and cons of Israel's acceptance of monarchy; the prophetic demythologization of the royal mystique) down to the final reinterpretation of the idea in an age when monarchy was no longer and when surrogate figures for the hope of salvation had to be found. Such a perspective is to be welcomed: first of all, because it properly locates Israelite messianism within a common cultural milieu as no exotic growth proper to Israel alone, and secondly, because it properly roots messianism within the OT and refuses to treat it as the postbiblical or intertestamental development that other distinguished modern scholars have wanted to call it[2].

It is true, "messianism" is not an OT term: in fact, as it is

---

[1] Cf. "Biblical Messianism", in *Studia biblica 1978 I* (Sixth International Congress on Biblical Studies, Oxford, 3-7 April 1978), *Journal for the Study of the Old Testament*: Supplementary Studies, 11; Sheffield: The University, 1979, pp. 49-58. Cf. H. CAZELLES, *Le Messie de la Bible*, Tournai-Paris 1978.

[2] For example, Joseph KLAUSNER, *The Messianic Idea in Israel*, New York: Macmillan, 1955; Sigmund MOWINCKEL, *He That Cometh*, New York: Abingdon, 1956.

commonly used, it is if anything the result of a Christian reinterpretation of the OT[3]. Certainly no OT person could but have been puzzled by such an expression as "messianism without a messiah", the designation which M.-J. Lagrange coined to refer to that OT and later Jewish eschatological hope which refrained from what he assumed was the normal procedure, to center its expectation in a designated soteriological figure[4]. Nevertheless, even though it would probably be impossible to defend the proposition that "messiah" ever appears in the OT in the technical sense which later Christian theology has endowed it—not even in Is 45,1, which in this acceptation is actually an "antimessianic" reference—there is no doubt that Cazelles is right when he speaks of an OT messianism, and there is no doubt that he rightly finds its origin in Israel's adoption and adaptation of the Near Eastern myth of the savior-king.

It is generally supposed that the tradition of a "Davidic covenant" mediated by the Prophet Nathan was necessary to domesticate the Near Eastern royal myth into Israelite theology (2 Sm 7,8-16; Ps 89,20-38: the latter is usually thought to represent the older witness to the tradition). But this is far from certain. The "royal" Psalms, if they are read dispassionately, seem to celebrate kingship as salvific in itself. They are, in Bernhard Lang's term[5], examples of "present messianism". Psalm 45 particularly, which seems to be, even though it is not certainly[6], of northern Israelite origin and therefore independent of any Davidic tradition, is in its most obvious reading a paean to a quasi-divine figure (the *ʾelōhîm* of v. 7 is surely one of the most prestigious titles ascribed to any living mortal in the OT). The

---

[3] Rightly so recognized by John L. MCKENZIE, *A Theology of the Old Testament*, Garden City: Doubleday, 1974, pp. 23-24, 28-29, etc.

[4] Lagrange's magisterial treatment appears in *Le messianisme chez les Juifs*, Études bibliques, Paris: Gabalda, 1909.

[5] "Messias und Messiaserwartung im alten Israel", *Bibel und Kirche* 33 (1978). pp. 110-115.

[6] Cf. Hans—Joachim KRAUS, *Psalmen I-59* (Biblischer Kommentar Altes Testament XV/1), Neukirchen-Vluyn: Neukirchener Verlag, ²1978, pp. 488-489.

OT, we know, in its final form is a Judahite document edited in conformity with Deuteronomic theology. The Nathan oracle, whether historically factual or of later theological devising, we may assume to have been an attempt at legitimation in peculiarly Israelite terms of a common cultural conviction that had already been accepted in Israel on its own terms. The king was *eo ipso*, savior and redeemer of his people.

If the king, actually reigning or imminently awaited, provided this "present messianism", what happened to the myth when it became apparent that it was to play no further role in a continuing history of Israel? What, in other words, happened to messianism when there was no longer any king to be messiah? Commonly it is asserted that the title was now transferred to other soteriological figures of expectation, prophetic or, especially, priestly (*hakkōhēn hammāšîaḥ!*). One such development is supposed to have eventuated in a "levitical messianism" (Cazelles speaks of an "Aaronic messianism") verifiable in late OT texts, in some of the intertestamental literature, and at Qumran with its "Messiah of Aaron and Israel." Elsewhere I have argued in some detail against this position[7]. While there is no doubt that in the postexilic community the Aaronic high priest assumed the function of government that had once been acquitted by the king, and no doubt at all that in this community the present priestly office was exalted at the expense of the vanished kingly office, there seem to be no grounds for imagining that the messianic myth survived the monarchy and found a locus elsewhere in other Israelite institutions. The postexilic situation I think more properly should be characterized as one of "realized messianism": messianism was considered to have run its course, whether it had succeeded or failed. Nothing else was considered to have taken over its function. At the very most, something else may have been substituted for it, but if so only on its own, very different terms.

Perhaps the earliest example of realized messianism — on the

[7] See my "Levitical Messianism and the New Testament", in J.L. McKENZIE, ed., *The Bible in Current Catholic Thought* (Gruenthaner Memorial Volume), New York: Herder & Herder, 1962, pp. 83-99.

part, that is, of those who had shared the royal mystique and had not, as other voices had, resisted—is to be found in Lm 4,20: *rûaḥ 'appênû mᵉšîaḥ yhwh* || *nilkad bišᵉḥîtôtā* || *ᵃšer 'āmarnû bᵉṣillô* || *niḥᵉyeh baggôyîm* || " Our breath of life, the messiah of the Lord"—the poet speaks the language of international as well as of Israelite messianism[8]—"has been caught in our enemies' snares: he of whom we said, 'In his shadow we shall have life among the nations'." This disillusionment with messianism is complete: nowhere in the book of Lamentations is there any indication of a retrieval of hope from any of Israel's institutions, and no substitutionary institution is suggested. Hope is in the Lord, but even that is faint. There is not even a "messianism without a messiah."

Not much different is the realized messianism of Ezekiel. Virtually any modern version of the text of Ez 21,31-32 (alternatively, vv. 26-26) will recognized that we have here a repudiation of the traditional Israelite kingship, even though not all might be willing to read v. 32 as an explicit reversal of the "messianic" Judahite passage of Gen 49,10[9]. I do not find, as others have found, in Ezekiel some kind of alternative messianism. I do find, in the idealized Israel of the future imagined by Ezekiel, that while there will be, as though from force of habit, a Davidic "prince" (34,23-24), he will be as thoroughly deprived of a sacred character as it would have been conceivable from any prince of the time to be (cf. 46,1-2.8-12, etc.; 43,7*b*-9 may or may not be original with Ezekiel). Ezekiel's restriction of the sacred to the priests and levites does not constitute the institution of a new messianism, only the denial of an exhausted one. As Jean Steinmann once put it[10], Ezekiel's only messiah is the temple itself.

What of the "Cyrus oracle" of Isa 44,24—45,13? It is easy enough to agree that key-terms like "shepherd" and "messiah"

---

[8] Cf. Jean DE SAVIGNAC, "Théologie pharaonique et messianisme d'Israël", *Vetus Testamentum* 7 (1957), p. 82.

[9] Cf. W.L. MORAN, "Gen. 49,10 and its use in Ez 21,32", *Biblica* 39 (1958), pp. 405-425.

[10] *Le prophète Ezéchiel et les débuts de l'exil*, Paris: Cerf, 1953, p. 263.

have here been appropriated to this foreign savior much in the manner that Ezekiel sarcastically applied a messianic oracle to Nebuchadnezzar: to signify the total passing away of old sureties which have been replaced by what is entirely new. It is hard, on the other hand, to agree with Graham S. Ogden's rather elaborate extrapolation from these appropriations into a presentation of "the Persian, perhaps, not as the 'New Moses', but certainly as one fixed firmly within YHWH's salvific activity after the manner of Moses[11]." Quite apart from the difficulty of fitting this construct to the character of the great exilic prophet, the recent careful study by Klaus Kiesow of the exodus theme in Second Isaiah[12] is persuasive that there is to be found here no such systematic development of a "Mosaic messianism", let alone the question of its application to Cyrus.

The idea that messianism survived the demise of kingship in some other form or forms has been nurtured by certain undeniable facts. One of them is that messianism was alive and well and prospering in intertestamental times, as both the intertestamental literature and the NT eloquently testify. This messianism was that of the strictest Judahite acceptation, of a political/religious savior who would be a Davidic scion: Rabbi Akiba's proclamation of the non-Davidic Bar-Cochba's messianism was an exception of this rule[13]. This messianism, however, was hardly a survival; it was a revival. It was a revival made possible by the apocalyptic as a literary form, a form which was only one manifestation of the apocalyptic mentality. The apocalyptic mentality, a phenomenon which we obviously have no possibility of investigation afresh at this juncture, appeared in late OT intertestamental Judaism as a reaction against rather than to the course of history (the latter having been the reaction of earlier prophecy), resulting, among other things, in the resurrection of some ancient ideals, including the ideal of the

---

[11] "Moses and Cyrus", *Vetus Testamentum* 28 (1978), pp. 195-203.

[12] *Exodustexte im Jesajabuch* (Orbis Biblicus et Orientalis, 24), Göttingen: Vandenhoeck & Ruprecht, 1979.

[13] KLAUSNER, *The Messianic Idea*, p. 395.

royal mediator, which would occur *despite* rather than as an outcome of historical developments[14].

Other undeniable facts are the alternative soteriological figures which were featured in intertestamental Judaism, figures which have in part been subsumed in the *christos* title which the NT has ascribed to Jesus. While again it is impossible to argue the point within the compass of this article, it seems safe to say that none of these figures was ever considered to be "messiah" by pre-Christian Judaism. The only exception to this general assessment is the assumption entertained by numerous scholars of the "priestly messianism" of which we have spoken above. It is to that assumption that I now and finally return, since it has affected so much of OT interpretation as well as having supposedly supplied a background to the NT. Under the influence of this assumption, for example, Psalm 110 has been denominated a composition of the time of Qoheleth and the Chronicler, a work of the Jerusalemite priesthood, professing a priestly messianism justifying (like Genesis 14) the payment of priestly tithes[15]. Such an interpretation is judged by a modern commentator on the Psalms, on the other hand, to be "heute überwunden und fast schon vergessen", since the psalm must belong to an early period of the Israelite monarchy after which its recall of pre-Israelite traditions would have been unthinkable[16]. Whence has this supposed priestly messianism derived?

I suggest that it came about by a redactional accident, when the oracle of Zech 6,9-15 originally designed for Zerubbabel's coronation was altered (in v. 11) to apply to the high priest Joshua[17]. It is not necessary to rehearse how the postexilic na-

---

[14] See Klaus KOCH, *The Rediscovery of Apocalyptic*, tr. Margaret Kohl, Studies in Biblical Theology, Second Series, n°22, Naperville: Allenson, 1971, pp. 31-32.

[15] Cf. R. TOURNAY, "Le psaume cx", *Revue biblique* 67 (1960), pp. 5-41.

[16] See KRAUS, *Psalmen 60-150* (BKAT XV/2), pp. 929-930.

[17] I am aware of and consider worthy of notice Margaret Barker's contrary assessment of the situation in her "The Two Figures of Zechariah", *Heythrop Journal* 18 (1977), pp. 38-46, and "The Evil in Zechariah", *ibid.*, 19 (1978), pp. 12-27.

tionalist prophets Haggai and Zechariah attempted on a regained Palestinian soil the restoration of Judahite messianism, in the person of the Zerubbabel who was presumably the Davidic heir apparent. What happened as a sequel to this nationalist activity we do not know, but we may easily imagine in view of Zerubbabel's quick disappearance from the chronicle that the Persian imperium took speedy action to remove the menace[18]. Once this had taken place, what followed was inevitable. Whereas Ezekiel and the Second Isaiah (and Obadiah 21, too, probably) had given up on messianism somewhat before, it remained for other, perhaps more naive prophets to hold for a Davidic messianism to the end, or even beyond the end. It could never survive again, not until an apocalyptic world view would assume (as in Am 7,8b-15; Isa 11,1-9, etc.) that it possibly could. Obviously, it would be foolish to pretend that messianism under any ever diluted form and with any ever transformation ceased forever to exist in Israel, since we know how much the idea influenced both the NT and the intertestamental literature. What is clear, however, is that it is hard to discover any direct connection between what the last of the OT was looking for, and what the first of the NT had thought it had found there.

What the last of the OT was looking for, apart from the apocalyptic exception just noted, was a continuation of what had been realized, not for a new messianism. Ben Sira, whose work never became part of the canon of the Hebrew OT (though apparently it was part of the canon at Qumran and certainly

---

[18] Our historical sources are less than minimal. With characteristic ingenuity Julian Morgenstern attempted to fill in the gaps of the history of this period of resurgent nationalism under the Persians. See his "Jerusalem – 485 B.C.", *Hebrew Union College Annual* 27 (1956), pp. 101-174; 28 (1957), pp. 15-47; 31 (1960), pp. 1-29; "The 'Oppressor' of Isa 51,13: Who was he?" *JBL* 81 (1962), pp. 25-34. Also "The Message of Deutero-Isaiah in its Sequential Unfolding", *HUCA* 29 (1958), pp. 5-9. According to his theory, there was an attempt in the time of "Trito-Isaiah" to mount a rebellion against Xerxes under a Davidic king " Menachem". In reprisal, after the failed revolt, Xerxes had Judah overrun by Edomites, Moabites, Philistines, and Ammonites.

was part of the canon accepted by the Jewish Christian church)[19], probably represents as adequately as any the testimony of a Judaism of the II[d] century B.C. This was the Judaism of Judith and Tobit, the Judaism of ultimate restoration which thought to have resolved its problems of accommodation and identity, safe and secure in its religious institutions with no need to be concerned one way or the other with regard to a benign or at least harmless political overlordship which it could afford to treat with indifference (cf. Qo 5,8; 8,2). It was a Judaism that had not yet known Antiochus IV Epiphanes, apocalypticism, or the Maccabean political explosion which occurred only after unexpected and incredible provocations: all of which occurrences had no precedents. In Si 45,25, Ben Sira probably wrote, in those relaxed and deceptively optimistic times: *w*egam berîtô 'im dāwîd || ben yišay lemaṭṭeh yehûdâ, naḥalat 'iš libbenô lebaddô[20] || naḥalat 'aharôn lekol zar'ô*. Which is to say: While the covenant with David had been made only for his immediate son (or for his sake only with the tribe of Judah), this covenant with Judah counts for nothing against the covenant with Aaron (Dt 33,9), which is for all time. In other words, messianism is dead. What remains in its place is not another messianism but rather a safe, cultic life, a comfortable religion with no political pretensions to interfere with other established ways.

It could not last for long, for the world did not allow it to last for long. But as long as it lasted it was no messianism but rather an attempt to live as a religious society which had surpassed messianism.

---

[19] See Jack N. LIGHTSTONE, "The formation of the biblical canon in Judaism of late antiquity", *Studies in Religion/Sciences Religieuses* 8 (1979), pp. 135-142. His position is that the LXX, Qumran, the Samaritans, and the NT are equally with the MT valid witnesses to what was regarded in Jewry as canonical Scripture at the beginning of the current era, and further, that the eventual canon of the MT has no traditional warrant other than that supplied by later imagination.

[20] Reading with the LXX in place of the *lipenê kebôdô* of the extant Hebrew.

14. A Tale of Two Cities: The Old Testament and the Issue of Personal Freedom

It was the best of times, it was the worst of times, it was the age of wisdom, it was the age of foolishness, it was the epoch of belief, it was the epoch of incredulity, it was the season of Light, it was the season of Darkness, it was the spring of hope, it was the winter of despair, we had everything before us, we had nothing before us, we were all going direct to heaven, we were all going direct the other way.

The reader may recall that Dickens went on to note among the benchmarks of this best and worst of times not a few that we have come to regard with almost proprietary interest as we enter the third century of the American Republic.

Plus ça change, plus c'est la même chose is a piece of cynicism that hardly appears in the Bible. On the contrary, that history does not and, indeed, cannot repeat itself seems to be the constant and consistent affirmation of both the Old and the New Testament, the "wheel of being" or "cycle of nature" of Jas. 3:6 forming only an apparent exception to this rule.[1]

---

[1]On the *trochos tes geneseōs*, see Horst Balz-Wolfgang Schrage, *Die katholischen Briefe* (NTD 10: Göttingen: Vandenhoeck & Ruprecht, 1973), p. 39, and Jean Cantinat, C.M., *Les Epîtres de Saint Jacques et de Saint Jude* (Sources Bibliques; Paris: Gabalda, 1973), p. 175. Originally the term

History, as the Bible understands it, has neither been inscribed in human genes nor programmed by any scenario of nature; it is a record of the unexpected and of the unpredictable in which God, though Lord of history, is such not as Fate (*fatum* = "that which has been [once for all] spoken") but as the sometimes reluctant partner in a contractual relationship of God's own devising with a people which engages with God in continuous dialogue in which God can and does often repent and change a decision. The only sense in which history can be said to repeat itself derives from its character as being a history of humankind, because human beings, to the extent that we have been able to observe them in some critical degree over the past seven millennia or so, have proved to be fairly predictable creatures, for good and for ill, whatever may be the cause.

Recently Carl F. H. Henry wrote to the effect that "a nation concerned with exploring the Bible as energetically as exploring the moon could have avoided Watergate and certainly would not have been as lastingly crippled in spirit by it."[2] I tend to agree with the first of the clauses, which is no less true for its triteness in other contexts. I am not so sure of the second clause, nor of the commentary with which Henry has embellished it:

> Few nations in the world historically matched America's moral authority even when her military strength was untried and unsure. Today, rich and strong in everything but moral stamina, America's influence is at a global crossroads. . . . Concentration on this-worldly pleasures, on the accumulation of material things, on sensate experiences as the measure of joy, has dulled any appetite for the transcendent and eternal.[3]

---

was at home in Orphic teaching where it meant the successive reincarnations within a course of fixed destiny; but in the times of New Testament Judaism it had become a casual phrase to signify nothing more or less than the ups and downs of human life. Hence there is little point to deciding whether James wrote *tróchos,* cycle, or *trochós,* wheel.

[2]"Reflections on a Nation in Transition," *Interpretation* 30 (1976): 58.
[3]Ibid., p. 59.

Whatever is to be said of this vision of human life and progress in light of the puritan virtues, Henry's final conclusion does
seem worth pursuing:

> The Bible still supplies the principles for just community life
> and personal dignity; it exhibits the new man and the new
> society able to lift the American dream out of its nightmarish
> present.[4]

The grounds for this pursuit rest in the commonality of human
beings, those of Dickens' England and of Jefferson's America
and of Jeremiah's Judah. The two cities whose tale we tell are
London and Paris, and they are also Washington, New York,
Chicago, Boston, Peoria, or Junction City on the one hand, and
Jerusalem, Shiloh, Bethel, Samaria, or Shechem on the other.
They conspire to tell us a story that can haply locate us in the
present by defining our *locus* in the past.

Watergate, I fancy, is for us a symbol not unlike the symbol
of Jezreel for Hos. 1:5, of Gilgal and Beth-aven (Bethel) for
Hos. 4:15, of Baal-peor for Hos. 9:10, of Bethel and Gilgal
for Amos 4:4, of Gilgal, Beer-sheba, and Bethel for Amos
5:5 – additional and perhaps even more apposite examples could
be imagined without difficulty. I have not researched the matter at all, but I would deem it a safe bet that in the Bible the
names of places and happenings that have become slogans for
triumphs and success are less in number than those that recall
a defeat, a shame, or a mischance. The Bible is not unaware
of human achievement and prowess, and indeed it could not
be, itself being a chief one of these; but the Bible always had
as its first task to lesson human beings and to lesson is to in-
struct and admonish out of experience, especially out of experience that has been unpleasant and humbling.

As an isolated event in human annals, the Watergate of
Washington, DC, is undoubtedly of far less importance than
the Watergate of Neh. 12:37, or at any rate would be so in that
imaginational and never-to-be-written total history of the
phenomenon of humanity. So paltry can the squalid little affair

[4]Ibid.

be made to appear, in fact, that not only the cynics among us but also some of our idealists have been provoked to ask why so much should have been made of it, since it probably did not transgress ground rules that had long been tacitly agreed on in the *Realpolitik* of this country's business. Or, if it did transgress them, it did so only through a natural impetus of gradation: a difference of degree and not of kind; or it transgressed them only by being found out while other, perhaps deadlier, assaults on our rights and liberties have remained and will remain undiscovered and unpunished. These objections may be very well founded. Watergate is important not because of what happened there or what was intended to happen there, which in either case was relatively trivial, but because of what it eventually began to reveal had been going on apace in the American Republic not in only one of the administrations of its executive authority but in several, and not in the executive authority alone, though this was the one immediately vulnerable to legislative and judicial scrutiny. Watergate also led to reflection on the extent to which the Congress and the courts of the United States have likewise, and perhaps not exclusively in these latter days, failed to accord with the expectations held up for them by the American ideal as expressed in the American constitution. I make no attempt to discuss these issues to the particular discredit of any one political party or even of any one political person or cabal of political persons. One of the Old Testament facts of life of which Watergate has reminded us is that fault can be collective, popular, and national, and that frequently we can single someone out for blame simply because he or she epitomizes a blame that is common to us all.

On March 11, 1976, the responses of former President Richard Nixon to seventy-seven questions posed to him on the preceding February 5 by a select committee of the United States Senate (the Church Committee) were made public by the former president's attorneys.[5] These answers were supplied, the former

---

[5]See *The New York Times* for Friday, March 12, 1976, p. 14. Paradoxically, Nixon's "answers" were published in the absence of corresponding "questions," which had been labelled "top secret" by the committee.

president stated, altogether voluntarily, without his conceding that Congress had any right to compel him to account for the conduct of his office as president. His reply to question 34 of the committee expressed first of all a political theorem, then some practical applications of it. The theorem:

> It is quite obvious that there are certain inherently governmental actions which, if undertaken by the sovereign in protection of the interest of the nation's security, are lawful but which, if undertaken by private persons, are not.

After instancing as precedents for this principle President Franklin D. Roosevelt's executive order setting up concentration camps for Japanese Americans during World War II, various actions of wartime seizure by President Lincoln, and his own acknowledged warrantless wiretapping, Nixon concluded:

> In short there have been—and will be in the future— circumstances in which Presidents may lawfully authorize actions in the interest of this country, which, if undertaken by other persons or even by the President under different circumstances, would be illegal.

This is, in several ways, a curious bit of prose. It does, on the one hand, seem to assert a concept of personal political sovereignty that has rarely been uttered to an English-speaking people since the reigns of the Tudors and the Stuarts, rarely since Sir Edward Coke's judgment against the pretensions of James I "that the King hath no prerogative but that which the law of the land allows him."[6] It also seems to assume that a sovereignty which the American constitution recognizes to reside in the people of the United States and in such state and federal governments as they devise has somehow come to have an exclusive depositary in that elected official in whom Article Two of the Constitution declares that merely the executive power has been vested and whom the Federalist Papers refer to as the Chief Magistrate of the Union. (The two terms add up to the

---

[6]Cf. Leonard W. Levy, *Origins of the Fifth Amendment* (New York: Oxford University Press, 1968), p. 249.

same thing, of course, since a magistrate is by dictionary definition simply an executor of laws.) Unfortunately, what seems
to be asserted in these lines was no doubt what was intended
to be asserted. They reflect that notion of the presidency which
has recently come to be termed "imperial," though that notion
is by no means a recent importation into American political
experience. Mr. Nixon inherited, he did not invent, this notion
of the presidency. It was foreseen at least as early as 1865 by
Orestes Brownson in *The American Republic*, and on the right
prognosis: namely, the tendency of extraordinary wartime
powers to become ingrained habit for an executive no more
disposed than any other in history to relinquish prerogatives
once accorded, and, on a more enduring basis, the "growing
disposition on the part of congress to throw as much of the
business of government as possible into the hands of the
executive."[7] The imperial presidency which Mr. Nixon inherited
and exploited will be discarded by his successors only through
a quixotic renunciation for which history has not prepared: not
after 1865 and not after Watergate have the Congress or the
courts of the United States done very much about it.

This is not a study of constitutional law. Therefore, I am
not about to speculate on the degree to which a maximized
presidency can sit comfortably with the division of powers principle that is fundamental to the American system of government. My concern is not with theory but with practice, with
the consequences which this assumption of power has had for
personal liberties in this country, not simply through the individual activities of the president but through the activities of
individuals and of governmental agencies accountable to the
president who have shared in the same assumption. Those activities, some of which have been criminal and others not demonstrably so, have had as their common premise the assessment
of such liberties as subordinate to the business of government,
subordinated sometimes in the name of national security, but
frequently enough simply because they have interfered with what

[7] *The Works of Orestes A. Brownson* (Detroit: H. F. Brownson, 1905),
vol. XVIII, pp. 189-190.

the executors of our laws have considered the most efficient way of doing their job. It is with this premise and assessment that we must deal, since the liberties of which we have been speaking are supposed to make government more difficult and not easier.

Because we are on the level of practice and not of theory in this discussion, I am not disposed to think that much light will be shed on our subject by exploring the Old Testament theology of kingship, the only area of the Old Testament in which a theory of government is espoused which corresponds in any way with our own. I am much impressed by the studies that have been made of this theology earlier[8] and lately, most recently, perhaps, by John H. Eaton,[9] which have demonstrated how pervasive has been the royal ritual and mystique in Israelite thought and piety (though hardly as pervasive, I would fancy, as Eaton claims). The title of Eaton's fourth chapter, however, rather gives the game away: "The Ideal of the King's Office in the Psalms." It was an ideal, and no doubt often a fructifying ideal, this concept of a king who would make justice reign, who would be God's child and servant, guided by God's spirit to be the beneficier of the people, which in turn became a model democratizable for everyone to whom the Pentateuchal traditions have lavishly ascribed the royal prerogatives of divine image in creation, destiny, and dominion. Withal, however, it remained an ideal. Was the ideal ever realized? The question needs only to be asked to be answered, and the answer is readily available in the Old Testament historical books and the prophets. The royal ideal of the Old Testament, not essentially different from the royal ideal of Canaan, Hatti, Mesopotamia, or Egypt, to all of which it was tributary, could be a hopeful inspiration to government, as it has always remained, but it never became its protocol.

Far more help from the Old Testament, I might suggest, will

[8]For example, Jean de Fraine, S.J., *L'aspect religieux de la royauté israélite* (*Analecta Biblica* 3 [Rome: Pontifical Biblical Institute, 1954]).

[9]*Kingship and the Psalms* (*Studies in Biblical Theology* 2:32; Naperville: Allenson, 1976).

be forthcoming from its antimonarchical tradition, a tradition which it did certainly acquire by bitter experience but which it also had vicariously before the fact from its observation of the ways of the Gentiles among whom its lot had been cast. The "rights of the king" of 1 Sam. 8:11-17, the antimonarchical diatribe ascribed to Samuel by the Deuteronomic author of this work, doubtless owes something to the recollection of certain less-than-praiseworthy Israelite kings, both of the North and of the South, but it has also been long recognized that precisely as it stands it could be, on the historical evidence we now possess, "an eloquent appeal to the people by a contemporary of Saul not to impose on themselves a Canaanite institution alien to their own way of life."[10] It would obviously be anachronistic to turn the prophets of Israel and its historians into civil libertarians and to interpret their opposition to monarchy as an earlier exemplification of the concerns of John Locke. Neither, however, is it entirely preposterous to suggest that the Israelite attitudes were motivated by values closely akin to those which I am seeking to defend here. The Deuteronomic theologians and historians, I think it fairly evident, would have preferred to reject kingship out of hand (the law for the king in Deut. 17:14-20, accepting kingship as a *fait accompli*, rationalizes its position by defining as a proper king for Israel exactly the kind that it never had, one born of its own ethos rather than from imitation of the Gentiles); Deuteronomy accepted kingship reluctantly only because it succumbed to the romanticism of the Davidic ideal.[11] A religious and cultic reason having been given for the acceptance of the institution, it is not inappropriate that a religious and cultic reason should thereafter be given by Deuteronomy for its condemnation of practically every Judahite king and of every northern Israelite king without exception; yet we may suspect that its opposition to kingship went down to

[10]So Isaac Mendelsohn in *Bulletin of the American Schools of Oriental Research* 143 (1956): 17-22.

[11]Cf. R. E. Clements, "The Deuteronomic Interpretation of the Founding of the Monarchy in 1 Sam. VIII," *Vetus Testamentum* 24 (1974): 398-410.

deeper levels than those of cult and rubric. 1 Sam. 8:11-17 says nothing about cult and rubric but rather that the king

> will take your sons and assign them to his chariots and horses, and they will run before his chariot. He will also appoint from among them his commanders of groups of a thousand and of a hundred soldiers. He will set them to do his plowing and his harvesting, and to make his implements of war and the equipment of his chariots. He will use your daughters as ointment-makers, as cooks, and as bakers. He will take the best of your fields, vineyards, and olive groves, and give them to his officials. He will tithe your crops and your vineyards, and give the revenue to his eunuchs and his slaves. He will take your male and female servants, as well as your best oxen and your asses, and use them to do his work. He will tithe your flocks and you yourselves will become his slaves.

If this is not an indictment of government in the name of freedoms which government destroys, I find it hard to conceive of how the indictment could be otherwise phrased. And what of the prophetic opposition to kingship? We are frequently told that the prophets did not oppose the monarchy "in principle," and this is a true statement, though also largely a meaningless one. Without exception, however, the prophets who lived under the monarchy did condemn Israel's and Judah's kings. Is it only by chance that they condemned them first and foremost for the corruption of justice under royal administration, for the rise of a class of grasping landlords and the breakdown under their regime of the ancient Israelite proprietary system and the acquisition by the ruling class of vast landed estates, for the reduction of the peasantry into a state of perpetual debt, for the restoration over a free people of the chariot aristocracy of Canaanite feudalism, and for the destruction of local and tribal power and the delivery of all administrative and judicial power to the creatures of the king?[12] These are surely considerations not

[12]Cf. John L. McKenzie, *A Theology of the Old Testament* (New York: Doubleday, 1974), pp. 256-257.

unlike those brought to the attention of a candid world by the American Declaration of Independence in respect to the conduct of the king of Great Britain. Neither can it be accidental that in the two best-known confrontations between prophet and king in the Old Testament — Nathan with David over the spoliation of Uriah (2 Sam. 11:1-12:25), and Elijah with Ahab over the spoliation of Naboth (1 Kings 21) — we have to do with the violation of those inalienable human rights of which the Declaration speaks, not with any narrow dogma of Israel, and we have to do with a violation of those rights possible only to kings — even as Jezebel the Phoenician taught her royal husband.

Kingship came to Israel as a piece of political pragmatism, a more or less inevitable development out of tribal confederation in the face of external threat.[13] The royal theology of the Old Testament was a later luxury. Similarly, we may safely conclude that the postexilic Deuteronomic bias against the monarchy related to Israelite cultic proprieties was not the primordial reason for the antimonarchical sentiment that runs throughout the Old Testament traditions early and late. Israel's prejudice against monarchical government seems to have been motivated by the same instinct and experience that provoked Lord Acton's melancholy judgment: power does, indeed, tend to corrupt, and absolute power does corrupt absolutely. The Old Testament never asserted this principle, but it did not need to; it demonstrated it instead.

Freedom, whether as a national or a personal possession, is not an Old Testament term.[14] This does not mean that the

---

[13]Cf. A. D. H. Mayes, "Israel in the Pre-Monarchy Period," *Vetus Testamentum* 23 (1973): 151-170.

[14]Under *eleutheros*, etc., *Theologisches Wörterbuch zum Neuen Testament* 2, 484ff. lists no Old Testament or Jewish background. In medieval Hebrew *ḥērût*, derived from the common Semitic (and also biblical Hebrew), *ḥr*, "freeman," "noble," took on this significance; cf. Charles F. Jean-Jacob Hoftijzer, *Dictionnaire des inscriptions sémitiques de l'ouest* (Leiden: Brill, 1965), p. 95. Hence Rabbi Joshua ben Levi's word-play on the text of Ex. 32:16, that the tablets of the Law should not be read as engraved (*ḥārût*), but rather as freedom (*ḥērut*), "since you have no true freeman except him

concept did not exist, but rather that it need not be named, since it was taken for granted. It was necessary to designate Egypt "that place of slavery," because that was an unnatural and unusual place, but it was not necessary to designate Israel a place of freedom. It was necessary to legislate, here and there in the ancient Covenant Code of Ex. 20:22-23:33, for both foreign and native slaves, since they were a case apart; but it was not necessary to specify in these same laws as free those whom God and nature had constituted free.[15] When the Jews (according to John 8:33) said to Jesus, "We are descendants of Abraham: never have we been slaves to anyone," they uttered an historical truth which is not dissolved by the Johannine irony, and they affirmed a proud tradition to which the Old Testament is witness.[16]

Without any intention whatever of reasserting the pseudobiblical civil religion of America, whose scriptures Robert N. Bellah has traced from Thomas Jefferson's second inaugural address, it is nevertheless possible to draw a real parallel between the Old Testament affirmation of freedom and the personal freedoms acknowledged by the American constitution in what is commonly called the Bill of Rights. On the one hand,

---

who is engaged with the Torah"; see Strack-Billerbeck, *Kommentar zum NT aus Talmud und Midrasch* (Munich: Oskar Beck, 1924), Vol. 2, p. 522. Another term, *ḥufšâ*, also derived from a common Semitic root (*ḥpš*; cf. Jean-Hoftijzer, p. 94) for "freedman," occurs in Lev. 19:20 of a freed slave, as does *ḥōfeš* in Sir. 7:21, etc. Including the *ḥofšît* of 2 Kings 15:5 = 2 Chr. 26:21, all these derivatives (not excluding Sir. 13:11) contain the idea of "freeing" or "to make free."

[15]Neither the Bible nor Babylonian law had a proper word for "slave." Slavery in the Semitic world was never a *status* as it became in Roman law. The Hebrew *'ebed* was a term also used for royal officials and of the service of the Lord. The Babylonian *wardu* or *ardu,* which corresponded, meant simply "one who has come down" in social position. Cf. G. R. Driver and John C. Miles, *The Babylonian Laws* (Oxford: Clarendon Press, 1952) Vol. I, p. 223, note 6.

[16]See the excellent discussion of this Old Testament background in José O. Tuñí Vancells, *La verdad os hará libres, Jn. 8, 32* (Barcelona: Herder, 1973), pp. 41-63.

we have a conception of human dignity that was first sensed in the experience of a liberating God whose redemptive action over some of humankind was eventually seen to have been patterned in the creation of humankind itself (Job 31:13-15 well illustrates the conclusion of the process). The elaboration of this conception was aided, perhaps, by common Near Eastern or Semitic presuppositions about humanity concerning which we can do little more than speculate. On the other hand, there is a philosophy of the rights of human beings rooted in a contemplation of the laws of nature and of nature's God, usually the contemplation of thinkers consciously influenced by the Old Testament and always of those who were unconsciously in tribute to it, a philosophy which had undergone a liberating experience of its own in its vindication over the hostile pretensions of kings and princes, parliaments, and star chamber proceedings.

Loose and inaccurate language, even on the part of our highest court, persists in referring to the provisions of the Bill of Rights as privileges. Privileges, however, they are not. Privileges are variously concessions, exceptions to general rules, favors granted by writ or rescript from the government to the governed. The Bill of Rights is not this at all, but rather an enumeration of the limitations imposed on government by the acknowledged rights of free men and women. They appear as the first ten amendments to the Constitution, but they are not amendments as are, say, the Sixteenth Amendment allowing the federal government to levy income taxes without apportionment among the States or the Seventeenth Amendment providing for the popular election of United States senators, both of which are genuine alterations of the original provisions of the written constitution. The Bill of Rights was attached to the Constitution because the legislatures of the several States would have it so as the price of ratification, because they were habituated to such specifications in the tradition of Magna Carta, as in the Petition of Right of 1628 or the Bill of Rights of 1689. It was precisely because such instruments had been construed as privileges wrested from reluctant princes that in the 84th of the Federalist Papers Alexander Hamilton would have had no Bill of Rights in the American constitution:

It is evident, therefore, that, according to their primitive signification they have no application to constitutions professedly founded upon the power of the people, and executed by their immediate representatives and servants. Here, in strictness, the people surrender nothing; and as they retain everything they have no need of particular reservations. . . .
I go further and affirm that bills of rights, in the sense and to the extent in which they are contended for, are not only unnecessary in the proposed Constitution, but would even be dangerous. They would contain various exceptions to powers not granted; and, on this very account, would afford a colourable pretext to claim more than were granted. For why declare that things shall not be done which there is no power to do? Why, for instance, should it be said that the liberty of the press shall not be restrained when no power is given by which restrictions may be imposed?

As we know, Hamilton's view did not prevail. The Constitution as finally adopted does contain a formal bill of rights. The incorporation of the so-called first ten amendments into the written document did not, however, change their nature in any way: they are exemplifications of what Orestes Brownson called (in distinction to the written constitution which "is simply a law ordained by the nation or people instituting and organizing the government") the unwritten constitution which is "the real or actual constitution of the people as a state or sovereign community, . . . providential, not made by the nation, but born with it."[17] They are exemplifications of that "higher law" which Edward S. Corwin found at the background of American constitutional law, whose origins reach back into the Middle Ages;[18] they are, as it happens, a fairly inspired summation of the common law tradition of human rights as it had painfully emerged through several centuries of often-one-sided dialogue and was eventually inherited by our founding fathers.

Not only professional libertarians but also various bar associa-

[17]*Works (The American Republic)*, pp. 18-113.
[18]Cf. Edward S. Corwin, *The "Higher Law" Background of American Constitutional Law* (Cornell University Press, 1955, 1959).

tions, constitutional lawyers, members of Congress, and judicial opinions, including those of the minority in Supreme Court decisions, have commented on the marked tendency, since the late 1960's in the aftermath of pronounced civil dissent, usually pacific but sometimes violent, of both the legislative and judicial branches of the government to come down hard on the side of law and order at the expense of personal freedom.[19] The Nixon Court—a term accepted by the White House itself as fairly applied in view of the former president's announced intention of shifting the ideological balance of the Supreme Court through his appointing power—has certainly played the major role in this process, both by upholding the constitutionality of certain congressional acts and by allowing or disallowing in sensitive areas of civil rights the decisions of inferior courts.

I shall mention only a couple of instances of the thing I have in mind. The Fourth Amendment to the Constitution guarantees the right of the people "to be secure in their persons, houses, papers, and effects, against unreasonable searches and seizures." The Watergate hearings before the select committee of the United States Senate were much concerned with violations of this right. The Fourth Amendment likewise states that "no warrant shall issue, but upon probable cause, supported by oath or affirmation, and particularly describing the place to be searched, and the person or things to be seized." Despite this language and despite this right, it is well known that the search warrant plays a role more in detective fiction than it does in actual life; at least ninety per cent of all searches in this country are warrantless.[20] Up to and including the day of its adjournment on July 6 of 1976, and with ominous precedents and portents subsequent, the Supreme Court has consistently ruled in a score of decisions to the effect of making search and seizure

[19]Cf. Leonard W. Levy, *Against the Law: The Nixon Court and Criminal Justice* (New York: Harper & Row, 1974).

[20]According to Richard Harris (writing in *The New Yorker* of November 10, 1975, p. 111), between 1929 and 1961, a period of thirty-two years, only two search warrants were issued by the Minneapolis Police Department, while tens of thousands of suspects were meanwhile searched.

even easier than it now is, allowing as admissable evidence obtained by lawless means, and widening the opportunities for surreptitious surveillance, the last mentioned having been given broad scope by the 1968 Omnibus Crime Control and Safe Streets Act of the Congress, which Senator Hiram Fong of Hawaii said began as the Right to Privacy Act and finally emerged as an End to Privacy Act.

My second instance concerns the Fifth Amendment, and again I shall restrict myself to something quite specific. The Fifth Amendment, of course, protects against self-incrimination; to invoke its provisions is not, as some have ignorantly imagined, to acknowledge guilt, but simply to take refuge in what is one of the supreme achievements of the common law, which will not compel a person to testify against himself or herself. One way that government has found of circumventing this provision of law is the granting of immunity from prosecution: this takes place, obviously, when its interest is in testimony that will involve and lead to the prosecution of third parties, since otherwise the process would be self-defeating. Whatever may be thought of this device, the courts have long held that having been granted immunity a person cannot invoke the Fifth Amendment with regard to the matter at hand, since effectively at least one can no longer incriminate oneself. The immunity in question has been called transactional, that is, exempting the person from prosecution in respect to the entire transaction about which he or she testifies. In 1970 Congress passed the Organized Crime Control Act which for the first time authorized "use immunity" in obtaining testimony otherwise barred by the Fifth Amendment. Use immunity precludes the use of a person's actual testimony against oneself but does not bar one's prosecution for the offense of which one accuses oneself should other, supposedly independent, evidence of the crime be forthcoming. The bar associations which viewed this Act with dismay — not for this feature of it alone — felt that it presumed on the part of prosecutors rather a higher degree of restraint or a lower degree of ingenuity than was to be justified by experience. Use immunity had been tried before but had been disallowed by the Supreme Court. The present Court has upheld the constitutionality of the law.

I have deliberately limited myself to these examples and shall therefore pass over many other, perhaps even more disturbing, illustrations of my meaning. Neither, of course, am I about to suggest that the Old Testament offers any direct guidance on these specifics—even though I find it at least interesting to reflect that Talmudic law did on Old Testament principles develop a statute against self-incrimination remarkably like that of the Fifth Amendment and centuries before our common law provision would take on its historical form.[21] What the Old Testament can do for us in these regards is, I think, twofold.

It can, first of all, as noted earlier, remind us to mistrust government. Mistrust of government is not denial of authority, which comes from God, but refusal to idolatrize the persons, the means, and the methods through which authority is administered. Mistrust of government is not motivated by a suspicion of evil intent or criminal act on its part but by that healthy cynicism about human beings and their ways with which the Old Testament is filled. "Be not just to excess," said the Preacher, "and be not overwise, lest you be ruined" (Eccl. 7:16). Mistrust of government is Isaiah's repudiation of "the wise" and Jeremiah's rejection of Zedekiah, who was not an evil man but an extremely inept one; and it is Ezekiel's law for the prince of the restored Israel (Ezek. 45:6-8, 46:16-18, etc.), not to mention Deuteronomy's law for the king. It is a fine old American tradition, which accounts for our having a Bill of Rights in the first place, though it has tended to take second place in recent times to another American tradition, which would have it that the solution to every problem is a new law. When this latter tradition is coupled, as it seems to have been, with the unexamined assumption that police, princes, and prosecutors will on their own recognizance observe those restraints which

---

[21]See Levy, *Origins* 433-441; *Encyclopedia Talmudica* (Jerusalem: Talmudic Encyclopedia Institute, 1969–) Vol. I, pp. 672-674; Strack Billerbeck, Vol. 3, p. 420. The Talmudic principle (San. 9b) *'en 'ādām mēśim 'aṣmo rāšā'*, "no man convicts himself of evil," was explained on the score that *'ādām qārōb 'eṣel 'aṣmô*, "a man is a neighbor in his own respect." There was debate as to whether the principle held equally well for women and slaves.

earlier Americans thought had to be imposed from without, the combination can make for doleful prognoses. I would hope, with or without the help of the Old Testament, that we might return to the older tradition.

The other thing that the Old Testament can do for us is to encourage us to prize and reexamine our heritage. "We do not do such things in Israel," Tamar's words to Amnon in 2 Sam. 13:12 (cf. Gen. 34:7), express a principle as unspecified as some* of those in the Bill of Rights—what are "unreasonable" searches, what is "excessive" bail, what are "cruel and unusual" punishments?—but they also expressed for all that a principle whose here-and-now purport was in no doubt, which drew its meaning from its being a living tradition enlivening the people who cherished it and who could find in it from generation to generation new inspiration. So it is with the common law principles which are our heritage. It has become fashionable in a debunking and cynical age to question the motives of such as our founding fathers in view of the obvious disproportion between the freedom which they so passionately espoused and the freedom which they actually brought forth on this continent, a freedom "to expand economically, unfettered by British restraints . . . precious only to a small segment of the population . . . not meant to encompass the lower orders of the white citizenry," let alone the black slaves in bondage, forty per cent of whom were in Virginia, where Thomas Jefferson brooded deeply over the "rights of man."[22] This is to miss the point of what our common law heritage is all about. Abraham Lincoln was not in error when he traced the genius of the American Republic from its Declaration of Independence, though life, liberty, and the pursuit of happiness meant to him something rather different from that they had meant to Edward Rutledge, let us say. Like the entwining of people and tradition in the Old Testament, so has been the entwining under our common law: our best instincts derive from it and in turn our best instincts

[22]See the review of Edmund S. Morgan's *American Slavery—American Freedom: The Ordeal of Colonial Virginia* by Alden Whitman in *The Chronicle of Higher Education* for January 12, 1976, p. 15.

feed into it new insights, new vitality, and new expansions and application. Recently John Coleman, in a study of the contributions to theology of Orestes Brownson, John A. Ryan, and John Courtney Murray, noted that it is one of the strongest weapons in the North American arsenal, by no means to be thrown away in the dialogue with Marxist social anaylsis of liberation theology, which is strangely silent on the issues of social pluralism, subsidiarity, and civil liberties.[23]

Gibson Winter has described America as

> nurtured by two faith communities—a community of natural right and a community of biblical faith. . . . In the American experience, civil and confessional heritages have furnished renewing transcendence one for the other in different historical periods. We now seem to be at a stage where the confessional heritage is a last hope for renewal and liberation; but this requires a retrieval of the religious heritage.[24]

If this is true, and I think it may very well be true, I propose that we begin to take another, perhaps more thoughtful, look at the original book of our religious heritage.

[23]Cf. John A. Coleman, S.J., "Vision and Praxis in American Theology," *Theological Studies* 37 (1976): 3-40.

[24]*Being Free. Reflections on America's Cultural Revolution* (New York: Macmillan, 1970), p. 140.

15. Are the Gospels Anti-Semitic?

Precis

The recognition that many Christian attitudes and actions have been anti-Semitic should lead to a refined theology of Judaism. Anti-Semitism may be defined as discrimination, contempt, and hatred for Jews as Jews. The Christian gospel which should be incarnated in every Christian affirms love rather than derogatory feelings toward others.

Many have discerned at least some roots of anti-Semitism in the Gospels in the way Jews are portrayed. The Gospels, being polemical in nature, are often oversimplified, one-sided, easily misunderstood writings. The ecumenical age should correct the misunderstandings as well as explain the origin and purpose of these words, written as an apology in an age of religious conflict.

Historically the following factors contributed to the tone of the Gospels: 1. Jewish hostility toward Christianity of the first century, which was part of a mutual emnity. 2. The tendency of Biblical writers to express themselves in absolute terms. This is true of some but certainly not of all references about Jews. Certain Gospel references use the term "Jews" as representing the unbelieving generation which confronted Jesus and the early church. 3. The apocalyptic tone of New Testamental thought which pitted the forces of good against the forces of evil in uncompromising terms condemning all those who did not accept Jesus (new Israel vs. old Israel).

The discovery of the Qumran scrolls enables the contemporary scholar to place primitive Christianity in its proper *milieu*.

Striking parallels can be made between Essene and Christian literature, even in respect to the derogatory remarks about fellow Jews. Thus the Gospels reflect a sectarian Jewish anti-Jewishness but certainly not anti-Semitism.

Many of the conflict-stories about Jesus and the Pharisees reflect the polemics of Christians and Jews of a later age which gradually led to complete separation of the two faiths. The Gospels accurately present Jesus in opposition to the ruling segments of the Jewish priestly hierarchy (Sadducees) which collaborated with the Roman authorities in the execution of Jesus. The Romans, however, rather than the Jews are responsible for the death verdict, though some Jews undoubtedly contributed to the crucifixion.

The Gospels contain unquestionable hostility toward Jews. Later Christians, reading them uncritically, interpreted this wrongly, which led to anti-Semitism that was not intended by the Gospel writers. This misinterpretation must be terminated. So, too, should suggestions linking the Gospels with anti-Semitic atrocities be stopped. Most of the anti-Semitic racist myths have been produced relatively recently and largely by anti-Christians, and were definitely not inspired by those who formulated or followed the teachings of the Gospels.

That much of the anguish of the Jews through the centuries has been due to the ignorance, the malice, sometimes to the well-intended but clumsy meddling of Christians, scholarly and unenlightened, clerical and lay, is hardly in need of documentation for any literate Christian today. In varying degrees of candor and with more or less happy choices of formulation the fact has been acknowledged officially by virtually every representative national and international body of Christian churches.[1]

---

[1]As regards the Declaration on the Jews of Vatican II, major breakthrough though it was in the history of the Catholic Church, one may certainly object to (1) its inclusion, on other than theological grounds (and the failure to acknowledge this candidly), in a general declaration on nonChristian religions, as though the attitude of Christians to Jews were *a pari* with their attitude

Though we may be skeptical about the immediate value of such declarations which—often with cause—invariably seem to disturb more Jews than they please, it is undoubtedly true that their ultimate effect will be to the betterment of Christian education, once their implications have been refined theologically as will surely take place the more serious we are about translating them into action. Christians are badly in need of a theology of Judaism just now, not only to replace the Christian myths from which both Jews and Christians have so often suffered in the past, but also to serve as a more substantial basis for brotherly understanding than the vaguely guilt-inspired desire to please that now prevails and which, unfortunately, seems to satisfy a great number of Jews.

Mainly it has been taken for granted by both Jew and Christian that anti-Semitism in the cruder sense as distinguished from mere dogmatic hostility and exclusivism has always been a perversion rather than an expression of the Christian spirit. By anti-Semitism "in the cruder sense" I mean, of course, hatred of and contempt for Jews as Jews, whether the attitude is disguised or overt, whether it contents itself with hostile thoughts or erupts into hostile actions, whether it acts with foul means or fair, or what it has persuaded itself are fair. I am not suggesting that there is an anti-Semitism that is less crude or not crude at all, but I am trying to identify what everyone will agree is anti-Semitism as distinct from other attitudes about which there may be less agreement or no agreement at all. "A good many studies have been willing to consider *any* acknowledgment that Jews are in *any way* different from non-Jews as being fundamen-

to Muslims and Buddhists, (2) the lack of any expression of contrition for Christian anti-Semitism, the unspoken cause of the declaration in the first place, and (3) the verbal weakening of the declaration in various ways done in the full light of worldwide publicity. No amount of rationalization can justify, for example, the elimination of the term "deicide" (cf. *The Documents of Vatican II*, ed. by Walter Abbott, S.J. [New York: Guild Press, etc., 1966], 666, ftn. 23). The term was needed precisely because it is terrible theology, precisely because it has been and is now, after the Council, being used (by such as Bishop Luigi Carli of Segni) as a term of indictment of the Jews of Jesus' time and our own.

tally anti-Semitic."[2] If this is anti-Semitism, it is not what I mean by anti-Semitism. Some Jews look on any missionary gesture of the Church as anti-Semitism: that the Roman liturgy has expunged from its Good Friday prayer for the Jews the offensive language that it once contained is to them less significant than that there should be a prayer in the first place. If this is anti-Semitism to some, however, it is not to those who pray the prayer, whose motive, however misguided it might be judged to be, is love and not hatred or contempt. By "the Christian spirit" I obviously mean the Christian Gospel, which admittedly has been perfectly incarnated only once and which frequently enough has not been incarnated at all in many who have called themselves Christian. Surely this is not too ambiguous an affirmation. Expressing his own reservations with regard to the Vatican Council's Declaration on the Jews, Abraham J. Heschel said: "I expected a document unconditioned, without ambiguities, just love and reverence, which the Gospels stand for."[3] This is what I understand the Gospels to be, too, bringing a message that is wholly incompatible with hatred or contempt for anyone.

Polemics In The Gospels

Rabbi Heschel's statement, however, can now bring us to the subject of this paper. Especially in these days of ecumenical goodwill we have become more and more sensitive to implications in the Gospels that have long been apparent to Jews, which have caused them to contend that in the Gospels themselves are

---

[2]Charles Y. Glock and Rodney Stark, *Christian Beliefs and Anti-Semitism* (New York: Harper & Row, 1966), 107, italics the authors'. They cite two questions used by Charles H. Stember, *Education and Attitude Change* (New York: Institute of Human Relations Press, 1961) as affirmative indices to anti-Semitic feelings: "Do you think there are any differences between Jews and other people?" "Do you think Jews are different from other people in any way?"

[3]Quoted in *The Dialogue,* Bulletin of the National Conference of Christians and Jews, No. 34, Sept. 1966, p. 3.

to be found the roots of anti-Semitism. Few have actually applied the label anti-Semitic to the Gospels, unless in one of the extremely broad and catch-all senses discussed above; but they have seen in them the beginnings of the pattern of myth and misrepresentation that leads to anti-Semitism or that feeds it. Among other things, it has been noted that "Pharisee"—an honored title for Paul—most often in the Gospels appears as a religious hypocrite, roughly a synthesis of everything that the Old Testament prophets opposed as retrograde and perverse. The suggestion is that the normative Judaism of Jesus' time has been systematically parodied as a soulless legalism in order to set in relief the supposed novelty of his own teaching (most of which, at least, can be duplicated in the sayings of the rabbis). Certainly it is difficult to justify historically a reference like that of Lk. 16,14 to the Pharisees as notorious money-lovers; such an indictment applies more properly to their bitter enemies the Sadducees. But as a matter of fact throughout the Gospels, despite their vaunted acquaintance with the Palestinian scene of the first Christian century, there is a bewildering confusion of Pharisees, Sadducees, scribes, chief priests, and Herodians, all of whom are represented singly and in concert as the enemies of Jesus. Such coalitions, while not impossible, have the antecedent likelihood of a liaison of the A.D.A. with the John Birch Society.

Nowhere has the truthfulness of the Gospel accounts been more seriously attacked than in respect to the Passion story, and in recent times no one has led the attack more successfully than the Jewish New Testament scholar Paul Winter.[4] Winter's conclusions, some of them, have themselves been carefully criticised, sometimes quite adversely,[5] but no one will ques-

---

[4]First in his *On The Trial of Jesus* (Studia Judaica, Forschungen zur Wissenschaft des Judentums I; Berlin: Walter de Gruyter, 1961),subsequently in various articles and responses, notably in *Commentary* of 1964 and 1965.

[5]Cf. (by a Jew) A. Schalit, "Kritische Randbemerkungen zu Paul Winters 'On The Trial of Jesus,' " *Annual of the Swedish Theological Institute* 2 (1963), 86-102. A fairly complete and certainly representative summary of the critical reaction to this book may be surveyed in the issues of *New Testament Abstracts*

tion his mastery of the form-critical studies on which his conclusions depend and the general integrity of his approach. At the very least, he has shown anew that none of the Gospel narratives of the Passion is scientifically historical as it stands. That is to say, these narratives are theological interpretations, all of which contain at least some details that could not have factually occurred. Without sharing Winter's skepticism regarding the basic historicity of the Gospel accounts, it is seemingly necessary to agree with his contention that the Passion story tends to transfer guilt for the crucifixion of Jesus from Romans to Jews, and that in doing so it partakes of a Gospel characteristic of waging polemics against contemporary Judaism.

Polemics, of course, is not ecumenism. Neither, however, is polemics necessarily malicious, uncharitable, or untruthful, though it is doubtless always somewhat one-sided and prone to *simplisme*, and it is obviously capable of being easily misunderstood by both friend and foe. Some of the misunderstandings open to readers of the New Testament have been countered with high success by Father Gregory Baum in his study of its attitudes towards the Jews.[6] To correct misunderstandings, however, is only part of the task in an ecumenical age. However important it may be to ensure that no would-be Christian bigot may derive aid and comfort from Gospel words like Mt. 27,25 ("His blood be on us and on our children") or Jn. 8,44 ("Your [the Jews'] father is the devil"), it is equally important to explain why the words are there in the first place and what they really do mean. It is no good to say with Frederick C. Grant, even if it were true, that these are "dreadful utterances, which ought to find no place in any sacred book."[7] They *are* in a sacred

6 (1961/62), 118f., 238f., 378f.; 7 (1962/63), 106f., 240, 364f.; 8 (1963/64), 116, 257f., 437; 9 (1964/65), 32, 117; 10 (1965/66), 110.

[6]Gregory Baum, O.S.A., *The Jews and the Gospel. A Re-examination of the New Testament* (Westminster, Md.: Newman, 1961); revised edition, *Is The New Testament Anti-Semitic? A Re-examination of the New Testament* (Glen Rock, N.J.: Paulist Press, 1965).

[7]*Ancient Judaism and the New Testament* (New York: Macmillan, 1959), 14.

book, and there they will remain. Perhaps in an ecumenical age they would never have been written, but the Gospels were not written in an ecumenical age. They are words that, even if we would, we cannot translate away.[8] Rather, we must face up to the fact that, for better or for worse and among many other things, the Gospels are polemical and apologetic literature that came out of an age of conflict, and while it is necessary to understand them in this light neither do we have cause to apologize for them or to try to make them say something other than they actually say. Rather, we must respect the spirit and the forms in which they have been written,[9] and we must recognize the individual purposes of the men who authored them.[10]

The Historical Background

In order to understand better the polemical character of the Gospels in respect to the Jews, we ought to have carefully in mind at least these following factors of historical relevance.

1. First of all, the Gospels are the product of an era in which the Church had suffered and continued to suffer from hostility and persecution which for all practical purposes were exclusively

[8]Michael D. Zeik, "Anti-Semitism and the Gospel," *Commonweal* 86 (Mar. 24, 1967), 16-18, makes a good point of the need of interpretive translation for the vast majority whose sole contact with the Bible is through its bare word without either commentary or context. But translation can go only so far, and in some instances it can alone do nothing at all except present us with problems for interpretation. I know of no convincing way of translating John's *Ioudaioi* except "Jews," whatever context the word has in the text. One of the responsibilities we must increasingly acknowledge towards those whom we expose to the word liturgically or otherwise is that it must not be proclaimed as a bare word. "How can I understand, unless someone shows me?" (Acts 8,31) needs asking by more than the Ethiopian, and answering by more than Philip.

[9]Cf. Dominic M. Crossan, O.S.M., "Anti-Semitism and the Gospel," *Theological Studies* 26 (1965), 189-214.

[10]Cf. Joseph A. Fitzmyer, S.J., "Anti-Semitism and the Cry of 'All the People,' " *Theological Studies* 26 (1965), 667-671.

Jewish. At the end of the apostolic age, it is true, the menace of the deified Roman State was both sensed and felt by the Christian community, and its reaction can be seen in the second half of the Apocalypse of John. (Yet even here, contrast the first part of the Apocalypse, which speaks only of Jewish persecution and a Jewish menace.[11]) By and large, throughout most of the New Testament, and especially perhaps in the Gospels, Rome is regarded as a force for good rather than for evil, the peace-keeper, the guarantor of law and order, to which tribute was to be paid. This situation obviously could not long outlast Christianity's loss of status as a *religio licita* when it came to be viewed no longer as another Jewish sect and when more than taxes were demanded by Caesar; but this time had not yet come when the Gospel materials were being formed.

On the other hand, from the very earliest of the New Testament documents, say around A.D. 50, Jewry is seen as the enemy to the Church's survival (cf. 1 Thes 2,14-16). Paul's utterances on this occasion are perhaps not models of that Christian patience which he otherwise extolled, but neither is it just to ignore their provocation. The provocation had begun in the synagogues of Palestine and the Diaspora, where Christianity was first preached and whence its early adherents were cast out as *mînîm,* heretics (proleptically recorded in John's Gospel, 9,22; 12,42; 16,2). And what Paul had observed in the 50's did not abate but rather increased in the 60's and the 70's.

> It is a tragedy that "the Israel of God" should have found its chief opponents from within Judaism—a tragedy made the more poignant when pre-Christian Judaism itself had had so noble a roll of martyrs to its credit, and indeed non-Christian Judaism was to continue to suffer at least obloquy and ridicule for its faith concurrently with Christianity. But that is the fact. . . . To make the situation more complicated, it appears to be true that the non-Christian Jews were most prone to persecute the Christians when Judaism was itself under attack by the Roman imperial authorities. The times

[11]Cf. Martin Hopkins, O.P., "The Historical Perspective of Apocalypse 1-11," *Catholic Biblical Quarterly* 27 (1965), 42-47.

when there was most tolerance were precisely the times when external pressure was at its least. Relations between Christians and Jews were strained to breaking-point most naturally when it was dangerous for the one to acknowledge any contact with the other.[12]

There is no thought here of suggesting that the provocation was all one-sided. We are merely making the point that the undeniable hostility to normative Judaism manifested in the Gospels did not come out of a vacuum of gratuitous malice. The mutual antagonism of Christians and Jews found reflections in both Jewish and Christian literature. In the Gospels it certainly accounts for a proclivity to speak well of the Romans in opposition to the Jews. No less certainly does it account for the prevalence of the conflict-story, the Gospel form in which Jesus is so often pictured at odds with the leaders of Judaism, opposing his teaching to theirs. There can be no doubt that this literary form owes its popularity in the Gospels to the controversies between Christians and Jews and to the need of the Church, especially the Palestinian Church, to find a precedent for its beliefs and discipline in the analogous situations of the life of Jesus.[13] For the same reason, the antagonists of Jesus have so often by preference been identified as "the Scribes and Pharisees," i.e., those who were *par excellence* the intellectual leaders of Judaism. At only a small remove from this has been the tendency of the later tradition to mix Scribes and Pharisees together with Sadducees and High Priests fairly indiscriminately. All of them had opposed Jesus and all of them stood for the

[12]C.F.D. Moule, *The Birth of the New Testament* (New York: Harper & Row, 1962), 105f. The reader may be referred especially to pp. 105-124. Cf. also Howard Clark Kee, Franklin W. Young, and Karlfried Froehlich, *Understanding the New Testament* (Englewood Cliffs, N.J.: Prentice-Hall, 1965), 239-246.

[13]Cf. Rudolf Bultmann, *The History of the Synoptic Tradition* (tr. John Marsh; Oxford: Blackwell, 1963), 39-54. Bultmann, it should be noted, considers these stories to be fictional as to narrative details, made to order for the occasion, though perhaps reproducing authentically the sayings of Jesus that are imbedded in them. We return to this matter below.

synagogue that now opposed his Church; their historical differences, if they were remembered, no longer greatly mattered to a Christianity that had now grown far beyond Palestine. The last stage is to be found in John's Gospel, where Jesus' adversaries can more often than not be identified simply as "the Jews."[14]

2. A second point, not unrelated to the preceding, must be made in regard to the thought processes of the writers of the Gospels. There is in the Bible, Old Testament and New, a manner of speech that follows a bent of mind that has been variously called "the Semitic relative absolute" or "totality thinking."[15] Neglect of it as a principle of interpretation can be disastrous. We can read, for example, in the Book of Samuel:

> Samuel took a stone and erected it between Mizpah and Jeshanah and gave it the name Ebenezer, saying, "Thus far has Yahweh aided us." So the Philistines were humbled and no longer came into Israelite territory; the hand of Yahweh lay on the Philistines all Samuel's lifetime. The towns the Philistines had taken from Israel were given back to them, from Ekron to Gath, and Israel freed their territory from the power of the Philistines. There was peace, too, between Israel and the Amorites (1 Sm. 7,12-14).

We may become somewhat disconcerted, several chapters on, at finding Samuel instructed by the Lord to anoint Saul king so that "he will save my people from the power of the Philistines; for I have seen the distress of my people and their cry has come

---

[14]It certainly ought to be remembered in this connexion that Paul, "a Hebrew of Hebrews and a Pharisee" (Phil. 3,5), can also refer to his persecutors in the third person as "the Jews" (2 Cor. 11,24) in the same breath with which he insists on his Hebrew and Israelite origin. See our observations under no. 3 of this section.

[15]Cf. Bernard J. LeFrois, S.V.D., "Semitic Totality Thinking," *Catholic Biblical Quarterly* 17 (1955), 315-323. The idea of "corporate personality" to which we refer below has been discussed quite thoroughly by Jean de Fraine, S.J., *Adam and the Family of Man* (tr. Daniel Raible, C.P.P.S.; New York: Alba House, 1965), though without specific reference to our problem.

to me" (1 Sm. 9,16). Not only were the Philistines not confined to their enclave bounded by Ekron and Gath during Samuel's lifetime, but most of the time they were in practical control of the heartland of Israel (cf. 1 Sm. 13f). We will be told,
and correctly, that variant sources have been combined here,
each of which for reasons of its own painted the age of Samuel
in extravagant colors. What we may easily overlook is the mentality of the biblical author who assembled these sources into
the Book of Samuel, who was at home with the temper of the
documents he employed and who shared it. The Bible does not
arrive at its conclusions by synthesis but by laying one con-
tradictory alongside another.

Biblical language, accordingly, is rarely nuanced; it is more
often absolute. "There is not one good man left, not a single
one" (Ps. 14,3). "I have loved Jacob, and hated Esau" (Mal.
1,3). "If any man comes to me without hating his father, mother,
wife, children, brothers, sisters, yes and his own life too, he
cannot be my disciple" (Lk. 14,26). Especially is this true in
respect to what has been called "corporate personality" whereby
the individual, or the few, readily stand for the whole. In the
exilic poems of the Second Isaiah (Is. 40-55) the one and the
same Israel appears now as a poor worm, a broken people
destroyed for its sins, now as the servant of the Lord whose
undeserved suffering has atoned for the sins of others.

Within this style of thinking and writing are to be placed many
of the Gospels' references to the Jews. The Gospels do not, as
a matter of fact, represent Jesus as rejected by the Jews of his
time or as handed over by them to execution by the Romans.
On the contrary, without exception they record his enormous
popularity with "the people" or "the crowds" both in Galilee and
in Judea, and they portray the circumstances of the crucifixion
as precipitated by a small and desperate cabal of men who had
to do their work covertly for fear of arousing against themselves
a general rebellion of their own people. The anti-Jewish hostility
of the Gospels, in other words, is selective.[16] However, in view

---

[16]This is especially apparent in Luke, who both before and after the Passion represents "the people" as at odds with "the leaders" over the disposition

of the tendencies we have just been discussing, neither is it surprising that so often for John the opponents of Jesus are "the Jews" *tout court*, and it is left for us to determine from the context or circumstances what Jews are involved. In somewhat the same way Luke has made "the crowds" (usually his term for the friendly following of Jesus) the targets of the Baptist's bitter denunciation in Lk. 3,7 (parallel in Mt. 3,7 has "many of the Pharisees and Sadducees"), doubtless by assimilation with the scene with "the crowds" of vv. 10-14 which is unparalleled in the other Gospels, though a literalist interpretation of the term in v. 7 would set it in profound contradiction with its use in v. 10.

Of a somewhat different situation, but in the same framework of thought, is Matthew's cry of "all the people" in Mt. 27,25. For Matthew as for John "the Jews" are the unbelieving generation confronting the Gospel: note the reference to "the Jews" in Mt. 28,15. (By all accounts, the Gospel of Matthew emerged from a church which had had a particularly tense relationship with the Jews and which felt the need of a strongly Jewish-directed apologetic. Antioch in Syria, which had a large Jewish population, is generally thought of as its place of origin.) Accordingly, there is no doubt that he seized on the episode of renunciation which he found in his sources—"his blood be on us and on our children"—as symbolizing the moment at which in his conception of salvation history the age of Israel passed, leaving the unbelieving synagogue.[17] Through corporate personality the "crowd" (v. 15) or "crowds" (v. 20) gathered before Pilate have assumed the character of "the whole people." As for the cry itself, there is no reason to question its factuality,

---

made of Jesus (cf. Lk. 19,49; 20,1.6.9.16.19.26.45; 21,38; 23,27.35.48; 24,19f.). The sole seeming exception is Lk. 23,13, which for that reason is corrected by some modern scholars. Cf. G. Rau, "Das Volk in der lukanischen Passionsgeschichte, eine Konjektur zu Lk. 23:13," *Zeitschrift für die Neutestamentliche Wissenschaft* 56 (1963), 41-51. Or there may be a situation like that of Lk. 3,7.

[17]Cf. Georg Strecker, *Der Weg der Gerechtigkeit. Untersuchung zur Theologie des Matthäus* (Göttingen: Vandenhoeck & Ruprecht, 1962), 106f., 115-117.

though it must be admitted that we have no evidence independent of the Gospels for the historical background that it presupposes. Matthew represents it as the cry of a mob of undetermined size which had gathered to petition for the release of Barabbas, evidently the popular leader of a nationalistic uprising, and which was easily persuaded to the concomitant action of calling for the crucifixion of Jesus.[18] The words echo Old Testament formulas (cf. Jer. 51,35; 2 Sm. 1,16; 3,29) and signify the assumption of legal responsibility for the execution of a criminal.[19]

3. A final consideration has to do with the cultural milieu in which the Gospel materials were formed and which has necessarily influenced their language and concepts. That was the milieu of eschatological and apocalyptic thought—a way of thinking in which good and evil appear locked in final and definitive combat, in which there is an imperative call to decide between light and darkness (as ethical rather than gnostic alternatives), between "this world" (under the judgment of God) and "the world to come" (that is, the kingdom of God coming in power). This is a way of thinking in blacks and whites, hardly in grays: there is no room whatever for the gentle agnostic, the disinterested bystander, the no-opinion residuum of the opinion polls. The only alternative to saving faith is willful unbelief: "He who believes and is baptized will be saved; he who does not believe will be condemned," it is written in the supplement to Mark's Gospel (Mk. 16,16). The alternative to the

---

[18]So is the situation also as recorded by Mk. 15,6-15, which Mt. follows closely. Neither Lk. nor Jn. have anything about the special delegation. Luke, in view of 23,13, is unclear (see note 16 above), but it is likely that in his mind the call for the crucifixion was that of "the chief priests and leaders of the people." For John, of course, it was "the Jews," whom, however, he has consistently identified in the Passion narrative as the plotters among the leadership opposed to Jesus.

[19]Cf. Strack-Billerbeck, *Kommentar zum Neuen Testament aus Talmud und Midrasch* (Munich: Beck, 1922), I, 1033, which cites among other references the tractate *Sanhedrin* 4, 5. See thereto *The Babylonian Talmud* (tr. Michael J. Rodkinson; Boston: The Talmud Society, 1918), vol. 8, p. 111.

acknowledgment of God's fatherhood through acceptance of his Son is to profess oneself of the progeny of Satan (Jn. 8,44). One belongs either to the new Israel, God's assembly (*synagōgē*) of the eschatological times, or he allies himself to the synagogue of Satan (Ap. 2,9; 3,9).[20]

Fortunately we have been afforded a means of re-setting the primitive Christianity of the Gospels in its contemporary milieu through the comparative material made available through the discovery of the Qumrân literature beginning in 1947. This literature, pertaining to a Jewish sect of Essenian stamp centered in the Judean desert west of the Dead Sea which co-existed with the nascent Palestinian Church, displays many striking parallels with the literature of the New Testament, in language, concepts, and institutions.[21] Like the first Christians, the sectaries of Qumrân regarded themselves as the true Israel of God, the heirs to Israel's prophetic heritage, the chosen remnant. They were, in their view, "the children of light": in the New Testament John, Paul, and Peter found it most natural to use this terminology for Christians. And who were, therefore, "the children of darkness"? Obviously, all who rejected the light (cf. Jn. 3,19f.). Specifically, both for the Qumrânites and for the first Christians, this meant in practice (the rest of) their fellow Jews. Just as John, restricting himself to the purview of Jesus' lifetime, identifies with "the Jews" the unbelieving world which has not accepted the new light of revelation,[22] so it is with the Qumrân sectaries whose geographical and religious perspectives were similarly restricted. It should be remarked in this connexion that in none of the Gospels is to be found as bitter and as inexorable a rejection of normative Judaism as we find in the

[20]In this undeniably harsh language used by a Christian author of certain Jews of Smyrna and Philadelphia, it ought not be overlooked that in each instance "Jew" itself is for him a term of respect.

[21]The reader may find a balanced and careful study of some of the parallels with Frank M. Cross, Jr., *The Ancient Library of Qumrân and Modern Biblical Studies* (New York: Doubleday, 1958), 146-180.

[22]Erich Gräser, "Die antijüdische Polemik im Johannesevangelium," *New Testament Studies* 11 (1964), 74-90.

literature of Qumrân. In both cases there is anti-Jewishness, but a Jewish anti-Jewishness that certainly does not add up to anti-Semitism, however sectarian it may be judged to have been.

Furthermore, the kindred anti-Jewishness has expressed itself in somewhat divergent practical attitudes. In the *Serek hayyaḥad*, the "Manual of Discipline" of the Qumrân community, we read:

> Everyone who wishes to join the community must pledge himself to respect God and man; to live according to the communal rule; to seek God [. . .]; to do what is good and upright in His sight, in accordance with what He has commanded through Moses and through His servants the prophets; to love all that He has chosen and hate all that He has rejected; to keep far from all evil and to cling to all good works; to act truthfully and righteously and justly on earth and to walk no more in the stubbornness of a guilty heart and of lustful eyes, doing all manner of evil; to bring into a bond of mutual love all who have declared their willingness to carry out the statutes of God; to join the formal community of God; to walk blamelessly before Him in conformity with His various laws and dispositions; to love all the children of light, each according to his stake in the formal community of God; and to hate all the children of darkness, each according to the measure of his guilt, which God will ultimately requite.[23]

In this sonorous and generally admirable series of propositions it would doubtless be unfair to seize on the injunction to hatred in isolation from the Old Testament precedents in whose spirit it has been formulated, execrations which are properly directed towards the existential presence of evil rather than to nurse any personal animosity (so also Ap. 18,20). Nevertheless, it is instructive to compare the parallel Gospel formulations that undoubtedly rose from the same life situation, namely, from the consideration of the attitude to be adopted towards those

---

[23]*1QS* 1,1-11a. I have quoted the translation of Theodor H. Gaster, *The Dead Sea Scriptures* (New York: Doubleday, 1956), 39.

who were conceived as the enemies of God's Church and people:[24]

You have heard how it was said, "You shall love your neighbor and hate your enemy." But I say this to you: love your enemies and pray for those who persecute you; in this way you will be sons of your Father in heaven, for he causes his sun to rise on bad men as well as good, and his rain to fall on honest and dishonest men alike. For if you love those that love you, what credit do you have? Do not even the publicans do this much? And if you greet only your brothers, what do you do that is so exceptional? Do not even the Gentiles do this much?	But I say this to you who are listening: love your enemies, do good to those who hate you, bless those who curse you, pray for those who treat you badly. For if you love those that love you, what thanks do you expect? Even sinners love those who love them. And if you do good to those who do good to you, what thanks do you expect? Even sinners do that much. . .
You must therefore be perfect just as your heavenly Father is perfect (Mt. 5,43–48).	Be compassionate just as your Father is compassionate (Lk. 6, 27-28.32-33.36).

Conclusion: The Jews in the Gospels

Without doubt there are more complexities to the question of the Jews in the Gospels than we are capable of dealing with in a treatment as brief as this one necessarily is. Nevertheless, in some fashion we have been able to touch on the major issues connected with the problem.

[24]Cf. Werner Foerster, *Theologisches Wörterbuch zum Neuen Testament* II, 813f. (*s.v. echthros*).

1. The polemic which the Gospels wage against the Pharisees certainly cannot be separated from early Christian apologetics directed against the Jews. The prevalence of the conflict-story, resulting perhaps in an overstress of this situation as respects the historical circumstances of the ministry of Jesus, owes much to this *Sitz im Leben* of primitive Christianity in Palestine and the Diaspora. This does not mean, however, that these stories have no authentic situation within Jesus' own life; rather do they reflect true disputes over the meaning of the Law that echo the Shammai-Hillel controversies within the bosom of first-century Palestinian Jewry.[25] What has happened in the process of transmission of these stories by the Christian community is, of course, that controversies over the spirit and interpretation of the Law have more and more been seen as precedents for its abandonment entirely, in keeping with the Church's growing awareness of its separation from Judaism.[26]

2. Jesus is likewise shown in the Gospels to have been in the most profound opposition to the highpriestly caste of Jewish society and to have attracted their fatal attention. The likelihood of this situation in the context of its time is beyond question: if only a small fraction of what is described in the Gospels of Jesus' deeds and sayings were factual, such a confrontation would have been inevitable. Everything that is said in the Gospels about the family and person of Joseph Caiaphas is perfectly

---

[25]Cf. Asher Finkel, *The Pharisees and the Teacher of Nazareth. A Study of Their Background, Their Halachic and Midrashic Teachings, The Similarities and Differences* (Arbeiten zur Geschichte des Spätjudentums und Urchristentums, 4; Leiden: Brill, 1964), 129-175.

[26]Thus in Mk. 2,23-28, a conflict-story ending in a pronouncement with which many other rabbis would have concurred ("the Sabbath was made for man and not man for the Sabbath") is capped by what was probably originally a later Christian commentary: "so the Son of Man is Lord even of the Sabbath." Into a pronouncement resulting from a similar controversy over law and tradition (Mk. 7,14-23) has been interpolated in v. 19b "(this he said) pronouncing all foods to be clean," suggesting the abolition of the Mosaic distinctions and thus going beyond the limits of the controversy.

consonant with verdicts that have been passed by Jewish historians, ancient and modern.[27]

3. The Gospels represent the crucifixion as a Roman execution precipitated at the initiative and with the complicity of some highly placed Jews, chiefly of this highpriestly, Sadducean element. Here it is not possible to go into detail concerning the literary form of the Passion narrative, basically three versions of which are represented in our Gospels. As already indicated, theological considerations have played a large part in its formation, together with a lack of enduring concern for many of its statistical aspects. As the accounts now stand, a factual history of the crucifixion and trial of Jesus has to be reconstructed rather than read from them. There seems to be no doubt that Jewish responsibility has been heightened at the expense of the Roman, for reasons that have been indicated above. In particular, the governor Pontius Pilate as portrayed in the Gospels appears to be credited with a greater degree of disinterested justice in his makeup than other historical sources concerning him would cause us to suspect. On the other hand, it should be observed that John, who is the most often charged with anti-Jewishness in his handling of the Gospel narratives, very clearly ranges Pilate along with "the Jews" as representative of the unbelieving world that will not accept the truth (cf. Jn. 18,38), and it is John alone of the evangelists who speaks of Roman intervention from the very beginning of the Passion story, at the time of Jesus' arrest (cf. Jn. 18,3).[28]

4. Under the conditions noted, therefore, it is an inescapable fact that a hostility to the Jews is manifest in various ways in the Gospels. When the Gospels have been uncritically read and

[27]Cf. Heinrich Graetz, *History of the Jews* (Philadelphia: Jewish Publication Society, 1941), II,237: "Avarice and greed of power were the mainsprings of the actions of those who were elected to represent the highest ideal of morality; the Temple was despoiled by its dignitaries even before the enemy forced his way into it with his weapons of murder."

[28]By mentioning the presence of the Roman cohort. In the versions of Matthew (25,47) and Mark (14,43) Jesus is arrested by a nondescript mob, though sent by the Jewish leaders inimical to Jesus; Luke (22,47.52) says that members of the Temple police were present.

explained, there can be no doubt that this hostility has been further increased and distorted in Christian minds and has been made the occasion of an anti-Semitism of a kind the Gospels never intended. It is imperative that we guard against the recurrence of any such thing by every educational and catechetical means at our disposal, and that we rigorously root out every vestige of medieval legend and bogus theology that have fed on a simplistic hearing of the Gospel message. It may be doubted, for example, whether even the very best Passion Play can ever entirely avoid travesty of the Gospel story in precisely the same way that, by its literalism in dealing with poetic themes, Hollywood periodically travesties the Bible as a whole with its "biblical" movies.

At the same time, it would be hoped that we be spared some of the counterexaggerations that have been offered in the name of ecumenical understanding and setting the record straight. The warmed-over rationalist mythology of *The Passover Plot* is only one such extreme. To suggest, as some seem to be prepared to do, that no Jew had anything to do with the crucifixion, and that there is a straight ideological line linking the Gospels with the furnaces of Auschwitz, is another extreme that is obvious nonsense. Gruesome as are the annals of anti-Semitism, Christian and other, it is doubtful that the Gospels have had very much of a real part to play in any of them. The terrible myth of ritual murder for which so many Jews suffered innocently in the Middle Ages was devised by men who called themselves Christians; but the myth is hardly older than the 12th century, not notoriously a time influenced by the Gospels, but subject to many other less Christian influences. The myth of Jewish world conspiracy rose in the 18th century, in the age of the Enlightenment. The Protocols of the Elders of Zion were not fabricated till the end of the 19th century and gained no credence till the early 20th century.[29] The nationalistic and other considerations that provoked these excrescences had little if anything

---

[29]Cf. Norman Cohn, *The Myth of the Jewish World-Conspiracy and the Protocols of the Elders of Zion* (New York: Harper & Row, 1967). A generous preview of this study was published in *Commentary* for June of 1966.

to do with Christianity, let alone the Gospels. The myth of racism is the creature of the Nietzsches, the Gobineaus, the Chamberlains, of men more often anti-Christian than not. Without the myth of race the horrors of modern anti-Semitism could never have been, and this is a myth of which the Gospels are entirely innocent. The cause of understanding will not be furthered by making the Gospels either more or less or other than what they are. To explain what they are is a great task that still mainly lies before us. One thing that they are not, is anti-Semitic.

16. Divorce and the New Testament

1. State of the Question

Preoccupation with the NT teaching on divorce has been constant and continuous since the present author first became interested in the subject well over twenty years ago,[1] just as it had been constant and continuous long before that time. Despite all the intellectual and literary effort brought to bear on the matter during this period, however, it is hard to discover much that has happened to compel practically anyone to alter the substance of his previous position to suit another. What was generally agreed on once seems to be generally agreed on still, and what was then debatable has not yet been taken far from the forum of legitimate dispute.

What appears to be certain is that there was a teaching of Jesus, or at least what was confidently assumed by the early church to be a teaching of Jesus, that spoke against divorce in quite absolute terms. The teaching is attested to directly by three sources of NT witness and indirectly, perhaps, by an additional one. The three direct witnesses are, first of all, an isolated *logion* or saying of Jesus that was found in that putative source of the synoptic tradition which is known to the critics as Q, that sayings-source which together with Mark (or a proto-Mark) is

---

[1]Cf. my "The Divorce Clauses in Mt 5, 32 and 19, 9," *CBQ* 16 (1954) 155-67. That article contained a fair summation of the relevant bibliographical material up to that date. Additional material was noticed in my 1967 article mentioned below. In the present writing I cannot pretend to have caught up with all the subsequent literature that I would like to have consulted. The articles which I cite below, especially those by Fitzmyer and Vargas-Machuca, are rich in bibliographical detail and cite additional sources, though I have also found a few that escaped their vigilance.

supposed to have been a quarry of primary material for the composition of the gospels of Matthew and Luke. This *logion*, now with suitable modifications on both sides, is what we read in Matt 5:32 and Luke 16:18. The second witness is contained in the conflict story of Mark 10:2-12 = Matt 19:3-12 encapsulating, again with appropriate modifications in narrative detail and purport, the same or a similar saying of Jesus thrown into the context of a debate between himself and the leaders of Judaism. The third witness is that of Paul in 1 Cor 7:10-11, the Apostle's ascription to the Lord of a prohibition of divorce on the part of either husband or wife which may be a reminiscence of the *logion* of Q or of Mark-Matthew or maybe of another one much to the same effect. The indirect attestation comes from the Pastoral Epistles, which in 1 Tim 3:2 and Titus 1:6 with regard to religious men (*episkopoi*) and in 1 Tim 5:9 with regard to religious women ("widows") envinces a distaste for multiple marriages even when the freedom of remarriage was not in question in view of the death of a previous spouse (cf. 1 Cor 7:8-9, Rom 7:2-3). The implication seems to have been that there was something about Christian marriage that somehow constituted it once for all, something that declared it indissoluble even beyond death, at least under certain circumstances, whatever the accepted legalities might otherwise be.

These are the facts that are not at contest in the subject that lies before us. What is debatable in the matter are all the conclusions that have been drawn from these many texts together with most of the interpretations that have been offered them. We shall try to take up these questions one by one in the order in which we have listed them, offering in the process our own commentary as a small contribution to the ongoing discussion, and at the end we shall venture some conclusions.

2. *The NT Texts*

(1) The isolated Q *logion* (Matt 5:32 = Luke 16:18) is precisely that, isolated, and we are afforded no opportunity of judging where, if ever, it played any part in the teaching of the histor-

ical Jesus of Nazareth. In the Q collection of *logia* it presumably was given no historical context at all, provided that Q was indeed the kind of sayings-source that scholars generally consider it to have been. In Matthew it has been made one of the antinomies of the Sermon on the Mount, where the evangelist makes Pharisaical practice of the Law a backdrop on which to feature Jesus as a greater than Moses, as Teacher of the true Way of Righteousness. In Luke it appears almost out of the blue, one of a series of aphorisms tacked on the Parable of the Shrewd Steward (16:1-8), immediately introduced by the derisory reaction of the Pharisees to the parable (v 14), a reaction which invites a contrast between their doctrine and that of Jesus (vv 15-18). What is common to both versions of the saying is the close connection made between divorce and adultery. But there is also a significant difference. To paraphrase the two texts:

Matthew	*Luke*
who puts away his wife[ ]	who puts away his wife and marries another woman
makes her an adulteress	becomes an adulterer
who marries a divorcée	who marries a divorcée
becomes an adulterer	becomes an adulterer

I find it hard to agree with Fitzmyer[2] when he suggests that Luke has preserved the older form of this *logion*. It is true, the Matthean *parektos logou porneias* omitted above where it is represented by brackets undoubtedly constitutes a modification of the primitive text: these words add up to an "exceptive" clause like the one found in the later Matt 19:9 which has similarly modified the text paralleled in Mark 10:11. We shall speak to the *porneia* issue below. As regards the substance of the saying, however, while I find its Lucan form easy to explain as an adaptation to the Marcan version that appears in the conflict story of Mark and Matthew—a story which Luke knew, of course, even though it did not find its way into the Third Gospel—it is rather incomprehensible to me that Matthew should

[2]Cf. Joseph A. Fitzmyer, S.J., "The Matthean Divorce Texts and Some New Palestinian Evidence," *TS* 37 (1976) 197-226, here referring to 201-2.

have so curiously altered the direction of the Q *logion* when he did nothing of the kind in his acceptation of the Marcan story.

Certainly the direction of the Q saying has been radically changed by someone, either by Matthew or by Luke. In its Matthean form a man who repudiates his wife is said to make her an adulteress. That is, he puts her in jeopardy of adultery by declaring her free of a bond which he has no right to dissolve. Whatever his declaration, she remains his wife and therefore by remarriage she will become an adulteress against him. Correspondingly, another man who marries such a repudiated woman will become an adulterer, because he sins against this bond that continues to exist. Luke's is another situation, according to which the husband himself becomes an adulterer by marrying another woman after repudiating his wife. There should be little question about which version of this pronouncement has the better chance of originality in a Palestinian scene. At least in theory, marriage and divorce were in that context entirely the prerogative of the male. A man could become an adulterer only by tampering with another man's marriage (so the second part of the Q saying, where both Matthew and Luke are at one), not by anything he could do with his wife or with any other woman who did not belong to another man. The "and marries another woman" of Luke, therefore, has changed the focus of the *logion* far more fundamentally than has the "exceptive" clause introduced by Matthew.[3] Luke's version of the saying is entirely compatible with his proclivity to Gentilize the alleged *logia* of Jesus, even as the Marcan conflict story has obviously Gentilized into a universalistic *casus conscientiae* what appears in Matthew as the challenge to resolve a rabbinical debate. Both Matthew and Luke presuppose the indissolubility of marriage. Only Matthew looks at it entirely from the male standpoint, and by this token it may be assumed that Matthew

---

[3]Cf. D. Heinrich Greeven, "Ehe nach dem Alten Testament," *NTS* 15 (1968-69) 365-88. In Greeven's reconstruction, "makes her an adulteress" into "becomes an adulterer" would have entailed only a slight recasting of the same Aramaic verb. Fitzmyer, without specifying why, considers Greeven's arguments to be "forced and unconvincing."

is closer to what a Palestinian Jesus or his spokesman may have said.

It may be added at this point—though we renew our intention of discussing the subject below—that if the *porneia* of Matt 5:32 and 19:9 really meant "adultery," as both traditional Protestant and now some Catholic commentators want to insist, the Matthean "exceptions" would take on rather different acceptations in their separate contexts. In 5:32 we would be left simply with a banality: He who divorces his wife, unless she is already an adulteress, now makes her liable to become an adulteress.[4] In 19:9, however, where the husband makes himself an adulterer through divorce and remarriage, *porneia* really says something about the liceity of divorce. Is it likely that the Matthean redactor would have intended that these two *porneia* additions should have served such disparate ends, or, if such ends had in fact been served inadvertently, that such a fact would indeed have escaped his attention?

(2) In Mark 10:2-12 and Matt 19:3-12 there is pictured a conflict situation between Jesus and the Pharisees, in which the question of divorce is raised and a response is given by Jesus that on the basis of God's intention in creation, monogamous and permanent marriage was to be the rule for mankind. Into both passages something very like the Q *logion* associating divorce with adultery has been incorporated. We can consider the narrative first and then the *logion* and what has been done with it.

The narrative represents Jesus under inquisition (the Pharisees *peirazontes auton)* concerning the legalities of divorce. In Mark the question is about the liceity of divorce as such: "Is it lawful

---

[4]Friedrich Hauck and Siegfried Schulz (*TWNT* 6 [1960] 590-94 [*s. v. pornē ktl]*)) rightly defend the originality of the Matthean version of the Q logion (historically, it does not seek to radicalize the Law, as is Matthew's wont, over against Pharisaical practice, nor to denigrate the latter in terms of later church practice). They also make *porneia = moicheia* according to Sir 23:23, a very difficult thing to prove, if it is to be taken in the sense of marital infidelity. Correctly, they explain the exceptive clauses in the Matthean texts as giving no grounds for divorce but rather as excusing the man who was forced willy-nilly by Jewish custom to divorce by reason of *porneia*.

for a man to put away his wife?" In Matthew the question is rather about the legitimate grounds for divorce, divorce itself being taken for granted as a fact of human life and of law: "Is it lawful for a man to put away his wife for any cause whatever *(kata pasan aitian)?"* Now we may properly ask whether in either of these versions we have to do with a genuine happening in Jesus' life or rather with a story that was devised to accompany a dominical saying meaningful in the life of the early church; and we shall probably be forever unable to decide the question one way or the other. A well-founded scholarly consensus would have us assume that here as elsewhere the Marcan gospel material antecedes the Matthean parallel, since the Matthean parallels are generally clearly tributary to Mark. In this instance, however, it would appear that Mark has handed on in a Gentilized refraction (the question of divorce in principle, the possibility of a wife's divorcing her husband, the possibility of a man's committing adultery against his wife) the account of a Palestinian controversy which in Matthew retains its original flavor of rabbinical disputes over the grounds of divorce, divorce itself being placidly assumed to be an exclusively male prerogative. Do we have here an exception to the rule of Matthean dependence on Mark, in which case Matthew would have had access to his Marcan conflict story in another and putatively more original form? Or has Matthew simply "re-Palestinized" the Marcan story by introducing into it for purposes of his own the motif of rabbinical dispute and the assumption that divorce could be initiated by a husband only? Neither of these responses especially attracts us. It would appear that Matthew no less than Mark, and Mark no less than Matthew, has redacted a common tradition to such an extent that its original connection with a *Sitz im Leben Jesu* must remain problematical.

Joseph Fitzmyer has recently argued for a realistic historical setting of the Marcan passage even in the context of Jesus' very life. He reminds us[5] that the texts of the Jewish military colony at Elephantine reveal that there a wife was empowered to divorce

---

[5]"The Matthean Divorce Texts," 205. Cf. L. Hannequin, "Eléphantine," *DBSup* 2 (1934) 1017.

her husband, though he wisely refrains from suggesting that this maverick and eclectic community in Egypt necessarily indicates anything that was going on in the normative Judaism of Palestine in the first Christian century. More to the point, he proposes some lines from the so-called Temple Scroll of Qumran (11QTemple 57:17-19) as evidence of "a clear prohibition of divorce in a first-century Palestinian Jewish text," therefore as providing the basis for a question posed to Jesus: "Do you side with the Essenes or with the Pharisees?" (the Essenes being the Qumran people rejecting divorce, the Pharisees allowing it).[6] I am not comfortable with this proposal for several reasons. The Temple Scroll, after all, remains unpublished except in a generic and quite unsatisfactory way, so that it is precarious to draw large conclusions from it until it is clearly understood how its various parts are supposed to contribute to its over-all thrust. For one thing, we have been assured that "Temple" is as obvious a misnomer for this scroll as "Lamech" was for the scroll that eventually came to be designated a Genesis Apocryphon.[7] While the lines cited by Fitzmyer seem to be relatively straightforward,[8] they are at the same time simply an elaboration of Deut 17:17, the "law of the king," prescribing that "he [the king] shall not multiply wives unto himself." The intent, in other words, is to strengthen the prohibition against royal polygamy of the Solomonic stamp. The text really says nothing pro or con the contingency of divorce, for "the king" or for anyone else, any more than the formula "till death us do part" in the conventional marriage ritual of the Western world (including Washoe County, Nevada) proves that those who pronounce it by that fact renounce any recourse to divorce. Would anyone care to interpret Eccl 9:9 as constituting a prohibition of divorce? Obviously it has nothing to do with the question; still, "all the days" of Qoheleth hardly differs from "all

---

[6]"The Matthean Divorce Texts," 216, 223-4.

[7]Cf. Yigael Yadin, "The Temple Scroll," *BA* 30 (1967) 135-9.

[8]Literally: "And he shall not take beside her (ʿlh) another wife, for she alone (lbdh) shall be with him all the days of his life; but if she die, then he shall choose for himself another."

the days" of Qumran. Naturally, nobody could be expected to propose divorce as an ideal at any stage of human development. Permanent marriage is always the ideal. Any ideal, however, admits by its very assertion to realities that will fall short of it. These realities may be strongly disapproved, but it is still a long step from moral disapprobation to legal prohibition.

Thus, the Temple Scroll does not want divorce for the king, naturally, but neither does it exclude the possibility of divorce simply because it does not mention it. Neither is it evident that Qumran's fictive law for a nonexistent king was intended by its sectarians to reproduce their notion of a sensible rule for everyday life. Also, nothing elsewhere in the Marcan tradition seems to have turned up to persuade us that for the Second Evangelist "the Essenes" were viewed as an option for Jesus in face of "the Pharisees." When Fitzmyer interprets the ambiguous CD 4:20-21 ("taking two wives during their lifetime") as excluding divorce,[9] his reading is conditioned by his understanding of the Temple Scroll and is therefore precarious. At the same time, what is in CD termed *zĕnût* probably conforms to the *porneia* of the Matthean version of the conflict narrative.

If it cannot be proved that the Marcan form of this narrative could ever have had a realistic setting in the life of Jesus,[10] neither can it be determined that the Matthean version has retained the genuine recollection of such an authentic setting or has archaized the story by recasting it in terms of the Shammai-Hillel controversy of the time of Jesus (presupposing, too, that

[9]"The Matthean Divorce Texts," 218-21. He says nothing about CD 13:17-18 which stipulates that the "Essenes" should seek the permission of their *mĕbaqqēr* (bishop) before divorcing their wives.

[10]Paul Hoffmann ("Jesus' Saying about Divorce and its Interpretation in the New Testament Tradition," *Concilium* 55 [1970] 51-66 [American edition]) argues that the story has been created out of the Q (Lucan) version of the *logion*. The Marcan story envisages an unreal question put to Jesus (in the language of LXX), but also Matthew has "Judaized" the story to put it in the context of the Shammai-Hillel controversy. For that matter, Paul the Apostle has also modified the severity of the dominical pronouncement in order to bring it in touch with the radical differences presented by a pluralistic society.

Matthew would have had to suppose any parallel to Mark 10:12). It should be said, however, that if the author of the First Gospel archaized the Mark-Matthew story, he did it very skillfully. Aidan Mahoney, whose ultimate thought about the Matthean divorce clauses and their implications on the teaching of the NT about divorce I regret to be unable to second,[11] has had the merit of reaffirming that the *logos porneias* of Matt 5:32 (and the paraphrase *mē epi porneią* of Matt 19:9) represents the *'erwat dābār* of Deut 24:1, a position which I defended in 1954 and find still defensible.[12] It is true, I do not defend this interpretation quite in the same fashion as I did then. I would not now hold that Matthew introduced the consideration of Deut

---

[11]Cf. Aidan Mahoney, C.P., "A New Look at the Divorce Clauses in Mt 5,32 and 19,9," *CBQ* 30 (1968) 29-38. His position is that Jesus set up for the Pharisees a dilemma opposing Genesis to Deuteronomy which he resolved in his explanation to his disciples: legitimate marriage is indissoluble by man but can be dissolved in the faith community when it involves something displeasing to God (the *aschēmon pragma/'erwat dābār* of Deuteronomy). Paul in 1 Corinthians was only following this precedent in declaring marriages void *in favorem fidei*.

[12]Cf. "The Divorce Clauses," 166, citing Kittel (*TWNT* 4 [1953] 105). I would now add on this side Hauck-Schulz (*TWNT* 6 [1960] 591), though with the reservations noted above. The Shammai-Hillel debate, as Mahoney points out, was not about adultery on the one hand *versus* anything at all on the other hand as constituting the grounds for divorce, but rather about the relative weight that was to be ascribed to *'erwâ* (so Shammai) over against *dābār* (so Hillel) in analyzing the Deuteronomic formula. Admittedly, *dābār* seems to be limitless in its possibilities while *'erwâ* (nastiness, impropriety, especially sexual impropriety) seems to be more precise, corresponding with the rabbinical *zĕnût* (literally, "whoredom") and therefore the NT *porneia*. The *logos porneias* of Matt 5:32 has been ridiculed as an impossible translation of the Deuteronomic *'erwat dābār*, reversing the *regens* and the *rectum* of Hebrew grammar; yet Shammai's restatement of the Deuteronomic phrase was precisely *debar 'erwâ*, i.e., *logos porneias* cf. Str-B, 1.313). The LXX of the expression is *aschēmon pragma*. In the Greek of the LXX *'erwâ* generally turns out as *aischynē, aschēmosynē, aschēmōn,* and *kakia,* and in non-moral contexts as *apokalypsis, gymnōsis,* or *ichnos.* The relation to *zĕnût* = *porneia* should be evident. What is meant is variously whoring, dissoluteness, idolatry, abominations of diverse kinds, cf. Ezek 23:27,29; 43:7,9, etc.

24:1 only to prescind from it.[13] The text does, however, speak to a situation that was live in Jesus' time, whether or not Jesus was ever called on to address himself to it.

Let us assume, as most do, that the introduction of the *porneia* clauses are redactional insertions on Matthew's part modifying the original *logion* ascribed to Jesus which simply ruled out divorce without qualification. This would not be the only indication of development that has taken place in the Matthean version of the pronouncement.[14] These clauses must, in such an acceptation, certainly be regarded as exceptive, but it would be totally erroneous to ascribe to Matthew the intention of constituting adultery the grounds to permit a divorce on the part of an "injured" partner in the marriage, as though such a contractual concept of marriage had been stipulated by the Teacher of Nazareth and amended by the First Evangelist. Rather, it is far more in keeping with Matthew's general purposes and

[13]As flattering as it is to find one's published opinions continually cited (Wijngaards, mentioned below, refers to my 1954 article as having been uttered "recently"), it is even more gratifying when the citations bother to be up to date. Not for the past ten years have we sought to defend a "preteritive" interpretation of the Matthean *porneia*-clauses. See our "The Biblical Theology of Divorce," *Proceedings of the Catholic Theological Society of America* 22 (1967) 223-43, esp. 235, n. 30.

[14] Matt 19:9, apart from the "exceptive" clause, seems to reproduce Mark 10:11 rather precisely, omitting, however, the *'ep'autēn* ("against her") which Mark has following *moichatai*. In both Matthew and Mark the pronouncement speaks to adultery of the male perpetrated by remarriage after divorce (*kai gamēsē allēn*) rather than to the putatively primitive construction of his constituting the wife an adulteress by repudiating her as Matt 5:32 has it. There is respectable MS evidence (p[25] ,B, etc.) for other readings of Matt 19:9 (not for Mark 10:11) that would bring it in line with Matt 5:32, but they may probably be dismissed as harmonizations. If we follow Greeven's argument ("Ehe," 377-8), Matthew has further "re-Palestinized" his text by turning Mark's *sklērokardia*, originally in Jesus' mind a self-condemnation before the stipulated two witnesses that the divorcing male was violating the law of marriage revealed in creation, into an explanation of the concession of divorce made by Moses in Deuteronomy which had become the occasion of the Shammai-Hillel controversy.

the context in which he has set the *logion* to conclude that he has simply adapted the dominical saying to the mores of a society in which *porneia* had long been regarded as making divorce mandatory, not optional. Thus understood, Quentin Quesnell's reading of the following Matt 19:12, the saying about those who have made themselves eunuchs for the sake of the kingdom of heaven, makes eminently good sense,[15] and it becomes clear that Matthew has in no way diluted the absoluteness of Jesus' prohibition of divorce and remarriage.

(3) Much the same kind of conclusion is to be drawn from an examination of the Pauline doctrine on Christian marriage in 1 Cor 7:10-11 (the word of the Lord) as contrasted with the so-called Pauline privilege (Paul's own word *tois loipois*, "to the others" not united in Christian marriage) in 1 Cor 7:12-16. Paul knows a dominical prohibition of divorce that is absolute and very similar to that of Matt 5:32: the husband is forbidden to divorce his spouse, while the wife, for whom divorce under Jewish law was unthinkable, is proscribed from separating from her husband.[16] On the other hand, when it is a question of a

---

[15]See " 'Made Themselves Eunuchs for the Kingdom of Heaven' (Mt 19,12)," *CBQ* 30 (1968) 335-58. Quesnell correctly observes that it is the redactional pattern of Matthew not to have Jesus agree with his misunderstanding disciples (who in this case are saying that "it is better for man not to marry") and therefore effect a case for celibacy, but rather to have him counter their misunderstanding by insisting on the hard consequences of indissoluble marriage. The "eunuchs for the kingdom of heaven," who might even be derisively termed eunuchs by uncomprehending unbelievers, are those forced to separate from their spouses because of *porneia* and now bound by the creational decree not to remarry.

[16]J. K. Elliott, "Paul's Teaching on Marriage in 1 Corinthians. Some Problems Considered," *NTS* 19 (1972-73) 219-25, makes a good case for distinguishing in these verses *aphiēmi* = "divorce," from *chōrizomai* = "separate." The distinction makes equally good sense for vv 12-14. I cannot, however, agree with Elliott's reading of v 15, since it seems plain to me that the *ou dedoulōtai* of this verse is the perfect counterpart of v 11 which requires the separated Christian spouse to remain *agamos*. It is curious that there is, really, no technical vocabulary of divorce in the MT, the LXX, or the NT; nor is there much if any relationship between the three. In particular, the NT shows

mixed marriage that threatens Christian tranquility, either the believing wife or husband may make avail of the law of nations and institute divorce *in favorem fidei*; such is the opinion of Paul. In other words, Paul was either unaware of the Mark-Matthew tradition surrounding the *logion* against divorce which held the latter to be a contravention of the intention of nature's God revealed in creation, or he assumed that in any case and regardless of its premises a word of the Lord known from tradition or delivered through prophecy was intended exclusively

no dependency with respect to the LXX. (1) *chōrizō ("separate")* used in Matt 19:6, Mark 10:9, 1 Cor 7:10, and by Hellenistic authors and the papyri to mean "divorce," never means this in the LXX even though the LXX uses the verb in other senses. (2) *apolyō* means "divorce" in Matt 1:19, 5:31-32; Mark 10:3-4, 11-12; Luke 16:18, but in many other contexts it is simply "release," "set free," etc. In the divorce-passages it replaces the LXX *exapostellō*, which is never used in this sense in the NT (where it rather means to send someone on a mission: so the *apostolos*); in turn the LXX word (Deut 24:1-4, cf. Deut 22:19; Jer 3:1) translates the piel of the Heb *šālaḥ*, "send (away, about one's business)," here meaning divorce but elsewhere referring to an infinite variety of other things (in Mal 2:11 *šillaḥ*, construed as a piel construct infinitive, serves as a substantive for "divorce"). (3) *apostasion* in Matt 5:31 is the *biblion apostasiou* of Matt 19:7-9, Mark 10:4, and the LXX of Deut 24:1-4, the "bill of divorce" (though, as we have seen, the verb for divorce is *apolysai* in the NT and *exapostellein* in the LXX). This expression translates the Heb *sēfer kerîtût*, "document of sundering." *Kerîtût* appears only in this sense in the Hebrew OT (cf. Isa 50:1, Jer 3:8), but it is derived from a verb which has a multitude of meanings. (4) In Sir 25:26 for "divorce" we have for one time only in the Greek *apoteme*, "cut away." There is no extant Hebrew for this verse. On the basis of the "larger" Greek reading (that is, of codex 248 which adds *didou kai apolyson* to the conventional text) and the Syrian (*bsrk qṣṣ hb lh wsryh mn bytk*: "sever her from your flesh, give unto her, and send her from your house"), Moses H. Segal conjectured that Ben Sira's original Hebrew would have been (cf. *ad loc.* in *Sēfer ben Sirā' hassālēm* [Jerusalem: Bialik, 1953, [2] 1958]) *mibbeśārekā gezor ten wesallēaḥ*, that is, "from your body separate (her), give (her the bill of divorce) and send (her away)." The Syriac suggests one cognate verb (*qṣṣ*), Segal another *(gzr)*. By Aquila, Symmachus, and Theodotion *apotemnein* was the word chosen to reproduce the *gzr* of Ps 87(88):6, Isa 53:8, and

for the governance of the Christian community (cf. 1 Cor 14:22 and 5:12).[17] Even though 1 Cor 7:12-15 admittedly does not deal with precisely what later Christian tradition would term the Pauline privilege, nevertheless both this and other like dispositions of ecclesiastical discipline declaring for the marital freedom of a Christian spouse when weighing the ideal of indissoluble marriage against other pastoral values have, it would seem, more in common than not with this Pauline precedent.

(4) Finally, what are we to say of the later NT theology reflected in 1 Tim 3:2, Titus 1:6, and 1 Tim 5:9 which decrees for certain members of the Christian community that they should have had but one spouse only? It should be obvious that this stipulation was not concerned with prohibiting polygamy, for even if polygamy had remained a theoretical possibility in the society out of which the NT grew, polyandry had not. Neither, for that matter, does it necessarily have anything to do with divorce and remarriage, which is there neither extolled, con-

---

it is entirely possible that Ben Sira employed neither of these words but rather a form of *krt* or something else – in any case, none of these words appears anywhere else in his established vocabulary. It is more than evident that he has no professional language for marriage and divorce. (5) *aphienai* is used in 1 Cor 7:11 (forbidding the setting aside of a Christian marriage partner) and in 1 Cor 7:12 (*tois loipois*, permitting the dissolution of a mixed marriage). BAG (p. 215) and Rudolf Bultmann (*TWNT* 1 [19] 506-9) note the use of the word for divorce in Herodotus 5,39, though apparently it does not occur elsewhere in Greek literature. (6) Finally, the divorcée of Lev 21:7, 14; 22:13; Num 30:10 (all in the Law of Holiness) is simply the passive participle of a verb (*grš* and *ekballō* respectively) which means "cast out." Again, there is no attempt at a technical language.

[17]Is something of the same kind insinuated by Mark 10:10-12 (contrary to Matt 19:9) which has the actual pronouncement against divorce made privately to the disciples? This construction agrees with a recognizable Marcan device, by which a Christian "mystery" is revealed. We do not feel called upon here to take up the positive Pauline doctrine of Eph 5:22-23 on marriage. Even if this text should be indisputably Pauline, it regards exclusively the marriage of Christians within the church, where divorce is excluded by definition.

demned, nor condoned.[18] All that these texts need say is that for some determined classes within the church it was deemed improper that there be a second marriage, even though for others such a marriage would be quite possible in view of the decease of an earlier spouse (cf. 1 Tim 5:14). What exactly lay behind this discipline, we can hardly say. Neither do we know the precise reason for the prohibition of Deut 24:1-4 (cf. Jer 3:1) against a man's taking back as his wife a woman whom he has once divorced, or the reason for the prohibition of Lev 21:7 inhibiting a priest from marrying a divorced woman. All that we can conclude is that there was ample precedent in Judaism for Christianity to adopt various taboos concerning the remarriage of some of its members, male and female. But we do not even know whether the taboos in question derive from the example of Judaism or from some other source.

3. Some Conclusions

Where are we left at the end of this NT survey? On the one hand, there seems to be no doubt whatever that the primitive Christian communities who produced the NT documents were of a single mind with regard to the thought of Jesus in the matter of divorce. Jesus had excluded divorce, they were all agreed. He had excluded it without qualification, they were all agreed. Even the Matthean "exceptive" clauses, as we have seen, were probably not intended to dilute the principle of marital indissolubility. Neither did Paul, presuming to decide in cases that were not clearly anticipated by the dominical pronouncement, question this principle; rather, he affirmed it. What kind of tradition the Pastoral Epistles drew on to justify their insistence on monogamous bishops and widows, we leave undecided.

---

[18]Joachim Jeremias proves to his own satisfaction that only the case of divorce and remarriage, common in the Hellenistic world for both men and women, could be involved in these passages. See Joachim Jeremias and August Strobel, *Die Briefe an Timotheus und Titus. Der Brief an die Hebräer* (NTD 9; Göttingen: Vandenhoeck & Ruprecht, 1975) 24, 38, 69.

And what of the magisterium of these texts as regards subsequent and present Christian discipline? J. N. W. Wijngaards has recently exhorted his fellow Catholic theologians to give up their misguided attempt to explain away as other than exceptive the Matthean *porneia* clauses, to acknowledge that the attitude of Jesus to divorce does not partake of the inflexibility of law in any case, and therefore to urge the church to do now what it has done in the past, following Paul, that is, dispense in favor of its faithful when the occasion warrants from the obligation of living to the letter the undeniable ideal of indissoluble Christian marriage.[19] Wijngaards' position is well chosen, though not entirely on his own premises. The exceptive clauses of Matthew are not, as he supposes, concerned with the "grounds" for divorce in the modern sense but rather with a complexity of imperative values with which nothing can probably be compared in our own culture. Still, his principle is doubtless correct. The *logion* of Jesus, whatever its historical context, was construed by the earliest Christianity to be gospel and not law.[20] We have

[19]"Do Jesus' Words on Divorce (Lk 16:18) Admit of no Exception?" *Jeevadhara* 4 (1975) 399-411.

[20]In this connection I have found rather stimulating the article by Gerhard Lohfink, "Jesus und die Ehescheidung. Zur Gattung und Sprachintention von Mt 5,32," *Biblische Randbemerkungen: Schülerfestschrift für Rudolf Schnackenburg* (eds. Helmut Merklein and Joachim Lange; Bonn: Echter, 1974) 207-17. Lohfink agrees that Matt 5:32 is the oldest form of the dominical *logion* and, without citing Greeven, concurs with him. It was the challenge of Jesus to confront his society by equating divorce (commanded by the Law) with adultery (a capital crime under the Law). Doing so, he vindicated the dignity of woman against legalism and the Law, just as in Mark 7:9-13 (=Matt 15:4-6) he did the same for the natural rights of parents. Matt 5:32 is legal in form, but actually it is a prophetic parody of law showing the absurdity of law as the ultimate arbiter of human relations (just as 5:21-22 suggests the same absurdity by invoking the Sanhedrin to rule on verbal injuries). In comparing divorce with adultery, therefore, Jesus issued a provocation to challenge the conscience, but he promulgated no law. Also helpful in the same volume is the article by Armin Kretzer, O.S.A., "Die Frage: Ehe auf Dauer und ihre mögliche Trennung nach Mt 19,3-12," 218-30. Kretzer understands *porneia* to mean "a continuous state of whoredom or of infidel-

seen what Matthew and Luke did with it in its Q version, what Mark and Matthew did with it in narrative context, and what Paul did when it was a question of adjusting it to an entirely new scene in the Gentile churches. At the very least, we should be able to say that on the NT precedent other situations can be envisaged in a twentieth-century Western world that are every bit as demanding of accommodation as those that occurred so long ago in the Matthean, the Lucan, the Marcan, and the Pauline churches.[21] What these situations might be, it is not our present task to specify. In 1967 we wrote:[22]

> Jesus' command regarding divorce was not the promulga-
> tion of a divine law, and obviously it was never intended
> to serve as a model for the civil regulation of marriage. It
> was and is a word addressed to the Christian conscience in-
> formed by divine grace. As with other similar commands,
> Christian tradition and ecclesial magisterium have helped the
> Christian conscience in understanding some of its specifica-
> tions. Such help will surely continue to be given as the
> Church brings to bear on the question other insights that re-
> spond to other situations that did not occur in the NT or in
> subapostolic Christianity.

Antonio Vargas-Machuca, after reviewing the discipline of the Latin church in its usage of the so-called Pauline privilege

---

ity" and therefore, like Wijngaards, believes that Matthew truly introduced an exception to Jesus' absolute prohibition of divorce. Not, however, as a laxist but as a realist; the evangelist recognized that the ideal of indissoluble marriage depended more on the grace of God than on the capability of man (hence the meaning of "not everyone can accept this teaching, only those to whom it is given to do so" in 19:11). It should be evident from the above that some of these arguments are not our own; but it should also be evident that they are arguing in what we think is the right direction.

[21]Cf. George W. MacRae, S.J., "New Testament Perspectives on Mar-
riage and Divorce," *Divorce and Remarriage in the Catholic Church* (ed. Lawrence G. Wrenn; New York: Newman, 1973) 1-15. Also Antonio Vargas-Machuca, S.J., "Los casos de 'divorcio' admitidos por S. Mateo (5,32 y 19,9). Consecuencias para la teologia actual," *Estudios Eclesiásticos* 50 (1975) 5-54.

[22]"The Biblical Theology of Divorce," 243.

(an unscientific but pastoral interpretation of 1 Cor 7:10-16);
the Eastern church's permission of divorce and remarriage in
the face of an adulterous spouse (an unscientific but pastoral
interpretation of the Matthean "exceptive" clauses) — a discipline
deliberately overlooked by a Western ecumenical council eager
to condemn Luther but not the East;[23] the Roman church's extension of its power to dissolve a less than "sacramental" marriage "in favor of the faith" — dissolution of a marriage *ratum
non consummatum* in view of religious profession, exercised
as early as the twelfth century (*Codex Iuris Canonici*, canon
1119); dissolution of a marriage *ratum non consummatum* in
any case as early as the fifteenth century; dissolution of a
"natural" marriage since the sixteenth century (canon 1125);
dissolution by pontifical dispensation of even a consummated
marriage between a baptized and nonbaptized partner when no
dispensation had been obtained from the impediment of disparity
of cult (done since at least 1924); dissolution of the same marriage even when the impediment had been dispensed from (done
since at least 1946); and finally, since 1958, the dissolution by
pontifical dispensation of even a consummated marriage entered
into by non-believers, neither of whom was subsequently converted or received baptism — this last dispensation having been
declared theologically impossible by competent canonical authorities a decade before the Pope did it — concludes quite logically
that it would require no broadening of the Roman church's
asserted powers for it to proceed ultimately to the dissolution
of a sacramental marriage *ratum et consummatum*. He suggests
two routes by which this step might be taken. The first, the
route that one might prefer, is to remove the concept of *"consummatum"* from the purely physical to the psychological and
interpersonal plane. The other, the route that one might more
realistically expect the Roman mind to prefer, would be to
broaden the juridical casuistry surrounding the concept of a null
marriage.[24] Other more conservative and perhaps more prag-

---

[23]Cf. Piet Fransen, "Divorce on the Ground of Adultery — the Council of
Trent (1563)," *Concilium* 55 (1970) 89-100 (American edition).

[24]Cf. "Los casos de 'divorcio,' " 52-54.

matic voices within the church[25] have urged that at least if the church cannot be brought to contravene the theory of its adherence to a law of total indissolubility of Christian marriage, it may be encouraged to follow the gentler disposition of the East which has pastorally favored the sacramental rights of the sinful and fallible Christian over against the "rights" of a matrimonial *sacramentum* defined as law.

4. A Terminal Animadversion

The biblical exegete and theologian tends to end a discussion of this kind with a certain feeling of frustration.[26] To rehearse the history of marriage and divorce in the Christian churches is to describe an experience that has been very little tributary to the NT and has listened very little to its expositors. Christian tradition, earlier and later, has honored the ideal of indissoluble monogamous marriage as a decree of its Lord, and Christian tradition, earlier and later, has never hesitated to compromise this ideal by adapting it to human realities. What par-

---

[25]Cf. Karl Lehmann, "Indissolubility of Marriage and Pastoral Care of the Divorced Who Remarry," *Communio* 1 (1974) 219-42 (American edition).

[26]Cf. *The Bond of Marriage* (ed. William W. Bassett; South Bend: University of Notre Dame Press, 1968), published by the Canon Law Society of America "encouraged by the Commission for Canon Law of the National Conference of Catholic Bishops to sponsor a symposium of experts in theology, scriptural studies, sociology, history, psychology, canon and civil law to reexamine all that is implied in the fundamental issue in the renewal of the marriage law, the question of indissolubility." In this volume the article "Divorce and Remarriage in the New Testament," 1-33, by my colleague Dominic Crossan, differs in no substantive way from the conclusions reached by me in the pages above. It would be hard to demonstrate from any ecclesiastical pronouncement that a semi-official gathering of the Bassett kind, or the Wrenn colloquium (n. 21 above), or any unsolicited scholarly contribution mentioned here or elsewhere has had any appreciable influence on hierarchical thinking about divorce and remarriage in the Catholic church and/or the pastoral care of the divorced Catholic.

ticular purpose is to be served by reviewing yet again the NT doctrine on the subject, is often hard to see.

The Christian communities which have accepted divorce as a deplorable but an inevitable fact of life have taken some guidance, admittedly, from NT exegesis, but far more they have taken their guidance from other indices to the realities of the human condition in their times; and this is perhaps partly as it should be. I speak here not particularly of the Protestant churches, for of no Christian community is this fact truer than of the Roman Catholic Church, which despite its reputation for an adamantine opposition to divorce in any form yet in fact has asserted to itself more than any other Christian body the prerogative of dissolving—that is, divorcing—practically every conceivable bond of marriage save one: and that one, as it happens, which should be the chief focus of its pastoral concern, the sacramental marriage *ratum et consummatum*, of course. As far as practical utility to the church is concerned, therefore, the biblist often feels pushed to the sidelines, puttering about with his colleagues regarding the niceties of Greek vocabulary when he would prefer to assist the church to grow under the instruction of the inspired word. If he cannot be allowed to lend his voice to the ear of him who would hear what the Spirit is saying to the churches, however, at least he must be permitted to continue to putter with his peers.

17. Levitical Messianism and the New Testament

It is frequently asserted that in the late biblical Judaism, especially under the early Hasmonean influence on Jewish thinking, a Levitical messianism tended for a time to displace the Davidic. In some instances, it is alleged, this Levitical messianism was the only one conceivable to men who had given up all hope of a Davidic restoration; in others, tradition reasserted itself, either to crowd out the Levitical idea altogether or to combine with it in a dual messianic expectation, the priestly together with the royal.[1] The so-called Zadokite document of the Damascus covenanters and, more recently, the Qumrân literature, have strengthened this position by their apparent references to an expectation of two Messiahs, the one "of Israel" and the other "of Aaron." It is the purpose of this paper to examine the sources in which this priestly messianism has been found, and to see how, if at all, such a conception has influenced the NT.

[1]Cf. Sigmund Mowinckel, *He That Cometh*, tr. by G. W. Anderson (New York: Abingdon 1956) 286-290.

Jeremiah 33, 14-26

Jer 33, 14-26 is the longest continuous passage of Jer completely missing in the Greek. This is only one of the reasons that compel virtually all modern scholars to regard it as a post-Jeremian addition. It bears, in fact, various of the traits we have learnt to associate with such additions in the prophetic collections. The style is anthological of other passages of Jer: vv. 14-16 are a pastiche of 29,10 and 23,5f.; v. 17 comes from 35,19; 31,35-37 have served as the model of v. 19ff. and v. 25f.; and there are other reminiscences. Furthermore, Jeremiah's words have been used partly in a sense different from that of the authentic passages: the *Yhwh ṣidqēnû* and *ṣemaḥ ṣaddîq* of 23,5f. turn up in v. 14f. (MT has *ṣemaḥ ṣᵉdāqâ* in v. 15, but 4 MSS have *ṣaddîq,* and this was read by Theodotion), but the former now means Jerusalem rather than the messianic king, and the latter in turn refers to the kingship itself rather than to a scion of David.

The language of the passage appears to be late and retrograde.[2] An exception that impressed some earlier commentators is the Deuteronomic expression "Levitical priests," a term that is properly pre- rather than postexilic, in respect to the canonization of the Priestly legislation. But, as is the case with the Chronicler's similar usage, this now appears to be a deliberate archaism.[3]

We do not, it is true, have to agree with Rudolph's contention that such a prophecy would have been impossible for Jeremiah. Like Ezekiel, Jeremiah would have thought most naturally of a restored covenant in terms of the sacrifice and priesthood without which the worship of God was impossible.[4]

---

[2]Cf. F. Giesebrecht, *Das Buch Jeremia* (HKzAT; Göttingen: Vandenhoeck & Ruprecht, 1907) 186 on v. 20.

[3]Giesebrecht 183; Wilhelm Rudolph, *Der Prophet Jeremia* (HZAT; Göttingen: Vandenhoeck & Ruprecht, ²1958) 201.

[4]C. von Orelli, *Der Prophet Jeremia* (KKzHS; Munich: Oskar Beck, 1905) 142f.; Albert Condamin, S.J., *Le Livre de Jérémie* (EB; Paris: Gabalda, 1920) 250.

But the author is not thinking simply of a continued priesthood in a renewed covenant. He is, rather, insisting that a covenant of perpetuity has been made with the tribe of Levi in its priestly function just as a covenant had been made with Judah in the royal function. The passage dates from a time when the priesthood had assumed an importance for the life of the nation equal to or even surpassing that of the kingship. This situation was not verified before the exile, but it was afterwards, particularly after hopes for a Davidic restoration were dashed with the passing of Zerubbabel and there was a consequent shift of political emphasis to the high priesthood.[5] We can probably be more precise than this: as Nötscher observes, it appears from the author's tone that he is encouraging those that had already been disillusioned with the priesthood.[6] Though Nötscher himself was disposed to date the passage as shortly after the exile, we may perhaps see in it a culmination of the disillusionment with the Zadokites that is reflected in the postexilic prophets and the work of the Chronicler, possibly of the time of Ezra and Nehemiah or even later.[7] Perhaps like the Chronicler the author awaited from the faithful Levites a priesthood of renewed fervor to replace the Zadokites, and perhaps, therefore, like the Chronicler again, his reference to "the Levitical priests" was not merely a piece of archaism.

[5]Cf. William F. Albright, *The Biblical Period* (Privately printed: Pittsburgh, 1950) 49f.; reprinted from *The Jews: Their History, Culture and Religion,* ed. by Louis Finkelstein, 1949.

[6]Friedrich Nötscher, *Das Buch Jeremias* (HSAT; Bonn: Peter Hanstein, 1934) 248-250).

[7]Cf. Roland de Vaux, O.P., *Ancient Israel* (New York: McGraw-Hill, 1961) 390-394 [= *Les Institutions de l'Ancien Testament II* (Paris: Éditions du Cerf, 1960) 263-266]; Henri Cazelles, P.S.S., *Les livres des Chroniques* (B.J.; Paris: Éditions du Cerf, ²1961) 12. Rudolph believes the passage should be referred to this "literarisch dunkle Zeit."

Malachi 1, 6-2,9; 3, 1-5

At all events, it seems clear enough that Jer 33,14-26 belongs temporally as well as conceptually in the category of the texts which follow.[8]

As it now seems to be generally agreed that Mal must be dated to shortly before the reforms of Ezra and Nehemiah — without entering into the fretted question of the relative chronology of these postexilic leaders — and obviously after the prophets Haggai and Zechariah,[9] these texts must belong roughly to the same era as the preceding; they perhaps even predate it. Much more explicitly than the preceding do they reflect a dissatisfaction with the Jerusalem priesthood. In 2,4.8 mention is made of the covenant with Levi, and in 3,3 a purification of the priesthood is promised.

The covenant with Levi is that found in Dt 33,9.[10] This covenant is invoked to give sanction against the unworthy priestly performance condemned in 1,6-14 and contrasted with the pure sacrifice ascribed to the Gentiles in vv. 11 and 14. Martin Rehm, in a recent article on the celebrated Mal 1,11, has rightly stressed the necessity of relating this prophecy to the messianic future.[11] In doing so, however, he seems to leave out of perspective the prophecy of 3,1-5 on the Levitical priesthood. According to Rehm, Mal 1,11 looks forward to a messianic age in which the prescriptions of the law of the single sanctuary and the Levitical priesthood will be impossible, when the plan of salvation must

---

[8]T. Chary, *Les prophètes et le culte à partir de l'exil* (Tournai: Desclée, 1955) 166-171, finds the beginning of a covenant with Levi in Mal 3 and makes Jer 33,14-26 depend on this text.

[9]Cf. Otto Eissfeldt, *Einleitung in das Alte Testament* (Tübingen: J.C.B. Mohr, ²1956) 545f.; R. Pautrel, "Malachie," *VDBS* 5, 739-746.

[10]Cf. Ernst Sellin, *Das Zwölfprophetenbuch* (KZAT; Leipzig: A. Deichert, 1922) 548; S. R. Driver, *A Critical and Exegetical Commentary on Deuteronomy* (ICC; New York; Scribners, 1895) 400f. A non-messianic expression of the covenant is the *berît hakkᵉhunnâ wᵉhalᵉwîyīm* of Neh 13,29.

[11]"Das Opfer der Völker nach Mal 1,11" *Lex Tua Veritas: Festschrift für Hubert Junker* (Trier: Paulinus-Verlag, 1961) 193-208.

revert to former institutions, as when sacrifice was the prerogative of every family head.[12] As a kindred text he cites the postexilic Is 19,19 concerning the altar-to-be in Egypt. But Is 19,18-23 precisely regards an extension of *Israelite* covenant and law to Egypt. Furthermore, the entire passage has now taken as its model the description of the conquest in the Deuteronomic book of Joshua.[13] The altar of Is 19,19f. which is *le°ôt ûle°ēd lYhwh* is patterned after the altar *°ēd hû'* of Jos 22,27ff. – a passage that expressly upholds the Deuteronomic law of the single sanctuary!

When we take into account the obvious devotion of the author of Mal to the Israelite cult and priestly purity, it is hardly realistic to interpret his messianic teaching apart from these. Whatever they might be in a Christian view, for him they were certainly no interim economy.[14] If 1,11f is to be taken (rightly, I think) as a reference to the messianic age, it must be reconciled with 3,1-5; but just as certainly the solution is not to be had in denying the manifestly messianic character of 3,1-5.[15] It is not our

---

[12]So also Pautrel, *VDBS* 5, 744: the cult presupposed by Mal 1,11 "ne deviendra possible que par la substitution d'une loi nouvelle à l'ancienne, disons au temps de l'ère messianique." Cf. also A. van Hoonacker, *Les douze petits prophètes* (EB; Paris: Gabalda, 1908) 713, who asserts the same, though on p. 731 (on 3,3) he says the very opposite, insisting that there is no contradiction.

[13]Cf. Edward J. Kissane, *The Book of Isaiah* (Dublin: Browne & Nolan, 1941) I, 218-220.

[14]Cf. Rehm, *Junker-Festschrift*, 207, ftn. 67: "Die Fortdauer des levitischen Priestertums in der messianischen Zeit wird vom AT nicht gelehrt. Jer 33,18 handelt nicht vom Messias, sondern bezieht sich auf die Wiederherstellung nach dem Exil. Mal 3,3f erwartet die Beseitigung der augenblicklichen Missstände und die Besserung der Leviten in naher Zukunft." This judgment seems to disregard the context of Jer 33,18 entirely (an everlasting covenant paralleled with the everlasting Davidic covenant), to say nothing of what it implies Jewish messianism to have been.

[15]Cf. M.-J. Lagrange, O.P., "Notes sur les prophéties messianiques des derniers prophètes," *RB* 15 (1906) 81: "Il [the author of Mal 1,11] songe encore aux Lévites, mais aux Lévites purifiés (III,3), à un sacrifice offert au nom de Iahvé connu comme tel." Whatever is to be said of Lagrange's

task to make this conciliation here, but we might suggest that it would have lain in the line of thought of Is 66,21, and not in the abolition of a law which our author had constantly before him (3,22) as the ordinance of an unchanging God (3,6) of an eternal covenant.

Zechariah 12,12f. (3,1-10; 4,11-14; 6,9-15)

The so-called Trito-Zech (12-14) seems to be in reality the second of three anonymous prophetic collections, the other two being Zech 9-11 and Mal 1-3, all of which originally stood at the end of the Book of the Twelve, each bearing the title *maśśā' debar Yhwh*. In the present editing of the Bible, the first two have been gathered into Zech, whereas the third has been ascribed to the *male'ākî* of Mal 3,1, taken now as a proper name.[16] There would seem to be no doubt that the two supplements to Zech are by separate authors and that both are subsequent to Mal.[17]

insistence that *minhâ* here is an unbloody sacrifice, finding an echo in the aspirations of some portions of Judaism, I think his judgment on the meaning of 1,11 is the only one consistent with the prophecy as a whole. Chary, *Prophètes,* 178-189 also recognizes the need to conciliate the two passages and to leave Malachi a Jew; he also admits a universalist influence (Iranian), however, in the construction of 1,11.

[16]Cf. W. Nowack, *Kleine Propheten* (HKzAT; Göttingen: Vandenhoeck & Ruprecht, ²1903) 422; Pautrel, *VDBS* 5, 739; Eissfeldt, *Einleitung*², 542f.

[17]Von Orelli's attempt, among others, to establish a pre-exilic (late Hoseanic) date for Zech 9-11 is conceded to have failed, cf. *Die zwölf kleinen Propheten* (Munich: Oskar Beck, ³1908) 178f. So also van Hoonacker's attempt, argued at length, *op. cit.* 650ff.; to ascribe the entire canonical book to Zechariah: cf. Sellin *Zwölfprophetenbuch,* 488ff.; Eissfeldt, *Einleitung,*² 535-543. Both sections seem to presuppose the beginning of the Hellenistic period. Paul Lamarche, S.J., *Zacharie IX-XIV* (EB; Paris: Gabalda, 1961) 22f., 105-115, 148-157 defends an hypothesis of a single author for Zech 9-14, who was dependent on Deutero-Isaiah and whom he is inclined to date, contrary to the prevailing trend, in the period 500-480 after the (putative) death of Zerubbabel. However, he also concedes the possibility of an Hellenistic dating.

In "Trito-Zechariah" there is no covenant with Levi properly so called. Neither is there properly a Davidic messianic expectation. In 12,12f., however, in describing the Jerusalem of the messianic age, the apocalyptist-prophet divides the people into "the families of the house of David," "the families of the house of Nathan," "the families of the house of Levi," and "the families of the Shimeiites" as those of note; "the remaining families" account for the rest of the eschatological Israel. The Davidic and Levitical elements of the people thus retain their preeminence, though no specific messianic functions are ascribed to them, and they are evidently put on a par.[18]

Despite all attempts to find other candidates, it would seem clear that the Nathan of v. 12 is the son of David by Bathsheba mentioned in 2 Sm 5,14; I Chr 3,5; 14,4 (the Targum identified him with Nathan the prophet, whom it calls "son of David"), and the Shimei of v. 13 is the Gershomite Levite of Ex 6,17; Nm 3,21, etc. (in the LXX Symeōn appears, while the Targum identified "the Shimeiite" with the Mordecai ben Jair ben Shimei of the book of Esther). Van Hoonacker's "conjecture assez hardie" to get rid of these names of no apparent importance[19] may, as a matter of fact, have been motivated by what precisely was their significance to the prophet. We are in the period long after the passing of Zerubbabel, when there was no longer any hope of a Davidic restoration from the normal line that had descended through Solomon. In "the house of Nathan" paired off with "the house of David" we may have the author's suggestion that the Davidic oracle will yet be fulfilled through another line of descent. Similarly, the pairing of "the Shimeiites" with "the house of Levi" can be another expression of dissatisfaction with the Zadokite priesthood, ideally descended from Aaron,[20] and the

---

[18]Cf. Chary, *Prophètes* 226f.

[19]*Les douze*, 685.

[20]On the Zadokite priesthood, cf. E. Auerbach in *ZAW* 49 (1931) 327f. It is generally thought that this was the priesthood of Gibeon (cf. 1 Chr 16,39), which remained a chief sanctuary during the time of David and Solomon (1 Chr 21,29; 2 Chr 1,3; 1 Kgs 3,4) after a long Canaanite history (2 Sm 21,9), cf. Henri Cazelles, "David's Monarchy and the Gibeonite Claim," *PEQ*

suggestion that another Levitical line will be substituted. This, in fact, is precisely the kind of apocalyptic fulfilment we might expect of this author.

We may now note several passages in Zech proper which have a bearing on the text we have just examined. In the vision of 3,1-10 the highpriest Jeshua is pictured as purified of the former sins of priesthood and people and elevated to a dignity beyond that ever enjoyed by the pre-exilic priesthood. He is endowed with many of the prerogatives possessed by the kings before the exile, though exclusively in the sacred domain. He is given (v. 7) "access" (probably read *mahᵉlākîm*) to the divine along with those who stand by, i.e., the angels. Sellin saw in this an absolute equation of Jeshua with the Davidic Messiah, and for him this was another reason to transfer 3,8-10 to a different context, after 4,10.[21] However, it does not appear that Zechariah has made such an advance over Haggai. The priesthood has, it is true, been given some of the royal prerogatives

---

87 (1955) 165-175; J. Dus, "Gibeon— eine Kultstätte des Šmš und die Stadt des benjaminitischen Schicksals," *VT* 10 (1960) 353-374. Brought to Jerusalem by David with the Ark, it was later given the artificial genealogy of the Chronicler (1 Chr 5,29-41) associating it with the Aaronite and Eliite priesthood. Auerbach thinks these facts exclude the reliability of the data of Sm, according to which (2 Sm 8,17) Zadok was the son of Ahitub, one of the Eliite priests (1 Sm 14,3), apparently a younger son in view of Ahimelech's preeminence (1 Sm 21f). But whatever is to be said of the relation of the Eliites to Aaron, it is not impossible that in Israelite times the relations between Shiloh and Gibeon were as pictured in the Bible. After the loss of Shiloh, presumably in the Philistine wars, part of the Eliite priesthood may as readily have been transferred to Gibeon with the tabernacle as to Nob. No further light is shed by Sm on the origin of the Eliites save in the later 1 Sm 2,27. Cf. also de Vaux, *Ancient Israel*, 390-394.

[21]*Zwölfprophetenbuch*, 448: "In Unterschiede von Haggai, der ausschliesslich den Serubbabel in ein solches unmittelbares Verhältnis zu Jahwe rückt, hat er gerade hier zunächst nachdrücklich dem Josua ein analoges Recht zuerkannt, and von da an immer zu vermitteln gesucht, jedem der beiden Ämter, dem weltlichen wie dem geistlichen das Seine gebend und beide als gleich berechtigt und notwendig im Gottesreiche der Zukunft hinstellend vgl. 4,14; 6,13."

and there is a "separation of church and state"; but it is still the Messiah who will inaugurate God's kingdom.[22] All of this corresponds to the new responsibilities of the postexilic priesthood independent of royal interference in obedience to the prophecy of Ezekiel. Zechariah, however, professes a personal Davidic messianism, and the entire grandiose vision has as its climax the introduction of the theme of the *ṣemaḥ*. The highpriestly office is glorified, but not to the detriment of the hoped-for kingship, to which pre-eminence is still ascribed. The priesthood of the messianic age will be able to realize its potentialities only through the coming of the Davidic scion.

In 4,11-14, the explanation of the imagery in 4,1-3, it is evident that the two olive trees are Zerubbabel and Jeshua. They are called *benê-hayyiṣehār* doubtless in reference to their separate anointings, Jeshua's in fact and Zerubbabel's in expectancy. The spirit is that of Jer 33,17f. The two serve their separate functions, however, each as the anointed of Yahweh, with neither equality nor subordination being implied. The olive trees do not represent equal suppliers of oil for the lampstand (v. 12 is a gloss), since the lampstand is (probably) designated in v. 10b as the eyes of Yahweh.[23]

It is hardly open to question that 6,9-15 originally referred to a symbolic crowning of Zerubbabel as king. According to v. 13, a priest (LXX: the priest) would stand by his throne (probably read *mîmînô* with LXX for the second *'al-kiseʾô*), and between the two there was to be peace. Again, it is Zerubbabel, the *ṣemaḥ*, who would build the temple of Yahweh and make possible the functioning of the priesthood.

This restoration of the original text from tendentious alteration is so axiomatic in view of the rest of Zech, there is no need

---

[22]Chary, *Prophètes*, 148-152 more aptly observes that this marks the emancipation of the priesthood and the beginning of its glorification. It would be difficult to understand an alteration of the received text in the manner that Sellin imagined, in view of the opposite course that was followed in c. 6.

[23]Cf. van Hoonacker, *Les douze*, 619f.; Albert Gelin, P.S.S. *Aggée – Zacharie – Malachie* (BJ; Paris: Éditions du Cerf, ²1951) 33.

to argue in its justification.[24] This alteration need not have been made only in Hasmonean times, of course; it could belong to any period after Zerubbabel, when the highpriest had by default become the sole depository of power in the postexilic community. It has resulted in what is verbally the only clear-cut example of Levitical messianism that lies in the texts before us. I need hardly add, however, that as this is the result of a purely mechanical substitution of a name without even an attempt to harmonize it with its conflicting context, it would be rash in the extreme to appeal to it as pointing to any elaborate theological development.

Ben Sira 45,15.23-26

Ben Sira mentions the covenant with Aaron in v. 15, and in the praise of Phinehas in vv. 23-26 he compares with the covenant made with David the everlasting covenant made with Aaron. The comparison is not to suggest their equality: he minimizes the Davidic covenant by contrasting it with the Levitical.[25] This is clear even if the Hebrew text of v. 25 is read as it stands:

> w^{e}gam b^{e}rîto 'im dāwīd
> ben yišay l^{e}mattēeh y^{e}hûdâ
> naḥalat 'îš lip^{e}nê k^{e}bôdô
> naḥalat 'aharôn l^{e}kōl zar^e'ô

The covenant with Aaron, says Ben Sira, is a covenant with all his descendants, whereas the covenant with David was with

---

[24]Among those who have tried to preserve the received text, von Orelli, *Propheten* 196-198, made some sort of case for vv. 11-12, but foundered completely in trying to explain away v. 13, attested by LXX, which clearly demands two parties, of which the priest is a second. LXX has preserved enough of the original to make its restoration more than probable. Lagrange, "Notes" 71f. also tried to defend the received text of Zech 6,9-15 as original.

[25]Norbert Peters, *Das Buch Jesus Sirach oder Ecclesiasticus* (EHzAT; Münster: Aschendorff, 1913) 391-393, following the uncorrected Hebrew text, makes it a simple comparison.

one man only. LXX and Syr further indicate that *lip^enê k^ebôdô* should be read *lib^enô l^ebaddô*, in which case the sense is that the Davidic covenant was made in view of Solomon only, even as the Deuteronomic interpolator of 2 Sm 7,13 interpreted it. In either case, it is plain that the Davidic covenant has ceased to have any messianic significance for Ben Sira, and that in its place is the covenant with the priesthood.

This does not mean, however, that Ben Sira professed a Levitical messianism. Rather, he saw in the existing highpriestly office that was so soon to be degraded by the rivalries prior to the Maccabean age, something that had taken the place of messianism. Ben Sira's messianism, if it can be called that, is a realized messianism. By the same token, his covenant with Aaron is something quite different from the Levitical covenant we have seen in the preceding examples.[26]

Testaments of the Twelve Patriarchs

As is well known, in the Testaments of the Twelve Patriarchs Levi is given a pre-eminence over all the other tribes. This is generally explained as due to the Maccabean fervor of the time of the composition of this work.[27]

The pre-eminence of Levi, however, would appear to be one of the few things certain about this conjecture-ridden and puzzling book. It was in view of it that Charles concluded to the idea of a Levitical Messiah who had replaced the Davidic Messiah under Maccabean influence; with the break of Hyrcanus with the Pharisees, however, this aberration was abandoned,

---

[26]It is possible that Sir 48,10f. is a reference to the *Elias redivivus* of Mal 3,23f., as CCD takes it to be. LXX differs widely from the Hebrew, and the crucial words *lip^en [ê (bô) yôm Yhwh]* have to be supplied in v. 10, which in turn must be depended on the tense to be assigned *rō'ekā wāmēt* in v. 11. In any case, if Sir follows Mal here, it is in the original sense of Elijah as a forerunner of the Day of the Lord, not of the Messiah, and still less does it identify Elijah with the eschatological highpriest.

[27]Cf. Hermann Strathmann, *"Leu(e)i," ThWNT* 4,242f.

and first-century additions to the book have restored the traditional Messiah from Judah.[28] In the light of the Qumrân evidence, Karl Georg Kuhn has corrected this position: the two Messiahs from Judah and Levi co-exist in the Testaments, making them agree with the messianic expectation of the Qumrân sectaries. The Testaments, like the Damascus document and the Qumrân literature, are all Essenian, the only form of Judaism that held to this dual messianic idea.[29]

It is true that an imposing list of qualities is ascribed to Levi in the Testaments. To begin with what is certain, Test. Reub. 6,7 ascribes supremacy to Levi, and it is easy to agree that the rest of the words in this verse (ascribing the same supremacy to Judah, Reuben, Dan, and Joseph) are what Charles called them, "a foolish interpolation." The rest of the passage down to v. 10 inclusive extols Levi as the anointed highpriest (or, in the unamended text, "highpriest of the anointed one") who shall fulfil his priestly office *until* (*méchri*) the consummation: his function, in fact, as in v. 11f., is to bless the messianic line of Judah. The *en autô* of v. 11 chosen to be king over all the nation, however, is probably the Judah just mentioned, not Levi. Even if "anointed highpriest" is the title given to Levi, this does not mean Messiah in the technical Jewish sense: the title is that of Lv 4,3, etc., *hakkōhēn hammāšîaḥ*. In this passage there is not, therefore, at least necessarily, any eschatological Levitical highpriest.[30] It is true that v. 12 can as easily apply to Levi as to Judah, but here the Armenian text indicates that Levi(?) will be "eternal kings," not an eternal king, i.e., that he will continually fulfil the functions of warlike leadership ascribed to

[28]R. H. Charles, *The Apocrypha and Pseudepigrapha of the Old Testament* (Oxford: Clarendon Press, 1913) II, 294.

[29]"The Two Messiahs of Aaron and Israel," *The Scrolls and the New Testament*, ed. by Krister Stendahl (New York: Harper Brothers, 1957) 54-64. Lagrange appears to have been the first to identify the Testaments as Essenian.

[30]G. R. Beasley-Murray, "The Two Messiahs in the Testaments of the Twelve Patriarchs," *JTS* 48 (1947) 1-12 thinks that only in this passage is there an unambiguous portrayal of a Levitical Messiah. He also finds this idea in Test. Lev. 18, but dismisses the other texts alleged by Charles.

Levi (the Maccabeans) in Test. Sim. 5,5f; Test. Dan 5,10-13 (corrected).

In Test. Lev. 8 Levi is given a crown as well as the diadem of priesthood and the ephod of prophecy (Moses). Probably the crown refers to the third stage in Levi's priestly career, which is also called a new priesthood, namely the Maccabean succession that replaced the Zadokites. Probably, too, this entails an assimilation to Levi of the role of Melchizedek, the association of temporal and priestly rule, as in Jub. 32,1 (in praise) and Ass. Mos. 6,1 (in reprobation).[31] But once again there is no eschatological priest or priestly Messiah. As Lagrange long ago pointed out, the reference to a king who will rise *from* Judah (so all the Greek MSS) in v. 14 must be a Christian interpolation in this much interpolated book; it is, at all events, at war with its context.[32]

The parade examples from the Testaments to prove a Levitical messianism are Test. Lev. 18 and Test. Jud. 24: in the former, a routine celebration of the new (Maccabean) priesthood becomes, in v. 6 and onwards, the prediction of an eschatological figure who will be a universal savior; in the latter, to a Judahite Messiah figured in vv. 4-6 another messianic figure is joined

---

[31]For a quite different interpretation, cf. T. W. Manson, "Miscellanea Apocalyptica III," *JTS* 48 (1947) 59-61. Manson takes the three stages to be Moses—Aaron—*bᵉnê ṣaddôq*: the king in v. 14 would be Solomon. If the figure of Melchizedek is invoked here to justify a change of priesthood, it is interesting to compare the view of H. H. Rowley, "Melchizedek and Zadok (Gen 14 and Ps 110)," *Festschrift für Alfred Bertholet* (Tübingen: J.C.B. Mohr, 1950) 461-472. According to Rowley the Zadokite priesthood, which he conceives to have been the Jebusite priesthood of Jerusalem accepted by David, itself was first legitimated by an appeal to the ancient story of Gn 14, and it is this legitimation that is reflected in Ps 110.

[32]Cf. M.-J. Lagrange, O.P., *Le messianisme chez les Juifs* (EB; Paris: Gabalda, 1909) 72f. Similarly, v. 11f. of Test. Dan 5,10-13 appear to be Christian. When they are removed, together with the Judah of v. 10 which is doubtless due to the same interpolator (rather than to the "first-century Jewish" influence seen by Charles), the passage becomes merely a reference to the Maccabean wars and not messianic. Test. Lev. 17,2f. has undergone an interpolation of the same kind.

in vv. 1-3 who can only be (so goes the argument) the Levitical Messiah. But once again, when the crucial verses are recognized as fairly obvious Christian interpolations (Test. Lev. 18, 6-12; Test. Jud. 24,1-3), the Levitical Messiah disappears.[33]

What remains in the Testaments, certainly, is the supremacy of Levi, but a purely priestly supremacy (Test. Lev. 4,1-6; 13). The kingship, it is made plain, resides with Judah (Test. Jud. 12,4). The author also takes pains to explain how it is that Judah has, for a time, forfeited his kingship (Test. Jud. 15,2f; 17,3), but he also insists that it is to be restored (Test. Jud. 17,5f.). Part of Levi's supremacy is that the priesthood should outrank the kingship; nevertheless, the kingship is Judah's eternally, and from it, not from Levi, will come the Messiah (cf. Test. Jud. 21f.; 25,1f.; Test. Iss. 5,7; Test. Naph. 5,3-5). In Test. Jos. 19,11 it is said that *a* savior (Armenian: "salvation") is to come from Levi and Judah, as a dual principle, and Levi and Judah together (Levi habitually mentioned first) are frequently coupled as this twofold source of salvation (Test. Sim. 7,2; Test. Lev. 2,11; Test. Gad 8,1; Test. Dan 5,4.7; Test. Naph. 6,6; 8,2). However, it appears to be clear enough what role each is to play in bringing about this salvation, and the role of the personal eschatological savior is assigned to Judah, not to Levi.

The tendency already discerned in Ben Sira has come to full term in the Testaments, to glorify the Levitical succession at the expense of the Davidic, for the reasons that have been seen. However, whereas messianism was of little or no concern to Ben Sira, it meant much to the apocalyptists. They, too, recognized that God had blessed Levi and diminished Judah. But when they look forward to the Messiah, the eschatological savior, they continue to look for him from Judah, whatever role

---

[33]Cf. Lagrange, *Messianisme*, 74-77. The verses can hardly be other than Christian: Test. Lev. 18,6 has a parallel only in the Gospel accounts of Christ's baptism; v. 11 recalls Ap 22,2, and v. 12 recalls Ap 20,2f. and Lk 10,19; v. 8 is the doctrine of Heb 7,23f.; the text further speaks of the conversion of the Gentiles and the probation of the Jews, etc. Test. Jud. 24,1-3 depends on the Gospel descriptions of our Lord's baptism and the Pauline doctrine of adopted sonship.

they may assign to the priesthood in leading to him. This teaching of the Testaments, recognized for what it is, is not isolated. Precisely the same doctrine is taught in Jubilees, cc. 30-32, where Levi is given supremacy over Judah as the reward (contrary to Gn 49,5-7) of the slaughter of the Shechemites — but a savior is still awaited from Judah.

In the foregoing I have followed the hypothesis that I believe still has the greater probability, namely, that the Testaments of the Twelve Patriarchs is a Jewish work that has undergone considerable Christian interpolation.[34] We must also reckon with the possibility, however, that it was a Christian work in its inception. This position, not a new one, has recently been supported by new evidence from Qumrân.[35] Among the extensive apocrypha and pseudepigrapha possessed by the sectaries of Qumrân, no fragment of the Testaments of the Twelve Patriarchs has yet been identified. However, fragments of a Testament of Levi in Aramaic were found in Cave I, and still more extensive fragments in Cave IV; also in Cave IV were found fragments of a Testament of Naphtali in Hebrew. In both cases, the material of the fragmentary testaments is more extensive than the corresponding testaments in the Testaments of the Twelve Patriarchs. Thus it may be supposed that the fragments belong to some of the source material of the Testaments of the Twelve Patriarchs. The identical material — Testament of Levi in Aramaic and of Naphtali in Hebrew — was also recovered from the Cairo Genizah that yielded the Damascus document.[36] Presumably it, too, comes ultimately from Qumrân, from one of the earlier discoveries, probably that of c. 785 AD., as related by Mar Timotheos I. Thus Qumrân may provide evidence of

[34]Cf. M. de Jonge, "Christian Influence in the Testaments of the Twelve Patriarchs," *NT* 3 (1960) 182-235. The author has returned to this position after previously defending the thesis of Christian authorship.

[35]Cf. Eissfeldt, *Einleitung*², 784f.; J. T. Milik, *Ten Years of Discovery in the Wilderness of Judaea*, tr. by J. Strugnell (Naperville, Illinois: Allenson, 1959) 34f.

[36]Monsignor Patrick W. Skehan has kindly called my attention to the significance of this fact.

a pre-compilation state of at least part of the Testaments of the Twelve Patriarchs. Correspondingly, the compilation date of the finished work would have to be lowered considerably from the Maccabean or Hasmonean age that is usually considered.[37]

If the Testaments is a Christian work in the ultimate analysis, then of course the "interpolations" must be seen as the author's original intention in composing the work. This intention would then obviously be to show that Jesus Christ is the fulfilment of both a royal (Davidic) and a priestly (Levitical) messianism. In part, this would correspond to other early Christian attempts to find a Levitical as well as a Davidic ancestry for Jesus.[38] Such attempts need not have a more complex explanation than the fact that Luke could be interpreted as ascribing Levitical ancestry to Mary, the *syngenís* (1,36) of Elizabeth, who was *ek tôn thygatérōn Aarōn* (1,5). In the same line is the messianic conception of the third-century Hippolytus of Rome.[39] It seems to me more reasonable to suppose the Christian theorizing to be the result of this interpretation of Luke than to imagine Luke and the theorizing together to be dependent on some Jewish tradition of a Levitical Messiah. For if Luke did intend to make such an insinuation, it is strange that it was never followed up. The idea is foreign to the rest of the NT, and it is deliberately excluded by the teaching of Hebrews.

[37]An alternative hypothesis has been sustained by Marc Philonenko. *Les interpolations chrétiennes des Testaments des Douze Patriarches et les manuscrits de Qumrân* (Cahiers de *RHPhilRel*; Paris: Presses Universitaires, 1960): that the Testaments are integrally a Jewish work, the product of a Qumrân type of Judaism. The soteriological figure is not Jesus Christ but the Teacher of Justice. Besides the other obvious objections to this early-Dupont-Sommer kind of hypothesis, the absence of the Testaments at Qumrân is a decisive argument.

[38]Cf. Strathmann, *ThWNT* 4, 244f.

[39]Cf. L. Mariès, S.J., "Le Messie issu de Lévi chez Hippolyte de Rome," *Mélanges Jules Lebreton I*=RechSR 39 (1951) 381-396.

Qumran

It has by now become virtually *sententia communis scholarum* that the Qumrân sectaries professed a Levitical, more properly an Aaronic, messianism which they had incorporated into the "normative" messianic expectation.[40] As the evidence, however, is somewhat ambiguous, we are not surprised to find a wide variety of opinion in the interpretation of this messianism.

Certainly, the existence of a priestly Messiah cannot be deduced simply from the famous passage 1QS 9,11, which speaks of *nābî' ûmešîḥê 'aharôn weyiśrā'el*, since *māšîah* is patient of a double meaning in such a connection: it can mean the Messiah of Israel in the technical sense on the one hand, and it can also be the coventional highpriestly designation.[41] Rather, we must look to the qualities that are ascribed to the supposed priestly eschatological figure in the Qumrân expectation. 1QS 9,11 doubtless refers to the (literally: "a") prophet who was needed to settle so many religious questions in the contemporary Jewish world now bereft of the prophetic word (cf. I Mc 4,46; 14,41). One of the prophet's functions, for the sectaries, would be to restore the Zadokite priesthood, "the anointed of Aaron." Possibly, but not certainly, therefore, the prophet and the priest

---

[40]Cf. J. T. Milik, *Discoveries in the Judaean Desert I. Qumrân Cave I* (New York: Oxford University Press, 1955) 121f.; Raymond E. Brown, S.S., "The Messianism of Qumrân," *CBQ* 19 (1957) 53-82; F. M. Cross, Jr., *The Ancient Library of Qumrân and Modern Biblical Studies* (Garden City, New York: Doubleday, 1958) 165-173; A. M. Habermann, *Megilloth Midbar Yehuda* (Tel Aviv: Mahberoth Lesifrut, 1959) 188.

[41]Millar Burrows, *More Light on the Dead Sea Scrolls* (New York: Viking, 1958) 297-311 apparently believes such a distinction to be captious, reminding us that the sectaries had no way of making a written distinction between Messiah and messiah. While this is quite true, it should be no less evident that *māšîah* was nevertheless capable of being employed in ways other than as the technical term for the object of messianic expectation. The *hakkōhēn hammāšîah* of Lv, at Qumrân or elsewhere, is neither *a* nor *the* Messiah. In a comparable situation, Burrows himself is quick to point out that the *benê-hayyiṣehār* of Zech 4,14 are " 'sons of oil,' not 'Messiahs.' "

of this passage are eschatological figures. We have no assurance that the reference is not to a restored priestly line rather than to an individual eschatological priest.

Is the priest of 1QSa, who appears to be called *rôʾš kôl ʿadat yiśrāʾēl* (2, 12), an eschatological figure? This might appear to be the case in view of the *bᵉʾaharît hayyāmîm* of 1,1.[42] However, this conclusion is not peremptory. As Cross has pointed out, the apocalyptic community of Qumrân is at one and the same time the future congregation of the elect and the present sect whose communal life foreshadows the new age.[43] The "messianic banquet" of 1QSa is simply the common meal of the sectaries, at which the Messiah, however, will be present (it is to be noted that "Messiah" and "Messiah of Israel" in this text are synonyms). The priest, therefore, may be simply the priest who *de facto* will be the head of Israel at the time of the Messiah's coming, who is represented here and now in the head of the Qumrân community. In a sense he could be called an eschatological figure, but he is hardly messianic. The role of the (presumed) highpriest in the formula of blessings (1QSb) is even more ambiguous, though it does seem likely that the *nᵉśî hāʿēdâ* of the blessings is the Messiah, or Messiah of Israel, elsewhere mentioned. Surely no one would attempt to establish the messianic character of the highpriest on the basis of 1QSb alone; those who find it there do so because of other considerations in other texts.

It might be thought significant that nowhere in the Qumrân literature do we find the expression "Messiah of Aaron" standing alone; the expression itself, as a matter of fact, occurs only the one time, if it occurs at all, as part of the designation of

---

[42]Theodor H. Gaster, *The Dead Sea Scriptures in English Translation* (Garden City, New York: Doubleday, 1957) 307-310 takes *both* the anointed king and the priest to be simply representatives of the two orders who will be present in the indefinite future. This seems improbable; *beʾaharit hayyāmim*, which Gaster translates "in the future," doubtless means "at the end of time," given the eschatological preoccupations of the sectaries.

[43]*Ancient Library*, 64, ftn. 63. Cf. also Edmund F. Sutcliffe, S.J., *The Monks of Qumran* (Westminster, Maryland: Newman, 1960) 111.

the Messiah of Israel in 1QS 9,11.[44] It is true, in the Damascus document the expression "Messiah of Aaron and Israel" occurs four times (12,23-13,1; 14,18;19,10f. [Charles 9b,10]; 20,1 [Charles 9b,29]: "Messiah from Aaron and from Israel"). The expectation that the fragments of this same work found in 4Q would show the singular Messiah of the Damascus document to be a medieval orthodox correction of a primitive plural Messiahs has not been realized: the singular occurs in the oldest exemplar of the document, which Milik dates 75-50 B.C.[45] This also rules out the suggestion that the repeated preposition of 20,1 indicated two Messiahs; the Damascus document clearly knows but one. That one, according to Milik, is the priestly Messiah who has taken over the title of the royal Messiah. The evidence does not seem to justify this assertion. "Aaron and Israel" appears to have meant simply "all Israel," that is, as embracing both the priestly and the lay elements (cf. 1,4-7, where *mîyiśrā'ēl ûmē'aharon šôreš = šᵉêrît lᵉyiśrā'ēl*; cf. also 10,5f.; in 1QM 3,12f. *yiśrā'ēl wᵉ'aharôn = 'am 'ēl*; cf. also 5,1); therefore, "the Messiah of Aaron and Israel" corresponds to "the Messiah of all Israel." He may, indeed, have been conceived as a priestly Messiah, but there is no proof of this. In view of the extraordinary denigration of David in 5,2-6 it may very well be, as Charles suggested,[46] that a non-Davidic Messiah was expected. The Damascus document, in other words, could be projecting the thought of Ben Sira into the eschatological future. It is perhaps worthy of note that the *nᵉśî' kol hā'ēdâ* of 7,20 (cf. the *nᵉśî' hā'ēdâ* of 1QSb), presumably the Messiah of Aaron and Israel, had an echo in the *nᵉśî' yiśrā'ēl* title of Bar Kochba, the non-Davidic Messiah proclaimed by Rabbi Akiba. All in all, though their affinities are plain, the Damascus document and the Qumrân literature contain too many obscurities

---

[44]And for this reason it can scarcely be said that "the coming of two anointed chiefs" is "the main doctrine of the sect" on which supposition the whole of its messianism is to be restored. So Yigael Yadin, "A Crucial Passage in the Dead Sea Scrolls, 1QSa ii.11-17," *JBL* 78 (1959) 238-241.

[45]Cf. Milik, *Ten Years* 125f.

[46]*Apocrypha and Pseudepigrapha*, 2, 795f.

to permit us as yet to explain the messianism of the one by the other.[47]

The rest of the original Qumrân material sheds no further light on an Aaronic Messiah. The War scroll makes frequent enough reference to the *kôhēn hārō'š*, but the highpriest of this document is no more eschatological than are the Levites, the other priests, and all the others who take part in the battle array. Strangely, the Messiah of Israel is not mentioned in connection with this eschatological battle; it is not immediately evident that the *nᵉśî' kôl hā'ēdâ* of 5,1 is the Messiah. Once again, as with the "messianic banquet," we seem to have merely a projection of existing Qumrân institutions (or would-be institutions) into the eschatological future.

Neither has the later Qumrân material provided as yet any solution to our problem. Documents published by John M. Allegro have satisfactorily defined the character of the Messiah of Israel, but say nothing of a Messiah of Aaron.[48] 4QpGen 49 (provisionally termed 4Q Patriarchal Blessings by Allegro), a *pēšer* on Gn 49,10, makes it quite clear that the Qumrân Messiah was the standard Davidic one of the tribe of Judah — something that, surprisingly enough, is not clear from the material that we have surveyed above. A second document, entitled by Allegro 4Q Florilegium, couples a *dôrēš hattôrâ* with the Davidic Messiah (*ṣemaḥ dāwîd*). Allegro identified this expounder of the Law with "the Messiah of Aaron." However, *dôrēš hattôrâ* is a fairly common figure in the Qumrân literature and the Damascus document, a figure who is not necessarily eschatological or even individualized. There seems to be no reason whatever to make him an Aaronic Messiah.[49] 4QpIsᵃ appears to speak of the Messiah (again explicitly identified as

[47]Cf. Morton Smith, "What is Implied by the Variety of Messianic Figures?" *JBL* 78 (1959) 66-72. The writer, however, would not accept Smith's conclusion that no systematization was attempted by the sectaries or should be attempted by us.

[48]"Further Messianic References in Qumran Literature," *JBL* 75 (1956) 174-187.

[49]Cf. Brown, *CBQ* 19 (1957) 80f.

Davidic) as receiving priestly instruction (Fragment D, line 7f.), but priests are in question (*kôhanê haššēm*), not a priestly Messiah. 4Q Testimonia, doubtless the most important document of the lot published by Allegro, is a catena of texts (from Ex, Nm, Dt, and an apocryphal 4Q Psalms of Joshua) which combine the prophetic, priestly, and royal aspects of messianism without distinguishing Messiahs; in view of the last text, which is not messianic, Allegro himself concludes that the common denominator of the texts is not messianism but eschatological doom.[50]

That the priesthood should figure largely in the eschatology of these true sons of Zadok is hardly to be wondered. However, to reconstruct from this the doctrine of a priestly *Messiah*, in all the technicality that we have the right to associate with this term, is, in the writer's opinion, an adventuresome step that has been too hastily taken.

The same judgment may be offered in respect to this entire investigation of the Judaism of the late biblical and intertestamental periods. Throughout the postexilic age the priesthood preoccupied the life and thought of Judaism, and this preoccupation inevitably affected Jewish eschatology in various ways. There is, however, no invariable pattern to this preoccupation, which was capable of quite disparate affirmations. It does not appear that in these affirmations there was sufficient consistency to allow us to speak of a Levitical messianism that either supplanted or shared the Davidic messianic expectation. We can speak of a priestly Messiah only by making the word "Messiah" mean something quite different from the meaning it has traditionally had both in Jewish and in Christian thinking.

The New Testament

If the line of reasoning we have followed above is correct, we should expect to find it confirmed by what we discover in

[50]Cf. also Patrick W. Skehan, "The Period of the Biblical Texts from Khirbet Qumrân," *CBQ* 19 (1957) 435-437.

the NT. There was, as we saw, a strand of Jewish thinking that brought a priestly figure into conjunction with the Davidic Messiah. We find that strand in the Gospels in the figure of John the Baptist, who is represented as Elijah the "restorer" of Mal 3,23f. (cf. Mt 17,12 *apokatastései*, Mk 9,12 *apokathistánei*, Mal 3,24 [LXX 4,6] *apokatastései*; also *apokathistâneis* in the question addressed by the as yet uncomprehending disciples to our Lord in Acts 1,6). It is true, the main emphasis of the Gospels is on John's and Elijah's prophetical status, not the priestly. Luke, however, is insistent on the Baptist's priestly origins: not only is he the son of a priest, but also of a mother who was a daughter of Aaron. John, therefore, was of priestly birth in the fullest sense.[51] That the Elijah-to-come would also be the eschatological Levitical highpriest who would anoint the Messiah was one form of the Jewish Elijah-expectation.[52]

This identification of the Baptist with Elijah the highpriest is certainly not one of the major emphases of the NT. What is equally clear is that when the NT attributes a priestly character to our Lord it is in no way dependent on the Levitical speculation of which we have been speaking above. Quite to the contrary, this attribution is premised on precisely the denial of what this speculation presupposed. The speculation, in whatever form it took, presupposed a covenant with Levi that would endure; the priesthood of Christ supposes that the Levitical priesthood has been definitely superseded. The Levitical speculation understood a renewed covenant whose priesthood preserved its ancient privileges and was restored to a pristine purity; the priesthood of Christ is incomprehensible apart from a new covenant with an entirely new priesthood.

According to Hebrews, Christ's priesthood is that of

[51]Cf. Alfred Plummer, *A Critical and Exegetical Commentary on the Gospel According to St. Luke* (ICC; New York: Scribners, 1920) 9.

[52]Cf. Joachim Jeremias, " *'El (e) ias," ThWNT* 2, 934f.; Strack-Billerbeck, *Kommentar zum Neuen Testament aus Talmud und Midrasch* (Munich: C. H. Beck, 1928) IV, 789-798; Joseph Klausner, *The Messianic Idea in Israel,* tr. by W. F. Stinespring (New York: Macmillan, 1955) 456. This identification was based, in part, on the association of Mal 3,1-3 with 3,23f.

Melchizedek. Despite the claim that the author of Heb was dependent on the Alexandrian school of Philo for his Melchize-dekian doctrine,[53] it should be quite evident that the resemblances are purely verbal.[54] It is hard to see how Cullmann—who, for that matter, completely confuses the Levitical and Melchize-dekian highpriestly concepts in his search for a background for the NT doctrine—can instance Philo among those who treated of Melchizedek "eschatologically."[55] Philo's Melchizedekian "doctrine" (in *Leg. All.* III, 79-82 [*lógos*]; *De Cong.* 99 [*automathê kaí autodídakton*]; *De Abrahamo* 235, etc.) is the purest allegorism, totally unrelated to any history or eschaton. The treatment in Heb, on the contrary, exploits an historical typology, whose controlling term is throughout the antitype, and whose purpose is to explain the disappearance of Levitical cult and covenant. There is in Heb no Melchizedekian specula-tion for its own sake. It is to be noted, too, that Philo's cele-brated dictum, *"légomen gàr tòn archieréa ouk ànthrōpon allà lógon theîon eînai pántōn ouch 'ekousíōn mónon allà kaí akousíōn adikēmátōn amétochon,"* was written as an allegoriza-tion of Nm 35,29 (in reference to the Levitical highpriest), the literal sense of which Philo considered an absurdity (*De Fug.* 108).

The doctrine of Heb is not the end result of a Jewish specula-tion, but a new revelation. Ps 110 and its Melchizedekian figure, when taken messianically, could only be an embarrassment to

[53]Cf. H. von Soden, *Hebräerbrief* (HCzNT; Tübingen: J.C.B. Mohr, ³1899) 6, 60f. This hasty conclusion of the older commentators has been almost completely abandoned today, cf. C. Spicq, O.P., *L'épître aux Hébreux* (EB; Paris: Gabalda, 1953) I, 39ff.; Otto Michel, *Der Brief an die Hebräer* (KEKNT; Göttingen: Vandenhoeck & Ruprecht, ¹¹1960) 16-27, 159f., 372f. However, Jean Héring, *Le royaume de Dieu et sa venue* (Neuchâtel: Delachaux & Niestlé, ²1959) 74 still makes Ps 110, Philo, and Heb together depend on a "mythe melchisédechien."

[54]Cf. H. Windisch, *Hebräerbrief* (HzNT; Tübingen: J.C.B. Mohr, 1913) 58f.; Otto Michel, *"Melchisedék,"* *ThWNT* 4, 574f.; Gottlob Schrenck, *"archiereús," ThWNT* 3, 275f.

[55]Oscar Cullmann, *The Christology of the New Testament*, tr. by Shirley Guthrie and Charles Hall (London: SMC Press, 1959) 85.

Judaism.[56] What made it an embarrassment and what made it impossible to integrate Melchizedek into the Jewish messianic expectation, are capitalized on by the author of Hebrews. Faced with a new fact, that the awaited Savior had combined in himself both the Davidic hope and a priestly character, this author did what Judaism could not. He dispensed with the Levitical priesthood and consequently with the Mosaic Law, and appealed for his justification in prophecy to the typology of Melchizedek.

The other parts of the NT that identify Jesus as priest must also be independent of and in conflict with any conception of the continuation of a Levitical priesthood, for the reason made explicit in Heb 7,13f.[57] Jesus' depreciation of the temple in favor of his own mission (Mt 12,6), his substitution of himself for the temple (Jn 2,19; Lk-Acts), his repeated application to himself of Ps 110 (Mk 12,35ff. par. 14,62 par.), and the highpriestly prayer of John's Gospel, all presuppose a new priesthood that was not that of Levi and Aaron.

One may say, with Condamin, that Jesus Christ has fulfilled the spirit rather than the letter of OT prophecy and has realized its priestly ideal.[58] This is very true. But it seems more important to insist that the Christ-event, in its unicity, so far transcends the OT expectation as to have made all its expressions an inadequate anticipation. If this truth can be seen with more clarity here than in the apparently more literal fulfilment of the Davidic hope which was exploited so enthusiastically by the NT, still, in the one as in the other, fulfilment brought with it quite as much of the unexpected as it did of the expected.

---

[56]Cf. Strack-Billerbeck, *Kommentar,* 4, 460-462.

[57]Cf. Cullmann, *Christology,* 87-89, 104-107.

[58]Condamin, *Jérémie,* 248: "On peut dire aussi que le prophète était éclairé par une lumière divine sur les traits essentiels du salut messianique, et non point sur le temps, les circonstances, les détails; pour ceci, il était laissé à ses conjectures probables, comme S. Pierre le note expressément I Pt 1,10-11."

18. The Development of the Expression of Faith in the Worshipping Community

It was Eduard Norden who some sixty years ago forged the form-critical tools that are now used to uncover the liturgical-hymnic source-materials redacted into the New Testament.[1] Neither liturgical influence on the New Testament nor the presence of hymns there was an original discovery by Norden, of course. Besides the obvious and explicit references to liturgy in Acts and the Epistles, and the many Gospel passages which have been shaped to allow for liturgical allusions, there has hardly ever been any serious doubt that—to take one example—the "Jesus is Lord" formula of Rom. 10. 9 and I Cor. 12. 3 was lifted by Paul straight from the liturgical experience of the Christian communities of Rome and Corinth. As for hymns, those of Luke and Revelation were always recognized as classic. What form criticism did was to bring the two together, liturgy and hymn, or rather, make it possible for us to see how the two had conspired together to make up one of the earliest Christian theologies, whose destiny it was to help create and at the same time be absorbed by the New Testament canon.

The hymns which appear explicitly and integrally in the New

---

[1] *Agnostos Theos: Untersuchungen zur Formengeschichte religiöser Rede* (Leipzig and Berlin, 1913).

Testament books may or may not have been original compositions by their canonical authors and may or may not have been
liturgically influenced in their beginning as they were later in
their use: the evidence is fairly evenly divided in either direction. The Lucan canticles, which serve a diagrammatic function identical with that of the sermons of Acts, are substantive
to the structure of the Third Gospel, the work of a consum-
mate artist who has so made them his own that their pre-
canonical character, if any, can only be guessed at and hardly
proved.[2] Something very similar must be said of the hymns of
Revelation, which badly need a thorough form-critical study.
In these "heavenly liturgies" we find doxologies, acclamations
of acceptance (*Würdig-Rufe*) and other forms of a cultic flavour
which show the author to have been at home with liturgical
thought, but they cannot be certainly related to any existing practice of the Church.[3] The hymns, or hymnic fragments, of which
form criticism has apprised us, are rather those which the canonical authors found already to hand in the credal and liturgical
life of their churches, which therefore affected their theology
in the very act of being modified or revised by redactional use.
Norden's criteria for the isolation of these passages, aside from
their evident poetic character and pecularities of vocabulary,
were principally their high incidence of participles and relative
clauses,[4] traits that suited them admirably to be the expansions
of prayers of blessing or thanksgiving. To be sure, he did not
then know all the conclusions that would ultimately be drawn
from his insights; his criteria had to be sharpened by another
long generation of literary study. Nevertheless, he deserves full
credit for our being able today to point with modest certainty

[2]See the discussions of P. Minear, C.F.D. Moule, E. Schweizer, among
others, in *Studies in Luke-Acts* (Paul Schubert Festschrift) (Nashville and New
York, 1966).

[3]Cf. Gerhard Delling, "Zum gottesdienstlichen Stil der Johannes
Apokalypse", *Novum Testamentum*, 3 (1959), pp. 107-37. On the role of the
doxologies in the structure of Rev., see Ugo Vanni, *La struttura letteraria
dell' Apocalisse* (Rome, 1971), pp. 149-67.

[4]*Op. cit.*, pp. 166-76, 254-63, 380-87.

to the remains of a respectable corpus of early Christian hymnody imbedded mainly in the epistolary of the New Testament which may very well put us in touch with some of the first language uttered by the Church in its christological prayer.

The passages with which we are concerned, if we restrict the list to those that are beyond debate (most of which were identified by Norden), are Phil. 2,6-11, Col. 1. (12-14), 15-20 + 2. 10; Eph. 2. 14-16, 5. 14 + (?); I Tim. 3. 16; Heb. 1. 3; I Pet. 3. 18-22; John 1. 1-5 + 9-11. All of them, with the exception of the Johannine hymn, have the literary characteristics we have just mentioned. For most of them the term "homology" has been found appropriate: that is, as distinct from the "creed" which proclaimed to the world as objects of faith the saving acts of God, these were acclamations in the Church of the Lord in whom salvation had been accomplished. The distinction is a useful one but must not be pressed. Obviously it was for their credal values that Paul and the other New Testament authors saw fit to incorporate such acclamations into their works; and it is for those values that we now deal with them.

What kind of christology was presupposed in these confessions? We might offer the following as elements of a composite,[5] presuming that even though all do not occur in any single example, they are sometimes implied there, and their recurrence is well enough distributed to postulate one doctrine rather than random and discrete pieties (remembering, too, that our examples are fragmentary at best):

1. The Redeemer is united with or equal to God (Phil., Col., Heb., John).
2. He is mediator or an agent in creation (Col., John).
3. He sustains creation (Col., Heb., John).
4. He descends from the heavenly to the earthly realm (Phil., John).
5. He dies (Phil., Col., I Tim., I Pet.).
6. He is made alive again (Col., I Tim., I Pet.).

[5]We use here the eightfold division of J. T. Sanders, *The New Testament Christological Hymns* (Cambridge, 1971), pp. 24-5. He does not include Col. 2. 10 or Eph. 5. 14 in his inventory.

7. He is reconciler (Col., Eph., I Tim., I Pet., Heb.).
8. He is exalted, enthroned, over the cosmic powers (Phil., I Tim., I Pet., Heb.).

It is not sufficient, however, merely to note the elements; they must also be evaluated. The death of the Redeemer, for example, in this christology is not the equivalent of the Pauline doctrine of the Cross. It has been adjusted to that doctrine only by evident redactional additions in the Phil. and Col. pericopes. For the rest, it remains a fairly statistical rather than a salutary event: it was destined, it happened, it was a *sine qua non*, the inevitable outcome of life in the flesh, the culmination of a self-abasement and subjection to the action of the powers of the world. We have an echo, then, of the primitive kerygma as it is represented in the first chapters of Acts, in which the crucifixion was largely a negative event cancelled out by the vindication of the resurrection. In these hymns, however, the resurrection itself, though central and all-informing in its effects, does not appear in explicit detail. Rather, what is featured is the exalted state of the Redeemer, his life of the spirit in which he effects salvation here and now, having achieved a cosmic reconciliation. The resurrection is not a vindication, but, at the most, the implied means that led to a vindication; vindication, as matter of fact, is less what is meant by this exaltation than simply another sphere of existence in a divine economy. It goes without saying, of course, that the resurrection does not figure, as it does for Paul, as the ground and exemplar of the Christian's eschatological hope. The eschatology of these hymns is "realized."

Even in Eph. 5. 14, which some believe to have been part of the hymn continued in I. Tim. 3. 16, and in which alone there is mention of a resurrection—of the believer, not of Christ—the exhortation is to a present, not a future awakening. The *epiphausko* of this verse is *hapax legomenon* in the New Testament, but the idea of "illumination" as well as its other content strongly indicates a baptismal liturgy as a likely setting for the composition. Paul, for whom "light" is a term for the present reality of the Christian life (Rom. 13. 12, 2 Cor. 4. 6, 6. 14, I Thes. 5. 5), while always retaining his eschatological perspective on salvation, nevertheless in his sacramental references is very mindful of proleptic realization: "alive to God" (Rom. 6. 11), "eats and drinks judgment" (I Cor. 11. 29). Indeed, we may ask whether we should not expect those theological utterances which originated in the liturgy, with its twin concern to "presentify" past event and future fulfilment, to have been a well-spring of realized eschatology here and elsewhere in the New Testament.[6] This supposition may be the more readily entertained when we recognize, as most seem to do these days, that there was no necessary descent of realized out of final eschatology, even though this development did take place, but that the former could coexist with the latter and be of equal antiquity with it. (By the same token, it is not required of us to go along with more recent hypotheses such as that of John A. T. Robinson, according to whom the dominant eschatology of early Christianity was an apocalypticized version of one that with Jesus had been originally "realized".) Another factor that must be taken into account is the genius of Christianity itself working instinctively in its liturgy as the faith and thanksgiving response to the saving acts of God. The genius of Christianity is that of a cosmic event which has altered the course of the world with consequent impact on its own awareness of its universal Saviour.[7]

If there has been general agreement concerning the liturgical provenance of these hymns, however, there is also a singular reluctance on the part of most scholars to venture opinions about what precise kind of liturgy it was.[8] For practically any one of the examples with which we have been dealing equally plausible settings have been suggested in both the baptismal and the eucharistic rituals of the first Christian communities. This ambiguity must also be taken into account as part of the phenomen-

---

[6]The thesis of D. E. Aune, *The Cultic Setting of Realized Eschatology in Early Christianity*. Supplement to *Novum Testamentum*, 28 (Leyden, 1972).

[7]Cf. Reinhard Deichgräber, *Gotteshymnus und Christushymnus in der frühen Christenheit* (Göttingen, 1967), pp. 208-14. He dates all the hymns in the Hellenistic period of the Church.

[8]*Ibid.*, pp. 131-3, 137, 140, 154-5.

ology of these hymns. What it indicates is a mould of thought
and language predating the liturgies in which the hymns served,
a mould that has shaped both their pre-canonical christology
and also the language of the liturgy.

There seems to be no doubt that the moulding influence we
are seeking was a wisdom tradition of some sort. Not unnat-
urally, the wisdom tradition of the Old Testament, including
its development in the Alexandrian Judaism represented in the
Wisdom of Solomon, has been ransacked for its store of words
and themes in order to account for the intellectual climate in
which this kind of Christian thinking took form. Some scholars
cling to the view that one need look no further than the Old
Testament, but such a position is increasingly difficult to defend. "Image of God", "firstborn of every creature", the hy-
postasis of creative wisdom, and so on, can certainly be derived from the Old Testament tradition, but probably not in exactly the form they achieved in the New Testament. Intertestamental studies have rendered old-fashioned any concept of
a monolithic Judaism single-mindedly devoted to the Old Testament as the matrix from which the nascent Church emerged.
For the same reason it is unnecessary to follow Rudolf Bultmann's lead, as many do, in seeking a non-Jewish or off-beat
Jewish[9] origin of this christology in an equally closed off world
of gnostic or pre-gnostic thought. Some of it does correspond
with this thought: "head of the body", "flesh and spirit", *Logos*,
the inimical powers, etc., while the closest parallels so far found
for Eph. 2. 14 occur in the Hermetic and Mandean literatures.
But it also contains much that is quite incompatible with a gnostic
point of view, including its most basic assertions which are of
far greater consequence than any amount of linguistic similarities. We feel that the best evidence still favours a composition of these hymns in light of the Christ-event, not a Christian
adaptation of a previously existing redemptive theology; but
the composition took place within the complex of speculation
and catch-words which passed for philosophy in a syncretistic
age, which liturgy found peculiarly adaptable to its needs.

[9]The conclusion ultimately reached by Sanders.

It seems to be entirely appropriate that the earliest language of liturgy should have been ready-made and not its own creation. If *lex orandi lex credendi* is a genuine principle – if the liturgy gives expression to a faith held by the community and is not, as is often the case nowadays, the attempt to form a faith by changing the terms of liturgy – then the language which liturgy chose must have already existed as one option among others and was plastic to uses other than the liturgical. It is also entirely appropriate that the choice should have descended on the language of wisdom. The participles and relatives which for the most part characterize the first Christian liturgy were acts of blessings or thanksgiving appended to acclamations of the Church's Lord. It was in wisdom circles, before and after the coming of Christianity (as we know from the Odes of Solomon, for example), that the thanksgiving hymn found a particular repository; and it was the same circles that were the most hospitable to speculation in those spheres where worship celebrated its thanks for God's saving activity: nature, creation, man, the cosmos.

At the same time, it is surely not without significance that probably in no single instance does any one of the liturgical hymns of which we have been speaking appear now in the New Testament in the exact language in which it was first composed. The redactional changes introduced by the canonical authors extend in almost every instance not merely to editorial adjustments demanded by new contexts but also to the actual substance of the material. Is this phenomenon related to the inadequacy of language taken in the whole, the principle that "speech is bounded by silence",[10] that theological formulations in each successive stage require further translation and rearticulation? Or is it an indication of the inherent inadequacy of the theology caught up by the hymns, of its unsuitability for kerygmatic proclamation? Of Phil. 2. 6-11 Hans Conzelmann has said, "no gospel could be written in the light of this christology", because of its minimization of history and susceptibility to myth.[11] Prob-

---

[10]Sanders, *op. cit.*, pp. 140-41; cf. also Deichgräber, *op. cit.*, p. 206.
[11]*An Outline of the Theology of the New Testament* (New York, 1969), p. 80.

ably we should answer both of these questions affirmatively.

The theology of the hymns was not only adapted by the New Testament authors but also changed. In Phil. 2. 8 "death on a cross" may perhaps be considered a minor amplification, but "of the church" in Col. 1. 18 certainly is not. At the same time, what took place in redaction should not be exaggerated into a correction of heterodoxy. Had this been the situation, we should doubtless never have had the hymns preserved for us in the first place: they were preserved because of the respect accorded them, even though it was a critical respect.[12] The christology they professed was not timeless and unhistorical, though it dealt with a minimum number of events selectively. What accounts for the discrepancies between the pre-canonical and the canonical texts are mainly the separate requirements of prayer on the one hand and credal articulation on the other. Externally, too, there was an undeniable pressure in the Pauline churches in favour of the more "standard" theological expression to which they had become accustomed, coupled, no doubt, with a growing suspicion against wisdom formulations because of their greater openness to gnostic and docetic thought.

The liturgical experience of early Christianity, as seen in the development of the christological hymns and their subsequent literary history, was unique, and it might be perilous to extrapolate from it to later liturgical experiences which may in part resemble it. We can only recapitulate the stages of the experience for what they show to have been New Testament convictions. It adapted rather than attempted to formulate anew the language in which it chose to express itself, falling back upon concepts which it found most congenial to its needs and tastes, some of which were especially congruent with the liturgical life-setting. The existential rather than the eschatological aspect of that setting was favoured, whether by design or natural affinity. The derivation of its speech, together with its easy redaction before and after its incorporation into the canonical texts, encourage us at least to recognize that on this precedent it is not language itself that is sacred but only what is done with language.

---

[12]As the present author has argued in "The Colossians Hymn and the Principle of Redaction", *Catholic Biblical Quarterly* (1971), pp. 62-81.

19. The Colossians Hymn and the Principle of Redaction

1. Redaction in the Canon

Anyone who has ever accepted a biblical canon and has had, at the same time, more than a passing acquaintance with the biblical text, is witness to the truth of a formulation which has become popular in recent times describing the canon as a unity in diversity. Of the two terms unity and diversity, furthermore, most everyone would doubtless be disposed to agree that the latter is more immediately applicable than the former. More applicable, that is to say, in respect to what the canon contains; for if the very existence of a canon is testimony to some kind of unity, its contents testify strongly to the diversity of the unity that somehow concurred in its making. Only a dogged disposition to harmonize at all costs, motivated by dogmatic bias or doctrinal naïveté, can be the alternative response to recognizing and striving to cope with the variety and contrariety of views that one encounters on all sides within the pages of the Bible, views that touch on profound things as well as reflect trivial differences, which go to the very heart of what the Bible is concerned with as well as lie on its periphery. There is no countering this fact by observing that the ordinary unsophisticated reader of the Bible is usually unaware of these inconsistencies, even when they are of the graver sort, and must have them pointed out to him. This phenomenon speaks, perhaps, to the higher unity of spirit that accounts for the canon, but it affords no critical basis for examining its contents. The existence of a canon has inevitably brought about for the ordinary reader a predisposition to find a basic harmony in the Bible, even when he has been educated out of the cruder forms of literalism.

There is no denying that the disposition to harmonize, to refuse to see or at least to fail to see the diversity in the unity of the canon, has prevailed throughout most of the long history of biblical religion. There was always some recognition of discrepancies within the canon, of course, even of internal discrepancies within various of the contributions to the canon. S. Bonaventure arrived at a fair approximation of the resultant literary form of Qoheleth when he concluded that "Ecclesiastes conducts a debate, as it were, to the very end of the book . . . so that it cannot be understood until it has been heard as a whole."[1] Even earlier S. Jerome could distinguish authors in the Johannine corpus[2] and think it possible that Mk 16:9-20 had been added to the Marcan text.[3] Such isolated conclusions, however, were certainly atypical not only of the age in which they were drawn but also of those who drew them. Divergencies in the canon were frankly acknowledged by Martin Luther, certainly, but only with the result that the canon, for him, became shortened on the procrustean bed of books "die Christum treiben": it was no solution to the problem of internal inconsistency in the canon to use a yardstick that ruled in favor of only one of its stresses. Luther's religious genius was undeniable, but it was also in conflict with the other religious geniuses which had shaped the canon. The Protestant orthodoxy that succeeded Luther ignored his limitations on the canon—acting less boldly than he had done but more boldly and forthrightly than those who would later call for "a canon within the canon"—and reverted to harmonization. But for that matter, Luther himself

---

[1]*Comm. in Eccl., prooem. q. 3, S. Bonaventurae . . . opera omnia* (Florence, 1893) 6, 8. "Ecclesiastes procedit quasi disputando usque ad finem libri . . . et ideo non potest sciri liber iste, nisi audiatur totus." This judgment is hardly affected by a contemporary verdict that the work may be the result of a redactor's modifying hand rather than of an author arguing with himself.

[2]*De viris illustr.* 9; *PL* 23, 623f.

[3]*Ep.* 120, 3; *PL* 22, 987.

had thought out no reasoned approach to deal with the canonical question: his reservations with regard to the NT, sparked by religious instinct, did not prevent his otherwise sharing to the full the concept of literal biblical unity that was the unchallenged assumption of his age.[4] For all practical purposes, the recognition of the problem that we have before us, and the attempt to arrive at some principles for its solution, belong to the age of biblical criticism and specifically to the vision of the Bible that has been opened up by form- and redaction-criticism.

Both form- and redaction-criticism were first applied to the OT before their applicability to the NT was seen in all of its ramifications. The implications which they had for interpretation were also seen somewhat differently, both because of the disparity in the kind of material that was revealed by critical analysis and because of the different presuppositions with which the text had been approached. The form-critical studies of Genesis, for example, which isolated the cult-sagas, the mythological and other etiological tales that had been woven into the fabric of its source material, also brought out how thoroughly these forms had been transmuted in their long transmission through the mouth of storytellers who were no longer concerned about the original motifs.[5] The hermeneutical relevance of such forms to the message of the biblical text is evidently rather different from that of an apothegm or paradigm of a saying of Jesus which has been provided with a narrative setting. The very remoteness of the material's origins from its utilization by a biblical author, together with a presumption that

[4]Despite the effort made by Heinrich Bornkamm, *Luther and the Old Testament* (tr. Eric W. and Ruth C. Gritsch; Philadelphia: Fortress Press, 1969), the present writer is hardly persuaded that Luther's understanding of the historical process of biblical formation and its consequent normative role ever transcended that of his contemporaries, Catholic or Protestant.

[5]Cf. Hermann Gunkel, *The Legends of Genesis* (tr. W. H. Carruth; New York: Schocken, 1964) 18-36; Sigmund Mowinckel, *The Psalms in Israel's Worship* (tr. D. R. Ap-Thomas; Oxford: Blackwell, 1962) 1, 166-169. See also Bruce Vawter, C.M., "Response to Arvid S. Kapelrud's 'The Role of the Cult in Old Israel,' " in *The Bible in Modern Scholarship* (ed. J. Philip Hyatt; New York/Nashville: Abingdon, 1965) 57-64.

its constitutive motifs had largely lost their interest for the biblical author, conspired to make the redacted text appear to have the sole *biblical* significance for *Sachkritik,* while the constituent forms might intrigue the student of ancient oriental history and religion.[6] As the witticism went, the R of the critical apparatus ought to be read *rabbēnû.*

Yet there has always been a large area of biblical material where redactional activity, though acknowledged, has been discounted or even ignored as though having no theological significance. The Psalms are a case in point. Despite the obvious fact that as a canonical book the Psalter is a work of much editing and redaction that have affected both its format and its theology down to relatively late times,[7] the Psalms continue to be interpreted almost exclusively in terms of their evident or assumed *Sitz im Leben* which first produced them as individual

[6]One cannot always feel entirely at ease with this solution. Oswald Loretz, *Schöpfung und Mythos* (Stuttgarter Bibelstudien 32; Stuttgart: Katholisches Bibelwerk, 1968), using Gen 6:1-4 as a paradigm, has made a thoughtful analysis of Gen 1-3 in support of a thesis that both J and P employed myth to illustrate theologoumena corresponding to Israel's contemporary historical experience. While his conclusions appear to be generally unexceptionable, one may wonder whether the biblical redactors always drew their distinction between received material and functional usage quite as cleanly as he does. In respect to Gen 2-3 he ends with the judgment that "als unausweichliche Folge ergibt sich hieraus, dass in diesem Text weder eine historische Beschreibung der Sünde des ersten Menschen vorliegt noch irgendeine naturwissenschaftliche Auskunft über den ursprünglichen Zustand der Menschheit. Wir haben es vielmehr mit einem Text zu tun, der nur von der besonderen religiösen Lage Kanaans und der Geschichte Israels in diesem Lande her verständlich ist." Is this "nur" really justified: is it consistent with J's interest in origins, manifested alike in his choice of sources and the exercise of his own imagination, that he intended to say nothing about beginnings? If he did intend to say something, his mythology must be coped with, not ignored.

[7]Cf. A. Arens, "Hat der Psalter seinen 'Sitz im Leben' in der synagogalen Leseordnung des Pentateuch?" in *Le Psautier* (Orientalia et Biblica Lovaniensia 4; Louvain: Publications Universitaires, 1962) 107-131; Jean Daniélou, *Etudes d'exégèse judéochrétienne* (Théologie historique, Etudes . . . à l'Institut Catholique de Paris 5; Paris: Beauchesne, 1966) 28-41, 141-169.

compositions. That this must be the first and indispensable stage at which exegesis is attempted, there can be no doubt. But when, following Hans-Joachim Kraus, we can see within the inner development of a psalm itself how an original *Sitz im Leben* became superseded, how, for example, the varied literary forms which had converged to make Ps 68 a cult-song of Tabor were later adapted to the worship of the Jerusalem temple, or how Ps 107 was converted from a thanksgiving liturgy of individuals into a national thanksgiving for delivery from the exile,[8] we may be persuaded of the need to consider other changes in meaning in psalms where redaction is less clear or even is merely implied by reason of their inclusion in the Psalter. To think of one instance only, what was the new meaning taken on by the royal psalms when they became part of the songbook of the kingless second temple? When words that rose in response to one setting are made adaptable to quite another, something redactional has taken place, even if not a single syllable has been altered. It would seem that it is the task of exegesis to ascertain what has occurred here, as long as we are working within a canon of Scripture and not simply translating a piece of ancient Semitic poetry.

Consider, too, the prophetic literature of the OT. With hardly any exceptions we have inherited the utterances of those who were once called the literary prophets in a redacted form, the canonical text. When we study these writings we find ourselves obliged to look behind their canonical form, however. We break up redactional units to recover the separate components that had distinct *Sitze* in prophetic careers, restore the occasional Judah to an undoubtedly original Israel, segregate the *Heilsorakel* that has been added or inserted to temper or nullify a message of doom and retribution, point out what are expansions and elaborations of the prophetic word introduced by later hands, in keeping with or in opposition to its pristine intent. Modern translations of the Bible have followed us in some or all or these procedures, in footnotes or by revising the received

---

[8]*Psalmen* (Biblischer Kommentar AT 15; Neukirchen Krs. Moers: Erziehungsverein, 1960) 468-472, 736f.

text. Once again, critical work of this kind is absolutely indispensable if we are to perform our exegetical duty: we want to know, and we must know, first of all, what sort of man was Amos or Jeremiah and to whom each prophesied and what he said, unencumbered by later interpretations occasioned by the changed circumstance of place, time, and religious development. All well and good. But then the commentators, having pared away the "non-authentic" redactional passages, have tended to treat them as so many defacements of the biblical text, unworthy of any serious consideration in their own right. Yet these elements stand as the testimony to the manner in which the prophetic word continued to live among a people. They are part of the canon, part of the OT's reflection upon itself.[9] In the OT as in the NT, word and interpretation are found together. The interpretation may be right or it may be wrong in relation to the prophet's original message, but in any case, it must be contended with and not simply dismissed.

Ernst Haenchen not too long ago accurately posed the problematic we have been discussing in a penetrating analysis of the prologue to John's gospel.[10] He, too, recognized the parity existing between the NT and the OT situation. Following the not uncommon view that the Johannine prologue resulted from the reworking of a christological hymn in the personified-wisdom tradition, Haenchen found the first redactor to have been the author of the fourth gospel who added Jn 1:18 to an original work that consisted of vss. 1-5, 9-11, 14, 16-17 in order to make it the introduction to his own writing. But there was also a second redactor, for the hand that was likewise responsible for the supplementary ch. 21 of John, mistakenly assuming that already in vs. 5 ("the light shining in the darkness") rather than only with vs. 14 the hymn had to do with the *logos*

---

[9]The expressed or unexpressed disposition of many Christian scholars to consider Israel or Israel's interpretation of itself an irrelevancy to the NT is, of course, a factor here. One thinks immediately of Rudolf Bultmann, Franz Hesse, Friedrich Baumgärtel. Cf. the discussion in my "History and the Word," *CBQ* 29 (1967) 512-517.

[10]"Probleme des johanneischen 'Prologs,' " *ZTK* 60 (1963) 305-334.

ensarkos, proceeded to contribute the references to the witness of the Baptist in vss. 6-8 and 15, as well as the motif of acquiring sonship with God through faith in the name of the Word expressed in vss. 12-13. The correctness of Haenchen's analysis and interpretation does not concern us here; whether or not it is verified in this case, the construction he put on the situation is doubtless instructive for many others that are to be found in the Bible. Therefore, he aptly raised the question of final meaning on a broader basis. As he observed:

> It has often been maintained that for the Christian reader *the* definitive sense of a biblical passage is that which the final redactor gave it. But when an OT redactor (for example, in Isa 6:13) has blunted the edge of a prophetic threat and turned it into a promise of salvation, surely it must be debated whether the prophet or the redactor is to be allowed the last word.[11]

His judgment coincides with our own expressed above that we do not seem to be of one mind concerning the hermeneutics of redaction. It is almost as though we make our choice of normative meaning, the redactor's or his source's, where these are in tension, on the basis of which we prefer to be heard. This is certainly to create a canon within the canon, and that a fairly arbitrary one.

2. The Colossians Hymn

The preceding has been prefatory to the examination we now propose to make of what is surely one of the NT passages that most epitomize the hermeneutical quandary revealed by redaction-criticism. This is the question of the christological hymn that is now embedded in the first chapter of the Epistle to the Colossians.

Gabathuler has exhaustively traced the history of interpretation of Col 1:15-20 all the way from Schleiermacher to Conzel-

---

[11]*Ibid.* 332 ftn. 95.

mann.[12] This interpretation has certainly been varied, in detail and in substance; yet there seems to have been a kind of inexorable logic according to which the basic literary form has become ever more sharply defined. Once the parallelism of the verses had been noted (Schleiermacher), only a short step was required to recognize that here was something possessing a hymnic character, with a content evidently dependent on some kind of *sophia* or *logos* speculation (von Soden, Artur Weiss, the *religionsgeschichtliche Schule*). Eduard Norden perceived that in its context the passage was used doxologically: he thought that Paul had assembled its motifs from the Stoic world of the time, mediated to him through Hellenistic Judaism.[13] He was followed rather closely by Günther Harder, who was the first to decide that the hymn was a citation and not a free composition.[14] Another kind of provenance was argued by C. F. Burney[15] and Ernst Lohmeyer,[16] both of whom thought of a wholly inner-Jewish genesis of the hymn, unaffected, or affected very little, by outside influences: for Burney it was a Pauline midrash derived from Prov 8:22ff. as a commentary on Gen 1:1 applied to Christ; for Lohmeyer it (Col 1:13-20) was the extension to Christ (by Paul) of a cosmic redeemer motif with roots in the day of atonement ritual. Subsequent studies have continued to divide over the issue of Jewish or extra-Jewish background, but a consensus of opinion clearly designates Col 1:15-20 a hymn or a hymn-like composition which the author of Colossians has redacted to fit his work, even though some would insist that this author and the author of the hymn (or his school) are one and the same.[17]

---

[12]Hans Jakob Gabathuler, *Jesus Christus, Haupt der Kirche — Haupt der Welt* (*ATANT* 45; Zürich/Stuttgart: Zwingli-Verlag, 1965) 11-124.

[13]*Agnostos Theos* (Berlin: Teubner, 1913) 250-254.

[14]*Paulus und das Gebet* (*NTF* 10; Gütersloh: Gerd Mohn, 1936) 46-51.

[15]"Christ as the ΑΡΧΗ of Creation," *JTS* 27 (1926) 160-177.

[16]In his *Die Briefe an die Kolosser und an Philemon* (Meyers Kommentar 9/2; Göttingen: Vandenhoeck & Ruprecht, 1930) 40-68.

[17]For André Feuillet, *Le Christ sagesse de Dieu d'après les épîtres pauliniennes* (*EBib*; Paris: Gabalda, 1966) 166-273; the author of Colossians had adapted a hymn that he had composed at an earlier time: "the apex of Pauline

First of all, setting aside for the moment the question of theological meaning and/or adaptation, it seems necessary to side with the majority view which on literary-critical grounds alone designates the original hymn as non-Pauline. It is true, the rhythmic pattern of the verses in question presents of itself no peremptory argument in favor of a citation: the preceding vss. 12-14, which certainly do not pertain to the original hymn, appear in a similar rhythmic pattern. This fact can be accounted for in various ways. A redactor about to cite the hymn could have adjusted his style to fit it in anticipation, surely, but it would have been even more natural for him to have done this had the hymn been his from the beginning.[18] Below we shall adopt what is to us the more convincing explanation, that vss. 12-14 represent an earlier redactional stage by which vss. 15-20 had been readied for their eventual inclusion in the epistle. For the same criteria which clearly mark the *Wortschatz* of vss. 15-20 as non-Pauline hold equally well for vss. 12-14. As far as vss. 15-20 are concerned, only in the formulaic aside of 2 Cor 4:4 does Paul elsewhere speak of Christ as the image of God (1 Cor 11:7; 15:49; 2 Cor 3:18; Col 3:10 reflect the concept of image [of God] that we more readily associate with Paul); *'oratos* (only here in the NT) is nowhere else contrasted with the invisible; Paul nowhere else speaks of thrones or of *kyriotētes* (the singular of the latter appears in the related Eph 1:21); *synistanō* is practically a technical term in the Pauline vocabulary (12x) with a clearly defined meaning, but only in Col 1:17 is it used intransitively and in a quite different sense; elsewhere Paul never speaks of Christ as an *archē*, though he does call him an *aparchē* — a

christology." Nikolaus Kehl, *Der Christushymnus im Kolosserbrief* (Stuttgarter Biblische Monographien 1; Stuttgart: Katholisches Bibelwerk, 1967), who sees the hymn as having undergone progressive amplification, is of the same mind: "Die Grundform des Hymnus steht fest in der paulinischen Theologie, und es ist ziemlich belanglos, ob die literarische Formulierung von Paulus selbst oder aus seinem Kreise stammt. In seiner Gründform hat er vor der Abfassung des Kol-Briefes existiert und die im Christusereignis eingetretene Verwirklichung des Heilplanes Gottes besungen."

[18]Kehl, 50.

quite different thing; the verb *katoikein* is found elsewhere in
the Pauline corpus only in Col 2:9 (possibly a displaced part
of the hymn, but in any case certainly related to it) and Eph
3:17 (related); the same may be said of the verb *apokatallas-
sein* (only in the related Eph 2:16). This is not the entirety of
the evidence.[19] As for the Semitically flavored vss. 12-14, it
may be noted that *klēros* is not a Pauline word; that "the lot
of the holy ones in the light," a *hapax* in the NT, demands a
meaning for *'agioi* (i.e., angels) used elsewhere by Paul excep-
tionally only in the apocalyptic stereotype of 1 Thes 3:13, since
this is his habitual term for Christians (as it is found in Col 1:26);
that while Paul often uses *rhyomai* for salvific deliverance, it
is always in the future and not, as here, in the aorist; that the
basileian tou 'uiou tēs agapēs is both un-Pauline and an anomaly
in the NT: that Paul does not use the term *aphesis*, though it
is common in the gospels. Again the evidence is not exhausted
by these examples.

    It is our contention, therefore, that the Pauline author of
Colossians — whether the apostle himself or an *alter ego* is of
little material consequence for our purposes — incorporated into
his writing a hymn, or a composition having a hymnic structure, that was not originally of his own devising. Whether we
can entirely reconstruct the composition as it first existed is
another matter altogether. We know that it did exist: enough
of the strophic pattern and the peculiar vocabulary remain to
convince us of this. But can we confidently proceed from these
bases to offer a convincing *Vorlage* of Col 1:15-20? James M.
Robinson has made a valiant effort in this direction, building
on Norden's pioneer research.[20] These is no doubt that by
relentlessly pursuing the verbal parallels and introducing a few
plausible alterations he has produced a well-balanced composi-

---

[19]Cf. Eduard Lohse, *Die Briefe an die Kolosser und an Philemon* (Meyers
Kommentar 9/2; Göttingen: Vandenhoeck & Ruprecht, 1968) 78f.

[20]James M. Robinson, "A Formal Analysis of Colossians I 15-20," *JBL*
76 (1957) 270-287. Ernst Bammel, "Versuch zu Col I 15-20," *ZNW* 52 (1961)
88-95, has also undertaken a reconstruction based on a chiastic structure
presumed but hardly demonstrated.

tion in two equal parts in which cosmic and soteriological concerns are evenly divided. However, as Kehl has pointed out,[21] the balance is more visual than substantive: despite the recurrence of formulas or catchwords, when some of the parallels are heard it becomes evident that there is no genuine correspondence between them. Furthermore, it is difficult to conceive of the redactional interests that would have motivated the dismembering of the harmonious structure which Robinson has reconstructed. The fact is, of course, that though Col 1:15-20 falls into a fairly well defined pattern which can be discerned elsewhere in the materials that have gone into the make-up of the NT canon, we do not really know what function this distinctive form served in the ecclesial communities that made use of it. Structurally, this form recurs as the elaboration of one or more relative clauses (the *'os*-formula); by this determination Col 1:15-20 is only one of a series of similar passages which seem to share the same character of early confessional poetry, or quasi-poetry, incorporated with or without changes into their present NT contexts (among them, Phil 2:6-11; 1 Tim 3:16; Heb 1:3; 1 Pet 2:22-25; 3:18f.,22). Besides their linguistic affinity these passages have other affinities as well. They are all confessional acclamations of the homology type,[22] that is, they concentrate on the person of the object of the church's faith and his attributes. Almost beyond doubt they had their origin in the liturgy. But how they functioned in the liturgy is another question, and one that we can hardly answer. Were they really hymns in their own right: songs of acclamation sung in chorus or antiphonally? Or were they rather pieces for recitation, having from the beginning the function they later assumed of accompanying or replacing credal formulas proper to the sacramen-

[21]*Op. cit.* 40f.

[22]We adopt this definition of Hans Conzelmann, cf. *Grundriss der Theologie des Neuen Testaments* (Munich: Kaiser Verlag, 1967) 81f. The homology is thus distinguished from the creed, wherein the history of salvation is affirmed. The distinction is not perfect: the Savior can hardly be acclaimed without advertence to the salvific acts worked through or by him, as we shall see; but it is sufficiently fine to be serviceable, and it does undoubtedly point to a distinct *Sitz im Leben formationis*, as is claimed.

tal liturgy?[23] If the former be the case, we might the more confidently reconstruct on the basis of strophic, syllabic, or metric balance. But if the latter was true, then undoubtedly content would have been the decisive factor, however much parallelism may have been an incidental technique. It might appear that what limited evidence there is favors the second alternative.

In dealing with Col 1:15-20, therefore, we propose to do no more towards reconstruction than see the existing text as it divides into sense lines, bracketing those words and phrases which appear to be redactional on the part of the author of Colossians. On the assumption, however, that vv. 12-14 represent an even earlier redaction of the christological "hymn" prior to its use in Colossians we also include them for discussion.

12 εὐχαριστοῦντες τῷ πατρὶ τῷ ἱκανώσαντι (ἡμᾶς)
    εἰς τὴν μερίδα τῶν ἁγίων ἐν τῷ φωτί:
13 ὃς ἐρρύσατο ἡμᾶς ἐκ τῆς ἐξουσίας τοῦ σκότους
    καὶ μετέστησεν εἰς τὴν βασιλείαν τοῦ υἱοῦ τῆς
    ἀγάπης αὐτοῦ,
14 ἐν ᾧ ἔχομεν τὴν ἀπολύτρωσιν,
    τὴν ἄφεσιν τῶν ἁμαρτιῶν:
15 ὅς ἐστιν εἰκὼν τοῦ θεοῦ τοῦ ἀοράτου,
    πρωτότοκος πάσης κτίσεως,
16 ὅτι ἐν αὐτῷ ἐκτίσθη τὰ πάντα
    ἐν τοῖς οὐρανοῖς καὶ ἐπὶ τῆς γῆς,
    τὰ ὁρατὰ καὶ τὰ ἀόρατα,
    εἴτε θρόνοι εἴτε κυριότητες εἴτε ἀρχαὶ εἴτε
    ἐξουσίαι,
    τὰ πάντα δι᾽ αὐτοῦ καὶ εἰς αὐτὸν ἔκτισται.
17 καὶ αὐτός ἐστιν πρὸ πάντων
    καὶ τὰ πάντα ἐν αὐτῷ συνέστηκεν,
18 καὶ αὐτός ἐστιν ἡ κεφαλὴ τοῦ σώματος [τῆς ἐκκλησίας].
    ὅς ἐστιν ἀρχή, πρωτότοκος ἐκ τῶν νεκρῶν,
    ἵνα γένηται ἐν πᾶσιν αὐτὸς πρωτεύων,
19 ὅτι ἐν αὐτῷ εὐδόκησεν πᾶν τὸ πλήρωμα κατοικῆσαι

---

[23]Cf. Werner Kramer, *Christ, Lord, Son of God* (SBT 50; tr. Brian Hardy: London: SCM, 1966) 64.

20 καὶ δι᾽ αὐτοῦ ἀποκαταλλάξαι τὰ πάντα εἰς αὐτόν,
   εἰρηνοποιήσας [διὰ τοῦ αἵματος τοῦ σταυροῦ
   αὐτοῦ] δι᾽ αὐτοῦ
   εἴτε τὰ ἐπὶ τῆς γῆς εἴτε τὰ ἐν τοῖς οὐρανοῖς.

Before turning to the question of redaction, however, we should
say something about the theology of the christological passage
and its thought background.

3. The Theology of the Hymn and Its Redaction

Col 1:15-20 and the other confessional poetry we have associated with it as having a like form (and also Rom 1:3f., which
appears in a different form) expound a theology of an exalted
Savior which evinces interest in the person of Christ only as
respects his death, resurrection, and universal lordship. Ulrich
Wilkens assigns the earliest version of this *kerygma* to the church
of the "Hellenists," whence it continued to develop as a theology
much subject to Hellenistic concepts and ideas.[24] Its ultimate
achievement is a cosmic christology which associates the Savior
as Son of God preexistent with the creator of the universe, his
function as universal mediator, his descent to earth where he
has effected redemption, and his return to heaven where he is
exalted as cosmic ruler. As has been noted above, the ideological
tradition which supplied the thought patterns for this kind of
theology continues to be the object of lively debate. On the one
hand, nobody seems to be in doubt that OT and later Jewish
wisdom speculation has provided a great number of the motifs
and even the vocabulary. The amount of these is, indeed, impres-
sive, and it is not surprising that many authors have, explicitly
or by implication, looked in this direction almost exclusively
to find the ideological origins of this christology.[25] Especially

[24]"The Tradition-History of the Resurrection of Jesus," in C. F. D. Moule,
ed., *The Significance of the Message of the Resurrection for Faith in Jesus
Christ* (SBT 2dS 8; tr. R. A. Wilson; Naperville: Allenson, 1968) 55f.
   [25]Examples: Jean Héring, *Le royaume de Dieu et sa venue* (Neuchâtel:
Delachaux & Niestlé, 1959) 163, did not think it impossible that extra Jewish

when the spectrum of the tradition is broadened to include Philo
as well as the less syncretistic kind of Hellenistic Judaism found
in such other Alexandrian works as the Wisdom of Solomon,
it has been easy for commentators to take this path.[26] Others,
however, have not been so sure. "Image of God," "firstborn
of every creature," "beginning," "head": this is all language extracted from the OT Wisdom vocabulary, just as pre-existence
and participation in creation are wisdom themes. But only in
some artificial sort of way can the personified-wisdom idea be
seen as the model for the portrayal of a cosmic redeemer, one
who has reconciled earth with heaven. Hence, some have looked
for at least a partial background of the hymn in the gnostic
redeemer-myth as reconstructed from Plato, Philo, Plutarch,
and the *Corpus Hermeticum*. In its most extreme form, perhaps,
this hypothesis has been defended in the seminal study of Ernst
Käsemann, for whom the hymn *is* the gnostic myth *tout court*,
a pagan composition later christianized by its introduction into
a baptismal liturgy.[27] Though the hypothesis has much to com-
mend it in a general way as providing suggestive parallels,[28]

tradition was quite sufficient to account for it all. Charles Masson, *L'Epître
de Saint Paul aux Colossiens* (Commentaire du NT 10; Neuchâtel: Delachaux
& Niestlé, 1950) 97-107, felt it unnecessary to go outside the OT to explain
the hymn's language and themes. This has also been the assumption of Feuillet,
both in his *Le Christ, sagesse de Dieu* and in numerous articles, such as those
on *plēroma and prōtotokos* in *DBS* 8, 18-40, 491-511.

[26]Cf. Eduard Schweizer, "Kolosser I, 15-20," in J. Blank, *et al.*, ed.,
Evangelisch-Katholischer Kommentar zum NT. Vorarbeiten Heft I (Zürich:
Benziger/Einsiedelin, Cologne & Neukirchen: Neukirchener Verlag, 1969) 10.

[27]"A Primitive Christian Baptismal Liturgy" (first published 1949), in
Essays on NT Themes (*SBT* 41; tr. W. J. Montague; Naperville: Allenson,
1964) 149-168.

[28]In respect to the imagery of Phil 2:1-11 much more so than to that of
Col 1:15-20. Cf. Ernst Käsemann, "Kritische Analyse von Phil. 2,5-11," *ZTK*
47 (1950) 313-360 [= *Exegetische Versuche und Besinnungen* (Göttingen:
Vandenhoeck & Ruprecht, 1960) 1, 51-95]; Kevin Smyth, "Heavenly Man
and Son of Man in Paul," *Studiorum Paulinorum Congressus Internationalis
Catholicus* 1961 (*AnBib* 17-18; Rome: PBI, 1963) 1, 219-230; Charles H.
Talbert, "The Problem of Pre-existence in Phil 2 6-11," *JBL* 86 (1967)

it has also been sharply attacked: for even in its pristine, unredacted form the hymn reflects some strikingly ungnostic concepts, including the key one of a reconciled heaven and earth.[29]

We are doubtless trying to preserve an anachronism if we insist on an all-or-nothing explanation of the world of ideas behind the hymn imbedded in Col 1:15-20, if we demand that it be either "Jewish" or "gnostic." What we have been compelled to recognize more and more through recent discoveries and studies is the strongly syncretic character of the world into which Christianity was born, a syncretism that was not confined to the Hellenistic-Roman world that prized it as an ideal life, but a syncretism that had permeated even such supposedly closed societies as that of Palestinian Judaism.[30] There were no taps marked "Jewish: Aramaic-speaking" or "Jewish: Hellenist" or

141-153; R. P. Martin, *Carmen Christi, Philippians ii. 5-11 in Recent Interpretation and in the Setting of Early Christian Worship* (Cambridge University Press, 1967); J. A. Sanders, "Dissenting Deities and Philippians 2 1-11," *JBL* 88 (1969) 279-290. The *Poimandres* 12-15 (*Corpus Hermeticum* 1, 12-26) presents a particularly interesting parallel.

[29]Cf. Lohse, 102 ftn. 1. See also Robert Haardt, "Gnosis und Neues Testament," in Josef Sint, ed., *Bibel und Zeitgemässer Glaube II* (Vienna: Klosterneuburger Buch- und Kunstverlag, 1967) 140-144; H. Langhammer, "Die Einwohnung der 'absoluten Seinsfülle' in Christus. Bemerkungen zu Kol 1,19," *BZ* 12 (1968) 258-263.

[30]Qumrân has surely shown how much that was once thought alien to OT processes had been taken into at least one form of Palestinian Judaism. Because of its dualism and other parallel features Qumrân was capable at one time of being regarded as a kind of Jewish bridge to gnosticism. It was not that at all, but rather had in its own way exploited current ideas that gnosticism exploited in another way. A case in point is the Melchizedekian savior-figure which appears at Qumrân, parallel in some respects both to the gnostic redeemer myth and to the Melchizedek myth of Philo. Cf. Joseph A. Fitzmyer, "Further Light on Melchizedek from Qumran Cave 11," *JBL* 86 (1967) 25-41. The Melchizedek of Hebrews may owe something to Qumrân, but with equal likelihood he may be in that respect totally *sine genealogia*. Certainly it is no longer necessary to try to connect him with Philo, who was once, as far as was then known, the only other contender in the lists.

"Hellenist: non-Jewish" which writers and thinkers could turn on to supply themselves with ideas and categories; what may have once been separate tributaries had long flowed into a common stream. The syncretism could be purely functional: we did not need the evidence of Chenoboskion, we already had it in the patristic literature, to recognize how words and ideas at home in one ideology could be equally at home in another, where they became grist for an entirely different mill. The author of Wis 3:1-9 found in his Hellenistic thought-world certain terms and ideas that were functionally useful to him in developing OT doctrine without, it seems, being affected by the underlying Hellenistic philosophy of a naturally immortal soul.[31] In like manner, Col 1:15-20 appears to have made use fairly indifferently of language and thought-patterns available from various sources without necessarily committing itself unreservedly to the intellectual background of any of them.[32] When read without presuppositions the Colossians hymn can hardly be taken simply as a paean to the personified creative wisdom of God found realized in Christ. Nor, *pace* Käsemann, is it the gnostic redeemer-myth newly identified with him. It contains elements that it may have derived from both streams of thought, but it is not explained wholly by either of them and in part it is in conflict with both of them. One may venture to suggest that it is, rather, really what it professes itself to be, a literary and thought form that has developed out of the Christian experience. As such it contains a theology which, as we have seen, turns up elsewhere in the NT canon. It is by no means the theology of Paul; indeed, wherever it has been utilized in a Pauline writing the need has been felt to Paulinize it. It is, for

---

[31]Cf. Addison G. Wright in *JBC* 34:6, 12f.

[32]What Siegfried Schulz, *Komposition und Herkunft der johanneischen Reden* (Stuttgart: Kohlhammer, 1960) seems to have shown successfully with regard to the discourse material of the Fourth Gospel would hold here equally well. The parallels can be quite close, especially as regards the *logos* figure, where one stream of thought has contributed the term and quite another has supplied the content.

all that, a theology that was formative of the NT, and for that reason it deserves examination in its own right.

This immediately raises the question, to what extent and with whatever qualifications Paul, or the Pauline author of Colossians, could have shared the theology of this christological hymn. We find it very difficult to believe with Schweizer[33] that he regarded it as skating perilously close to the edge of pantheism and making of salvation a thing of nature and not of grace. Psychologically, it is difficult to imagine an author attempting to build on a theology he found so radically wrong, and practically it is difficult to imagine him having thought to correct it with such a minimum of adaptation. It is much easier to agree with Rudolf Schnackenburg's analysis of the situation,[34] that the author of Colossians found in the hymn a christology with which he was in basic agreement but which he felt obliged to modify by adaptations which spoke a language with which he was more at home. Here we think it relevant to observe that the author of Colossians did not really redact a christological hymn as such, but a hymn that had *already* been redacted, simply by its inclusion in a sacramental liturgy, presumably in a baptismal liturgy: we are completely in agreement with Käsemann on this point. In other words, vss. 12-14 must be included together with vss. 15-20 as the material which the author of Colossians found to hand, not as two blocs of verses but a redactional unity. The implication of this fact is considerable. Whatever is to be said of the timelessness of the christology of the original hymn, a point which we reserve for the moment, it has been put firmly into the temporal sphere of a *Heilsökonomie* by the *'ikanōsanti 'ēmas*[35] of vs. 12, by the *errysato 'ēmas* and *metestēsen* of vs. 13, and by the parallels

[33]*Loc. cit.* 30f.

[34]"Die Aufnahme des Christushymnus durch den Verfasser des Kolosser briefes," in the same *EKK*, 33-50.

[35]Though *'ymas* is the preferred reading of the critical text and the *'ēmas* of the *textus receptus* is undoubtedly the result of an assimilation to vs. 13, the latter is also by serendipity probably what the original liturgy had to offer before it was redacted by the author of Colossians.

of vs. 14,[36] not to mention the fact that a sacramental liturgy by its very nature speaks to the historical and eschatological, whether it be a baptismal or a eucharistic liturgy. The transition had already been made from the hymnic situation with its allowable triumphalism uttered in praise and from personal experience for the ears of the object of cult to the rather different one of a credal statement intended to impress believer or nonbeliever alike with an objective statement of what God had wrought in Christ.[37] As far as we can see, the author of Colossians did no more than continue and perfect a process already begun in the liturgical redaction of the hymn.

The redactional changes introduced by the author of Colossians, at least as they affected the theology of the hymn/liturgical passage, we consider to have been slight.[38] The awkward *tēs ekklēsias* of vs. 18 is undoubtedly the more obvious of the adaptations: given the otherwise unbroken cosmological orientation of the hymn, there would seem to be no doubt that the *sōma*

---

[36]It is not necessary to regard vs. 14, which fits into the rhythmic pattern of the surrounding verses, as a redaction of the author of Colosians. Three uses in the primary Pauline material of the NT against seven uses elsewhere certainly do not constitute *apolytrōsis* a "Pauline" word (even though in two of the three instances, it is, as here, a term for present rather than eschatological salvation); and as we have seen, the quite common *aphesis 'amartiōn* is not Pauline at all.

[37]Schweizer 24f. is particularly helpful in explaining what is entailed in such a translation. He is thinking of the redactional work of the author of Colossians, but the same principle applies to the earlier liturgical redaction as well.

[38]We can leave aside the question whether the *eite . . . exousiai* of vs. 16 is redactional. Together with the *eite . . . ouranois* of vs. 20 which is its parallel, the expression has often been taken as a polemical expansion of the primitive text in view of the Colossian "errors." It may be admitted that an *eite . . . eite* phrase is eminently Pauline (1 Cor 3:21-23 among other examples), but so was it of many other Greek writers of the time; most of the other terminology in the context is not distinctive of the Pauline corpus. We tend to agree with Käsemann, 152 that vs. 20c is integral to the original hymn, and — if this is so — then the parallel in vs. 16 could hardly have been lacking. See the discussion in Lohse, 80f., and for a contrary view, Kehl, 45-48.

of this verse was originally the cosmic body of syncretic Hellenistic thought, pagan and Jewish.[39] To call Christ the head of this body was to epitomize what is said of him in vss. 15-17 as firstborn of every creature and the one in whom *ta panta* have order and meaning.[40] Less obvious but of the same order and purpose is the introduction of *dia tou 'aimatos tou staurou autou* into vs. 20b which now interferes with the original rhythmic pattern according to which the divine salvific power manifested (*en autō*) in the Christ-event[41] has reconciled all things *di' autou* and *eis auton*, making earthy and heavenly peace *di' autou:* again an event of cosmic dimensions has been specified.[42] The cosmos has been shrunk to the dimensions of the church, while cosmic reconciliation has been identified with the datable execution at accountable hands of an historically defined person.

We have called these redactional changes slight; others would doubtless disagree and insist that they are substantive. We can respond to this possible challenge only by defining what, in our opinion, the original christological hymn had intended to say, even before it had been (as we assume) incorporated into a sacramental liturgy.

First of all, we do not believe that it is entirely correct to characterize its concept of salvation as timeless. This might be true were we to consider only its first, and quantitatively its major part, down to vs. 18a. But between this first and the sec-

---

[39]Cf. Lohse, 93-95, and Schweizer in *TWNT* 7, 1072-5.

[40]It may be debated whether vs. 18a concludes the ctisiological part of the hymn or begins the soteriological. By the addition of *tēs ekklēsias* the redactor obviously understood it as soteriological, but in any case the entire unity with which he dealt had already been constituted soteriological through the prooemion of vss. 12-14. It is our view that the hymn originally intended a full stop after *sōmatos*, and that the soteriological strophe began, appropriately, only with the second *'os*.

[41]Whatever its original relation to the hymn, there can hardly be any doubt that Col 2:9 is the key to the meaning of the *plēroma* of vs. 19.

[42]So Lohse, 102: "Eine theologia gloriae, die die Vollendung als schon gewonnen betrachten möchte, wird durch die theologia crucis korrigiert."

ond, soteriological strophe, as Schnackenburg has pointed out,[43] something is presupposed, a falling away of the world from God which has disrupted the order otherwise triumphalistically hymned in the first verses, an insubordination that has necessitated the reconciliation of which vs. 20 speaks.[44] Salvation is not, therefore, a matter of nature but one of grace: it has *pleased* God that his saving fulness should reside in Christ to be the means whereby he reconciles and effects peace.[45] Secondly, and in continuation, it is not eternally, not as *pantokratōr* that Christ is savior, but as *prōtotokos ek tōn nekrōn*: despite all that has been said thus far of his primacy over all, only by this fact of divine intervention has he become the *archē*, truly holding first place *en pasin.*[46] In this respect, the Colossians hymn takes its place among the other acclamations of the glorified Christ which we have noted above (Rom 1:3f.; Phil 2:6-11; 1 Tim 3:16; Heb 1:3; 1 Pet 2:22-25; 3:18f.,22), all of which suppose some historical salvific action worked by or through him

[43]*Loc. cit.* 38.

[44]As the parallel with *eirēnopoiēsas* shows, *apokatallaxai* can hardly be made to fit any other meaning than that of a reconciliation produced by God (whether God or *plēroma* is the subject of *eudokēsen* in vs. 19). This is the meaning *katallassō ktl* has in Pauline usage, cf. Friedrich Büchsel in *TWNT* 1, 259.

[45]It can hardly be shown that *eudokēsen* refers to any specific divine intervention in time (e.g., to the incarnation); it is, rather, a reference to the eternal salvific will. Nevertheless, in context this is a will that has been effected in history, in the Christ *event.* Cf. Lohse, 99f.; Kehl, 120-124; Gottleb Schrenk in *TWNT* 2, 739f.

[46]Cf. Wilhelm Michaelis in *TWNT* 6, 879.883. The argument is somewhat weakened, to be sure, if the *'ina* clause of vs. 18c is considered to be yet another redactional addition of the author of Colossians. We see no need to consider it so, however, except on a theory of the theology of the hymn that is independent of its analysis. The *'ina* clause seems to be as integral to the development of these verses as is the comparable *'ina* clause of Phil 2:10 to the verses which surround it. The *'os estin archē* of vs. 18b introduces a wholly new dimension in which the *prōtotokos pasēs ktiseōs*, etc., of the earlier verses are to be viewed, and for this new dimension both the *'oti* of vs. 19f. and the *'ina* of vs. 18c are necessary.

whom the cult celebrates as the title by which he is celebrated.

This christology of glorification would, it is true, occur more readily to a Johannine than a Pauline author. Yet it is hard to imagine Paul repudiating it altogether; it is not all that removed from the theology of 1 Cor 15:45. The difference in the Pauline emphasis, which accounts for the Pauline adaptations, we conceive to be one of eschatological perspective. It should not be minimized, but neither should it be exaggerated. In the hymn and in Col 2:12 the eschatological life enjoyed as a share in the resurrected life of the Savior is spoken of *in a sense* as a present reality, whereas the "standard" Pauline view of it, as in Rom 6:4f., is of a hoped-for future. "For if we have become *symphytoi* with him in the fashion of his death, so shall we also be in the fashion of his resurrection." The same Paul, however, who in the next few verses speaks of the dual mystery of the death and resurrection as a once-for-all death to sin and life to God, can enjoin the Romans to consider themselves *nekrous men tē 'amartia zōntas de tō theō en Christō Iēsou* (Rom 6:10f.). Is it really a giant step from this formulation to that which relates Christians to Christ as *en 'ō kai synēgerthēte*, especially when it is quickly qualified: "through faith in the power of God who raised him from the dead"? (Col 2:12). A development, surely. But a development that it is not impossible to imagine Paul himself making,[47] and certainly one that has not betrayed Pauline thought. At the same time, we can easily see why the redactor felt it necessary to introduce into vs. 20 of the hymn the missing doctrine of the cross, thus maintaining the customary Pauline balance of death and resurrection (a balance which is carefully preserved in Col 2:12).

The same eschatological shift may be seen as the basis for the other Pauline adaptation of the hymn. In Col 1:16,20 and 2:15 the demonic and/or cosmic powers inimical to the reign of God's peace in the world are seen as having already been

---

[47]We are not presuming here to pass judgment on the complex question of the authorship of Colossians, but merely affirming that in this instance, at least, we find its doctrine to be Pauline.

subdued and pacified (properly, in the original intention of the
hymn, Col 1:16 speaks of a primeval harmony, prior to a "fall"),
whereas in 1 Cor 15:25 this is an accomplishment reserved to
the eschatological future. The difference in perspective is obvious, yet once again we believe we are in the presence of a
development in thought that is not un-Pauline. What is involved
is the concept of the kingdom of God. While for Paul this is
almost universally an eschatological term (1 Cor 6:9f.; 15:50;
Gal 5:21; 1 Thes 2:12, certainly), in 1 Cor 15:24 he speaks
of "the end, when Christ turns over the kingdom to God the
Father, when he has broken the control of every domination,
authority, and power." In the following verse, he calls Christ's
presence in the church a *basileuein*. Is it, then, a major departure from Pauline theology to conceive of the church as a *basileia*
which is not yet the kingdom of God, but in which has already
been achieved *in principle* the ultimate victory that will be revealed in the *eschaton*, in the *parousia*?[48] Surely such an idea
may be inferred from the Pauline usage of *aparchē*, of *arrabōn*,
his notion of the relation of election to grace and glory (Phil
1:6, for example): all of which suppose that the church is not
a prognosis but a beginning in kind of a work that is to be ended
only in degree. The liturgical redaction of the hymn adopted
this viewpoint by situating its theology, as had 1 Cor 15:24,
eis tēn basileian tou 'uiou tēs agapēs autou (vs. 13b), and the
author of Colossians did no more when he defined the "body"
of vs. 18a as "the church." As for the triumph of Col 2:14f.,
it is seen as achieved, indeed, but only "by the cross."

In summary, we believe that the author of Colossians took
at a second stage, and as basically acceptable, a christological
hymn that had already been redacted in a direction that he could
only choose to pursue to its final conclusions, which had been
firmly set within the limits of an historical concept of salvation. In making use of what was presumably the Colossians'
own liturgy he did not intend to deny a theology which he re-

48Cf. Gabathuler, 143f.

garded as heterodox[49] but to modify it with provisos which he thought necessary or at least highly desirable.

4. Conclusions

Having arrived at this point, it may be thought that we have bypassed the problem which we set ourselves at the beginning of this paper. If the redactor of Col 1:12-20 lightly altered a passage with which he was in basic agreement and which, therefore, theoretically he could just as well have left alone, does the passage itself or the hymn which it incorporated—always on the assumption that our interpretation of it is sound—cast any light whatever on the question of biblical authority in relation to the various layers of tradition that have gone into the composition of the canonical text?[50] We believe that it does, in several respects.

Firstly, we believe that exegesis confirms, in this instance at least, what antecedently might be thought likely of the spirit in which redaction was undertaken, namely, that it was an attempt to assimilate sympathetic material. Much more than a modern critic can hope to be, the redactor himself was aware

---

[49]See W. Foerster, "Die Irrlehrer des Kolosserbriefes," *Studia Biblica et Semitica* (Fest. Vriezen; Wageningen: H. Veenam & Zonen, 1966) 71-80. We find his argument persuasive that the intention of the author of Colossians was to shore up the Colossians' theology against the seductions of false teaching to which they had been exposed but to which they had not succumbed.

[50]In a necessarily quite limited way we are seeking to respond to an appeal of the Faith and Order Commission of the World Council of Churches stemming from a preliminary consultation held at Boldern, Switzerland, in October of 1968. The purpose of the consultation was to program a worldwide discussion of the authority of the Bible in all its aspects, and its recommendation was that this question be examined not by directly dogmatic methods, but by the interpretation of particular biblical passages in relation to some chosen theme. Among the "questions to be answered" as outlined by James Barr in his report on the proposed study (published by the Commission in February of 1969) we believe that several in his §§ 5.31 and 5.32 are at least given some further definition by this present paper.

of the differences between his theology and the theology of those whose work he redacted; his redactions are the witness to his awareness. That he chose to redact, however, rather than to denounce or to ignore, indicates that he found the alien theology at least tolerable and adaptable. Whether he was right in his judgment, and whether he succeeded in his endeavor, may be other matters entirely. Nevertheless, the effort involved in redaction has something to say with regard to the intention of those who formed the canon in the actual process of its formation, who made the later definition of the canon possible; and it is perhaps one of the earliest answers to the question of whether the principle of a canon within the canon ought to be recognized.[51] There was no compulsion, after all, that required an author to adopt any pre-existing theological formulations, particularly any that he felt had really departed from the essence of the gospel as he understood it.[52] He always had the option, which we believe Paul took in dealing with the Corinthians and others, of turning heterodox language against its own original purposes, but in new contexts and with new intents.[53] It still seems to be a fair conclusion that the usual purpose of a citation—without other than redactional comment—is to approve rather than disapprove what the *citator* has drawn from his source material.

Furthermore, we must observe that the author did not cite his passage simply as some available formulation from the past, but as *authority*, as an argument that was supposed to have some

[51]To speak of the canon as a unity in diversity is not always to make an affirmation of faith. The canon, and the steps that were taken to make it a possibility, are also objects of historical study. It is doubtful that history will verify that totally disparate groups espousing totally different ideologies are likely to collect and codify a mass of material upon which only a later community will impose a specious unity.

[52]In this respect we are unable to follow Käsemann, 164-168, in his rationale of how a heterodox hymn would have been utilized by the author of Colossians.

[53]Cf. Ulrich Wilckens, *Weisheit und Torheit* (Tübingen: J.C.B. Mohr, 1959), esp. 97-100.

telling effect. We fail to see any distinction in this regard (again *pace* Käsemann) between the undoubted Paul's citations of Rom 1:3f. and Phil 2:6-11 (both with redactions) and the doubted Paul's citation of Col 1:12-20. In each instance language was being used that was calculated to strike a responsive chord in the heart of a church that had long employed it and was accustomed to it as pertaining to its identity. The usage in each case was, we might say, in the order of a *captatio benevolentiae*: the authority in question existed in the eye or ear of the community that was addressed, not necessarily in the mind of the redacting author, though, as we have maintained, he must have found the underlying theology at least tolerable. We are not trying to argue from such a precedent, therefore, directly to the contemporary issue of biblical authority as we have stated it above. The authority, such as it was, that was being supposed was traditionary and ecclesial rather than specifically biblical.

Nevertheless, indirectly at least, we are brought to something very analogous to our problem by this biblical precedent. The Bible, considered as a canon of Scripture, can be rather accurately defined as a gathering of traditions or, if one prefers, as a Tradition that has found expression in various traditions. Whoever would want to limit "primitive Christianity" to some single existential response—justification by faith alone, let us say—against which all other responses and the traditions which inevitably derived from them must somehow be measured as departures from the pure gospel, has been impressed by a logic that does not seem to have been that of the Bible. To reduce the message of the NT to Paul, and at that only one bit of Paul, is not a procedure justified by the example of Paul himself or of the Pauline tradition.

Col 1:12-20, it appears to us, contains in microcosm a paradigm of the canon itself. Without destroying them or even making their recovery very difficult, the passage has incorporated diverse theological viewpoints, each of which has to be examined in its own right if we would understand what the ultimate redactor intended as a final, or provisionally final, elaboration. The primitive hymn which was adapted to the liturgy of the Colossian church was surely no isolated piece of private homework but represented a current of Christian thought that had been respected and was respected.[54] The author of Colossians, as we see it, chose an option which has made it imperative for his interpreters to interpret first the theology of which he made use rather than cast it aside as he could so easily have cast it aside. Biblical precedent itself, in other words, encourages us to examine the layers of the tradition and not merely the judgment that has been rendered on them in the canonical text.

This last point may perhaps be significant. There can hardly be any doubt that the final redactor considered his editorial efforts to have constituted an improvement over the *tradita* which he had received. One of the functions of *Sachkritik* will be to determine whether he was correct in this evaluation: that he left us the means of doing so is a measure of his openness. When Asiatic churches at the 1961 Faith and Order Conference at New Delhi manifested enthusiasm for a cosmic type of christology as opposed to an alleged "Kirchturmstheologie" of the west, they appealed to passages such as the Colossians hymn for their biblical justification. It hardly seems proper to deny them this right simply on the basis of the redactions which the hymn has undergone in its passage into the canon.[55] Despite its redactions, or even because of them, the hymn remains a part of NT theology.

Whether the conclusions we have reached will be supported by the examination of other redactional material in the Bible we do not venture to say. It is our suspicion that in many instances they will be, even in instances where it might first appear that the redactor has attempted to nullify the past. The key to our understanding of what the canonical text itself presents as normative we may find, though in a somewhat different sense than we have traditionally believed, still to be "what was intended by the final author."

[54]Cf. Lohse, 84 ftn. 6: "Der Hymnus ist sicher nicht nur in einer Gemeinde—etwa der von Kolossae—bekannt gewesen und gesungen worden. Er war zweifellos Gemeingut der kleinasiatischen Gemeinden, so dass man weder von einem 'kolossichen' noch von einem 'häretischen' Hymnus sprechen darf—ganz abgesehen davon, dass eine scharfe Unterscheidung zwischen Rechtgläubigkeit und Ketzerei noch nicht vorhanden war, sondern erst gefunden werden musste."

[55]As Lohse seems to think, 102 ftn. 7. See on the contrary Kehl, 20f., 165.

20. "And He Shall Come Again With Glory": Paul and Christian Apocalyptic

The course of Pauline studies has followed that of the Gospels.[1] The determination of the history-of-religions school of the past century to "ethicize" the Gospel had its equivalent in their picture of Paul the solitary genius, the unique spirit who had moulded Christianity much as the Prophets were thought to have moulded the ethical monotheism of Israel. With the rediscovery of the primitive Christian eschatology of the Gospels around the turn of the present century, there was a corresponding rediscovery of Paul's eschatological orientation, his inheritance from Judaism. In this connection, it would be hard to overestimate the significance of the study of Richard Kabisch,[2] who rightly insisted on the need of scholarship to re-examine

[1]Cf. B. Rigaux, O.F.M., *L'interprétation du paulinisme dans l'exégèse récente*, in A. Descamps et al., *Littérature et Théologie Pauliniennes* (Recherches Bibliques V; Louvain: Desclée de Brouwer, 1960) 17-46.

[2]*Die Eschatologie des Paulus in ihren Zusammenhängen mit dem Gesamtbegriff des Paulinismus* (Göttingen: Vandenhoeck & Ruprecht, 1893), esp. 2-5, 7-12, 71-76, 139-188, 214-218.

Paul in the light of the Jewish eschatological tradition that he shared. Though Kabisch in his own turn, as Albert Schweitzer pointed out,[3] went to an extreme in the application of his theory, nevertheless one must agree that his was a most important contribution to historical theology. Such studies made the conclusion possible that is today almost a commonplace: "Paulinismus und Griechentum haben nur die religiöse Sprache, aber keine Gedanken miteinander gemeinsam. Der Apostel hat das Christentum nicht hellenisiert"[4]

The authors who recalled critical attention to the eschatological origins of primitive Christianity, however, hardly did so from any appreciation of the values of eschatology. It was recognized as the viewpoint from which the New Testament authors had written, but as having in itself no enduring religious relevance. Rather, it had to be reinterpreted, even as today Rudolf Bultmann tries to reinterpret it in terms of the existential moment.[5] These were the times before the first World War that wrote a definitive end to nineteenth-century optimism. It is surely not mere coincidence that in our own times, now that an eschatological and even apocalyptic future no longer seems to be the remote eventuality it once was, the eschatology of the New Testament is being once more taken seriously and on its own terms.

Thus it is that Oscar Cullmann has listed as one of the marks of apostasy from true Christianity the "rejection of the primitive Christian eschatological expectation, whose characteristic distinction in terms of time between the present and the future age is replaced by the Greek metaphysical distinction between this world and the timeless Beyond".[6] So too, C. K. Barrett will

---

[3]*Geschlichte der paulinischen Forschung* (Tübingen: J.C.B. Mohr, 1911) 48f.

[4]*Ibid.*, 185. Cf. also W. Wrede, *Paulus* (Halle: Gebauer-Schwetschke, 1904), esp. 80-82, 86-88.

[5]On Bultmann's continuity with the old liberal theology, cf. E. Schmidt, *R. Bultmanns Programm der Entmythologisierung der christlichen Botschaft*, in *Zeitschrift für systematische Theologie* 23 (1954) 177-205.

[6]*Christ and Time. The Primitive Christian Conception of Time and History* (Philadelphia: Westminster, 1950) 56. Cf. also 144ff.

not have it thought that the realized eschatology of John's Gospel constitutes any real break with the primitive eschatology of Christianity,[7] a point that is being more and more emphasized by other scholars for other parts of the New Testament. Catholic authors as well have not been slow to underline the irreplaceable character of the eschatological imperatives of Christianity as a doctrine and as a way of life.[8]

However, if eschatology has come back into its own in our conscious appreciation of the essentials of Christianity, there has remained a reluctance to deal kindly with the apocalyptic in whose language and thought-forms the eschatology of primitive Christianity was articulated. Schweitzer accurately observed that one of the factors that encouraged the critics to dissociate Paul from the Judaism of his time was the belief that between a fantastic apocalypticism and a soulless rabbinism *tertium non*

[7]"To have abandoned it would have been to abandon the biblical framework of primitive Christianity, and to run all the risks to which a purely metaphysical Christianity, divorced from history, is exposed. The dangers of mysticism, perfectionism, and antinomianism are, in his gospel, held in check by the contraint of the primitive Christian eschatology, which is a constant reminder that the Church lives by faith, not by sight, and that it is saved in hope". *The Gospel According to St John* (London: SPCK, 1958) 58.

[8]Cf. Rudolf Schnackenburg, *Die sittliche Botschaft des Neuen Testaments* (Handbuch der Moraltheologie 6: Munich: Max Hueber Verlag, 1954) 97f.: "Man kann nur bedauern, dass dieses Motiv von der eschatologischen Teilnahme an Gottes vollendeter Herrschaft zu unserem heutigen 'In-den-Himmel-Kommen' abgeblasst ist. Um der individuellen Seligkeit jedes einzelnen nach seinem Tode willen wird so die grosse kosmische Schau verkürzt, und auch der Christ ist versucht, mehr an die Rettung der eigenen Seele als an die Vollendung der Heilsgeschichte, mehr an seine eigene Glückseligkeit als an die Verherrlichung Gottes zu denken-nur Akzentverschiebungen, gewiss, die aber für den Charakter des sittlichen Strebens nicht unwichtig sind". See also Karl Hermann Schelkle, *Biblische und patristische Eschatologie nach Rom* 13,11-13, in *Sacra Pagina. Miscellanea Biblica Congressus Internationalis Catholici de Re Biblica* (Paris: Gabalda, 1959), II, 357-372; M. Miguéns, *L'apocalisse secondo Paolo,* in *Bibbia e Oriente* 2 (1960) 142-148.

dabatur.[9] Clearly, apocalyptic has not yet been forgiven its "fantastic" associations.[10] Rather than to concede to apocalyptic its determining role in the eschatology of early Christianity, there is now a tendency to distinguish the eschatological from the apocalyptic, in which distinction the latter term has become a pejorative one.[11] Recently we have even seen the attempt made by John A. T. Robinson to revive the old "ethical" view of Jesus' teaching which divorced it from *parousia* expectation.[12] Robinson, it is true, does not deny eschatology to Jesus, but for him the *parousia* is an apocalyptic idea elaborated in primitive Christianity by a reinterpretation of the Lord's words. The realized eschatology of the later Paul and especially John's Gospel is, Robinson believes, a return to the authentic non-apocalyptic eschatology of Jesus.

Though one may agree with A. Feuillet that in certain respects Robinson's exegesis has liberated biblical theology from some of the impasses encountered in New Testament eschatology, one must also agree with him when he insists that Robinson has not proved his central thesis.[13] What Robinson has done,

[9]*Op. cit.,* 36.

[10]J.-B. Frey, "Apocalyptique", *Dictionnaire de la Bible Supplément,* I, 350f., seems to be quite harsh and negative in his judgment on apocalyptic as a hindrance rather than a help to the understanding of the Gospel, though he does point out (353) that the opposition between apocalyptic and the rabbis has been exaggerated. Cf. also James W. Parkes, *The Foundations of Judaism and Christianity* (Chicago: Quadrangle Books, 1960) 94, according to whom apocalyptic was a worthless literary genre "which Judaism was right to reject and Christianity to forget".

[11]Cf. Schnackenburg, *op. cit.,* 132 (Paul's moral teaching as motivated by the *parousia:* "Der dem Ende zugewandte Blick . . . versetzt [diese Christen] nicht in ein apokalyptisches Fieber"), 260 (even in the Apocalypse of John apocalyptic is only "a clothing"). This last view is also held by Antonino Romeo, "Apocalittica letteratura", *Enciclopedia Cattolica* (Vatican: Ente per l'Enciclopedia Cattolica, 1948), I, 1615-1626.

[12]*Jesus and His Coming. The Emergence of a Doctrine* (New York and Nashville: Abingdon, 1957).

[13]Cf. André Feuillet, S. S., *Les origines et la signification de Mt 10,23,* in *Catholic Biblical Quarterly* 23 (1961) 182-198.

we may suspect, and that something that he did not in any way intend, is to demonstrate anew the inseparability of eschatology and apocalyptic. "The teaching of Jesus", he writes, "underwent the same sort of shift of key that occurred in the Old Testament in the transition from the eschatology of the prophets to that of the Apocalyptic writers".[14] Now it may be questioned, and has been questioned, whether the "historical" eschatology of prophecy is really separated from apocalyptic in the biblical mind to the degree that has appeared so obvious to modern exegetes.[15] Be that as it may, in Robinson's hypothesis we are asked to believe that, between the years 30 and 50, when New Testament eschatology is first encountered in Paul's letters to the Thessalonians, a completely non-apocalyptic eschatology had become a thoroughgoing apocalyptic one, and that through no devising of Paul's, who had merely taken his eschatology from the primitive Christian community. Not only this, this eschatology was already so much taken for granted by the year 50, it is impossible to "get behind" Paul's writings to discover its original contours. According to Robinson, this shows only "how soon this [apocalyptic] application came to be made".[16] It might indicate equally well that it was as natural for Jesus himself as for Paul and the first Christians to associate escha-

---

[14]*Op. cit.*, 94.

[15]Cf. George Eldon Ladd, *Why Not Prophetic-Apocalyptic?*, in *Journal of Biblical Literature* 76 (1957) 192-200; Bruce Vawter, C. M., *Apocalyptic: Its Relation to Prophecy*, in *Catholic Biblical Quarterly* 22 (1960) 33-46. History and beyond-history is a common rule of thumb for distinguishing the prophetic and apocalyptic futures, cf. Stanley B. Frost, *Old Testament Apocalyptic. Its Origins and Growth* (London: Epworth Press, 1952). Gerhard Von Rad, *Theologie des Alten Testaments* II (Munich: Kaiser Verlag, 1960) 314-321, who sees apocalyptic as the outgrowth of wisdom rather than of prophecy, also adopts this distinction, although (p. 121, ftn. 15) he acknowledges that the new age of apocalyptic can be represented, on the one hand, as the extension of time into an incalculable future, whereas on the other hand, such prophetic texts as Am. 9,13; Is 60,19f; Zech 14,7 seem to conceive of a beyond-time.

[16]*Op. cit.*, 106.

tology with apocalyptic, to conceive of eschatology in apocalyptic terms.

As a matter of fact, there is no contradiction between the realized eschatology of John and the later Paul and the apocalyptic eschatology of the *parousia* — expectation; realized eschatology is inherent in the ministry of Jesus itself, without detracting one iota from a preaching that manifestly looked to a future fulfilment.[17] It is likely enough that a realized eschatology can be discerned even in the apocalyptic letters to the Thessalonians.[18] Certainly it is to be found in Rom 13,1-7, in an epistle in which the expectation of the *parousia* nevertheless is dominant.[19] It is very true that realized eschatology breaks with the viewpoint of the purely *Jewish* apocalypses, but then again so does the eschatology of the entire New Testament, including the Apocalypse of John. So, for that matter, does the very idea of the *parousia* itself. What is unique in the Christian revelation has sundered it completely from its Jewish antecedents; this is as true of the apocalyptic tradition as of anything else in Christianity. Realized eschatology is due to the resurrection of Christ and to the whole Christ-event, not to an abandonment of the apocalyptic mentality. Christian apocalyptic therefore differs from the Jewish, but it has not ceased to be apocalyptic.

The fantastic and other less "religious" elements in apocalyptic have been stressed to such an extent that it is easy to lose sight

---

[17]Cf. T. W. Manson, *The Life of Jesus: Some Tendencies in Present-day Research,* in *The Background of the New Testament and its Eschatology,* edited by W. D. Davies and D. Daube (Cambridge University Press, 1955), 211-221; Maurice Goguel, *Le caractère à la fois actuel et futur, du salut dans la théologie paulinienne,* ibid., 322-341; Joseph Bonsirven, S. J., *L'Évangile de Paul* (Paris: Aubier, 1948) 338-343; Albrecht Oepke, παρουσία, *Theologisches Wörterbuch zum Neuen Testament* V, 864-866.

[18]Cf. A. Feuillet, "Parousie", *DBS* VI, 1374f.

[19]Cf. Clinton D. Morrison, *The Powers That Be* (Studies in Biblical Theology 29; Naperville, Illinois: Allenson, 1960) 22. See also Heinrich Schlier, *Mächte und Gewalten im Neuen Testament* (Quaestiones Disputatae 3; Freilburg: Herder, 1958).

of its truly spiritual values.[20] Taken as a whole, Jewish apocalyptic should not be deemed unworthy to have formed the minds of the first Christians, including St. Paul.

And form their minds it surely did. Though it may be very true that in much of Paul's theology concepts that are clearly apocalyptic are "far from being a peculiarity of Jewish apocalyptic",[21] nevertheless, in such cases there can hardly be any doubt as to the source to which he was tributary. Nowadays there are few to question that Paul was what he claimed to be, a Hebrew of Hebrews, living in a Jewish world that had been thoroughly imbued with the apocalyptic tradition. The post-70 A.D. rejection of apocalyptic by Judaism must not be projected back into the Judaism before Christ. Rabbi and Pharisee that he was, was no deterrent to Paul's acceptance of apocalyptic. Apocalyptic was in no way outside the normative in Judaism, and rabbinism was heavily in debt to it as to other currents of thought in Judaism.[22]

What are confidently put down as the characteristics of apocalyptic are equally characteristic of Paul. From apocalyptic derives the conception of the two ages that figures so prominently in his thought, with the significant difference, of course, that for Paul as for all of the New Testament, the resurrection of Christ has inaugurated the new age already, "the world to come", as the author of Hebrews (2,5) actually calls the age of realized eschatology.[23] When Paul rejects the wisdom of this world and of its angelic rulers who are passing away (I Cor

[20]Cf. Frost, *op. cit.*, 242-258; H. H. Rowley, *The Relevance of Apocalyptic* (London: Lutterworth Press, ²1947) 13, 150-178; Oepke, ἀποκάλυψις, *ThWNT* III, 580f.

[21]Morrison, *op. cit.*, 130.

[22]Cf. Hans-Joachim Schoeps, *Paulus, die Theologie des Apostels im Lichte der jüdischen Religionsgeschichte* (Tübingen: J.C.B. Mohr, 1959) 3If. Note, for example, in Strack-Billerbeck's *Kommentar* IV, 977-986, the influence of the apocalyptic "sorrows of the Messiah" on the rabbinical literature.

[23]Cf. Schoeps *op. cit.*, 96-98; Hermann Sasse, αἰών, *ThWNT* I, 206f.; Cullmann, *op. cit.*, 104f. Before 70 A.D. the concept of the two ages is rare and uncertain with the rabbis, but common in apocalyptic. It is commonly asserted that it came into apocalyptic under Persian influence, though the characteristic terminology is lacking in Parsiism.

2,6), which in realized eschatology can be said to have passed away, he is firmly within the apocalyptic tradition.

The ministry of Paul itself is clearly conditioned by an apocalyptic concern. One does not have to agree with Schoeps[24] that Paul, like Rabbi Aqiba and Rabbi Eliezer ben Hyrkanos, anticipated a forty-year period from the coming of the Messiah to the end (Schoeps cites Rom 13,1); but it is certainly a fact that the expectation of the *parousia* was a determining factor in the urgency of his ministry. "The Gospel must first be preached to all the nations" (Mk 13,10) was the call to action of the apostle of the Gentiles—a call to action, it may be added, whose imperative remained unaffected, for Paul as for his successors, by the "delay" of the *parousia*.[25] The *parousia* itself is a doctrine formed within the framework of apocalyptic; thus far we can agree with Robinson, without concurring in his reconstruction of its elaboration. It is distinctively Christian apocalyptic, nowhere found *quâ talis* in Jewish apocalyptic;[26] the Old Testament origin of both the idea and the term seems to be the same Dn 7,13 (in which the verb πάρειμι appears twice).

From apocalyptic, too, is Paul's conception of the "tribulation" of the Christian life, the other side of the coin to realized eschatology, just as it is in the Apocalypse of John (7,14). The term θλῖψις almost qualifies as a specifically Pauline word in the New Testament (almost exactly half of its 45 occurrences), and it certainly represents an apocalyptic idea developed from Dn 12,1(צָרָה עֵת = καιρὸς θλίψεως).[27] The doctrine of the "sorrows of the Messiah" rules the thinking of Paul throughout his entire ministry, and Col 1,24 shows how compatible it was

---

[24]*Op. cit.*, 99. If there were no other reason, the aberrancy of this opinion from the normal would make Paul's acceptance of it doubtful. Cf. Ferdinand Prat, S.J., *La Théologie de St Paul* II (Paris: Beauchesne, ³⁸1949) 564f.

[25]Cf. Cullmann, *op. cit.*, 163-166. Cullmann's interpretation of 2 Thes 2,6 of the apostle's own ministry is well-known, cf. *Le caractère eschatologique du devoir missionnaire et de la conscience apostolique de S. Paul*, in *Revue d'Histoire et de Philosophie Religieuses* 16 (1936) 210-245.

[26]Cf. Feuillet, "Parousie", 1334.

[27]For the development in apocalyptic, see Schlier, θλίβω, θλῖψις, *ThWNT* III, 139-148.

with the realized eschatology of that epistle.

It has sometimes been asserted that Paul's lack of concern for the earthly life of Jesus reflects his apocalyptic viewpoint.[28] In a certain sense, this is doubtless true. The *merely* earthly life of Jesus was, of course, of no concern to any of the New Testament. But if it is permissible to think of the *kerygma* as apocalyptic in its concentration on the world to come as the object of Christian decision, and of Paul's preaching as always kerygmatic in this way, then it is possible to discern the function of apocalyptic shaping his message as it did not the more developed *didachè* of the Gospels. Paul's Jesus, in any case, was the resurrected Lord and Christ whom he encountered on the way to Damascus; apart from this vision we should hardly attempt to understand Pauline Christology.[29]

The attempt to "demythologize" New Testament eschatology by removing it from apocalyptic is not merely to select one of its emphases at the expense of another. It is, rather, to distort its entire message, which includes a truly religious judgment to be passed on this world. Christian apocalyptic is the expression of Christian hope and of Christian optimism.[30] Apocalyptic was, at the first, the assertion of pious Jews that the Scripture was not to be broken, that a God who was Lord of history would and could bring about all he had promised, despite all worldly signs to the contrary. Apocalyptic became, at the last, a proclamation of Christian hope resting on Christian faith, that the good work begun in man is but the 'αρραβών of God's kingdom when the last enemy will be destroyed and Christ is indeed all in all. Nor does it proclaim only; it also advances the kingdom. Both in Paul and in the Apocalypse the *eschaton* arrives through the prayers and the works of the saints (Col. 1,24; Ap 8,2-6).

---

[28]Cf. Schweitzer, *op. cit.*, 191. So also Schoeps. "Bedeutungslosigkeit" appears to be too strong a term to characterize Paul's attitude, however.

[29]Cf. Martin Brückner, *Die Entstehung der paulinischen Christologie* (Strassburg: Heitz & Mündel, 1903), who, however, can hardly be followed in all his conclusions.

[30]Cf. E. Käsemann, *Die Anfänge christlicher Theologie*, in *Zeitschrift für Theologie und Kirche* 57 (1960) 162-185.

ABBREVIATIONS

AAS	Acta apostolicae sedis
AB	Anchor Bible
AnBib	Analecta biblica
AnOr	Analecta orientalia
ATANT	Abhandlungen zur Theologie des Alten und Neuen Testaments
ATD	Das Alte Testament Deutsch
BASOR	*Bulletin of the American Schools of Oriental Research*
BHS	*Biblia hebraica stuttgartensia*
BibOr	Biblica et orientalia
BKAT	Biblischer Kommentar: Altes Testament
BZ	*Biblische Zeitschrift*
BZAW	*Beihefte zur ZAW*
CBQ	*Catholic Biblical Quarterly*
CBQMS	Catholic Biblical Quarterly Monograph Series
CurTM	*Currents in Theology and Mission*
DBS(up)	*Dictionnaire de la Bible, Supplément*
DISO	*Dictionnaire des inscriptions sémitiques de l'ouest*
EBib/EB	Études bibliques
EH(z)AT	Exegetisches Handbuch zum Alten Testament
HAT	Handbuch zum Alten Testament
HeyJ	*Heythrop Journal*
H(z)AT	Handkommentar zum Alten Testament
HK(z)AT	Handkommentar zum Nuen Testament
HUCA	*Hebrew Union College Annual*

ICC	International Critical Commentary
Interp	*Interpretation*
JAAR	*Journal of the Amgie und Kirche*
NAB	*New American Bible*
NCE	*New Catholic Encyclopedia*
NEB	*New English Bible*
NTD	Das Neue Testament Deutsch
NTF	Neutestamentliche Forschungen
NTS	*New Testament Studies*
PEQ	*Palestine Exploration Quarterly*
PL	J. Migne, Patrologia latina
RB	Revue biblique
RHPhilRel	*Revue d'histoire et de philosophie religieuses*
SBJ	*La sainte bible de Jerusalem*
SBS	Stuttgarter Bibelstudien
SBT	Studies in Biblical Theology
SEA	*Svensk exegetisk årsbok*
SJT	*Scottish Journal of Theology*
SR	*Studies in Religion / Sciences religieuses*
TDOT	*Theological Dictionary of the Old Testament*
TQ	*Theologische Quartalschrift*
TS	*Theological Studies*
TTZ	*Trierer theologische Zeitschrift*
TWAT	*Theologisches Wörterbuch zum Alten Testament*
ThWNT	*Theologisches Wörterbuch zum Neuen Testament*
TZ	*Theologische Zeitschrift*
UT	C.H. Gordon, *Ugaritic Textbook*
VDBS	*Dictionnaire de la Bible, Supplement*
VT	*Vetus Testamentum*
VTSup	Vetus Testamentum, Supplements
ZAW	*Zeitschrift für alttestamentliche Wissenschaft*
ZNW	*Zeitschrift für neutestamentliche Wissenschaft*
ZTK	*Zeitschrift für Theologie und Kirche*

Acknowledgments

"The Bible in the Roman Catholic Church" was first published in *Scripture in the Jewish and Christian Traditions*, ed. F.E. Greenspahn, ©1982 by Abingdon Press and is used by permission. "The God of Hebrew Scriptures" was first published in *Biblical Theology Bulletin* 12 (1982), 3–7, and is used by permission. "Salvation is a Family Affair," was first published in *Sin, Salvation and the Spirit*, ed. D. Durken, ©1979 by The Liturgical Press, and is used by permission. "The Scriptural Meaning of Sin," was first published under the title "Missing the Mark" in *The Way* 2 (1962) and is used by permission. "The Biblical Meaning of Faith" was first published in *Worship* (Aug-Sept, 1960) and is used by permission. "The Jerusalem Bible" was first published in the *Duke Divinity School Review* 44 (1979), 88–103 and is used by permission. "History and Kerygma in the Old Testament," was first published in *A Light unto my Path: Old Testament Studies in Honor of J.M. Myers*, ed., H.N. Bream, et al., ©1974 by Temple University Press and is used by permission. "Prophecy and the Redactional Question," was first published in *No Famine in the Land. Studies in Honor of John L. McKenzie*, eds. J.W. Flanagan and A.W. Robinson, ©1975 by Scholars Press, and is used by permission. "Israel's Encounter with the Nations" was first published in *Service and Salvation: Nagpur Theological Conference on Evangelization* by Theological Publications in India, 1973. "Intimations of Immortality and the Old Testament," was first published in the *Journal of Biblical Literature* 91 (1972) 158–171 and is used by permission. "Prov. 8:22: Wisdom and Creation," was first published in the *Journal of Biblical Literature* 99 (1980) 205–216 and is used by permission. "Postexilic Prayer and Hope," was first published in the *Catholic Biblical Quarterly* 37 (1975) and is used by permission. "Realized Messianism" was first published in *De la Torah au Messie* ©1981 by Desclee Editione, and is used by permission. "A Tale of Two Cities: The Old Testament and the Issue of Personal Freedom," was first published in the *Journal of Ecumenical Studies*, 15 (1978) 261–273 and is used by permission. "Are the Gospels Anti-Semitic?" was first published in the *Journal of Ecumenical Studies* 5 (1968) 473–487 and is used by permission. "Divorce and the New Testament," was first published in the *Catholic Biblical Quarterly* 39 (1977) 528–542 and is used by permission. "Levitical Messianism and the N.T." was first published in *The Bible in Current Catholic Thought*, ed. J.L. McKenzie, by Herder and Herder, 1962. "The Development of the Expression of Faith in the Worshipping Community." was first published in *Concilium* 82 (1973) 22-29 by Burns and Oats. "The Colossian Hymn and the Principle of Redaction," was first published in the *Catholic Biblical Quarterly* 33 (1971) 62-81 and is used by permission. "'And He Shall Come Again with Glory' Paul and Christian Apocalyptic," was first published in *Studiorum Paulinorum Congressus Internationalis Catholicus 1961* (*Analecta Biblica* 17-18) by the Pontifical Biblical Institute, 1963.

These essays, having appeared in such varied places, have followed various editorial conventions, thus accounting for discrepancies in transliteration, spelling, etc.